Defending the Masses

DEFENDING THE MASSES

A Progressive Lawyer's Battles
for Free Speech

Eric B. Easton

The University of Wisconsin Press

The University of Wisconsin Press
728 State Street, Suite 443
Madison, Wisconsin 53706
uwpress.wisc.edu

3 Henrietta Street, Covent Garden
London WC2E 8LU, United Kingdom
eurospanbookstore.com

Copyright © 2018
The Board of Regents of the University of Wisconsin System
All rights reserved. Except in the case of brief quotations embedded in critical articles and reviews, no part of this publication may be reproduced, stored in a retrieval system, transmitted in any format or by any means—digital, electronic, mechanical, photocopying, recording, or otherwise—or conveyed via the Internet or a website without written permission of the University of Wisconsin Press. Rights inquiries should be directed to rights@uwpress.wisc.edu.

Printed in the United States of America

This book may be available in a digital edition.

Library of Congress Cataloging-in-Publication Data
Names: Easton, Eric B., author.
Title: Defending the masses: a progressive lawyer's battles for free speech / Eric B. Easton.
Description: Madison, Wisconsin: The University of Wisconsin Press, [2017]
| Includes bibliographical references and index.
Identifiers: LCCN 2017012506 | ISBN 9780299314002 (cloth: alk. paper)
Subjects: LCSH: Roe, Gilbert E. (Gilbert Ernstein), 1865–1929.
| Lawyers—United States—Biography.
| Freedom of speech—United States—History—20th century.
| Progressivism (United States politics)—History—20th century.
Classification: LCC KF373.R557 E27 2017 | DDC 342.7308/53 [B]—dc23
LC record available at https://lccn.loc.gov/2017012506

ISBN 978-0-299-31404-0 (pbk.: alk. paper)

To

Susan,

with All My Love

Contents

Preface	ix
Introduction: A Free Speech Pioneer	3
1 Getting Started	12
2 The Muckrakers	30
3 The Anarchists	46
4 The Feminists	70
5 The Socialists	103
6 The Pacifists I	127
7 The Pacifists II	149
8 The Communists	167
9 Winding Down	189
Conclusion: Gilbert Roe's Legacy	201
Notes	205
Table of Cases	253
Index	257

Preface

I had never heard of Gilbert Roe.

As a professor of media law, however, I had long admired Judge Learned Hand's prophetic opinion in *Masses Publishing Co. v. Patten*. In the spring of 2012, I thought I might write something about that case, and I asked my research assistant to put together a bibliography. It was an extensive and intimidating bibliography, and I knew right away I would have to find a novel way into the case in order to contribute to the literature. My first thought was to write about Supreme Court cases that cited Hand's opinion to support modern First Amendment principles. A young colleague at the University of Baltimore, Professor Colin Starger, had developed software that would graphically display the citation history of seminal cases, and I was more than eager to use it. There was only one problem: no Supreme Court majority has ever cited *Masses*. That line of inquiry seemed to be a dead end.

My next thought was a series of biographical sketches of the principal actors in the case. Learned Hand and Max Eastman were very well known, of course, and already claimed serious biographies. I found some basic information on Postmaster Patten on the internet, though I did not find it very interesting. I'd never heard of the lawyers, Gilbert Roe for *Masses* and Earl Barnes for the Postmaster of the City of New York, but I did learn that Roe had graduated from the University of Wisconsin. I wrote to the law library there, only to learn that they didn't have much. But a librarian named Shucha Bonita ran a Westlaw listing of his reported cases. I could have done that myself, of course, but I did not, and I will forever be grateful that someone had the curiosity I lacked. As I looked over the list of cases, I spotted some familiar names: Sanger, McClure, Smedley, Eastman, Sinclair . . . could these be the colorful characters I knew? A closer look showed they were, and I had found my way in.

For the past five years, I have been steeped in the stories of Gilbert Roe and his clients. When people asked what I was working on, I was prepared for the quizzical looks I received when I told them. "You've seen the movie *Reds?*" I would ask. "Sure," they would say. "Well, everyone in that movie was Gilbert Roe's client." OK, so I exaggerated, but not by much, and it got the point across. In any case, I was having the time of my life, buried in archives in Washington, New York, and Madison, Wisconsin. More importantly, I was uncovering a record of exemplary service to the cause of free speech now all but forgotten. I have tried here to shine a light on one of the dedicated lawyers who devoted his time and labor to the application of First Amendment principles to the very real world of unpopular, radical, and even seditious speech. My fellow members of the legal academy, who usually seek wisdom in the opinions of judges, may be able to look more deeply into the legal issues, theories, and processes from which that wisdom emerged. Historians may find a new lens through which to consider the Progressive Era and the war years, and journalism scholars may get a new, perhaps unexpected, view of the mainstream press in a time of distress. I hope, too, that the lay reader finds compelling the many individual stories in this book.

My primary sources of material for this book are Gilbert Roe's correspondence and other papers, housed in the Library of Congress as part of the huge La Follette collection, and Netha Roe's papers in the Wisconsin Historical Society. In my view, Netha Roe deserves her own biography; rarely have I come across a longer, more interesting life. For the legal documents I could not find online, I found the New York office of the National Archives most helpful. And I could never have pieced everything together without the incredible collection at Newspapers.com. To all of the archivists who helped me find the material I needed, thank you. Gilbert Roe's own writings were indispensable, of course, and I want to thank my colleague Professor James Maxeiner for giving me a vintage copy of *Our Judicial Oligarchy*. Most of Roe's writings were readily available in the University of Wisconsin stacks. Many of the other characters in the book had written memoirs, autobiographies, or histories that provided welcome context, the inevitable "spin" notwithstanding, but none was more important than the two-volume biography of La Follette by his wife and daughter. Of the scholarly writings that contributed to my understanding of Roe's legal philosophy, Mark Graber's *Transforming Free Speech* and David Rabban's *Free Speech in Its Forgotten Years* stand out.

My colleagues at the University of Baltimore School of Law were unfailingly helpful. In addition to those already named, my thanks go especially to Professor C. J. Peters for giving me two opportunities to workshop the book, to Professor

Preface

Matthew Lindsay for commenting on the book at one of those workshops (and providing me a great meal during one of my research trips to Wisconsin), and to Professors Michael Meyerson and Garrett Epps, who helped with advice and support. Thanks, too, to Dean Ron Weich for funding some of those research trips to Madison and New York, and to the finest cadre of law librarians anywhere: Adeen Postar, Harvey Morrell, Joanne Colvin, David Matchen, Pat Behles, Jane Cupit, Bob Pool, and the magician of interlibrary loan, Bijal Shah. I also want to thank the research assistants who directly or indirectly contributed to the book: Katie Dorian, Kellye Beathea, Chris Stock, Rachele Norfolk, and Tom Geddes.

Finally, my gratitude to others who contributed in many ways to the manuscript at various stages of development: Blair Keltner for her help with the Schroeder Papers at Southern Illinois University; Jennifer Andruzzi for her outstanding proofreading and indexing work; Albert Copland, who read and improved early chapters; Cary Blankenship, who found just the right sources to fill the gaps in my historical knowledge; two anonymous reviewers who read and commented on the entire manuscript at two different points, each time making it far better than it had been before; and to Gwen Walker of the University of Wisconsin Press, who shepherded the manuscript every step of the way. Any mistakes that remain, of course, are exclusively my own.

Defending the Masses

Introduction

A Free Speech Pioneer

> There are worse calamities even than war. One of them would be the destruction of free speech and of free press—both of which have already been much restricted even in times of peace.
>
> Gilbert Roe

> [Gilbert Roe] has always looked upon the profession of law as one that involves to a high degree responsibility to the public, and it would be difficult to find a successful practitioner who combines with his legal skill a keener sense of duty to the public good.
>
> Robert La Follette

On December 18, 1914, a gentleman visited the third-floor apartment at 10 E. 15th Street in Manhattan and, finding that birth control advocate Margaret Sanger was not at home, left his card with a man who suggested he return around 9 a.m. the following day.[1] He came back the next day at 8 a.m.[2] and found William Sanger, Margaret's estranged husband. Sanger, still wearing his undershirt, opened the door about a foot.[3] "Is Mr. Sanger in?" the visitor asked. "That is my name," Sanger replied.

"My name is Heller," the visitor said. "I left a card here. I wanted to get some of Mrs. Sanger's books."[4] Heller said he sympathized with Margaret's work and specifically asked for her 1914 pamphlet *Family Limitation*.

"He seemed insistent, and finally said that if he could only get a copy of this pamphlet he would have it printed in different languages to distribute amongst the poor people he worked with and did business with," Sanger later wrote. "Thereupon I went and looked through the various books and pamphlets left in my care and found several copies, one of which I gave to him, and sent him, as I supposed, on his way rejoicing."[5]

Rejoicing he was, but not for the reason that Sanger supposed. One month later, on January 19, 1915, Heller returned to Sanger's apartment in the company of a "gray-haired, side-whiskered six-footer who lost no time in announcing, 'I am Mr. Comstock. I have a warrant for your arrest on the grounds of circulating obscene literature.'"[6] "Heller" was actually Charles J. Bamberger, an eighteen-year veteran agent of Anthony Comstock's New York Society for the Suppression of Vice.

Sanger was detained at the Yorkville Magistrate's Court, where one of his jailors let him use the phone. Sanger would logically have used the opportunity to contact Leonard Abbott, then president of the Free Speech League, an early precursor to today's American Civil Liberties Union formed in 1902, and a personal friend of the Sangers. Abbott, in turn, would tap the league's principal trial lawyer—Gilbert Ernstein Roe—to represent him.

By 1915, Roe had been practicing law for twenty-five years, the last fifteen in New York City. He had established a thriving Wall Street practice but had also carved out a niche for himself in Greenwich Village's radical society. Roe had already represented the *McClure's* "muckrakers," progressive-oriented investigative reporters; several anarchist editors, taking one to the U.S. Supreme Court; an iconoclastic feminist educator; and the leading Socialist journalists in New York. He had also written an important book on the judicial system and played a substantial role in the presidential campaign of 1912. But Roe's highest contributions to freedom of speech had been made in the trenches as a litigator. His experience and skill in the courtroom were indispensable assets to the Free Speech League and the activists it served.

After the Sanger case, Roe would go on to join that handful of dedicated lawyers who would challenge the repressive Espionage and Sedition Acts and the Red Scare that followed. The task of the free speech lawyers of Gilbert Roe's era was to find—and to sell, through motions, briefs, and oral arguments—an interpretation of the Constitution that would keep their activist clients in business and out of jail. It was largely a thankless struggle; they lost far more cases than they won and often received little or no remuneration for thousands of hours of hard work. In the early twentieth century, the cycle of conviction, appeal, and disappointment was repeated again and again in free speech cases, with small victories few and far between. Yet that continuing struggle was ultimately critical to the development of First Amendment protection for disfavored speech. For a quarter century, Gilbert Roe was in the thick of it all, and one of his cases, *Masses*

Introduction

Publishing Co. v. Patten, yielded an opinion that is still studied today from one of America's most important jurists, Learned Hand.

A list of Roe's clients and close acquaintances reads like a Who's Who of progressive America. Robert M. "Fighting Bob" La Follette, icon of the Progressive Era, was Roe's first law partner and a lifelong friend. During La Follette's many years in Washington, Roe remained his chief legal and political consigliere—fiercely loyal and dedicated to both the man and the movement. If La Follette was the heart of the movement, the "muckrakers" were its voice, and Roe worked with and for the best of them: S. S. McClure, Lincoln Steffens, Ray Stannard Baker, and Upton Sinclair. Roe also had intense personal and professional relationships with the fiery anarchist Emma Goldman and her sometime lover, the equally incendiary Alexander Berkman. Iconoclastic feminists like the Sangers and Henrietta Rodman rounded out Roe's prewar casebook.

Roe's most important client, at least from a historical perspective, was *The Masses*, a socialist magazine sometimes described as the soul of bohemian Greenwich Village. After defending editor Max Eastman and cartoonist Art Young in a criminal libel suit, Roe led the magazine's defense against federal charges brought under the Espionage Act, a statute enacted just as America entered World War I, ostensibly to combat espionage in the United States but effectively to criminalize any criticism of the war. Antiwar and Red Scare cases dominated Roe's caseload during and immediately after the war. He successfully defended La Follette against expulsion from the Senate for an allegedly seditious speech, and he unsuccessfully urged the U.S. Supreme Court to reverse the Espionage Act conviction of labor leader Eugene Debs. Roe's representation of Agnes Smedley was, perhaps, his only professional encounter with an actual Soviet agent, although he maintained a close personal relationship with journalist Jack Reed—chronicler of the revolution and a true believer. The "loyalty" issue spawned by the fear of communism prompted Roe's representation of Socialist assemblymen expelled from the legislature in Albany and New York City teachers expelled from their classrooms for leftist sympathies and Jewish faith. Roe represented the New York City Teachers Union until his death in 1929.

For all that, Roe remains relatively unknown. Despite playing a significant role in the history of free speech, he did so, as Mark Graber has pointed out, "in the field," leaving little in the way of academic writing on the subject. Lawyers like Roe "were far more interested in actually defending the rights of political dissidents than in detailing the philosophical and jurisprudential foundations of their libertarian beliefs," explains Graber.[7] Although Roe was a prolific writer, his overall orientation was far more practical than theoretical, which partly accounts for his relative obscurity today. Our understanding of First Amendment doctrine during this period has been shaped by far more dominating historical figures, including judges like Hand, Oliver Wendell Holmes, and Louis Brandeis, academics like Zechariah Chafee and Harold Laski, and even some of the litigants themselves: Goldman, Eastman, Debs. Of the lawyers, only Clarence Darrow is immediately recognized by name today. The Harry Weinbergers, Morris Hillquits, and Gilbert Roes are largely forgotten.

Gilbert Roe grew into maturity during a period of unprecedented social and economic changes "so alive with the promise of constructive change that they are known to history as 'the Progressive Era.'"[8] John Buenker describes the Wisconsin in which Roe began his legal journey as rapidly industrializing and urbanizing, with "teeming multitudes of southern and eastern European immigrants" working as unskilled labor in the growing manufacturing sector. The growing working class "reinforced, widened, and deepened existing social divisions—and created new ones." While some Wisconsinites dealt with the newly emerging social order by invoking such doctrines as "rugged individualism, natural law, laissez-faire, and Social Darwinism," others found this kind of nativism destructive of traditional "American ideals of equal opportunity and natural rights." Roe would soon join what Buenker characterizes as a "rising new class of 'professionals' [who] organized themselves, by occupation, to establish standards, to certify and discipline practitioners, to prescribe societal goals, structures, and behavior." Above all, they believed "that technological innovation, combined with the systematic application of expertise, must ultimately produce 'progress.'"

With the advent of these "progressives" came a "proliferation of trade associations, labor unions, producer and consumer cooperatives, municipal reform leagues, women's organizations, fraternal and benevolent societies, and professional associations." And political action. Wisconsin's progressives, Buenker writes, "sought to fashion a system that would ensure every citizen's economic security and enhance every citizen's quality of life without destroying the fundamentals of democracy and capitalism." Foremost among the political progressives was Robert M. La Follette, who advocated "equitable taxation, civil service, railroad regulation, and direct primary elections." While Gilbert Roe had exhibited liberal tendencies as far back as high school, his joining the La Follette law firm upon graduation from law school—indeed, his becoming an honorary member of La Follette's family—surely had an outsized influence on Roe's personal philosophy and the arc of his legal career.

Introduction

The post–Civil War jurisprudence that Roe would have witnessed in his early practice years was conservative in its regard for laissez-faire capitalism, but activist in its approach to promoting that philosophy. The "activist, interventionist posture"[9] that the Supreme Court had adopted by 1890, when Roe began working at the La Follette firm, valued most highly the liberty of contract as a fundamental right provided by Article I of the Constitution and the protection of life, liberty, and especially property through the due process clause of the Fourteenth Amendment.[10] Moreover, the Supreme Court had appropriated for the judiciary the power to determine what processes of law were "due" and to strike down regulatory legislation as substantively unreasonable or unwise, regardless of the processes by which the laws were enacted.

This "substantive due process" theory became the principal vehicle through which the court protected the economic interests of the railroads and other great corporations from state regulation of rail freight and other public utility rates. Expanded use of injunctive relief kept labor unions in check, and—beginning with the 1897 decision of *Allgeyer v. Louisiana*[11]—liberty of contract immunized labor practices from state health, safety, and welfare regulation, notwithstanding the unequal bargaining power between employers and workers. Thus, the court routinely struck down state regulatory measures that might interfere with corporate interests and, consequently, with untrammeled economic development.[12]

Freedom of speech was rarely an issue in the conservative decisions of this era but was often mentioned as another of the fundamental rights protected by the Fourteenth Amendment. The early conservative libertarians—late nineteenth-century thinkers who believed the role of government was limited to protecting "the property of men and the honor of women"[13]—accepted both freedom of speech and freedom of contract as two sides of the same coin; both were individual liberty interests to be insulated by the Supreme Court from legislative encroachment. Graber points out that in the twenty-five years following *Allgeyer*, the court "heard five cases in which the petitioner asserted a free-speech right and adjudicated all of them on the merits," rather than dismissing them on the ground that neither the Constitution nor the post–Civil War amendments restricted state power to regulate speech.[14]

The laissez-faire capitalism that thrived under this legal regime was anathema to the progressives, who saw their legislative reforms thwarted by judicial activism in defense of liberty of contract. Roe's book, *Our Judicial Oligarchy*, was typical of the progressive reaction to the *Lochner*[15] line of Supreme Court decisions. For many progressives, however, rejecting the substantive due process rationale justifying that activism also meant that the courts could no longer strike down legislative restrictions on speech. Gilbert Roe did not accept that limitation.

Roe's constitutional views on free speech grew out of his close association with Theodore Schroeder, a fellow Wisconsin law school alumnus, sometime legal colleague in New York City, and, most importantly, the philosophical heart of the Free Speech League. There is little evidence that Roe gave a great deal of deep philosophical thought to free speech issues before meeting up with Schroeder in New York; even afterward, his writings were far more doctrinal than theoretical as befits an eminently practical trial lawyer. As the league's principal legal representative, Roe generally shared Schroeder's views, which differed from those of both conservatives and progressives. Schroeder accepted the conservative view that free speech rights derived from the liberty interest protected by the due process clause of the Fourteenth Amendment. Judicial activism was not only permitted but required to protect those rights against any legislation that restricted speech, except for speech that caused actual material injury.[16] But he rejected the conservative view that freedom of contract stood on the same ground. Rather, he "insisted that private-property rights could not be derived from the more general right of equal liberty" and, therefore, were not protected by due process.

In taking that position, Schroeder differed from those progressives who did not distinguish between economic and expression rights and who accepted government regulation of both. Schroeder had little confidence in progressive legislation in any case; as a philosophical anarchist, he believed that only unlimited intellectual freedom would ultimately put an end to privilege and exploitation. Gilbert Roe, who was profoundly committed to the progressive political cause but also deeply influenced by Schroeder's support for free speech, seemed to find room for both ideas in crafting a practical approach to free speech litigation.

Perhaps the most complete articulation of Roe's prewar views on free speech, outside of the courtroom, came in the spring of 1915, when he testified before the Commission on Industrial Relations. The commission, also known as the Walsh Commission after its chairman, labor lawyer and activist Frank P. Walsh, was created by Congress in 1912 to study working conditions in the industrial economy throughout the country. Roe's testimony on May 10 covered a wide range of labor issues—including the legality of strikes, boycotts, and blacklists, and the use of martial law in labor disputes—and related legal doctrines, such as judicial review and due process. Roe explained his view that the common law was never designed to help the laboring class and that, absent a statute, judges who generally came from the upper classes were largely bound by unfavorable common law precedent.[17]

Amplifying his views on freedom of speech and assembly, Roe argued that "the courts have failed of their duties in respect to those fundamental rights" in several respects. "In the first place," he said, "so far as I am aware, the courts have upheld and enforced every statute that has been passed on the abridgment of those rights. Now, whether the courts are going into the business of passing upon the validity of statutes at all or not is another question; but if they are going to declare statutes unconstitutional that relate to property when they are in conflict with the Constitution, it would seem that they ought to apply the same principle to statutes which invade personal rights."

Commissioner Harris Weinstock, a California businessman, asked at what point public speech ceases to be lawful and begins to be seditious and lawbreaking in character. "Where would you draw the line?" Roe replied that he would not draw a line "short of the point where some overt act results from the abuse of free speech." Weinstock pressed: "You mean, if a man got up in a public place and denounced the Government and the authorities and charged them with all sorts of crimes and misdemeanors you would treat it with contempt unless some unlawful act followed, in which event you would hold them responsible?" Roe replied, "Yes. I would ignore it. I think that is the right way, in principle; and I think that in practice it is the best way to get along."

World War I and the Red Scare that followed gave rise to a new—in Graber's view—"civil libertarian" theory to justify judicial protection of free speech rights.[18] Under this theory, the freedom of speech was embodied in the First Amendment, not due process, and was less an individual liberty than a civic necessity in a self-governing democracy. The war had seriously divided the progressives. Some, like La Follette and Roe, were vehemently opposed to the war and to the legislation that essentially criminalized that opposition. No abstract principle of judicial acquiescence in democratically enacted legislation would persuade them that the Espionage Act and a package of draconian amendments that came to be known as the Sedition Act of 1918 were constitutional, at least as they were being construed by the courts. As a practical matter, however, the conservative libertarian defense of free speech—broadly protective in theory—was spectacularly unsuccessful in court. Although Roe asserted in *Masses* that the law violated the First and Fifth Amendments, his constitutional argument was perfunctory at best.

Those progressives who were neutral toward or supported the war, and were opposed to judicial activism, found themselves without any constitutional defense of free speech. Learned Hand found *The Masses* case raised no constitutional questions at all but turned exclusively on interpretation of the Espionage Act and whether the published articles and cartoons should have been barred from the mails by the postmaster as provided in statute. Hand would have allowed *The Masses* to be mailed because Congress surely could not have intended to bar "every political agitation which can be shown to be apt to create a seditious temper."[19] Of course, Hand was reversed because that is exactly what Congress intended to do, and there was no constitutional barrier to prevent it.

Even after Holmes articulated a "clear and present danger" test in *Schenck v. United States*[20] — the first of the Espionage Act cases to reach the U.S. Supreme Court — most progressive jurists continued to believe that it was up to Congress, not judges, to determine when such a danger existed. Brandeis pushed that standard closer to providing a degree of protection by requiring the danger to be serious and distinguishing permissible advocacy from punishable incitement.[21] But it was Zechariah Chafee who fully conceptualized the new constitutional justification for judicial activism to protect speech. Rather than a fundamental *individual right*, freedom of speech was a *social requirement* for the proper functioning of a democratic society, and judges were obligated to safeguard that process, even from majority opinion as expressed by legislatures.

In Graber's view, Chafee's conception was less protective of speech rights than the conservative libertarian doctrine but prevailed because Chafee was able to (mis)characterize it as a continuation of traditional principles. It is certainly true that the scope of protected speech was much broader in Schroeder's view than in Chafee's (or that of later scholars such as Alexander Meiklejohn or Thomas Emerson) — which might not have protected the sexual speech that interested Schroeder — but Chafee's strategy was much better suited to protecting political dissidents from majoritarian legislation.

Indeed, Roe's approach to free speech was already evolving to track the more successful doctrine; even before the Espionage Act was passed, he had made a democratic process argument in hearings. In April 1917, Roe posed the rhetorical question, "[How] is any voter to form an intelligent opinion unless there is the fullest discussion permitted of every phase of the war, its origin, its manner of prosecution, and its manner of termination?"[22] Later, condemning the Act in 1919, he wrote, "I insist upon freedom of speech and of free press not merely because it is a constitutional right, but because it is a necessity under our form of government. Today, the President of the United States and our other representatives in the Peace Conference are assuming to act for the people of this country without knowing what the sentiment of the country is upon the most vital matters to be decided at the conference."[23]

Introduction

Thus, Gilbert Roe straddled the old conservative libertarian approach to free speech and the new civil libertarian approach—probably without giving those abstract concepts very much thought at all. He made the free speech arguments he thought would win cases. Most of the time, he lost, never knowing that his perception of free speech would ultimately be accepted as the American perception of free speech. Still, he labored on, achieving modest recognition during his lifetime, and was all but forgotten after his death, except among those who needed his help.

1

Getting Started

> People who knew Mr. Roe will remember he always rose slowly in greeting anyone. Rather than coldness or reticence, it seemed a crescendo of warmth, all the more real for its slow tempo. It gave one time, as it did me now, to look deep into eyes one never forgot.
>
> Gwyneth King Roe

> My notion is that when election day comes, most of the real progressives will think it wise to vote for Wilson, and in that way, bury both Taft and Roosevelt; then we can reorganize the movement and put it back where it was before Roosevelt "butted in" and disorganized it.
>
> Gilbert Roe

The Madison Years

Gilbert Ernstein Roe was born to John and Jane McKeeby Roe on February 7, 1864, in the town of Oregon, Wisconsin, in Dane County.[1] The youngest of the three Roe children, Gilbert attended Evansville High School, graduating in 1883,[2] and many years later remembered the experience fondly.[3] Roe's liberal sensibilities were already apparent when he was in high school. His graduation oration was entitled "Stability of the American Government" and, while it tended to prolix, it clearly demonstrated his strong sense of political and social justice. Roe lamented the "social vices" as a "dark cloud that overshadows the brightness of America's future." Without moral development to match America's technological achievements, declaimed the young Gilbert Roe, "she, who has done more to advance the cause of humanity than any other nation on the face of the earth; she who has ever been the champion of the weak, and the refuge of the oppressed; the friend of truth and the founder of justice, shall she fall the victim of her own folly?"[4]

Roe received a Bachelor of Laws degree from the University of Wisconsin in 1890,[5] after taking an active role in campus activities—especially debate.[6] Of particular note was his participation in the eleventh annual joint debate between the Athenaean and Hesperion Literary Societies in 1887. The topic of the debate was Prohibition, specifically, "Is legal prohibition a true remedy for the evils arising from the traffic in alcoholic liquors in the United States?" Roe argued the affirmative for the winning Athenean team, and in so doing, he displayed the talent for legal argument that would stand him in good stead for the rest of his life.

Roe was admitted as "Attorney and Counselor at Law and Solicitor in Chancery" in January 1890,[7] even before he received his diploma in June. In June, he received certificates of admission to practice from the Wisconsin Supreme Court and the Federal Circuit and District Courts for the Western District of Wisconsin, as well as his degree from the university.[8] Most significantly, he joined the firm of La Follette, [Sam] Harper, Roe & [Albert] Zimmerman in the same year.[9] Robert M. La Follette, who had been admitted to practice ten years earlier, had much in common with Gilbert Roe. "It was always amusing to hear Bob and his law partner, Gilbert Roe, also a Dane County boy, compare their boyhood experiences in selling their farm products," La Follette's wife, Belle Case La Follette, would write.[10] For the next ten years, Roe would practice law in Madison. More than a hundred cases are recorded in the firm's archives between September 1890 and December 1895, including personal injury and contract claims, foreclosures, divorce, probate, criminal defense, and other general practice matters.[11] There was no hint of the civil liberties career to come.

In June 1891, after his first year in practice, the twenty-seven-year-old Gilbert Roe married Carolyn M. "Carrie" Drake, who was not yet nineteen.[12] The record contains little information about Carrie Roe. Gwyneth D. King, who would become Gilbert Roe's second wife, recalled meeting Carrie Drake at King's temporary "ladies gymnastics" studio in Madison in January 1895, where Carrie participated in King's classes.[13] "A sparkling-eyed young girl sat by her solicitous mother whose heavily lined face showed anxiety and tension. This young person introduced her mother . . . and then said gaily: 'Mine's short—R-O-E—you can't forget it.'"[14] Within five years of her marriage, however, Carrie Roe was dead. She had been diagnosed with tuberculosis in mid-November 1895, "without a shadow of hope for recovery."[15] Roe's professional as well as personal life changed dramatically after Carrie's death. The La Follette law firm was dissolved to give La Follette more time to devote to politics,[16] and Roe formed a new partnership with Albert Zimmerman. "There was no change in the close personal friendship of the firm members," Belle added. She said Roe devoted much of his time to helping La Follette prepare and try cases, so La Follette was free to give a few weeks each year to political campaigns.

Roe remarried in 1899. His second wife, Gwyneth D. King, was born in 1868 to Quakers John and Permelia King on the outskirts of New Providence, Iowa.[17] John King was elected to the Iowa state legislature in 1877 and reelected in 1879,[18] but he resigned in 1881 to found a new town in the Dakota Territory that would be called Chamberlain.[19] While the King family moved to Chamberlain in 1883, Gwyneth stayed in Hampton, Iowa, to finish high school and then moved on to Highland Hall, a "Young Ladies' College" in Highland Park, Illinois, a Chicago suburb.[20] While a student there, she met Emily Mulkin, a physical education teacher who would become her dearest friend and mentor. After King graduated, she took a position at Yankton College in what had become South Dakota. She taught at Yankton for two years. In the summer of 1887, Emily Mulkin Bishop was asked to teach at the famed "Summer School for Adults" at Chautauqua, New York, and invited Gwyneth to come with her. At Chautauqua, Bishop taught a course called Health and Self-Expression, based on the work of French pioneer François Delsarte, the progenitor of a school of modern dance movement epitomized by Isadora Duncan. After the first season, Gwyneth became a teacher as well, sharing the expenses and revenues with Bishop. Gwyneth taught at the University of South Dakota during 1889 and 1890, then moved to Washington, D.C., where she taught in a number of public and private schools during the 1890s.

King first met Gilbert Roe in 1895 when Emily Bishop asked King to take her place teaching a group of women in Madison, Wisconsin, who had formed an Emily Bishop League.[21] Mrs. Robert M. La Follette, the former Belle Case, was president of the league,[22] and Carrie Drake Roe was one of the students. In her draft autobiography, Gwyneth recounted her first meeting with Carrie's husband Gilbert, who had agreed to join a men's class organized by Judge Robert Siebecker, La Follette's brother-in-law. "From the depths of a huge arm chair two rooms away, a young man rose and came forward with outstretched, friendly hand," King would write much later. "People who knew Mr. Roe will remember he always rose slowly in greeting anyone. Rather than coldness or reticence, it seemed a crescendo of warmth, all the more real for its slow tempo. It gave one time, as did me now, to look deep into eyes one never forgot."[23] Gwyneth King returned to Madison the following year, not long after Carrie Roe's death. "Besides the thrill from success in work," she wrote, "there was the joy of close association with the La Follette circle."[24] On the second trip, she lived with the La Follettes, which brought renewed contact with Gilbert Roe. Soon, Gilbert and "Netha" were corresponding every day, sometimes twice a day, and openly talked about marriage. "We finished one of the hardest trials today I ever engaged in and won out with a verdict of fifty-five hundred dollars for our client—damages for breach of promise of marriage," Gilbert wrote. "Beware how you trifle with my affections."[25] On September 7, 1899, Gilbert and Netha were secretly married in New York City,[26] just before Netha and Emily Bishop embarked on a grand tour of Europe, visiting France, Italy, and Switzerland.[27] Upon Netha's return to New York on November 12, 1899, she and Gilbert were more formally married.[28] Fola La Follette lamented not having "Uncle Gil" around to talk to, but took the move gracefully. "I am glad you have decided to go to N.Y.," she wrote to Gilbert, "for I think you & Netha will be happier and when we really love people that is what we care for—I know you and Netha would be happy anywhere so long as you had each other. But I am glad you are to be where you will be the happiest."[29]

Starting Out in New York

Following a trip west to see family and friends, the newly wed Roes initially settled down in a Harlem apartment at 208 W. 116th Street,[30] near what is today called Adam Clayton Powell Boulevard. Gilbert opened his law office downtown at 96 Broadway and 6 Wall Street.[31] Gwyneth opened her own studio at 114 W. 72nd Street[32] with the help of Emily Bishop, who stayed in the Roe household for a time.[33] In January 1900, Roe was admitted to practice in the New York courts on a petition attesting to his admission and nine years' practice in Wisconsin. La Follette and Zimmerman provided certificates of "good moral character."[34] Later that year, La Follette would finally win the Republican nomination for governor; he won the election by 100,000 votes and would be reelected in 1902 and again in 1904. Roe's earliest New York cases were fairly routine business-oriented cases, several involving organizing businesses as corporations.[35] During that first decade in New York, Roe's reported decisions included a partnership accounting case;[36] a breach of contract case;[37] construction cases ranging from enforcing a mechanic's lien[38] to an accidental death in a building collapse;[39] and an estate case.[40] While he was not particularly fond of business cases, he did enjoy the fees they provided.[41]

Roe also began to invest his new income, although not always wisely. As early as 1901, Roe had invested $500 in shares of an Alaska gold-mining scheme that never panned out,[42] and Gwyneth Roe remembered an early investment in a pecan grove in Florida.[43] On the whole, she wrote, those "mistakes" were relatively few, perhaps because they began with so little money. By 1906, however, that was no longer the case, and Roe seemed eager to make new financial investments. That year, Roe offered to invest $5,000 in a Wisconsin real estate investment business with La Follette's partner Alfred Rogers.[44] "I am anxious to get what ready cash I have into dirt," he wrote Rogers, mentioning a real estate opportunity on Long Island.[45] By the end of the year, however, Roe was telling Rogers that he couldn't invest any more money in Rogers's Southern Wisconsin Realty Company because he was going into "an oil deal here, which will use up my spare cash."[46]

Insurance cases comprised a significant part of Roe's practice. As Gwyneth pointed out, he found himself on both sides of these cases but more often represented individuals against the companies. In his very first reported decision, Roe represented the Union Central Life Insurance Company, which had issued a $10,000 policy to one Isaac Levy.[47] Levy subsequently assigned the policy to Jacob Strauss, who failed to pay all of the premiums on time. When the company declared the policy forfeit, Strauss sued to have it reinstated on the ground that he was not properly notified of the premiums due. The company had notified Levy, but not Strauss, despite having knowledge of the assignment; all three New York courts that heard the case held against Roe's client.[48]

By far the most important and time-consuming of the insurance cases that Roe handled during his first decade in New York involved his representation of various clients against the Mutual Reserve Life Insurance Co., a New York company that sold insurance policies in several states. In his first reported case against the company, Roe won a pretrial motion requiring officers of the company to show whether the company had enough money on hand to pay the amount due under the policy to the estate of one Mary F. King.[49] Mutual Reserve was also the defendant in numerous lawsuits around the country, and Roe got a good share of the business representing successful plaintiffs seeking to enforce judgments against the company in New York.[50] One of those cases, *Birch v. Mutual Reserve Life Ins. Co.*, took Roe all the way to the United States Supreme Court.[51]

The issue in *Birch*, which was typical of many of these cases, was whether the insurance company could avoid paying plaintiffs who won lawsuits against it in North Carolina on the ground that the North Carolina courts lacked jurisdiction due to improper service of process.[52] While the issue presented to the

New York courts was highly technical, the lawsuits on which these judgments were based alleged such nefarious practices as imposing unlawful assessments on policy holders and declaring the policies forfeit if the assessments were not paid.[53] Roe's client, Henry C. Birch, was the assignee of seven such North Carolina judgments, which the company sought to void on the ground that it no longer solicited business there and had revoked the power of attorney it had granted the North Carolina insurance commissioner to receive service of process.[54] The New York courts gave the company's arguments short shrift, and on December 18, 1905, the United States Supreme Court affirmed the judgment for Roe's client.[55] The *Mutual Reserve* cases continued through the end of the decade.[56] Besides helping to put Roe's practice on a solid financial footing, the *Mutual Reserve* cases had yet another salutary effect: he had the opportunity to work on the same cases as Theodore Schroeder, who would become the guiding theorist of the Free Speech League, which Roe would serve as chief trial lawyer.

Schroeder was born in Dodge County, Wisconsin, a few months before Roe.[57] He entered the University of Wisconsin in 1882, a year before Roe, and graduated from its law school in 1889, also a year earlier than Roe. While Roe stayed in Madison for nine years after graduation, Schroeder immediately moved to Salt Lake City, Utah, where he opened his own law practice. As his hostility to the LDS Church grew, however, Schroeder increasingly found himself embroiled in politico-religious controversies in Salt Lake City. He even traveled to Washington, where he successfully pursued the exclusion of a Mormon congressman from the House of Representatives. In Washington, he also connected with Charles B. Landis, a like-minded congressman from Indiana. Around the turn of the century, Schroeder left Salt Lake City to establish a new law practice in New York City. By 1903, Schroeder had become involved in the *Mutual Reserve* cases. At the suggestion of Rep. Landis, Schroeder offered to provide information on those cases to Sen. John C. Spooner (R-Wis.) in connection with pending legislation to "prevent 'wild cat' insurance companies from using the mails as a means of soliciting business from States and in States with whose laws they have not complied."[58] In a letter to Spooner, Schroeder closed: "You will possibly remember me as having come formerly from Wisconsin. Mr. Gilbert E. Roe of 96 Broadway, also formerly a resident of your state, is interested with me in the [*Mutual Reserve*] litigation." How closely the two men worked together on these cases is not clear from the record. The letter suggests that Schroeder did not consult Roe before writing it. Spooner was a leader of the Stalwart faction that bitterly opposed La Follette, and mentioning Roe would hardly have won Schroeder any lobbying points. On the other hand, Spooner and La Follette had come to a modus vivendi whereby Spooner would stay out of state and local politics and La Follette would not oppose Spooner's reelection to the Senate in 1903.[59]

It is certain, however, that Schroeder and Roe found common ground in the radical milieu of New York City. As Schroeder's biographer put it, "here the terrain was permeated with many factions of radicalism, liberalism, and what not, each seeking to adjust its claims to constitutionality and restore to the people their civil rights. Naturally, this was fertile soil to Schroeder . . . and he launched a wide propaganda for free speech."[60] But where Schroeder soon abandoned the practice of law to plunge headlong into the radical "terrain," Roe entered those circles as a lawyer first and an activist second. Moreover, even as Roe represented and largely sympathized with his radical clients—anarchists, socialists, and eventually communists—his personal activism, particularly his work on behalf of women's suffrage and, later, against the war, remained grounded in progressive Republican politics and a rather conservative family life. Roe had partnered with William F. McCombs, another Wall Street attorney, in October 1904, but their offices remained at 96 Broadway and 6 Wall Street.[61] McCombs would serve as Woodrow Wilson's campaign manager in 1912.[62] The Roes had also moved house from Harlem to a fifteenth-floor apartment in the Ansonia Building, 2109 Broadway at 73rd Street, overlooking the Hudson River.[63] And by early 1906, Gwyneth was pregnant with their first child.[64]

Throughout 1906, Roe continued to be both legislative and political "consigliere" to La Follette, who had relinquished the Wisconsin governorship in January to succeed U.S. senator Joseph V. Quarles, who was appointed to a federal judgeship. In Washington, La Follette continued his interest in the kind of railroad rate regulation that he had implemented as governor of Wisconsin, and he sought Roe's counsel on the provisions he might submit as proposed legislation. On April 19, 1906, La Follette began his maiden speech in support of legislation to regulate freight rates. The speech continued for eight hours over three days, consuming 148 pages in the *Congressional Record*. By the end, there were almost no other senators in attendance. Belle remarked, "There was no mistaking that this was a polite form of hazing."[65] Polite or not, Roe wrote Belle to say he was glad to hear the speech went well. "More important even than its effect upon the present rate discussion, is the fact that it starts Bob off right in the Senate."[66]

Word of Gwyneth's pregnancy reached Belle La Follette in May. Belle wrote to congratulate her, while expressing sympathy for the loss of her father, who had died in April. "Motherhood is the supreme experience of life," Belle wrote. "I am glad for both your sakes that you have not let thoughts of self deprive you of the greatest joy life affords."[67] Belle was similarly effusive when John Ernest (Jack) Roe was born in September. "I want you to know however disappointed you may be, that the *Grandmother is entirely satisfied* with a *boy* and stands ready to adopt him at any time when he gets too much for you," she wrote.[68] Roe's personal life in 1906 also included a growing concern for his first father-in-law, Henry C. Drake.[69] Rogers had been trying to help Drake organize his assets and liabilities but told Roe he feared "that if things are allowed to drift along he will lose everything he has." He asked Roe to write Drake suggesting he follow Rogers's advice, and Roe replied that he would try to find a tactful way to do that.[70] Late in the year, Roe sent Drake $50 for Christmas, which Rogers said "made the old man mighty happy."[71] Drake died in May 1907 of what the coroner described as apoplexy, probably a stroke.[72]

The year 1907 also saw the publication of Roe's first book, *Selected Opinions of Luther Dixon and Edgar Ryan, Late Chief Justices of the Supreme Court of Wisconsin*. The book was suggested by members of the Wisconsin Society of New York, Roe said in his preface, "who desired in this manner to testify their admiration for these great jurists."[73] Roe had selected the nineteen cases included in the book and had written biographical sketches of the two jurists, as well as legal and historical annotations. Roe's political efforts turned toward promoting La Follette for president in 1908. At the same time, however, he began to feel the financial pinch from so many unproductive investments. "Needless to say," he wrote Rogers in July, "I fully approve of the scheme to boom the 'Boss' for President. I will also be one of twenty to put in $500, but I cannot promise any of it for several months, and cannot promise it all for several months more."[74] As it happened, Roe put both money and labor into the La Follette campaign during 1907 and 1908, organizing speaking engagements in and around New York[75] and working to get books prepared and articles placed to advance La Follette's prospects.[76] But La Follette's campaign for the Republican presidential nomination collapsed in June 1908 when the Chicago convention nominated William Howard Taft. La Follette came in sixth, with only 2.5 percent of the vote. Taft would go on to defeat William Jennings Bryan in the general election in November.

By 1910, the Roe family had moved back uptown but remained close to the Hudson River. They first rented an apartment at 620 W. 115th Street, then moved another block or so north and west, to 445 Riverside Drive, in September of that year.[77] Daughter Janet was born in October. Belle La Follette wrote her "Loved Ones" celebrating the birth: "You can only measure the happiness your telegram gave us by your own."[78] In 1911, Roe had moved his office a few blocks north to 55 Liberty Street, still in the Wall Street area, but farther away from his partner, William McCombs, who was disputing the division of proceeds from the *Mutual Reserve* insurance cases.[79] Netha retained her 72nd Street studio and was listed in a 1911 directory as an "elocutionist." Netha became pregnant again during 1911, and Belle was sympathetic: "My heart is with you Netha and I know these waiting days are long at best. But you will have your reward and this will complete and enrich your life as nothing else could and I believe you will have the easiest time yet—it will be so good when the waiting is over."[80] Daughter Gwyneth was born in November.

The Campaign of 1912

Gilbert Roe spent the latter part of 1911 and much of 1912 working on La Follette's next presidential campaign, only to see Theodore Roosevelt throw his hat in the ring,[81] divide the progressive movement, and destroy La Follette's chances. As early as 1910, Roe had written to Wisconsin governor Francis N. McGovern warning about Roosevelt. "Progressive Republicans do not pin their faith to Roosevelt," Roe wrote. "Roosevelt is not a 'Progressive' as we use the word. In his heart he does not believe in popular Government, except by roundabout methods. He is much more in accordance with Hamilton than he is with Jefferson. Real Progressives here are backing Roosevelt merely to kill off corrupt bosses. What they will do with Roosevelt later is a question."[82] By the summer of 1911, the hostility between Roosevelt and Taft had weakened the president politically,[83] and as long as Roosevelt stayed out of the race—as he insisted he would—there seemed to be hope for a La Follette candidacy. Roe was actively involved in fundraising for La Follette and helped develop a permanent National Finance Committee for the Progressive Republican Campaign Committee at the Chicago conference. The finance committee included lawyers Amos Pinchot of New York, Alfred Baker of Chicago, and Rudolph Spreckles of San Francisco.[84] Pinchot's brother, Gifford, endorsed La Follette as "the logical successor to Roosevelt" at an Insurgents Club dinner that fall. Roe also kept an eye on La Follette's public appearances and other publicity, negotiating with several companies on the publication of the senator's autobiography in book form. On December 30, 1911, for example, he blasted *Collier's National Weekly* for an article stating that La Follette was not a viable candidate to give the Democrats a serious challenge in the presidential primaries.[85] "In common with many thousands of readers of your magazine, who are earnest supporters of Senator La Follette's candidacy, I fully recognize the right of your paper to promote the candidacy of Mr. Roosevelt, by all honorable means," he wrote.

"I deny, however, that you have the right to do so by the method used in your article."[86]

But public support for a Roosevelt candidacy, always strong, grew even stronger toward the end of 1911, even as La Follette's campaign was gathering momentum.[87] In fact, work had already begun to undermine La Follette's candidacy to make way for Roosevelt's entrance. On January 2, 1912, the *Washington Times* carried a story speculating that La Follette would probably drop out of the race.[88] A convention of Ohio progressives, expected to endorse La Follette, abruptly decided to endorse no single candidate.[89] And William Allen White's *Emporia Gazette* formally declared for Roosevelt, saying he alone could keep the Republicans in office.

On January 22, La Follette and his family traveled to New York for a campaign speech at Carnegie Hall. Fola recalls they arrived in the late afternoon and were met at the station by Gilbert and Netha Roe, among others. They went to the Roe apartment on Riverside Drive for a "quiet family dinner" and then drove to Carnegie Hall.[90] More than two hundred members of the Insurgents Club were seated on the stage, and La Follette's speech was a great success by all accounts. La Follette spent the night and most of the next day at the Roe home and then went to Roe's office for a strategy conference. The conference reconvened at Roe's home and lasted through dinner until almost midnight. Roosevelt's candidacy was now seen as inevitable, and pressure on La Follette to withdraw was mounting. Amos Pinchot and his brother, Gifford, were among the earliest defectors from La Follette's camp, and they implored him to drop out of the race.[91] Angry at being treated like a "stalking horse" for Roosevelt, and bitter about the betrayal of the Pinchots, La Follette steadfastly declined to withdraw. It would only get worse.

On February 2, La Follette gave a disastrous speech in Philadelphia at the annual banquet of the Periodical Publishers' Association, alienating the audience of magazine and newspaper journalists, most of whom eventually walked out on him. Belle looked to Roe for consolation. "When I learned of the humiliation Bob had suffered in Philadelphia I longed for you Gilbert," she wrote. "And it is you and Alf [Rogers] who are needed here or men like you—if there are any."[92] Rumors began circulating that La Follette had suffered a nervous breakdown, and many of his remaining supporters used that excuse to defect to Roosevelt. Gifford Pinchot made a public statement of support for Roosevelt, saying La Follette's failing health "compromised the progressive cause."[93] La Follette wrote Roe, "I am likely to be attacked in every conceivable and underhanded way by the friends of another candidate in order to force me to quit the field. . . . There is not a thing wrong with me, excepting that I find myself dead tired."[94] There was little Roe could do to stem the tide. On the evening of February 4, meeting at Roe's home with California governor Hiram Johnson, George Record told Roe that he would join other New Jersey progressives in moving to Roosevelt.[95] Roe wrote La Follette on February 8 about his meeting with Johnson and other progressives. "I found it very hard to take any part in the discussion and keep my temper," he said.[96] On February 25, Roosevelt publicly declared that he would accept the Republican nomination.[97]

Despite all the setbacks, Roe soldiered on for La Follette during the spring of 1912. "We are just plugging along night and day," he wrote, "working about all the hours there are out of the twenty-four, confident that whatever the immediate results, we are on the right path, and ultimately our work will count."[98] Roe postponed much of his regular legal work to campaign for and with La Follette in California, New Jersey, and South Dakota—three of the handful of states then with direct primary elections that La Follette and his insurgents had worked so hard to promote.[99] The first primary was held on March 12 in North Dakota; La Follette received 58 percent of the vote to Roosevelt's 39 percent and Taft's 3 percent. La Follette would go on to win the Wisconsin primary as well, but no others, even after a concerted effort by the Roosevelt campaign to expand the number of primaries before the convention. By the end of the primary season, Roosevelt had 1.2 million popular votes; Taft, 866,000; and La Follette, 327,000. At the Republican Convention, however, more than half the votes needed for victory—254 delegates—were disputed by the Roosevelt and Taft forces. Roosevelt's forces thought that if they could control the convention with the help of the La Follette delegates, at least long enough to prevent Taft from winning a first-ballot victory, Roosevelt could still take the nomination.

In an effort to engineer just such a coalition, Roosevelt's operatives offered Gilbert Roe the temporary chairmanship of the convention while the committee was considering the disputed seats.[100] Roe turned them down, telling them the La Follette delegates "would keep absolutely clear of anything that could look like a combination with either Roosevelt or Taft."[101] Roe was subsequently invited to "have a conference with Roosevelt personally."[102] California's Johnson also asked Roe to act as temporary chairman. Roe refused both requests. In the end, the committee awarded 235 of the 254 disputed seats to Taft[103] and Taft won the nomination. Roosevelt supporters formed the Progressive Party, better known as the Bull Moose Party, and nominated the former president as their candidate. Following the Democratic Convention, La Follette and Roe threw their support to its nominee, Woodrow Wilson, hoping that a Wilson victory would clear the path for a resurgence of La Follette progressivism in the wake of a Republican implosion. "I believe the first task of all progressives is to eliminate

Roosevelt," Roe wrote to one La Follette supporter.[104] "My notion is that when election day comes, most of the real progressives will think it wise to vote for Wilson, and in that way, bury both Taft and Roosevelt; then we can reorganize the movement and put it back where it was before Roosevelt 'butted in' and disorganized it," he wrote another.[105] "I think Wilson is more or less of a fraud, and rather expect his administration will be a fraud; but so much the better for us," Roe wrote still another.[106] To La Follette, Roe confided, "I personally have made up my mind to support Wilson, though I do not expect to take any active part in the campaign." He did allow his name to be used in an organization of progressive Republicans for Wilson but told La Follette, "I am so rushed with law business, that I am not giving much time to politics now."[107]

New York Politics

During 1912, Roe published a progressive manifesto called *Our Judicial Oligarchy*—a vigorous condemnation of the *Lochner*-era[108] courts that struck down progressive legislation at the state and federal levels. The book charged that the courts had "usurped" the power to declare statutes unconstitutional, had "come to legislate generally" by reading their own opinions into statutes, and had treated the rich and poor unequally.[109] *Oligarchy* called for free criticism of the courts—which was largely stifled by the courts' use of contempt by publication—and, should that fail, the recall of judges. That year also saw Roe's eldest daughter stricken with multiple ailments. In early February, she was diagnosed with pneumonia and was suffering from pain in the aftermath of an ear operation.[110] In a February 8 letter to La Follette, Roe confessed that his nerves were already raw "because things have been going badly with Janet."[111] In October, the Roes abandoned New York City as their place of residence, purchasing a spacious estate at Pelham Manor in Westchester County to accommodate their growing family.[112]

But Roe spent a substantial portion of the next few years in the byzantine world of New York politics, largely the consequence of his own ambition to ascend the bench. Specifically, Roe had his eye on a seat on the principal state trial court, the New York Supreme Court, to be filled in the November elections. With the splintering of the Progressive Republican movement in 1912, the only way to displace Tammany Hall machine officials seemed to lie with a Fusion ticket that represented traditional Republicans, Bull Moose progressives, and independent Democrats. Such Fusion tickets had been successful in the past, defeating Boss Tweed's machine in the 1870s, and would be in the future, electing Fiorello La Guardia in the 1930s.[113] Roe threw his lot in with the Fusionists. Roe's candidacy for a Supreme Court nomination surfaced on July 23, when the *Times* reported that the "Gilbert E. Roe Non-Partisan Judiciary Committee" had formally urged the Fusion committee to place Roe's name on its slate.[114] A week later, in a long letter to La Follette, Roe confided that he did not think he had sufficient support to win.[115] In August, he wrote that he had had a "nice visit" with Louis Brandeis, who had been talking up Roe's candidacy among committee members he knew. "[He was] very much pleased with the way my candidacy had been received by everyone with whom he talked," Roe said, but "I did not get the impression . . . that he expected we would win this time."[116]

Brandeis was right about Roe's prospects. That very week, the committee unanimously decided to nominate an "unknown"—in Roe's words. "[He] is an agreeable chap," Roe wrote La Follette, "who has never taken any part in anything. His father was a judge in the time of Boss Tweed, and received some disagreeable notoriety at the time. This ought not to be held against the son, however, who up to the present time has never had an opportunity to show what he has inherited from his dad. If elected, he will have the opportunity."[117] To be sure, Benjamin N. Cardozo was largely unknown. Roe even misspelled his name as "Cardoza." Fusion routed Tammany in November, and Cardozo won by 2,300 votes out of 300,000 cast.[118] He would certainly have an opportunity to show his mettle: on the New York Supreme Court, the New York Court of Appeals, and eventually the United States Supreme Court. Cardozo would become one of the most highly regarded American jurists of all time.

Gilbert Roe also played a role in New York's second high political drama of 1913: the impeachment and removal of Gov. William Sulzer led by the Tammany forces in the state legislature. The impeachment was partly responsible for the anti-Tammany backlash that swept the Fusionists into power. Roe had a good relationship with the Democrat Sulzer, who had been elected with Tammany support. In May 1913, for example, Sulzer appointed Roe to the committee that would lead the fight for direct primaries in New York, based on his experience and success in Wisconsin.[119] But direct primaries posed an existential threat to Tammany power, and that was only one of the issues dividing the more populist Sulzer from his machine roots. Tammany boss Charles Murphy marshaled his forces in the legislature to remove Sulzer from office.[120]

Roe was retained by a close Sulzer aide, James C. Garrison, when Garrison was arrested for contempt of the State Assembly in early morning hours of September 19, 1913.[121] Some weeks earlier, Garrison, a former editor of the *New York Press*, had allegedly accused four members of accepting bribes to support the impeachment proposal and then refused to answer questions about the allegations before the judiciary committee.[122] "We are confident that the commitment will not stand a court review," Roe told the *Times*. "If this action is allowed to stand, no citizen's liberty will be safe."[123] On October 30, a court did indeed free Garrison, ruling that the assembly only had the power to punish Garrison for contempt committed in its presence.[124] Garrison called the decision a "landmark for the freedom of the press" and threatened to sue members of the Assembly.[125] But the case soon faded from the headlines, giving way to election stories. Sulzer was elected to the Assembly from the sixth district,[126] and Roe took a break from New York politics to practice law again.

Well, almost. The 1913 New York state ballot also included two Progressive Party candidates for the Court of Appeals, New York's highest state court. For associate judge, the party had nominated Judge Samuel Seabury, then sitting on the New York Supreme Court, and for chief judge, Judge Learned Hand, then a judge on the United States District Court for the Southern District of New York. Hand had no illusions about winning; he had accepted the nomination as part of an effort to keep the Progressives alive as a party in the wake of Roosevelt's 1912 defeat.[127] In a conversation with Roe, who had been before Hand on several occasions, Hand had predicted a serious drubbing. In the end, he was pleasantly surprised with the 195,000 votes he received, some 13 percent of the total. Two days after the election, Roe wrote a note to Hand congratulating him on the size of his "protest" vote. Roe said the vote showed that there is a "sentiment in this state demanding a change in the character of Judges."[128] Hand wrote back, condemning "the very ill-advised and lawless attitude of judges in the past in their constitutional decisions." Echoing the Progressive mantra that Roe had argued in *Oligarchy*, Hand insisted that a judge's "first duty is honestly to try to get at the legislative meaning when it is written."[129]

Meanwhile, an ailing La Follette had thrown himself into the 1914 Wisconsin gubernatorial race, backing the Democrat Paul Husting against his old Stalwart nemesis, Emanuel Philipp, who had captured the Republican nomination, and James Blaine, an independent Progressive. Roe's role in the campaign was largely advisory—opposition research based on his work in *S. S. McClure Co. v. Philipp*[130]—but he did play an active role in trying to rescue *La Follette's Magazine* from financial disaster.[131] Politically, it made no difference; Philipp defeated both Husting and Blaine on November 3, 1914.

In January 1915, Roe had another opportunity to leave private practice for public service. He had been suggested for an appointment to the Federal Trade Commission and, on January 5, met with President Wilson's chief political aide, Colonel Edward M. House.[132] Later that day, House wrote Wilson that

Roe had impressed him more strongly than any other candidate for the job. House noted Roe's "marked ability" and the likelihood that his appointment would be received with enthusiasm by both Progressives and progressive Republicans. In February, however, Wilson appointed progressive lawyer George Rublee to the post Roe had sought. Roe would never again seriously consider public office. In May 1915, Roe wrote La Follette to say he would testify before the Industrial Commission concerning the attitude of the courts in labor cases. Expressing concern about the 1908 Danbury Hatters' Case,[133] in which the Supreme Court had ruled that the hatters' union violated the Sherman Antitrust Act by initiating a national boycott of a nonunion hat manufacturer, Roe asked La Follette if Congress had done anything to exempt unions from the reach of the act.[134] In fact, the Clayton Antitrust Act of 1914 did just that, and, presumably, Roe and La Follette discussed it after Roe arrived in Washington on the evening of Sunday, May 9.[135] When he returned from Washington, Roe concentrated on a campaign to prevent the New York Bar Association from adopting a proposal to have judges appointed by the governor, rather than elected by the people. On June 24, Roe testified before the Judiciary Committee of the New York State Constitutional Convention, strongly supporting a proposed amendment to the constitution to provide for the election of judges in nonpartisan campaigns.[136]

In his private practice, Roe began representing a group of investors swindled by one Jared Flagg Jr., a notorious New York huckster who claimed to have invented the "no money down" sales pitch. Roe won major victories for his clients in the New York courts,[137] beginning in 1915, and the U.S. Supreme Court would ultimately deny Flagg's petition for certiorari.[138] "Oh, but I was glad to know Gilbert had won his case," Belle La Follette wrote to Netha. "He had put so much time on it and the stake was so large that it would have hit him hard to lose."[139]

In 1916, the Senate confirmed Louis D. Brandeis as associate justice of the Supreme Court. Brandeis had supported Roe's nomination for the New York bench,[140] and Roe had returned the favor. "There is no danger of Mr. Brandeis making the Supreme Court radical," Roe wrote Sen. William E. Chilton (D-W. Va.), a member of the Judiciary Committee that would vet Brandeis's nomination.[141] Despite the concern for his radicalism, and blatant anti-Semitism, Brandeis was confirmed, 47–22, on June 1, 1916. La Follette was one of only three Republicans to vote for him. Compared with other elections, Roe played a relatively small role in La Follette's 1916 campaign for reelection to the Senate. La Follette would be reelected in November, defeating Democrat William F. Wolfe by the largest margin ever received by any candidate for statewide office.[142] "We are, of course, delighted with the news from Wisconsin," Roe would write the senator.[143] "Next to the President himself, whoever he may be, you will have more power for the next six years than any other man in the country. It is great!"

Throughout this period, Roe's busy practice was repeatedly punctuated by family health concerns. In May 1916, for example, Roe wrote La Follette: "Janet is going to the hospital today, for an operation tomorrow.... It is for the gland trouble in her neck, which has become very much worse in the past few days and the surgeon says there is no time to wait.... We do not anticipate serious results from the operation, but I am afraid the swelling is in a measure tubercular, which makes it grave."[144] The operation was apparently successful,[145] but Roe told La Follette's secretary, John Hannan, that it went harder than anyone expected.[146] The child's recovery was very rough for the first week, but she showed marked improvement thereafter. "Today is the first time for just one week that we have smiled," Roe wrote to Belle.[147] "Yesterday was the worst day Janet ever had. Her temperature went up to 104 and as she had taken no nourishment for a week, she certainly looked to be about all in. Last night, however, the wound in her neck commenced to discharge again and her fever went down." As Janet improved, however, the Roes became concerned that little Gwyneth, 4, might be coming down with whooping cough. When Janet came home, they kept the girls separated, not daring to expose Janet to an infectious disease so soon after her ordeal.[148] A few weeks later, Roe reported that his family would stay in Pelham Manor, for the present at least, because they could control the children's activities in the face of an infantile paralysis scare.[149]

The Coming of War

Woodrow Wilson had won reelection in November 1916 on the slogan "He kept us out of war." By the beginning of 1917, however, it must have appeared to the antiwar left that President Wilson was rapidly losing his ability or willingness to hold out against pressure to enter the war. That pressure had been growing since the outbreak of war in 1914. It only intensified after the British passenger ship *Lusitania* was sunk in May 1915 with considerable loss of American lives. By 1917, the pressure had become irresistible. According to Fola La Follette, Gilbert Roe had been spending as much time in Washington as his law practice permitted, "working with Bob and Belle on questions of international law." These two men, former law partners and intimate friends, had entered upon one of the most important of their many collaborations. "[I]t is often difficult in this period to distinguish where the work of one leaves off and the other's contribution begins," she would write. "It never occurred to either to weigh the cost of differing with a powerful President on the eve of war."[150]

Despite their best efforts, the antiwar coalition was badly frayed. Some progressives were looking upon the war as an opportunity to launch sweeping social and political reforms.[151] Others may have calculated that continuing to oppose the war would work against their principal cause. Of particular interest to the Roes was the capitulation of the suffragist leadership, such as Carrie Chapman Catt, who had helped organize the Woman's Peace Party in January 1915. Two years later, Catt—as president of the National American Woman Suffrage Association—was offering "war service" to President Wilson.[152] A similar pledge was offered by Mrs. Norman de R. Whitehouse, who chaired the New York State Woman Suffrage Party.[153] Netha Roe was outraged. Her letters to Catt and Whitehouse protesting the pledges were couched in legal argument—questioning whether the organizations' constitutions permitted advocacy of any cause save suffrage—but the sense of betrayal was unmistakable. "I find myself not merely shocked by being handed over to the Governor and the President for war service but particularly humiliated by what I have done to other women," she wrote Catt, noting that many had joined the suffragist cause on her assurance that they would be serving no other cause.[154] Gilbert Roe praised his wife's efforts in a letter to La Follette. "In common with all the country, we are all, of course, watching events closely in Washington," he wrote. "Netha is much more wroth up about the situation than I am. . . . She has written what I regard as one of the best and briefest statements of the situation from the woman's point of view. . . . [T]hat has been prepared and sent to the suffrage leaders. Probably it won't do any good; possibly, nothing will do any good, but be that as it may, it relieves one's feelings to do their bit."[155]

Of course, it made little difference that the suffragists were divided on the war. Netha Roe's plea to support Wilson's quest for peace seemed naive when she wrote Catt; days after her response to Whitehouse, the president delivered his second inaugural address, asserting that, "Our own fortunes as a nation are involved, whether we would have it so or not."[156] On April 2, Wilson asked Congress for a declaration of war; two days later, despite the best efforts of La Follette and a handful of antiwar senators, the Senate approved the war resolution 82–6. The House followed on April 6, voting 373–50 for war with Germany.[157]

It is impossible to overstate the importance of World War I and its aftermath in the history of American freedom of speech. Not since the Alien and

Sedition Acts of 1798 and the Civil War's martial law decrees had this fundamental value been so seriously threatened. But unlike those previous episodes, the legal protections for seditious speech ultimately emerged stronger and more durable after World War I and the Red Scare that followed. It took time, of course; the early cases generally yielded terrible outcomes. But the activists and their lawyers persisted and earned a claim to some of the credit for today's robust First Amendment regime. Over a quarter of a century, Gilbert Roe became one of those lawyers, beginning with a case that grew directly out of his personal association with the progressive movement.

2

The Muckrakers

> "See here," he says, "what will you give me if we send our private cars exclusively over your road?"
>
> "Why," says the railroad freight agent, "we will pay you the customary mileage on your cars, which will give you a handsome profit."
>
> "Good morning, sir," we can imagine Mr. Philipp saying, "I can do better."
>
> Ray Stannard Baker

McClure's Magazine

The alliance among progressive Republicans, muckraking journalists, and Gilbert Roe can probably be dated to a 1904 letter to Roe from Robert La Follette, then governor of Wisconsin. "Say, Gil, Lincoln Steffens of *McClure's Magazine*, spent three days with me at St. Louis," La Follette wrote, referring to the St. Louis World's Fair. "He afterwards came here and was in Madison several days. . . . I gave Steffens your address and he expects to call on you. He is a man thirty-five to forty,—able, keen, high-minded, and I believe imbued with a lofty patriotism in the reform he is leading through his magazine work. His articles, several of them, are out in book form, entitled 'The Shame of the Cities.' Get it and read them. Also the last *McClure's* on Illinois if you have time. He is doing a great work."[1]

Among the many progressive reforms that La Follette advocated or achieved—including women's suffrage, direct election of senators, open primaries, workers' compensation, minimum wage—was a major overhaul of the way railroads did business in Wisconsin. From his first term in office to his last,

La Follette oversaw reforms in railroad taxation and rate setting, albeit with political compromises along the way.[2] That was especially interesting to Steffens, who had identified the railroads as one of the "Enemies of the Republic" for a series of articles he was preparing for *McClure's Magazine*.[3]

Steffens had joined *McClure's* in 1901, becoming an integral part of the editorial nucleus that propelled the magazine to muckraking glory. *McClure's* was launched in June 1893, in the teeth of the depression that began in February with the failure of the Pennsylvania and Reading Railroad. Its founders were Samuel S. McClure, a progressive editor and publisher; McClure's college friend and business manager, John S. Phillips; and another college friend and advertising manager, Albert Brady. McClure recruited a remarkable core team of writers, beginning with Ida M. Tarbell in 1894. Ray Stannard Baker, a hard-hitting Chicago newspaperman, joined the team in 1898, and legendary Kansas editor William Allen White was also considered part of the core when Steffens came aboard, although White never relocated from Emporia to New York City.[4]

The January 1903 issue of *McClure's* was the culmination of a trend toward investigative exposés that began a year or so earlier[5] and would earn the sobriquet "muckraking" three years later. That issue included Steffens's "The Shame of Minneapolis" as the lead article, Tarbell's "The Oil War of 1872," and Baker's "The Right to Work: The Story of the Non-Striking Miners."[6] President Theodore Roosevelt wrote to compliment McClure on the issue. By 1906, however, Roosevelt had become hostile to the crusading journalists, comparing them to the character in Bunyan's *Pilgrim's Progress* who could "look no way but downward, with a muckrake in his hands . . . who continued to rake to himself the filth from the floor."[7]

After Steffens's *Shame of the Cities* was published as a book in 1904, McClure decided Steffens should next undertake a new series on American political corruption, focusing on the states this time and bearing the overall title "Enemies of the Republic."[8] The railroads were high on the muckrakers' list of "enemies" for their collusion with monopolists like Rockefeller. La Follette's work to rein in the railroads would have naturally attracted the muckrakers' attention.

"Mr. Steffens's article on Wisconsin is being written now," La Follette wrote to Roe. "It is vitally important that it should be right. I think from what he told me that it will be right, but am mighty anxious. . . . I am sure you would like him and that Netha would like Mrs. Steffens, who is a novelist and very bright and handsome. . . . Your calling upon him at an early date may be important as to putting him in possession of facts before he gets his articles upon these subjects shaped out fully."[9] Roe and Steffens did meet and, in fact, became good friends and close political and ideological allies.[10] After Roe died, Steffens would write to Netha: "My grief (there is always a remorse) is that I can't remember having expressed to Gil my love for him; it's as if I had taken his and never thought that he might have liked to know about mine, which wells up warm and big now that it is too late for him."[11]

Whether Roe had anything to do with it or not, the article, "Enemies of the Republic—Wisconsin: A State Where the People Have Restored Representative Government—The Story of Governor La Follette," which appeared in the October 1904 issue of *McClure's*[12]—was extremely favorable, as Roe quickly wrote to Belle.[13] La Follette later told Steffens it would be impossible to exaggerate the effects the article had on the November elections. "The article settled things," he wrote. "It was like the decision of a court of last resort."[14]

In the fall, bolstered by the Steffens article in *McClure's*, La Follette took revenge on his political enemies. In one speech, on November 4, La Follette attacked Emanuel L. Philipp, who had defected from the Stalwarts briefly to support La Follette's 1900 election,[15] but who would later lead the conservative Stalwarts back to power as governor in 1914. At the time, however, Philipp was president of the Milwaukee-based Union Refrigerator Transit Company of Wisconsin.[16] The company owned some two thousand refrigerator cars that were used to ship beer and other foodstuffs by rail. In a November 3, 1904, report prepared by La Follette's railroad commissioner, John W. Thomas, Philipp was found to have taken substantial and illegal rebates from the Chicago, Milwaukee & St. Paul Railroad.[17] On November 4, La Follette incorporated the details of that report in a campaign speech in Milwaukee.[18] Philipp made no reply at the time, but *McClure's* Ray Stannard Baker would later use the report and speech as evidence in defending his railroad series. Baker's series ran in *McClure's* from November 1905 to April 1906, with the material about Philipp in the January 1906 issue, which actually appeared in late December 1905.[19] In that article, Baker detailed how the widespread use of specialty cars, such as refrigerator cars or oil tank cars, owned not by the railroads but by private companies, facilitated the rise of the trusts. This time, Philipp did reply, with a devastating libel suit against the S. S. McClure Publishing Co. in January 1906. McClure tapped Gilbert Roe to lead the defense.

In the middle of this detailed attack on the use of private refrigerator cars by the Armour Company of Chicago's "beef trust," Baker devoted a single page to illustrating "the power of a private car owner" with the story of the Union Refrigerator Transit Company of Wisconsin and its president, Emanuel L. Philipp. Baker explained that the private car company carried beer for Pabst of Milwaukee and that "brewery interests" owned all or nearly all of the stock.

In a mock dialog, Baker attempted to re-create how Philipp would negotiate with the railroads:

> "See here," he says, "what will you give me if we send our private cars exclusively over your road?"
> "Why," says the railroad freight agent, "we will pay you the customary mileage on your cars, which will give you a handsome profit."
> "Good morning, sir," we can imagine Mr. Philipp saying, "I can do better."

Baker backed up his claims with statistics from the Thomas report. The article alleged that the Chicago, Milwaukee & St. Paul Railroad was the favored bidder in the fiscal year ending June 20, 1903, and that it paid Philipp's company more than $73,000 in mileage rentals. Baker also claimed to have a list of vouchers showing that Union Refrigerator received another $34,000 in "commissions" in five of the months between December 1902 and June 1903. The article noted that Philipp had been a lobbyist against La Follette's efforts to reform the railroad industry. "At the very time that Mr. Philipp was denouncing La Follette as an 'inciter,' a demagogue, and the like, his company was receiving over $6,000 a month in rebates from a single Wisconsin railroad."

The series on railroads had two more installments, both entitled "Railroads on Trial," in the February and March 1903 issues. But the damage had been done. Both the Union Refrigerator Transit Co. and Emanuel Philipp filed libel suits in the Circuit Court of the Southern District of New York against *McClure's* in January 1906 alleging that Baker's article was false and defamatory.[20] The complaint insisted that neither Philipp nor the sole stockholder in Union Refrigerator, one Eugene Wuesthoff, had any interest in any brewery, nor did any brewery have an interest the company.[21] Furthermore, "[n]o rebates or unlawful, improper or unjust commissions, damages or favors, whether called such or by any other name, were ever received by [Union Refrigerator Company] or by this plaintiff . . . and no discriminations whatever were ever practiced in its favor or through it in favor of any brewer or other shipper of freight, as alleged in the publication hereinafter complained of." It then summarized the Interstate Commerce Act as amended, the Elkins Act, and a parallel Wisconsin statute to show that any allegations of such discrimination would be an accusation of criminal conduct, or libel per se, thus permitting the plaintiff to sue without showing any "special damages" or pecuniary loss.[22]

Philipp's complaint went on to charge that Baker's series on rebates, mentioned in a presidential address in December 1905, had promoted such "agitation of the question and the public discussion thereof" that "the payment and receipt of such rebates and the practice of giving and receiving such discriminations were made odious and justly brought into popular condemnation."[23] The complaint enumerated every allegation in the January article, particularly as read in conjunction with the December article, concluding that they were wholly false and "calculated to and did injure plaintiff in his good name and reputation and in his standing in the community and in his business" by giving the impression that he was "collecting secret, unlawful rebates and commissions or damages." Using classic libel terminology, Philipp's complaint charged that the allegations in Baker's article "give on their face the impression that the plaintiff is insincere in his writings, and a trickster and a hypocrite and a criminal who, while he preaches good things, at the same time practices evil things, and as aforesaid and otherwise in many ways hold up the plaintiff to public ridicule, contempt, scorn and obloquy, and by reason thereof the plaintiff has been injured in his business and in his credit, and in his reputation, and in his good name, to his damage in the sum of one hundred thousand dollars ($100,000)."

According to Steffens's biographer, McClure and his muckrakers lived with the constant threat of lawsuits and were forced to devise certain defensive tactics,[24] but none of them would have avoided this lawsuit. Since everything Baker had said about Philipp was ultimately sourced to La Follette or members of his administration, Roe was the logical attorney to handle the case in New York. Roe had already established a relationship with *McClure's*, apart from his personal friendship with Steffens, having ordered some ten thousand reprints of Steffens's La Follette article for distribution,[25] presumably to La Follette's substantial mailing list of supporters.[26] Roe worked closely with Alfred T. Rogers, La Follette's Madison-based law partner, in collecting materials to prepare the defense. "I am very much interested as attorney for *McClure's* here in getting the facts, exactly as they are, in the answers in the libel suits that I must prepare," Roe wrote Rogers in early February.[27]

In particular, he asked Rogers to send him an exact copy of a new report dated January 10, 1906, that Commissioner Thomas had prepared at Philipp's request that completely absolved Philipp and Union Refrigerator.[28] The *Milwaukee Sentinel* had printed a version of the report on January 11: "Nothing in the investigation indicates or discloses that Mr. Philipp, or the Union Refrigerator Transit Company of Kentucky, of which he was President at the time, or the Union Refrigerator Transit Company of Wisconsin, of which he is now President, ever received any commissions, rebates or refunds of any kind."[29] The *Milwaukee Free Press* had published a different version, however, inserting the words "barring above statement of vouchers" after the word "investigation." Roe told Rogers the addition completely reversed the meaning of the sentence, and he needed the original document.

Unfortunately for *McClure's*, the *Sentinel* had it right. Thomas and his experts had misattributed the rebate vouchers to Union Refrigerator Transit Company; they were actually signed by Philipp in his capacity as vice president of the Northern Refrigerator Transit Company.[30] While the accusations against Philipp remained unresolved, *McClure's* had no good defense to Union Refrigerator's lawsuit. Roe had filed a demurrer based on the company's failure to show special damages, but it was overruled in mid-June,[31] and *McClure's* settled for $1,500.[32]

Roe filed his answer in *Philipp v. S. S. McClure Co.* on February 26, 1906.[33] He acknowledged the mistake in Thomas's original report but treated it as akin to a typographical error. Neither Baker nor *McClure's* could have known of the mistake before publication of the series, he said, pressing the defense that the republication by *McClure's* of Thomas's original report was a "fair and true report of a public and official proceeding, published without malice, in the belief that they were true, and that the publication thereof was and is absolutely privileged." The answer also asserted that Baker was a disinterested and highly competent journalist seeking only the facts in a "matter of great interest vitally concerning the people of this country and in relation to which public policy requires the fullest statement of the facts." Both Baker and *McClure's* were without malice toward Philipp, Roe said, and corrected the error as soon as possible. Roe asked that the complaint be dismissed. It was not, and the case headed for trial.

In preparing his case, Roe felt handicapped by the absence of favorable discovery rules in New York and wrote to La Follette lamenting his inability to "grill" Philipp on the issue of rebates under Wisconsin's discovery rules.[34] That opportunity was lost, he said, when the *Milwaukee Free Press*—which Philipp had also sued for reprinting the *McClure's* article—agreed to run a correction in exchange for Philipp's dropping his lawsuit.[35] "If the *Free Press* had stood pat, they could have examined Philipp under the Wisconsin Discovery Statute as to every act of his life concerning rebates," Roe wrote La Follette. "It made me sick at heart when I saw that the *Milwaukee Free Press* had quit."[36] Roe told La Follette that *McClure's* was "standing up first rate" and that Al Rogers was helping collect what evidence he could. "[B]ut the back-down of the *Free Press* is a blunder that can't be corrected." Roe sent La Follette copies of the vouchers that Philipp signed, asking him to "keep Mr. Philipp and his rebates in mind, and if you can devise any way to uncover more fully his rebate practices, do it."

But he warned La Follette to steer clear of *McClure's* on the subject lest it be construed as malice and "go in aggravation of damages."

In March, Roe again wrote asking Rogers if there were anything further on Philipp and the rebates and expressing the hope that Wisconsin's new Railroad Commission would open an investigation.[37] He also sent three more "Philipp receipts" to La Follette in Washington.[38] Toward the end of the month, in its April 1906 issue, *McClure's* published an editorial by Baker with a view toward correcting the record. The editorial was entitled "Some of the Difficulties Encountered in Investigating the Railroad Problem: The Unreliability of Official Documents."[39] In the editorial, Baker described the series of events that led him to correct his account as it regarded Union Refrigerator Transit Company. But the editorial could hardly be called a retraction; rather, Baker treated the error as one of mere mistaken identity with regard to the corporation involved, but with Philipp still on the receiving end of the rebates. "Mr. Philipp and the Union Refrigerator Transit Company have both sued *McClure's Magazine* for libel—because of this error in names—which shows one of the dangers of following official reports and the importance of being legally accurate," Baker wrote.

In the spring and summer of 1906, *McClure's* suffered a dramatic upheaval. On May 11, the *New York Times* reported that John Phillips, Ida M. Tarbell, Ray Stannard Baker, Lincoln Steffens, and Albert Boyden had resigned from *McClure's* the previous day.[40] The *Times* linked the defection to Roosevelt's muckraker speech, but Steffens's biographer asserts that it was much more a reaction to what Steffens called Sam McClure's "big fool scheme of founding a new magazine with a string of banks, insurance companies, etc., and a capitalization of $15,000,000."[41] Added Steffens, "It was not only fool, it was not quite right, as we saw it." McClure bought back Phillips's and Tarbell's stock for $187,000 and continued to pay Steffens and Baker for work on ongoing projects. McClure parted company with his core staff on amicable terms,[42] and Phillips would later testify on Baker's behalf in the libel trial. William Allen White and Finley Peter Dunne joined the defectors soon thereafter. Together, they formed the Phillips Publishing Company on July 2 and acquired the failing *American Magazine*. The new company raised $400,000 in cash and pledges to purchase the magazine; Steffens had invested $10,000 of his own money and had talked Roe into contributing another $1,000. "Please find enclosed my check for $1,000 for stock in the new magazine," Roe wrote.[43] "Mr. Steffens, I think, has explained to me the different classes of stock and the different rights attaching to the different classes. I have not this explanation clearly in mind, and therefore, request you to send me such securities for this as Mr. Steffens directs." Roe continued to represent *McClure's*, of course, not only in the *Philipp* libel case, but in matters involving Mary Baker Eddy, founder of Christian Science,[44] and Maria Montessori, an educational pioneer.[45]

The Trial

The trial of *Philipp v. S. S. McClure Co.* finally got under way in March—more than two years after the complaint was filed. The Honorable Charles M. Hough presided over the jury trial on March 20–28, 1908.[46] Hough had been appointed by Theodore Roosevelt in 1906 to the newly created judgeship on the United States Circuit Court for the Southern District of New York. In 1916, Woodrow Wilson would appoint Hough to the United States Court of Appeals for the Second Circuit, where he served until his death in 1927. This would not be Roe's last important case before Hough; in 1917, Hough would stay the application of Roe's most significant, albeit fleeting, victory in *Masses Publishing Co. v. Patten*.[47]

Philipp was represented by the firm of Huntington, Rhinelander & Seymour; Roe's team for *McClure's* included his partner, William F. McCombs, and Charles L. Burr. Even before the trial got underway, Francis C. Huntington pulled the rug out from under *McClure's* by moving to strike the defenses of privilege and justification. Hough denied the motion to strike the defense of justification, which meant Roe was free to prove the truth of Baker's assertions. Given the mistakes Baker had taken from the Thomas report, such a proof would be all but impossible to make. Roe's best chance to get *McClure's* off the hook completely was the defense of privilege, but Hough granted Huntington's motion to strike it and deny Roe the opportunity to assert it as a complete defense.

Under the common law, a libel plaintiff needed to prove only three elements of the tort to make a prima facie case: publication, identification, and defamation. In this case, publication (that *McClure's* published the allegedly libelous statements in question) and identification (that the statements were about the plaintiff, Mr. Philipp) were not contested. It would not be difficult for Philipp to show that several of the statements in Baker's article were defamatory, and Roe's arguments to the contrary were aimed at reducing the number of such statements that the jury would consider. Once a prima facie case was made, the defendant could raise one of three defenses. Truth, or justification, was a complete defense, but to prevail on that defense, a defendant had to show that the statements in question were actually true; it would not be sufficient to show that they were accurately reported. An accurate report of an official government report, however, might give rise to the defense of privilege, which could also be a complete defense, if made without malice.

Roe argued that the Thomas report was just such a document, but that Hough had improperly excluded evidence of its statutory authority "on a false premise that it was only pleaded in mitigation and unknown to the writer at the time, when in fact privilege and justification were pleaded as a complete defense to specific charges in the complaint."[48] Indeed, Hough allowed the jury to consider Baker's reliance on the Thomas report in mitigation of damages.[49] Philipp argued, successfully, that the defense of privilege was properly stricken. Under common law and the statutory law of Wisconsin, he asserted, no privilege attaches to any such preliminary report until brought up in court or the legislature. Even if Philipp could not sue Commissioner Thomas for libel, the report could not be the basis of a privilege for any third party to publish it.[50]

The third affirmative defense, fair comment, is a qualified privilege usually reserved for literary or other artistic criticism or editorial opinion. Although Roe had asserted the predicate facts for fair comment in his answer to the complaint,[51] it appears that he did not plead that privilege as a complete defense. Again, Hough allowed the jury to consider those facts, particularly the general public interest in the issues discussed in the articles, in mitigation of damages— provided the otherwise fair and honest criticism did not constitute a personal attack on Philipp's character.[52] Thus, the trial began with Roe's best defenses already rejected as a matter of law.

After Hough denied a pro forma motion by Roe's associate, Charles Burr, to dismiss the case for failure to state a claim, William C. Quarles opened for the plaintiff, calling Philipp to the stand as the first witness.[53] Following a detailed description of his life and career, Philipp testified to his first and only meeting with Baker. "I met Mr. Ray Stannard Baker in my office in Milwaukee, in January, about the 24th or 23rd of January, 1906," Philipp testified. "This was after the action was commenced. . . . He came in with his hat in his hand. I did not know that he was coming. He said that he was Mr. Ray Stannard Baker, the gentleman who wrote the article in *McClure's* about which there seemed to be some trouble. He said he was very sorry that a mistake had probably been made, and that he came there to find out the facts in regard to it."

Philipp testified that he gave Baker access to his books, but all Baker wanted was a statement. "I told him I went to Madison and told Mr. Thomas that he had wronged me," Philipp said, "that the report which he had sent out was incorrect, that there was no authority for making any such statements as Mr. Baker had made." Philipp said he talked to Baker for a long time, discussing his efforts to comply with the law regarding commissions, including a visit to the Interstate Commerce Commission in Washington for clarification. "Mr. Baker in reply to these matters said, when he was about to leave, that he believed that he had made a mistake, and that he intended to write a retraction in which he would state the facts, and he thought I would be entirely satisfied with it." When Quarles asked Philipp how he felt when he read the January article, Roe objected, but was promptly overruled. "I was distressed because of the effect it would have upon my family," Philipp said. Asked how he felt after reading the April "retraction," again after strenuous objections, Philipp said he felt worse. Philipp also denied that he was ever a lobbyist, as alleged in the Baker articles. "I have never appeared at any time during my life before any legislature or any legislative committee for hire." Roe's cross examination was very detailed, focusing on the introduction of the vouchers Philipp signed, but he never seemed to shake Philipp's conviction that he had done nothing wrong.

Quarles then called Sam McClure as an adverse witness, principally to establish the circulation of the allegedly libelous articles. *McClure's* had a print run of just under half a million, with about 200,000 regular subscribers. With that, Quarles rested. Burr renewed his motion to dismiss, this time on three separate grounds: (1) the complaint failed to state facts sufficient to constitute a cause of action; (2) plaintiff failed to establish such facts in his case; and (3) plaintiff's own evidence proved that the allegations in Baker's articles were true. Hough denied the motion, and Roe opened for the defense.

Roe's first witness was John M. Winterbottham, secretary of the Wisconsin Railroad Commission, which had succeeded in function the Wisconsin Railroad Commissioner in 1907. Winterbottham had been a deputy railroad commissioner, and he authenticated the Thomas report of November 3, 1904. He testified further that the report was on file for anyone to see. Cross and redirect were inconsequential, and Roe called John Phillips as his next witness.

As general manager of *McClure's* when Baker's articles were published, Phillips could testify as to Baker's competence and *McClure's* lack of malice. "We had the highest regard for his reliability; we trusted him," Phillips said. "We trusted his reports of the materials he investigated. I don't remember of any case where Mr. Baker had ever been found inaccurate or unreliable in any respect in any matter that he had investigated and reported for *McClure's Magazine* previous to his undertaking the railroad articles." Phillips also asserted that neither he, nor any officer of the company, "had any feeling or ill will of any sort against the plaintiff." Phillips said he read over the January 1906 article before it was published and "believed it to be in all respects correct and true." As to the April correction, however, Phillips could only say he discussed it with

Baker. "Beyond that I had no part in it. I was away." On cross examination, Phillips was equivocal about the allegations in the January piece. "When I read that article I do not remember that it impressed me that it charged Mr. Philipp with having received private graft," he told Quarles. "I do not remember that I noted that the article charged Mr. Philipp with being a lobbyist. I remember that article saying something about criminal rebates. I know it is there. I do not remember anything about that being referred to Mr. Philipp in that article — applied to him. I do not remember that it applied to him."

Roe recalled Sam McClure as a defense witness, again to testify as to Baker's experience and competence. "His particular work that showed us his great qualities were investigations of great labor strikes, in Chicago, in San Francisco, and particularly the Haywood and Moyer trial in Colorado, and in Chicago and New York, the first article being on the great coal strike of 1902 and 1903 in the anthracite coal mines," McClure said. "He made an investigation of lynching in the South that attracted a great deal of attention, especially from the more progressive young Southerners, and brought the magazine a great deal of credit." McClure said he did "not remember that any complaint had ever been made to the defendant company concerning the accuracy or impartiality of Mr. Baker in any manner on these railroad articles."

Roe concluded his case by calling Baker to testify as to how the railroad articles were put together. Baker explained that he first met with Commissioner Thomas in October 1905, when he received a copy of Thomas's report to La Follette. Thomas also told him about Philipp's repeated appearances before the legislature in Madison on railroad and brewery company bills. "In writing up my article, I referred to Mr. Philipp in one place as a lobbyist," Baker told Roe. "I meant by the use of the term 'lobbyist' any man who appears before Congress or the Legislature to advance or defeat any given measure. I did not mean to imply in any way that it meant the defeating or advancing of legislation corruptly." Baker testified that soon after the first of January 1906, he learned of the mistake regarding the companies with which Philipp was associated. Roe introduced a letter from Thomas to Baker, dated January 9, 1906, stating that "the name of the corporation with which Mr. Philipp was connected that received the commission vouchers was the Northern Refrigerator Transit Co. instead of the Union Refrigerator Transit Co." and that Thomas had ordered a reinvestigation of the whole matter. As a result, Baker testified, he went to see Philipp and offered to correct any mistake the magazine might have published. His account of that meeting generally tracks Philipp's testimony, with one notable exception. "Mr. Philipp said, 'I don't blame you, Mr. Baker. It is that La Follette crowd' — that he blamed." Baker said he urged Philipp to sue them instead of the magazine.

Roe introduced Thomas's revised report of January 10, 1906, which absolved Philipp and the Union Refrigerator Transit Co. He also took Baker through an explanation of the April 1906 correction in *McClure's*. Among other things, Baker testified that he used the term "private graft" to mean "extra or secret payments," although not necessarily illegal payments. He also explained that when he wrote about taking commissions before passage of the Elkins Act as "outside the law," he meant they were essentially unregulated, not that they were illegal until the Elkins Act passed. He did not intend to apply allegations regarding "private car mileage" to Philipp.

Quarles's cross examination, however, focused more on the political aspects of the case — with devastating effect. Baker had testified on direct examination that during his meeting with Philipp, Baker asked why Philipp had not complained when the original report was issued. "He said that this report had been used by La Follette in the political campaign, and published in the newspapers, and he did not think it worthwhile to bother about it at that time." Quarles pressed the point on cross examination, getting Baker to concede that he knew of the split in the Republican Party between the La Follette faction, the Half-breeds, and the conservative Stalwarts; that he knew La Follette was running for reelection in the fall of 1904; and that he knew that La Follette and Philipp were "intensely, if you please, opposed to each other."

> Q: Now, I ask you, whether, in your judgment, a man with a proper regard for the truth, ought to accept and publish, broadcast in a magazine a statement made in a political campaign, that tends to injure another in his reputation, without corroborating the accuracy of such statements?

Roe's objection that the question was hypothetical and unfair was promptly overruled, and Baker answered from his experience.

> A: Nearly all of the investigations in the different States and in Congress have been the result of political campaigns; the evidence has been brought out as the result of those campaigns and if the investigator should cut off the facts brought out for that reason, the public would never get them through the magazines. I think it is perfectly justifiable to use such statements if they bear on their face the evidence of having passed between the proper authorities.

When Quarles asked, "Did it occur to you that it would be a reasonably safe or fair thing to do to communicate with Mr. Philipp before publishing this article?" Baker responded, "I supposed that my use of an official document that had not been denied was sufficient. That is all the answer I want to make to that question." The testimony ended with an inconsequential recross and redirect of the plaintiff, E. L. Philipp.

Judge Hough's charge to the jury on March 26, 1908, destroyed any possibility, short of jury nullification, that *McClure's* would emerge from the trial unscathed. Following the practice of reading and ruling on the requested charges of both plaintiff and defendant, Hough accepted the plaintiff's proffered charge that "as a matter of law . . . no defense of justification has been made out by the defendant in this case." Roe would later write to La Follette asking whether there was any legislation pending to reform the federal courts, particularly by preventing judges from commenting to juries regarding the facts.[54] Thus, with the defense of privilege rejected on a pretrial motion, the defense of fair comment pleaded only in mitigation, and now the defense of justification or truth rejected as a matter of law, all that remained for the jury to consider was the amount of damages it would impose on *McClure's*.

With respect to the evidence in mitigation or aggravation of damages, Hough accepted much of the plaintiff's proffered language. For example, the Thomas report from which Baker had taken essentially all of his information on Philipp was characterized as the "so-called" report,[55] undermining its value in mitigation. And the April "correction" published in *McClure's* was presented as a repetition of the libel, asserting that the only mistake was an "error in names" and that Philipp was "just as much of a grafter as the January article imputed he was only for a different company." Of the defendant's proposed charge to the jury, Hough accepted the proffer that Baker had relied on the Thomas report, which was "not in all respects correct." He also accepted the charge that "receipt of commissions derived from freight money paid by shippers to railroads, on the part of the plaintiff as a representative of the Northern Refrigeration Transit Company, after the 19th day of February, 1903 [when the Elkins Act was enacted], was unlawful." And he accepted application of the innocent construction rule with respect to the word "lobbyist." Under that rule, when a word is susceptible of having a defamatory or innocent meaning, the innocent meaning is presumed; but the jury can overcome that presumption by finding the word was used in its defamatory sense.

In his concluding summary of the charge, Hough told the jury there was no complete defense before them, but only defenses in mitigation of damages—any evidence that tends to show an absence of malice. He told the jury there was no ill-will associated with the January article—the only article for which the jury could award damages—and that Baker was a highly regarded journalist who naturally trusted the Thomas report. Nevertheless, he said, the plaintiff was entitled as a matter of law to compensatory damages for some portion of the charges in the January article, and possibly punitive damages if the April editorial—as a reiteration and reassertion of the defamation—was evidence of malice. The amount of the damages was "wholly and absolutely in your discretion, guided, of course, by reason, and your oath to act impartially between the parties to this case."

Roe proceeded to enter a series of exceptions to preserve the issues for appeal, and the jury retired to deliberate. The following morning, March 27, the jury returned a verdict for Philipp and awarded damages of $15,000. The record does not show whether the amount included punitive damages. Roe moved for a new trial, but the decision on that motion was reserved until April 3 because Hough had taken ill. On April 4, Roe argued that the "verdict was contrary to law, and contrary to the evidence, and that the damages were excessive."[56]

On April 10, Sam McClure wrote to Roe suggesting that Roe write something for the magazine about the libel suit.[57] He suggested Roe point out that the $1,500 settlement with Union Refrigeration was the result of a mistake in the Thomas report, and that, notwithstanding the $15,000 verdict for Philipp, the court ruled that he had committed a crime for receiving payments after the Elkins Act was enacted. Roe replied to McClure that he did not think the magazine should publish anything about the case until it was fully resolved.[58] "A motion to set aside the verdict and for a new trial is now pending," Roe said. "The errors in the case are so numerous and obvious, as it seems to me, that I am rather of the opinion that the Judge will either set aside the verdict or very materially reduce it in the hope that you will pay up and not take the record to the appellate court." Roe was probably right to warn against publication, but entirely wrong about Hough's decision. In denying Roe's motion, Hough conceded that the amount of damages was "larger than I would myself have awarded had the question of damages been for the Court," but he found that no reason to award a new trial.[59] He stayed execution of the judgment, however, until May 15, to give Roe time to serve his bill of exceptions.[60] The judgment was signed and entered on April 27, 1908, showing costs of $69.40 in addition to $15,000 in damages.[61]

Shortly after the verdict, the *Milwaukee Free Press* carried an article ostensibly written from Philipp's perspective. On April 18, Roe wrote to H. P. Myrick, editor of the *Free Press*, criticizing the article and telling Myrick that he expected a reversal. Myrick wrote back that Philipp had threatened to renew legal action against the paper if he did not publish the article, and that his lawyers had advised publication. Myrick said he just couldn't afford to spend five or ten thousand dollars on defending a lawsuit that might conclude with an adverse verdict.[62] Myrick also said he hoped Roe was right about a reversal. "Such verdicts . . . do not encourage newspapers to seek to protect the public, nor do they hold out inducement for struggling newspapers to involve themselves in long and expensive litigation, in which even if they are finally successful, they are the losers."

Roe, meanwhile, was hard at work on the *McClure's* appeal and had compiled a list of dozens of "errors" to present to the U.S. Court of Appeals for the Second Circuit.[63] On June 29, Roe filed his petition for a writ of error;[64] the following day Judge H. S. Ward of the Second Circuit filed an order summoning Philipp to appear on July 27 pursuant to the writ to show cause why the judgment should not be corrected.[65] The appellate process was underway, but 1908 would be all but over by the time Roe prepared and transmitted the record of the case to the Second Circuit.[66] Briefs in the case were not filed until early 1909.

Roe's brief for *McClure's* (the plaintiff in error) began with a summary of what Roe characterized as undisputed facts[67] and then pointed out some twenty-seven errors made at trial.[68] Philipp's brief responded sarcastically, "Very few of these facts are undisputed and the statement as a whole is so unfair and misleading that we feel it incumbent on us to refer to the testimony. It is scarcely necessary to remark that on all disputed questions of fact the jury have found, or are presumed to have found, in favor of the plaintiff."[69] The brief then proceeded to refute each of Roe's assertions of error. In reply, Roe answered in kind, telling the court that he wished only to "lighten the labor of the Court," by pointing out "inadvertent" errors in Philipp's brief "which, if unobserved, would lead to confusion, and might improperly affect the result."[70] Roe stressed the trial court's failure to admit evidence of statutory authority for the Thomas report and its allowing testimony that the April 1906 editorial made Philipp feel worse, as if that were the legal test for liability. On May 19, 1909, little more than a month after his last filing, Roe got his response from the Second Circuit, showing once again that his confidence was misplaced.[71]

The appeal was heard by Judges Emile Henry Lacombe, Alfred Conkling Coxe, and Henry Galbraith Ward. Coxe wrote the unanimous opinion, which dealt with only a few of the points that Roe had raised. Coxe wrote that it was "well settled" that a jury could consider the mental suffering of the plaintiff in a libel case, so the remark "I felt worse" was properly admitted. Coxe also upheld the trial judge's decision to exclude testimony about rebates taken by the Schlitz brewing company while Philipp was traffic manager there, but long before it was legally clear that taking rebates was criminal. Such testimony "would have added no relevant fact and would have tended only to confuse" an already complicated issue. Further, Baker's knowledge or lack of knowledge about another judicial decision clarifying that issue would have had no bearing on the jury's decision in this case. Finally, Coxe rejected Roe's contention that the meaning of "graft" should have been left to the jury. "[N]o man of mature age and ordinary intelligence who has lived in this country for the past ten years could have a moment's doubt as to the meaning of the word 'graft' as applied to one who is charged with receiving unlawful compensation." Concluding, without further discussion, that none of the twenty-seven assignments of error referred to in Roe's brief was prejudicial or constituted reversible error, the appellate panel affirmed the trial court on every point.

Postscript

The rebate issue would surface again, several years later, when Senator La Follette was trying his best to undermine Emanuel Philipp's 1914 campaign for governor of Wisconsin. La Follette had sent Roe some draft campaign materials asking, rhetorically, whether progressive Republicans could "trust a man to enforce the laws of the state, who has made money by bargaining with the railroads to violate the law of the nation? Can you vote for a man for Governor of Wisconsin who accepted rebates when it was criminal for the railroad company to pay rebates?"[72] On October 16, 1914, Roe sent La Follette some additional information derived from the trial to use as ammunition against Philipp. "There is no doubt," Roe said, "that [the Northern Refrigeration Transit Co.] took rebates and that [Philipp] receipted for them." He cautioned La Follette against even discussing the Union Refrigeration Transit Co. or using actual quotations from the trial record to support the argument. The former might be too confusing, Roe wrote, and Philipp could raise the trial verdict as vindication.[73] As it happened, Philipp defeated two progressive candidates for the Republican nomination, one of whom, John J. Blaine, ran as an independent.[74] Philipp defeated both Blaine and the Democratic nominee, John C. Karel, in the general election. He twice won reelection and served from 1915 to 1921.

3

The Anarchists

> Clothing was made to protect the body, not to hide it. . . . One of the liberties enjoyed by Homeites was the privilege to bathe in evening dress, or with merely the clothes nature gave them, just as they chose.
>
> Jay Fox

> In our predicament I turned to my friend Gilbert E. Roe, a lawyer by profession, an anarchist by feeling, and one of the kindest of men it has been my good fortune to know.
>
> Emma Goldman

The Free Speech League

If Gilbert Roe's link to the muckrakers was a natural consequence of his relationship with La Follette and progressive Republican politics, his link to the American anarchist movement and freedom of speech issues is somewhat more attenuated. Roe was anything but a radical in his personal and professional life, although the Russian-born anarchist lecturer and activist Emma Goldman would later say that he was "an anarchist by feeling."[1] But the radical salons of turn-of-the-century New York City were quite eclectic, embracing all manner of liberals, progressives, Georgist single-taxers, feminists, suffragists, unionists, socialists, and anarchists of every stripe from libertarian to communist.[2]

One man, more than any other, was critical to Roe's involvement with the radicals: Theodore Schroeder. Schroeder and Roe, then two Wisconsin lawyers working independently in New York City, had collaborated on the *Mutual Reserve* insurance cases. Soon thereafter, however, Schroeder abandoned the practice of law to follow more radical philosophical pursuits. A periodical in Salt Lake City, where Schroeder lived between his Wisconsin and New York periods, uncharitably described his orientation as "the rankest, most intolerant, vicious kind of an atheist" who "diligently disseminates doctrines intended to overthrow the existing social and governmental forms in this nation. His teachings are undiluted anarchy."[3] Perhaps the highest priority on Schroeder's agenda was the defense of free speech against anti-obscenity laws, anti-anarchist laws, and other forms of censorship. He was drawn toward a relatively new organization called the Free Speech League around 1905 and soon became its philosophical and administrative center. Schroeder was not interested in practicing law, however, and when the defense of free speech called for a practitioner, Schroeder would call on Gilbert Roe.

The Free Speech League was formed in 1902, but Janice Ruth Wood traces its origins to the post–Civil War Free Religious Association founded by Francis Abbot, who edited the freethought newspaper *Index*.[4] In an effort to build a stronger national alliance, Abbot launched the National Liberal League in the 1870s, but the organization was divided over the response to the Comstock anti-obscenity laws. The most radical wing became the National Defense Association. Drs. Edwin Bliss Foote and Edwin Bond Foote, father and son, were both members of the Manhattan Liberal Club, the local affiliate of the National Liberal League. After Foote Sr. was prosecuted under the Comstock law in 1876, the Footes launched *Dr. Foote's Health Monthly*, which became the unofficial newsletter of the National Defense Association. The National Defense Association's principal target was Anthony Comstock and his vigorous prosecution of obscene speech and conduct, very broadly defined, under laws for which he had campaigned at the state and federal level. The federal Comstock law was enacted by Congress in 1873 and named for its chief proponent.[5]

Comstock was born in 1844, fought for the Union in the Civil War, and joined the Young Men's Christian Association during the last few months of his enlistment. Comstock served with the YMCA's Committee for the Suppression of Vice as a private policeman and prosecutor. His aggressive pursuit of pornographers, abortionists, and others he deemed morally corrupting prompted the YMCA to spin off the committee as an independent corporation. The New York Society for the Suppression of Vice was chartered in May 1873, with the backing of such establishment figures as J. Pierpont Morgan, Andrew Carnegie, and Louis Comfort Tiffany.[6]

Comstock was also a very effective lobbyist. The law he persuaded Congress to enact barred from the mails any "obscene, lewd, or lascivious book, pamphlet, picture, paper, print, or other publication of an indecent character, or any article or thing designed or intended for the prevention of conception or procuring of abortion, [or] any article or thing intended or adapted for any indecent or immoral use or nature, [or] any written or printed card, circular, book, pamphlet, advertisement or notice of any kind giving information, directly or indirectly, where, or how, or of whom, or by what means either of the things before mentioned may be obtained or made."[7] Within a week of enactment, Comstock was commissioned as special agent of the U.S. Post Office, charged with enforcing his own law. He also took his legislative proposals to the state capitals, where he enjoyed one victory after another.

The National Defense Association disappeared in the mid-1890s, and the Footes suspended publication of the *Monthly* in 1896. They would soon help to found the Free Speech League to combat both Comstockery and the widespread anti-anarchist harassment that followed President McKinley's assassination in 1901 by a self-styled anarchist. Anti-anarchist sentiment had been steadily growing in the United States since the Haymarket Square bombing in Chicago in 1886 and the attempted assassination of industrialist Henry Clay Frick by Alexander Berkman, anarchist philosopher and Goldman's erstwhile lover, in 1892.[8] Anarchist publications such as *Discontent*, the newspaper of the anarchist Home Colony near Tacoma, Washington, came in for particular attention. Four of *Discontent*'s principals were arrested under the Comstock Act on September 24, 1901, for reprinting an article entitled "Prodigal Daughter" by Rachel Campbell.[9] The article, first published in the late 1890s, made the argument that legal marriage was the cause of prostitution. In an editorial protesting the arrests, Moses Harmon, editor of the anarchist newspaper *Lucifer: The Light-Bearer*, called for the formation of an organization to fight against anti-anarchist laws,[10] such as the then-pending Alien Immigration Act of 1903.[11]

In response, the Free Speech League was formed on May 1, 1902, at a meeting of the Manhattan Liberal Club.[12] According to Goldman scholar, Candace Falk, "Edward Chamberlain and E. B. Foote, Jr., prominent members of the Manhattan Liberal Club, and previously president and secretary respectively of the National Defense Association, assumed the role of president and treasurer of the newly formed League. Arthur Pleydell, a prominent single-taxer, served as the League's secretary, along with several well-known anarchists on the executive committee, including E. C. Walker, Benjamin Tucker, and J. A. Maryson."[13] Formation of the league was announced by Harmon's *Lucifer* on May 15, 1902.[14] That issue carried a letter from E. C. Walker, stating that the object of the Free Speech League was to maintain the right of free speech "against all encroachments." The membership fee was one dollar annually, but that did not exclude "good workers to whom such payment would be onerous" and "who think outside the conventional ruts." Harmon added: "It is to be hoped that this League will grow into a powerful organization. We will print further information regarding it when received."[15]

In a 1903 brochure, Walker, who had become president of the Free Speech League, would elaborate on his brief description of the league's mission: "The League demands freedom of peaceable assembly, of discussion and propaganda; an uncensored press, telegraph, and telephone; an uninspected express; an inviolable mail. For these we work by means of the press and platform and the courts; by persuasion, argument, petition, protest, and demand; through the agencies of election and rejection. But the education of brains and quickening of consciences are first in order of time and effect."[16] The league's first formal event was a dinner honoring the release from prison of Ida Craddock, who had first attracted Comstock's attention in 1893 when she defended Little Egypt's belly dancing at the Chicago World's Fair in editorials for the *New York World*.[17] Craddock had been imprisoned for mailing her instructional sex booklet, "The Wedding Night," deemed so obscene under the Comstock Act that the jury should not be allowed to see it at trial.[18] She was re-arrested shortly after her release and committed suicide rather than spend more time in prison. Emma Goldman would call Craddock a "hero[ ] of the battle for free motherhood, for the right of the child to be born well," who, "hounded by Comstock[,] . . . paid the supreme price."[19] Ten years after her death, Craddock's story would capture the imagination of Theodore Schroeder, who would study her work intensively.

In 1903, the league undertook the defense of English anarchist lecturer John Turner, who had been arrested on October 23 in New York City under the new Alien Immigration Act of 1903 and ultimately became the first person deported under its terms.[20] The league temporarily reconstituted itself as the Turner Defense Committee to organize meetings and raise funds for Turner's defense. Emma Goldman, operating under the pseudonym Miss E. G. Smith, "became chief fundraiser and publicist for the case, raising about sixteen hundred of a total of two thousand dollars for Turner's defense and mailing out thousands of leaflets and fliers to mobilize opinion and publicize the case."[21] The league retained Clarence Darrow and his law partner, Edgar Lee Masters, to take Turner's case to the U.S. Supreme Court. Darrow made a First Amendment argument on Turner's behalf, itself a novel approach for 1903, but it went for naught. In a unanimous opinion by Chief Justice Melville Fuller on May 16, 1904, the court held that Congress had plenary power to decide which aliens to admit and which to refuse admission; that Turner was an anarchist and, thus, explicitly excluded by the 1903 act; and that any obstacle to Turner's ability to speak was a function of his exclusion, not an unconstitutional deprivation of his

First Amendment rights. "He does not become one of the people to whom [free speech rights] are secured by our Constitution by an attempt to enter, forbidden by law."[22] Turner was eventually deported, but the league obtained his release in time for him to deliver a number of lectures and stimulate widespread discussion of his case.[23]

As a result of the Turner case, Emma Goldman came to be closely associated with the Free Speech League—so closely, in fact, that she claimed responsibility for organizing the league on a permanent basis.[24] If that is an exaggeration, it is nevertheless true that the alliance ultimately strengthened the league. By the end of 1903, her biographer has written, Goldman—who had been shunned in the aftermath of the McKinley assassination—"once again found herself widely invited to lecture, particularly by middle-class liberals and radicals who gathered in groups such as the Manhattan Liberal Club, the Brooklyn Philosophical Society, and the Sunshine Club."[25] Among others she met and befriended were Theodore Schroeder and Gilbert Roe. Roe even attended a 1904 salon Goldman hosted for Catherine Breshkovskaya, better known as "Babushka, Grandmother of the Russian Revolution," who founded the Socialist Revolutionary Party in Russia in 1901.[26]

Roe and Schroeder seem to have been drawn into active participation in the Free Speech League around 1905, along with the muckraker Lincoln Steffens of *McClure's Magazine*, who had become a good friend of both men. Schroeder focused his energies on legal analysis and the writing of briefs, rarely entering the courtroom; Roe acted as the league's trial attorney.[27] For several years, Roe's work for the Free Speech League coexisted with his private practice, particularly his representation of *McClure's Magazine*. When that litigation ended in 1909, Roe seemed ready to focus more attention on league activities. In a November 9, 1909, letter to Foote Jr.—Foote Sr., died in 1906—Roe proposed organizing and, "preferably incorporat[ing], a society . . . which shall have for its objects the promotion of free speech and a free press, and the resistance generally to sumptuary and arbitrary legislation" at the federal or state level.[28] This organization, "a suitable name for which can be devised," would "gather up and solidify" favorable sentiment around the country and, "by education, [. . .] make more sentiment of the same kind." Roe recommended that Schroeder be appointed secretary. "Schroeder has a better acquaintance for this sort of thing than any other man in the country, and, I believe, could be gotten to undertake the job," he wrote. Roe said he believed the "time is ripe" for such a movement, given the "encroachments everywhere upon the freedom of speech and the press, and personal liberty of all kinds, during the last fifty years." The movement should be done "in a big way," if at all, Roe told Foote, asking whether he knew of any men who could help bear the expense.

"Apparently following Roe's advice," wrote David M. Rabban, the foremost scholar on freedom of speech in the pre–World War I period, Foote left Schroeder a secret fund in 1909 for the "Free Speech League and its propaganda, for defense of victims, for encouragement of papers that favor it and postal progress reforms, and lastly, for comfort and relief of its friends when 'down and out.'"[29] Foote also "encouraged Schroeder to provide that the fund would be passed to Roe if Schroeder died first."[30] In any event, Schroeder tapped Roe for the routine legal work of the league. Rabban—who called Roe Schroeder's most important collaborator in the Free Speech League[31]—wrote that Schroeder never wanted to be attorney of record in free speech cases; he thought briefs were too easily forgotten, at least compared to independent writings. "Schroeder himself, in confiding to Gilbert Roe the reasons he did not want to represent clients in free speech litigation, acknowledged that 'introspection persuades me that I take the world's troubles too seriously to enable me to do my best work if I must wage a war which involves contention at close quarters.'"[32]

The Free Speech League was formally incorporated on April 7, 1911, in Albany, New York. Leonard D. Abbott, associate editor of *Current Literature*, was named president. Vice-president was Brand Whitlock, then the reform mayor of Toledo, Ohio, who had previously been a sports reporter for the *Chicago Herald* and later became ambassador to Belgium. Foote Jr., identified in the incorporation announcement as an "author of medical books," was listed as treasurer, but he should more properly have been called "financier." Schroeder retained the title of secretary. Also among the incorporators were Lincoln Steffens, the muckraking journalist for *McClure's* and *American Magazine*, who was listed in the incorporation announcement as a "leading progressive economist"; Bolton Hall, author, lawyer, and single-tax advocate; and Gilbert Roe. The announcement, which was reprinted in all of the League's publications—many written by Schroeder—described the league's purpose:

> By all lawful means, to promote such judicial construction of the Constitution of the United States, and of the several states, and of the statutes passed in conformity therewith, as will secure to every person the greatest liberty consistent with the equal liberty of all others, and especially to preclude the punishment of any mere psychological offense; and, to that end, by all lawful means to oppose every form of governmental censorship over any method for the expression, communication or transmission of ideas, whether by use of previous inhibition

or subsequent punishment; and to promote such legislative enactments and constitutional amendments, state and national, as will secure those ends.

Noting that all the officers were unsalaried, the announcement solicited contributions to The Free Speech League, 56 East 59th Street, New York City.[33]

According to Goldman scholar Candace Falk, "The League sponsored meetings and lectures, organized free speech legal defense, and, under Schroeder's direction, published and circulated educational and political literature on free speech."[34] Among many others, the League would support anarchist editor Jay Fox in a battle that Roe would take to the United States Supreme Court, albeit in a losing cause. Roe's involvement in that case would not begin until the end of 1912, however, after Fox had already lost in the Washington Supreme Court. In the meantime, Roe remained busy with other matters, including writing a book and helping La Follette with the 1912 presidential campaign. With Wilson's election in November, Roe was free to take the *Fox* case to Washington and the United States Supreme Court.

The Nude and the Prudes

Just as the anarchist colony of Home, Washington, provided the spark that gave rise to the Free Speech League in 1902, so it also provided the league and Roe with their last major free speech case before World War I.[35] Like so many free speech cases of the time, the prosecution in *Fox v. Washington* could never have been brought (or even contemplated) today. But the First Amendment of 1911 was not the First Amendment of even two decades later, and neither Schroeder nor Roe was so prescient as to see what legal weapons their successors would have.

Home was an anarchist communist community located in a wooded area of Pierce County, Washington, near Von Geldern Cove. It was founded in 1896 by three families who were refugees from Glennis, a failed industrial cooperative community near Eatonville. The colony was named after the Mutual Home Association, which was established in 1898 to buy more land and "to assist its members in obtaining and building homes for themselves and to aid in establishing better social and moral conditions."[36] Under the original charter, land would be apportioned to members who accepted the colony's anarchist principles, although title to the land would remain with the association. In 1909, the association's charter was amended to allow for private ownership of the land and individual deeds. The change effectively eliminated the promise of land for

The Anarchists

incoming members and led to factionalism between radical and more conservative members. That factionalism, in turn, created the conditions for the state's case against Jay Fox.

Jay Fox was born in New Jersey in 1870, but his family moved to Chicago and settled near the stockyards. Fox quit school at age fourteen to work first in the stockyards' cabbage fields and then at the Malleable Iron Works. In 1886, at the urging of organizer Albert Parsons, Fox joined the Knights of Labor—just in time to participate in a strike scheduled for May 1. Two days later, while walking the picket line in front of the Iron Works, Fox wandered over to the nearby McCormick Reaper Works. There, strikers were throwing rocks at scabs until police reinforcements arrived and began firing on the retreating strikers. Fox was injured in the melee. The next night, Fox attended a meeting in Haymarket Square, where workers denounced police tactics at McCormick Reaper. A bomb was thrown into the crowd, and eight of the best-known radicals were arrested. Ultimately, five of them received a death sentence; four were hanged—including Albert Parsons—and one committed suicide. The Haymarket Affair, as the labor action and subsequent events came to be known, radicalized Fox, who became an outspoken advocate for anarchist causes through lectures, speeches, and publications in journals such as the *Demonstrator* in Home Colony, Washington, and the *Free Society*, then published in Chicago. He is known to have shared a stage with Emma Goldman on at least one occasion during this period, at the tenth anniversary of the Haymarket hanging on November 11, 1897.

Following the McKinley assassination in 1901, Fox was arrested and then released by the Chicago police. He moved to New York City briefly and then returned to Chicago, where he took Esther Abramowitz as his common-law wife. Both were active in Chicago anarchist circles, which included Clarence Darrow and his occasional client, Emma Goldman. In 1904, Fox and Lucy Parsons, Albert's widow, attempted to launch an anarchist newspaper to replace the *Free Society*. Parsons did launch the *Liberator* in 1905, but Fox accepted an invitation to become editor of Home's the *Demonstrator* that same year.[37] Home had seen a succession of anarchist publications dating from the short-lived *New Era* in 1897. The *Demonstrator*'s immediate predecessor, *Discontent*, published from 1898 to 1902, had provoked the crackdown that led to the formation of the Free Speech League. James F. Morton became editor of *Discontent* in 1901, changing the name to the *Demonstrator* in 1903 and continuing to publish under that name until Fox took over in 1905. Fox edited the *Demonstrator* until mid-1907, when Lawrence Cass replaced him. The *Demonstrator* lasted until early 1908,[38] when Fox actually arrived in Home with his wife and two children by her previous marriage. Eventually, Fox raised enough money to launch the *Agitator* in November 1910.

On July 11, 1911, Fox published the editorial for which he is best known. "The Nude and the Prudes" exposed the rift that had occurred between Home's conservatives and radicals, earned Fox a guilty verdict and sixty-day sentence, and brought Gilbert Roe to the U.S. Supreme Court. The subversive editorial that drew the wrath of state authorities read as follows:

The Nude and the Prudes

Clothing was made to protect the body, not to hide it. The mind that associates impurity with the human body is itself impure. To the humanitarian, the idealist, the human body is divine, "the dwelling place of the soul," as the old poets sang.

To the coarse, half-civilized barbarian, steeped in a mixture of superstition and sensualism, the sight of a nude body suggests no higher thoughts, no nobler feelings than those which the sight of one animal of the lower order of creation produces in another.

The vulgar mind sees its own reflection in everything it views. Pollution cannot escape from pollution, and the polluted mind that sees its own reflection in the nude body of a fellow being, and arises in early morning to enjoy the vulgar feast, and then calls on the law to punish the innocent victims whose clean bodies aroused the savage instincts, is not fit company for civilized people, and should be avoided.

These reflections are based on an unfortunate occurrence that took place recently in Home.

Home is a community of free spirits, who came out into the woods to escape the polluted atmosphere of priest-ridden, conventional society. One of the liberties enjoyed by Homeites was the privilege to bathe in evening dress, or with merely the clothes nature gave them, just as they chose.

No one went rubbernecking to see which suit a person wore, who sought the purifying waters of the bay. Surely it was nobody's business. All were sufficiently pure minded to see no vulgarity, no suggestion of anything vile or indecent in the thought or the sight of nature's masterpiece uncovered.

But eventually a few prudes got into the community and proceeded in the brutal, unneighborly way of the outside world to suppress the people's freedom. They had four persons arrested on the charge of "indecent exposure." One woman, the mother of two small children, was sent to jail. The one man arrested will also serve a term in prison. And the perpetrators of this vile action wonder why they are being boycotted.

The well-merited indignation of the people has been aroused. Their liberty has been attacked. The first step in the way of subjecting the community to all the persecution of the outside has been taken. If this was let go without resistance the progress of the prudes would be easy.

But the foolish people who came to live among us only because they found they could take advantage of our cooperation and buy goods cheaper here than elsewhere, have found they got into a hornets' nest.

Two of the stores have refused to trade with them and the members avoid them in every way.

To be sure, not all have been brought to see the importance of the situation. But the propaganda of those who do, will go on, and the matter of avoiding these enemies in our midst will be pushed to the end.

The lines will be drawn and those who profess to believe in freedom will be put to the test of practice.

There is no possible grounds on which a libertarian can escape taking part in this effort to protect the freedom of Home. There is no half way. Those who refuse to aid the defense are aiding the other side. For those who want liberty and will not fight for it are parasites and do not deserve freedom. Those who are indifferent to the invasion, who can see an innocent woman torn from the side of her children and packed off to jail and are not moved to action, cannot be counted among the rebels of authority. Their place is with the enemy.

The boycott will be pushed until these invaders will come to see the brutal mistake of their action, and so inform the people.[39]

Fox was not arrested for seven weeks following publication, suggesting that the prosecutor was uncertain of his ground.[40] On hearing rumors that Fox might leave Home to avoid arrest, however, authorities sent a special deputy to arrest him in the middle of the night and hold him at a Tacoma hotel. In the morning, Fox was taken to the sheriff's jail, where a state senator's offer to post a $1,000 bond was refused. Fox stayed in jail for two days before being released on bail. On his release, Fox addressed a meeting of the Tacoma affiliate of the Industrial Workers of the World, whose founding convention he had attended in 1905.[41] Although Fox had some reservations regarding IWW's revolutionary strategy of bypassing existing unions, he had covered IWW activities from Chicago for Home Colony's *Demonstrator* before moving to Washington. In addition to support from the IWW, Fox supporters in Home organized a Pierce County Free Speech League to solicit funds for his defense.[42]

The legal case against Fox was formally initiated by a criminal information charge filed in Superior Court for Pierce County, Washington, on August 23, 1911, by Grover C. Nolte, deputy country prosecutor, for his boss, J. L. McMurray.[43] The information—a charging document used when, as here, a grand jury is not available to indict—accused Fox of "committing the crime of editing printed matter tending to encourage and advocate disrespect for the law."[44] Specifically, the information charged that Fox "unlawfully and wilfully" edited the offending editorial.[45] Fox's lawyer, Col. James J. Anderson, filed a demurrer to the information—similar to the motion to dismiss used in most jurisdictions today—asserting that the information alleged no facts that would constitute a crime in Washington and that the statute under which Fox was charged was "unconstitutional and void." Superior Court Judge W. O. Chapman heard the demurrer on November 6, 1911, and overruled it the same day. Fox would later describe Chapman as "an eminently fair minded man, but a very conservative, old-fashioned moralist."[46]

The trial began on January 10, 1912, before a jury that had sworn, to a man, that they did not believe in anarchy. Anderson had objected to Nolte's asking the question on voir dire but was overruled. From the outset, it was apparent that the trial would turn on whether the editorial tended to encourage citizens to disobey the law against nude bathing. Testimony indicated that there had been an increase in nude bathing following the editorial, but other testimony attributed that increase to warmer weather. Judge Chapman reportedly kept the focus on effects, rather than motives. "It doesn't make so much difference what is in a man's mind, it is what comes out of his mind that counts," he reportedly said. On the second afternoon, Fox addressed the jury: "It is only by agitation that reforms have been brought about in the world. . . . Show me a country where there is the most tyranny and I'll show you the country where there is no free speech. This country was settled on that right, the right of free expression."[47]

At the close of the testimony, Judge Chapman instructed the jury to decide whether Fox in fact edited "The Nude and the Prudes" and whether the item tended to encourage and advocate disrespect for the law.[48] He also gave the jury a primer on the meaning of free speech under the Washington Constitution as of 1912: "[E]very person may freely speak, write and publish upon all subjects," he said; "they are, however, answerable and responsible for the abuse of that right." Chapman interpreted the clause as allowing publication with impunity only "truth, with good motives and for justifiable ends," not otherwise harmful or unlawful.

Chapman recited the statute under which the charges against Fox were brought and admonished the jury that it was no defense that Fox may have acted "with intent to produce what he might consider an ultimate good." He drew a fine distinction between nude bathing, which, he said, was not in itself a violation of law, and "indecent exposure of the person." Fox cannot be found guilty of merely defending nude bathing, Chapman said, unless he was advocating nude bathing "under circumstances amounting to indecent exposure" or other conditions violating the laws of decency and tended, by tenor or effect, to encourage disrespect for the law. Finally, Chapman warned the jury not to consider whether Fox believed in anarchy or not.

The jury received the case at 4 p.m., adjourning at 10 p.m. without a verdict. Various press accounts reported a 9–3 split for acquittal and, the following day, a hung jury.[49] In all, the jury deliberated for twenty-five hours before reaching a verdict, at 5 p.m. on the second day, of guilty with a recommendation of leniency. Anderson filed a motion for a new trial, based on misconduct by the prosecution and erroneous instructions by the judge. Judge Chapman ordered a hearing on the motion on February 3 but then denied it the same day. On February 6, 1912, Fox was sentenced to two months in the Pierce County Jail. On the same day, Anderson's motion in arrest of judgment was summarily denied, and he filed notice of appeal to the Washington State Supreme Court.[50] Fox's appeal would be financed, in large measure, by the Free Speech League. In September, the league published a fund-raising pamphlet reprinting Fox's editorial in full[51] and promising to take the case all the way to the U.S. Supreme Court if necessary. Estimating the cost of such an undertaking at $2,000, the League asked that contributions be sent to Theodore Schroeder, now living in Cos Cob, Connecticut. "As all of the officers of the Free Speech League contribute their time without one cent of compensation, you can feel assured that all of your contribution will go to Mr. Fox's defense and will be accounted for to you."

Anderson's brief to the state supreme court began by listing a series of procedural errors, including the admission of testimony as to the increase in nude bathing prosecutions after publication and, more significantly, submitting to the jury the question of whether the editorial tended to encourage and advocate disrespect for law.[52] Anderson turned next to an argument based on an erroneous construction of the statute under which Fox was charged. Specifically, he argued the court erroneously allowed the jury to believe that the law effectively forbade criticism of "any particular law," rather than disrespect for law generally.

Anderson made two principal constitutional arguments urging the court to void the statute. The clearest argument urged the court to void the statute for vagueness—a direct violation of Fox's Fifth and Fourteenth Amendment rights to due process. Without even a hint of irony, Anderson analogized the vagueness of the Washington statute to the vagueness found by various courts in striking down laws criminalizing unreasonable freight rates. "Where the law is uncertain," Anderson quoted Blackstone, "there is no law."[53] Anderson's First

Amendment argument, however, was much murkier, urging that the court void the statute for violating the "spirit" of the First Amendment's guarantee of freedom of the press. He attempted to distinguish the Washington statute from laws against advocating murder and similar crimes, or against criticizing the integrity of a court in a case pending before it, which had been routinely upheld. But the distinction was more conclusory than compelling, and ultimately, Anderson's First Amendment argument did little more than reiterate his procedural and statutory construction claims.[54] Asserting that no other state had gone as far in nullifying freedom of speech and press as Washington had done by this anti-anarchist statute, Anderson charged that "sustaining the law in question would be to make the said constitutional guaranty only a high-sounding phrase valuable for use only in Fourth of July orations." Unfortunately, the First Amendment of 1912 was little more than that.

The state's brief barely mentioned the First Amendment, choosing instead to address the free speech issue with the comparable provision in the Washington Constitution, on which Anderson also relied: "Every person may freely speak, write and publish on all subjects, being responsible for the abuse of that right."[55] As if to respond in kind to Anderson's non-argument, the brief simply quoted a New York sedition opinion to the effect that although government "cannot abridge freedom of the press, the legislature may control, and the courts may punish the licentiousness of the press."[56] Other issues raised by Anderson were competently rebutted in the state's brief, signed by prosecutor McMurray and deputies Nolte and A. O. Burmeister. But the most interesting aspect of the brief was its characterization of Home Colony as "a group of malcontents and discontents . . . composed of two factions, namely, the law and order element and the anarchistic element."[57] The editorial was prompted by a series of prosecutions initiated by the "law and order element," which had become "disgusted with the indecent exposures committed . . . where the parties walked about their premises in the nude."

In his reply brief, Anderson vigorously protested that characterization, "evidently made in the hope of prejudicing the minds of the court against the appellant . . . in line with the animus of this whole prosecution."[58] On the issue of press freedom, however, Anderson made almost no argument at all, merely stringing together a series of quotations for the court to consider. Among his sources was *Obscene Literature and Constitutional Law* by Theodore Schroeder, with whom he had been collaborating closely throughout the litigation.[59] The very last citation in Anderson's reply brief referred to Justice Harlan's pioneering dissent in *Patterson v. Colorado*, urging that the First Amendment be applied to state laws through the Fourteenth Amendment and construed to regulate not merely Blackstonian prior restraint but also subsequent punishment imposed by state legislatures when they deem the "public welfare" to be threatened.[60] "This is only a dissenting opinion," Anderson wrote. "However, since its rendition the court has entirely changed its personel [sic]. It is believed that the dissenting opinion should be, and will be, made the rule of the court when next the matter is presented." Anderson was ultimately correct, but overly optimistic as to timing by more than a decade. In any event, the Washington Supreme Court ignored the reference, and not merely because Anderson had directed the justices to the wrong page in the reporter.

The Supreme Court issued a unanimous decision on November 29, 1912, affirming the lower court judgment.[61] Again, the opinion sheds light on prevailing views of the limited free speech right afforded by the Constitution. "The appellant apparently concedes that the article does tend to encourage disobedience and disrespect for law, for it clearly does so," wrote Chief Justice Wallace Mount. "But he argues that the statute is unconstitutional because it abridges the right of free speech and of the press, and also because the statute is uncertain." Wrong on both counts. Acknowledging a right to publish freely on any subject, Mount characterized Fox's piece as an abuse of that right. In stark contrast to Harlan's dissent, Mount wrote that the "'punishment of those who publish articles which tend to corrupt morals, induce crime, or destroy organized society is essential to the security of freedom and the stability of the state.' This is the rule and the statute under consideration is not repugnant to the constitutional provisions relating to freedom of speech and of the press." As to Fox's uncertainty claim, Mount said that any reasonable person in similar circumstances would have known "the exact character of the offense with which he was charged." Mount also disposed of the procedural claim that the court should have dismissed the action because it was not brought to trial within sixty days on the ground urged by the state that any delay was caused by Fox. And he rejected Fox's objection to the admission of evidence of increased prosecutions for indecent exposure after the editorial appeared, because the editorial "clearly upon its face incited the commission of crime and disrespect of law relating to indecent exposure of the person."

On December 28, 1912, Anderson petitioned for a rehearing, asking the court to address the federal constitutional questions raised more specifically.[62] In the meantime, however, Gilbert Roe had taken notice of the Washington decision and wrote to Schroeder: "After examining the law somewhat further since I last saw you and much reflection, I believe if it is possible to get the matter up to the United States Supreme Court before Fox serves out his time, we ought to try it on. We may some time get a case where the Federal question is raised better but we will never get a better case on the facts otherwise, and if the Supreme Court of the United States either decides against us or refuses to take jurisdiction, the best possible basis will be laid for subsequent agitation and propaganda work."[63] Roe told Schroeder he would make up a statement of the time and disbursements made in the case through the end of 1912. "If we go on, we will start fresh from that point." They did "go on," of course, and on January 6, 1913, Schroeder sent Roe copies of the information, appellant's opening brief, and prosecutor's brief. Schroeder said he did not have the demurrer but recalled that it had been read to Roe earlier over the telephone.[64] Schroeder also sent Roe a check for $111.40, presumably from league funds to cover Roe's statement.[65] It was still Anderson's case, but Roe was now taking a very active interest, largely through Schroeder as interlocutor.

On January 13, Roe expressed some concern that Anderson might not fully understand the constitutional issues involved in the case, and said it was not clear what constitutional question the Supreme Court of Washington had actually decided. "Possibly, Anderson will get something on his motion for reargument that will strengthen us on the constitutional question."[66] Roe reiterated his desire to take the case to the U.S. Supreme Court but worried that Fox might serve his jail term and render the case moot before the court could hear the case.[67] Anticipating that the petition for rehearing would be denied, Roe and Schroeder had set to work on the Assignments of Error that Anderson would submit to the Washington Supreme Court in order to get the Writ of Error that would keep Fox out of jail pending appeal.[68] Recalling that they had been "obliged to leave" the Bar Association library at closing time, Roe told Schroeder he was not satisfied with the work they had done on the constitutional questions and urged that Schroeder give it more attention before sending it to Anderson.

As expected, Anderson's petition for rehearing was summarily denied, along with some twenty-seven other petitions, on Saturday, February 8, 1913.[69] On Monday, February 10, the court formally entered judgment affirming the decision of the trial court and ordered Fox to pay $34.50 in costs. The same day, Anderson filed his Petition for a Writ of Error with the Washington Supreme Court, which was duly allowed with an order staying the judgment and requiring Fox to post a $1,000 bond. Along with the petition, Anderson filed the Assignment of Errors on which Roe and Schroeder had collaborated, and the entire package was certified by Chief Justice Herman D. Crow for submission to the U.S. Supreme Court. Anderson submitted the Writ of Error to the U.S. Supreme Court the next day, via the U.S. District Court for the Western District of Washington. It was formally filed on February 19, as was Fox's bond to the

The Anarchists

Supreme Court of Washington. On March 3, Fox submitted the praecipe requesting documents from the Washington Supreme Court, and the state, now represented by Lorenzo Dow, who had succeeded McMurray as prosecuting attorney for Pierce County, acknowledged receipt of the writ on March 5. The required documents were filed with the U.S. Supreme Court on March 7.

On March 21, Roe received a letter from the clerk of the U.S. Supreme Court informing him that the case would not be heard for at least two years after it was docketed.[70] The letter noted that Roe could submit a deposit and enter an appearance earlier, and following Schroeder's instructions, Roe sent the $25 deposit to the court and effectively took over the case.[71] The following month, Roe and Dow entered a stipulation adding the written jury instructions from Fox's trial to the record.[72] The case would be considered in the October 1914 term.

Roe and Schroeder decided to stake everything on a Fourteenth Amendment argument, namely that the statute under which Fox was convicted deprived him of liberty and property without due process of law.[73] To be sure, the brief contains a one-paragraph reference to the notion that the First Amendment guarantees could be applied against the states through the Fourteenth Amendment, which was "left undecided" in *Patterson v. Colorado*. "[But] in our view," Roe wrote, "the Fourteenth Amendment is sufficient to give full protection to the rights of [Fox], which were invaded in state court." The view that freedom of speech is a fundamental individual right, protected by the Fourteenth Amendment's due process clause, was central to Schroeder's constitutional philosophy. Mark Graber has written that he shared that view with many conservative jurists. "[While] late nineteenth-century conservative libertarians and philosophical anarchists disagreed on applications, they shared common principles. [Justice Thomas] Cooley and Schroeder, in particular, can be said to be part of a common libertarian tradition" which held that "free speech was an individual right, that this right was one aspect of the broader right of equal liberty protected by the due process clause of the Fourteenth Amendment, and that federal courts were expected to protect such liberties from the whims of elected majorities."[74]

In the *Fox* case, Roe applied this due process theory in two different ways. The first seemed like a variant of the "uncertainty" argument advanced below, recast here as a constitutional issue. Roe asserted that the first element in "'due process of law' is that there shall be a '*law*'"; then he reiterated the maxim that "where the law is uncertain, there is no law."[75] He pointed out that the statute contained no standard for determining whether an article encouraged respect for law, or for any specific law, or even what might constitute indecent exposure.

Again, Roe cited several cases where the courts had struck down statutes that, he asserted, were more certain than the statute at issue here. Roe then addressed the Washington court's assertion that the law could properly punish speech having merely a "tendency" to bring about the harms proscribed by the statute. Specifically, the state court had cited the antitrust case of *Waters-Pierce Oil Co. v. Texas*[76] for the proposition that a conviction for acts having such bad tendencies does not violate due process. Roe pointed out that, in the same case, the court seemed to condition that proposition on the certainty of the legal standards. "In the case at bar, however, the statute in question [gives] the jury the absolute power to determine the criminal character of the act in accordance with their belief in the merits or demerits of the law subjected to criticism," he wrote.[77]

In addition to the "uncertainty" argument, Roe's Fourteenth Amendment argument also urged that the statute arbitrarily deprived the defendant of his protected liberty interest. Roe quoted from the majority opinion in *Patterson v. Colorado* to show that, whenever "innocent conduct has been laid hold of as an arbitrary pretense for an arbitrary punishment," the Fourteenth Amendment is properly invoked. "[What] can be more arbitrary," Roe asked, "than the verdict of the jury in this case, finding the defendant guilty of the shadowy and uncertain offense of editing the innocent article in question and thereby tending to create a mental attitude on the part of someone which the jurors would describe as 'disrespect' for some law, relating to nude bathing."

The state's brief rather handily disposed of the "uncertainty" argument, distinguishing the cases Roe presented from another list of cases where, as here, the state argued "there could be no serious difference of opinion as to what the Legislature meant."[78] It countered Roe's press freedom argument with *New York v. Most*'s dictum that the "legislature may control, and the courts may punish, the licentiousness of the press," without abridging its freedom. Signed by Washington attorney general W. V. Tanner, the brief insisted that Fox made "a direct appeal and a direct attempt to incite and coerce the members of the colony to 'action' against the law-abiding portion of the colony by exhortation, yes, by threats, by saying that the lines will be drawn, and those who profess to believe in freedom will be put to the test of practice." The statute under which Fox was convicted, Tanner wrote, "welcomes fair and reasonable criticism; but it is aimed at such appeals and declarations against our commonwealth as is found throughout this entire article."

In his perfunctory affirming opinion for a unanimous court, issued February 23, 1915, Justice Oliver Wendell Holmes Jr. reasoned that the Washington Supreme Court had construed the statute narrowly to reach only that speech that encouraged an actual breach of law.[79] "Therefore the argument that this act is both an unjustifiable restriction of liberty and too vague for a criminal law

The Anarchists

must fail," he wrote. Regardless of the wisdom of the defendant, the prosecution, or the act, Holmes said, there is no constitutional infirmity in the statute. Roe later called the opinion "apologetic."[80] When he received word of the affirmance, James Anderson, Fox's local lawyer, petitioned Washington governor Ernest C. Lister for executive clemency.[81] Both Judge Chapman and former deputy prosecutor Burmeister said they would not object, but the governor refused and ordered Fox to serve at least part of his sentence. Anderson continued to press Lister, and on September 11, 1915, twelve days before his sentence would have been fully served, Lister relented and granted a pardon. Fox continued to live in Home with his second wife, Cora. He became a communist in the 1920s and died in 1961.[82]

Paterson and the Boyd Sabotage Case

While the Fox case was pending, Roe became involved in another anarchist-inspired event—the 1913 IWW silk workers strike at Paterson, New Jersey. Paterson was the silk-weaving center of America, with a history of strikes dating back to 1828 and the reputation as a "hotbed of anarchy."[83] There had already been one strike in Paterson under IWW auspices, in 1907; in early 1913, IWW organizers Carlo Tresca and Elizabeth Gurley Flynn came to town to lead the silk workers' protest against attempts by employers to increase the number of looms for which each weaver was responsible to as many as four, with no increase in pay. At a mass meeting on February 25, they were arrested, along with the Socialist Party's Patrick L. Quinlan, and ultimately charged with "conspiracy to cause an unlawful assemblage of persons as well as to raucously and riotously and tumultuously disturb the peace of New Jersey." In addition to an end to the "speedup" system, the union demanded an eight-hour day, wage increases, and a guarantee of no retaliation against workers for union activities. Some twenty-five thousand workers were involved in the strike, and employers complained that "the entire fabric of the city's business interests and the Commonwealth itself is menaced to a point that should cause widespread alarm." More than a thousand strikers were arrested, not to mention the union leaders. Quinlan was tried first, and convicted, followed by Socialist newspaper editor Alexander Scott, for an editorial criticizing the Paterson police. The third trial was that of another outside speaker, a Socialist, IWW member, and friend of Jack Reed from New York City, Frederick Sumner Boyd.

In her autobiography, Flynn wrote disparagingly about Boyd, whom she called a "volunteer speaker on the strike platform over whom the [IWW] could exercise no control. Once the damage was done, the IWW reaped the blame and felt compelled to defend these embarrassing friends of the strike." In Boyd's case, the issue was sabotage—the subject of two speeches he made on March 31 and April 1. According to court records, Boyd told strikers on March 31 they could sabotage the operations by putting a kink in the warp, ruining the finished fabric.[84] On April 1, he allegedly suggested rubbing the reeds of looms operated by scabs with a cloth soaked in vinegar. Boyd was indicted on June 6, 1913, for two violations of a New Jersey statute that declared it to be a "high misdemeanor" for anyone "in public or private speech, writing, printing or by any other means [to] advocate, encourage, justify, praise or incite the unlawful burning or destruction of public or private property."[85] He was arraigned and pleaded not guilty on June 25. A jury trial was slated for July 7 but subsequently was continued until September 29. Four days before the trial was to begin, Boyd waived his right to a jury.[86]

At his bench trial, Boyd was represented by local counsel, Gustav Hunziker and Henry Marelli, with Gilbert Roe of counsel. In a letter to La Follette regarding the strike, Roe wrote: "A few of us have volunteered to do what we could in order to bring their case to the attention of the Congress." Noting that the strikers in Paterson "are certainly getting a rotten deal from the authorities and the contest is very unequal," Roe said the difference between Paterson and the West Virginia coal strike "seems to be that in West Virginia they have martial law, while in Paterson they do not have any law at all."[87] In pretrial motions, the court agreed to let the prosecution try both indictments together; it also allowed Boyd to withdraw his plea in order to present objections to the indictments.[88] Boyd next moved to quash the subpoenas on grounds that the indictments failed to state a violation of the law and that the law itself violated the New Jersey and U.S. constitutions. That motion was denied, and Boyd reentered a plea of not guilty. Finally, Roe was admitted *pro hac vice*, and the trial began.

The state called a stenographer who had apparently been assigned to a number of the IWW meetings; he testified that Boyd had indeed spoken the words alleged in the indictments. That testimony was further supported by a Paterson police officer. The state then called a chemist and a silk manufacturer to testify that the methods advocated by Boyd would have damaged the looms and the silk. The defense moved for acquittal on the ground that the statute required "destruction," not merely "injury," but the court denied the motion. The defense declined to mount an affirmative defense, and the court found Boyd guilty as charged. Sentencing was put over until October 3,[89] when Judge Abram Klenert sentenced Boyd to serve one to seven years at hard labor in the state penitentiary and pay a $500 fine on the first count, suspending sentence on the second count.[90]

In his appeal to the New Jersey Supreme Court, Boyd again argued that the indictment failed to state a crime and that the law under which he was indicted violated the New Jersey and United States constitutions.[91] The court disagreed. Both the indictments and the evidence showed very clearly that Boyd advocated the destruction of property, the court held, and the law did not require any actual destruction of property before criminal liability would attach.[92] As to the principal constitutional issue, Justice Charles Wolcott Parker wrote that "free speech does not mean unbridled license of speech, and that language tending to the violation of the rights of personal security and private property, and toward breaches of the public peace, is an abuse of the right of free speech. . . . Incitement to the commission of a crime is a misdemeanor at common law, whether the crime advocated be actually committed or not." To support his conclusion, Parker cited one case arising from the Paterson strike itself[93] and a New York case involving a much earlier anarchist, Johann Most.[94] Boyd's conviction was affirmed on July 27, 1914.[95]

Boyd visited Roe in mid-August in New York City, where Boyd was working with Reed at *Metropolitan Magazine*. "Nothing important came up in the conversation," Roe wrote Boyd's wife, "except he seemed desirous that the appeal should be taken, and the best use possible made of his case as a test case."[96] Roe and his New Jersey colleagues did appeal the decision, to New Jersey's Court of Errors and Appeals, making essentially the same arguments that they had made below.[97] On March 1, 1915, that court issued a per curiam opinion affirming Boyd's conviction "for the reasons expressed in the opinion delivered by Mr. Justice Parker in the Supreme Court."[98] On June 14, however, the court dealt separately with the second indictment, this time reversing on an argument the Supreme Court had rejected as untimely: that the indictment failed to state whose property might be subject to destruction if Boyd's advocacy were heeded.[99] Unfortunately for Boyd, the reversal involved the indictment for which sentence had been suspended; Boyd had begun serving his prison term on the first indictment on March 22.

Three days later, Boyd stunned the radical world by petitioning the New Jersey Court of Pardons for clemency rather than attempting any further appeal. According to the *Call*, a New York Socialist newspaper, the petition was probably the idea of Theodore Roosevelt, who, like Boyd, was affiliated with the *Metropolitan* and whose name headed the list of endorsers. The second name on that list was Gilbert Roe, followed by such luminaries as Lincoln Steffens, Jack Reed, Walter Lippmann, Finley Peter Dunne, and others. The Court of Pardons abandoned its usual policy to make the petition public in hopes of dissuading other agitators from advocating sabotage.[100] The petition gave numerous reasons to justify clemency, but the single most striking assertion was that Boyd had completely renounced his positions of 1913. Boyd said "he was convicted of advocating views he has now entirely abandoned, regarding them as anti-Social and detrimental to the general welfare; that he now looks upon the tactics he formerly advocated as certain to defeat the moral and social betterment of the working class." His endorsers also signed a statement attesting to their belief that "the ends of justice will have been met if at this time his petition is granted, thereby enabling him to become a good and useful citizen." That was not exactly how other radicals saw it.

Emma Goldman's *Mother Earth Bulletin* reprinted the *Call*'s coverage of Boyd's petition in its April 1915 issue. It also carried an editorial under the rubric "Observations and Comments," which began as a sympathetic salute to the Paterson agitators. "The cold chariot wheel of justice has ridden over Patrick Quinlan and Frederick Sumner Boyd. If proofs were needed, their cases have again shown us the utter futility—not to speak of the inconsistency—for the revolutionary element to hope for justice from the courts." But midway through the editorial, the tone changed dramatically, condemning Boyd's "cringing and slimy" appeal for pardon. "The most disgusting feature of the Boyd recantation is that such men as Gilbert E. Roe, John Reed and Lincoln Steffens should have put their names to such a document," she wrote.[101] Steffens did remove his name from the petition, writing a separate letter in support of Boyd,[102] but to no avail. Boyd was denied a pardon on April 26, 1915.[103]

Emma and Sasha

Roe continued to maintain his relationship with other anarchists, particularly Goldman and Berkman. The Free Speech League had always been critical to Goldman's ability to reach her national audiences by challenging local government efforts to block her lectures. By 1909, the situation had become so dire that a special Free Speech Committee of the league was formed to support the effort.[104] Roe was among the many advocates who signed the committee's manifesto "assert[ing] our right to hear any person upon any subject, and demand[ing] that our liberty to hear Emma Goldman or any other speaker shall not be infringed by the authorities."[105] But Roe's relationship with Goldman transcended the league connection and took on a much more personal character; she even spent time with the Roes at Pelham Manor.[106] In September 1910, for example, Roe wrote Schroeder that he had received a note from Goldman saying she was "flat broke" and needed money for rent. "Now I haven't even *one* dollar *cash* I can spare," Roe said. "If you can help her out as to *immediate* needs, I will stand in it with you & divide the burden whatever it may be. If you can use any of the Dr. Foote fund for the purpose, I am sure it will never be needed more."[107] It was not the last time Goldman would ask Roe for financial support.

The following summer Berkman completed his *Prison Memoirs*, but he had trouble finding a publisher and, with Goldman, decided to publish the book independently. Many years later, Goldman would recall, "In our predicament I turned to my friend Gilbert E. Roe, a lawyer by profession, an anarchist by feeling, and one of the kindest of men it has been my good fortune to know." Goldman went on to describe at length how "Gilbert and Mrs. Roe remained among my staunchest friends and most generous contributors to our work," even to the extent of giving a reading in their apartment to raise the money.[108] Berkman's book was published in 1912, but his activities and Goldman's *Mother Earth* were a constant drain on their finances. When Goldman returned from her West Coast tour in late 1914, she found the magazine and her own finances once again in dire straits.[109] "I decided to give up our house and to declare myself bankrupt," she would write in her autobiography. "My friend Gilbert E. Roe, to whom I confided my troubles, laughed at my strange notion. 'Bankruptcy is resorted to by those who want to get out of paying debts,' he said; 'it will involve you in year-long litigation, and your creditors will attach every penny you make to the end of your days.' He offered to lend me money, but I could not accept his generosity."

Instead, Goldman moved to a small place at 20 E. 125th Street in October 1914, and by May 1915, the magazine was strong enough that Roe would write a tribute in it to Goldman's "efforts and her achievement in keeping that magazine up to its high standard of excellence." Roe said the magazine had "earned for itself a distinct place in the literary and radical world. The next ten years should see its influence and its usefulness multiply many-fold."[110]

Both Goldman and the *Fox* case would figure prominently in a talk Roe presented at the annual meeting of the American Sociological Society on December 29, 1915, at Princeton, New Jersey. Entitled "Reasonable Restrictions on Freedom of Assemblage," the speech reiterated the position he had taken in *Fox* with respect to the uncertainty of the laws attempting to regulate free speech. He also recounted Goldman's 1909 lecture hall experiences with what would today be described as a "heckler's veto," that is, authorities' refusal to allow her to speak, not because her advocacy might incite her audience to adopt anarchism, but because her ideas "would be rejected so vigorously that a breach of the peace might result."[111] Roe warned that the courts "cannot be depended upon to protect the fundamental rights of liberty against the assaults of unconstitutional legislation with the same zeal with which they have defended the rights of property from somewhat similar attacks." Rather, he said, "where freedom of speech and freedom of assembly have been denied, some unpopular person or unpopular cause has usually been the victim," closing with Jefferson's famous observation that "a little rebellion now and then is a good thing."

Roe's relationship with Alexander Berkman was also a blend of the personal and professional. Goldman recounts a time in the fall of 1914 when Berkman was planning a western tour. On his way home from a farewell party in New York, he tried to stop a policeman from hitting an old friend and coworker with a billy club. Berkman was charged with assaulting an officer and inciting a riot, and he demanded a jury trial. Roe bailed him out and promised to look after the case during his absence. When Berkman reached Denver, however, Roe warned him to stop so he could return to New York within two days. Goldman remembered the situation as serious, with Berkman facing up to five years in prison.[112] Berkman spent about five months lecturing in Colorado, though he was eager to go to California to aid in the defense of anarchists Matthew A. Schmidt and David Caplan, who had helped the McNamara brothers buy the dynamite they used to blow up the *Los Angeles Times* building in 1910.[113] He wrote to Roe from Denver: "I suppose nothing has been heard so far in re my case. Do you think it safe for me to allow myself to be extradited, in case my return to N.Y. is demanded? I have no fare to return, but I do not want to risk forfeiting the bail. I should like your advice in this matter."[114]

About a week later, Berkman received a telegram from New York, Goldman recalled, "reading: 'Case against you dismissed. You are free to go where you please. Congratulations.' It was Gilbert E. Roe who had managed to have the indictments against Sasha quashed by convincing the new District Attorney of New York that the charges were the result of police enmity."[115] Berkman himself would recount this episode in a March 1930 letter to Netha Roe, written from exile in Paris, following Roe's death. The telegram, dated February 25, 1915, was from Harold Spielberg, an attorney who was to help Roe in Berkman's defense. "But it was Gilbert E. who had talked with the new District Attorney that had just assumed office. I forgot his name, but he was a college chum of Gilbert, I think, and G. E. succeeded in showing him that those indictments against me were nothing but police vengeance."[116] Actually, the district attorney was Charles A. Perkins, who was appointed to fill the unexpired term of Charles S. Whitman when Whitman was elected governor in 1914. Roe did not go to college with Perkins but would have had ample opportunity to make his acquaintance during Perkins's thirteen years in the D.A.'s office.

The Anarchists

Berkman had written to thank Roe for having the charges dropped, but lamented that he had no opportunity to thank him personally. He called the outcome a "wonderful achievement, for a trial of this notorious criminal would have been synonymous with conviction and a maximum sentence." Berkman told Netha that what Roe had done "he did out of friendship; and by no means in the interest of any professional service." His closing to that 1915 letter to Roe reflected that friendship: "Kindly remember me to Mrs. Roe & family, & be sure to kiss the kiddies for me. I often think of my visit at your place."[117] In fact, Berkman had built the "kiddies" a playhouse at Pelham Manor, which they were still using when Roe wrote to Berkman in San Francisco in September 1916.[118] Roe had sent Berkman a newspaper clipping showing that the police were trying to connect Berkman with the Preparedness Day bombing there in July. "I have seen nothing in the papers about it since," Roe said, "and hope that you will have no further trouble." Two labor organizers protesting the imminent U.S. entry into World War I were ultimately convicted of the bombing. There were limits to the relationship, however. In that same letter, Roe told Berkman that he had received a circular asking for help for the *Blast*, Berkman's San Francisco–based anarchist magazine. "I am sorry that I am not in a position to give financial assistance to any publication of this kind," Roe said. "I feel sure that any paper you edit has a real work to do and must eventually make a place for itself. I know that good wishes cannot take the place of cash, but sometimes they are all one has to give, and this you know you have."

Looking back on their relationship after Roe's death, Berkman assured Netha that it was "not ONLY [the legal] service of Gilbert that endeared him to me. In truth, I admired him for the unusual qualities of heart and mind that I had learned to appreciate in him. . . . He was a man of very keen intellect, broad view and great, even exceptional moral courage—a mighty rare trait among men, unfortunately. I do not need to add anything about his generosity and kindness: they were too well known among our people."[119] Our people? Anarchists, of course. But Roe's commitment to free speech for dissidents was hardly so limited. Almost exactly a month before the *Fox* case was submitted to the U.S. Supreme Court, a drama was unfolding near Union Square that would present Roe's best opportunity to attack the plague that Comstockery— by equating birth control with obscenity—had visited upon the rights of women. As a committed suffragist, Roe may well have shared some of that movement's ambivalence toward birth control issues. Even so, the evidence is clear that Roe's devotion to the cause of women generally was as great as his dedication to free speech.

4

The Feminists

> The law is so because men have made it so, and will remain so until women have an equal part with men in making the law, and in administering it.
>
> Gilbert Roe

> I hear you have taken charge of the Sanger case. Hope you'll wallop old man Comstock good and plenty.
>
> Alexander Berkman

Suffrage Plus

Gilbert Roe could not have avoided feminist causes even if he had tried. The most important political influence in his life, Robert La Follette, was a committed suffragist. La Follette's wife, Belle Case La Follette, was the first woman to graduate from the University of Wisconsin Law School, and she was involved in "securing the legislation and in making the appointments" of women to state office from the moment he became governor.[1] Belle was listed as "First Auditor" on the letterhead of the National American Woman Suffrage Association in 1912.[2] "I believe not only in using the peculiar executive abilities of women in the state service," Robert La Follette would write in his 1913 autobiography, "but I cannot remember a time when I did not believe in woman suffrage. . . . I am glad to say that the legislature of Wisconsin passed, at its last session, a suffrage law which will be submitted on referendum next November to the voters of the state. I shall support it and campaign for it."[3]

Both La Follettes campaigned for enactment of the Susan B. Anthony Amendment when Robert served in the Senate, even cutting short a California vacation in 1918 in case his vote was needed. When the amendment finally passed on June 4, 1919, La Follette wrote to his sons: "Mamma sat in the gallery all day and was rewarded as were the other fighters for suffrage and equal rights by seeing the Susan B. Anthony Amendment pass by 56 to 25—after a 70-year struggle. Six votes to spare. I started the applause on the floor and it swept the galleries again and again without any rebuke from the Chair. . . . All felt it was a great victory."[4]

The greatest influence in Roe's personal life, his wife Netha, was also an ardent advocate for women's rights. Netha's greatest influences, in turn, were Belle La Follette and Emily Bishop, who sent her a postcard in 1909 quoting Robert La Follette's responses to questions at a meeting in New York on women's suffrage. "I do not know of any reason why a woman should not vote," La Follette reportedly said. "I am satisfied there is a member of my family that can cast as intelligent a vote upon any question as I can. I am quite sure that the vote would be just as patriotic as mine. I don't know why it should be denied."[5] Netha Roe's own views on suffrage were adamantly expressed in a 1912 letter to Theodore Schroeder. Schroeder had sent her a draft of an article for *International Magazine* in which he expressed support for women's suffrage in a manner that Netha Roe found unacceptable. Netha interpreted Schroeder's article as a condemnation of the demand for suffrage for the "wrong" reasons, such as "lust for power," and took him to task in a long, handwritten letter.

"[Women's suffrage] is the first thing in history that has ever united 'all sorts & conditions' of women, of every creed & no creed—and it is simply inevitable that there should be as many reasons now set forth for the demand as there are women (or groups of women) demanding it," she wrote. "They *need* to set forth as many arguments as there are voters or groups of voters among the men to be influenced to grant it. . . . A woman should be allowed to vote for any reason whatsoever if she chooses just as a man is—whether it be for 'lust of power' or to fall down and fawn at the feet of power."[6] Schroeder's response was defensive, but he agreed to make some changes in the article, "just so the next fellow will have more difficulty in reading into my preachment what you almost saw there."[7]

For all that, Gilbert Roe did not participate in the first New York City suffragist parade in May 1910. The following month, a representative of the Collegiate Equal Suffrage League wrote to him, urging him to reconsider the negative view of demonstrations that he shared with Schroeder. Netha Roe later affixed a note to the letter: "Interesting because of change of mind that led Mr. Roe to march in the later parades."[8] Indeed, when the second major New York parade was held on May 6, 1911, Roe was among the eighty-seven men who joined some three thousand women marching up Fifth Avenue.[9] Roe marched with George Middleton, husband of Fola La Follette, who carried the banner for the actresses division.[10] Roe became an active member of the Men's League for Woman Suffrage of the State of New York and, during the winter of 1913–14, wrote a major speech for one of their meetings entitled "Memorandum Dealing with Cases Wherein Women are not on an Equality with Men Under the Law." The speech was so popular that the National Woman Suffrage Association decided to issue it as a pamphlet, simply called "Discriminations against Women in the Laws of New York."[11]

In his speech, Roe outlined thirteen laws of New York that discriminated against women. Several of these laws were facially neutral, that is, treated men and women the same way, but because women had no say in their making, Roe found them discriminatory nevertheless. These included taxation, takings, criminal penalties, enforcement of contract, and general personal and property rights. Roe was particularly critical of the inability of women to sit on juries, especially considering that men could gain the right to sit on juries solely by virtue of property owned by their wives. Other overtly discriminatory laws that Roe singled out included laws governing the custody and religious education of children, curtesy and dower, and descent and inheritance. In Roe's view, it all came down to suffrage: "Why should the male have the advantage in matters of inheritance, in the guardianship of children, in the administration of estates, in the education of children, and in the many other matters I have considered?" he asked. "There is no reason, but there is an answer. The answer is that the law is so because men have made it so, and will remain so until women have an equal part with men in making the law, and in administering it."

In December 1914, Roe agreed to chair, at least temporarily, a new Men's Campaign Committee "to assist in the present Woman Suffrage fight" in New York State. In a letter to Harriet Stanton Blatch, president of the Women's Political Union in New York City, Roe asked for advice on how the men's committee could help,[12] but it is clear from his correspondence throughout 1915 that his principal role would be making speeches and raising money for the effort.[13] Roe clearly enjoyed the work, suggesting to Fola La Follette that an evening of suffrage speeches could be "a real night of jollification,"[14] but it was taking its toll on his time and law practice. "I'm about all in with suffrage work, and trying to keep up my legal work at the same time," he told Commissioner of Immigration Frederick C. Howe, in a letter regarding one of his cases.[15]

Roe's speaking engagements were also taking a toll on his health by the end of 1915. "I think my cold is pretty well cleared up, however, and I am hoping to get my voice back very soon," he told La Follette. "I think probably I went back to speaking in the Suffrage Campaign too soon after my cold, and have had a good deal of trouble with my throat ever since."[16] The Suffrage Campaign might have absorbed much of Roe's time and energy during 1915, but the Sanger trials (and tribulations) had also taken their toll.

Birth Control, Progressives, and the Sangers

Roe's passionate commitment to women's suffrage also put him somewhat at odds with the birth control advocates. Nineteenth-century feminists who supported the concept of "voluntary motherhood" generally disapproved of contraception; to the extent that middle- and upper-class women (and men) came to participate in the suffrage movement of the early twentieth century, some of that disdain remained.[17] Margaret Sanger's writings of the period revealed the class-based schism between the progressive suffragists like Roe and the socialist birth control advocates like Sanger. Early in her transformation from nurse to activist, Sanger "consulted the 'up and doing' progressive women who then called themselves Feminists. Most of them were shocked at the mention of abortion, while others were scarcely able to keep from laughing at the idea of my making a public campaign around the idea of too many children. 'It can't be done,' they said. 'You are too sympathetic [to working-class mothers]. You can't do a thing about it until we get the vote. Go home to your children and let things alone.'[18] And, in a 1914 article for the *Woman Rebel*, Sanger ridiculed "the attitude of those fashionable ladies who are working for the suffrage 'cause.'" She reprinted a letter purporting to be from a working-class suffragist describing a meeting of the "rich . . . women who hold meetings in expensive hotels for other rich women. . . . Gold bags clatter, the mass of fur and feathers heaves—they tremble with the thought of the great things they are going to do for us, the workers."[19]

Roe's ambivalence was reflected in a 1916 letter responding to a request for support from Leonard Abbott, who had become president of the Free Speech League in 1911. "I don't quite feel that the Birth Control fight is my fight. It is a cause in which there is already enlisted people of prominence and wealth and while I want to do what I can in my small way, and anything I can in a legal way, to further the movement, I do not feel that it is a cause to which I can devote much time. As I have written you before, I want to concentrate on a few things where I likely feel my work is important, and with the able champions that Birth Control already has, I don't feel that it particularly needs me."[20]

Nevertheless, when William Sanger was arrested in 1915, Roe took on the case under Free Speech League auspices, presumably for a number of reasons: the obvious implications for freedom of speech and press; the thrill of combat against Anthony Comstock; and the many social and professional acquaintances whom the Roes and the Sangers shared. The Sangers and their three children had moved to New York City from suburban Westchester County in 1910, and it is likely that Gilbert Roe and the Sangers crossed paths several times between 1910 and 1914.

Although Margaret would become far more famous than her architect-artist husband, it was William who apparently attracted the "liberals, anarchists, Socialists, and I.W.W.'s" who gathered in their uptown living room on any given night. "They really came to see Bill," Margaret wrote. "I made the cocoa."[21] The circle included Emma Goldman, Alexander Berkman, Jack Reed, "Big Bill" Haywood, and other members of the leftist elite. Among them was Leonard Abbott, who was also a founder of the Ferrer School in which the Sangers enrolled their oldest child. Abbott would become the primary interlocutor between the Sangers and Roe in their legal struggles and between Roe and the contributors who paid the Sangers' litigation expenses.

Margaret was the first of the Sangers to run afoul of the Comstock law. She had joined the Socialist Party and put her nursing training and experience to work writing a regular Sunday column for the *Call* under the general heading "What Every Girl Should Know." One article about venereal diseases contained the words "gonorrhea" and "syphilis" and was declared unmailable by the postal authorities. The *Call* removed the column but derided the censorship by publishing in its place a box containing: "What Every Girl Should Know—Nothing—By Order of the Post-Office Department." Birth control information, techniques, and devices were particular targets of Comstock and his New York Society for the Suppression of Vice. Comstock believed sexual intercourse without a procreation purpose amounted to immoral masturbation. Emma Goldman had protested against "Comstockery" as early as 1898, but principally for the suppression of anarchist literature from the mails.[22] Her attitude toward birth control was initially quite ambivalent. While she lectured on the subject after her return from a Neo-Malthusian Conference in Paris in 1900, she "did not discuss methods, because the question of limiting offspring represented in my estimation only one aspect of the social struggle and I did not care to risk arrest for it. Moreover, I was so continually on the brink of prison because of my general activities that it seemed unjustifiable to court extra trouble."[23]

Goldman's attitude underwent a striking change, however, after her protégé, Margaret Sanger, and Margaret's husband, William, were ensnared by the Comstock laws. Goldman had taken young Margaret under her wing when the Sangers moved to New York in 1910. Although their relations became strained in later years, Sanger's arrest in 1914 prompted Goldman to focus on contraception—including methods—in her lectures. "[T]he time had come when I must either stop lecturing on the subject or do it practical justice," she declared. Ironically, Comstock seemed to ignore even Goldman's most explicit lectures. The Sangers had not been so lucky. In the late autumn of 1913, the Sanger family journeyed to Glasgow, then Paris, where Margaret collected practical information on contraception and William painted.[24] "Bill was happy in his studio," Margaret wrote, "but I could find no peace.... I could not contain my ideas, I wanted to get on with what I had to do in the world."[25] On December 31, 1913, Margaret and the children set sail for New York; the separation brought the Sangers' marriage to an end, but it was only the beginning of their legal problems.

On her return to New York, Margaret set to work publicizing what she had learned in Europe in a new magazine called the *Woman Rebel*. The first issue, dated March 1914, contained no contraceptive information but declared her intent to publish such information in subsequent issues. Nevertheless, Margaret received a letter from E. M. Morgan, postmaster, that the magazine had been declared unmailable under Section 489, Postal Laws and Regulations, by the solicitor of the Post Office Department. She knew if she continued to publish, she faced indictment, but continue she did. Two more issues—May and July—were barred from the mails. Margaret decided to launch a second front while awaiting further legal action against the *Woman Rebel*. She began collecting her European materials for a pamphlet on birth control to be called *Family Limitation*. Theodore Schroeder agreed to support the project from the fund left in his trust by Dr. Edward Bliss Foote, another founder of the Free Speech League, who died in 1906. In all, a hundred thousand copies were clandestinely printed and stored in three cities for future circulation.[26]

Margaret Sanger was indicted on August 25, 1914, for three violations of Section 211 of the United States Criminal Code[27] and arraigned the same day. She initially thought the judge in her case, U.S. district judge John R. Hazel, would be sympathetic to her cause; he gave her six weeks to prepare her case. When her case was called in October, however, she perceived a change in his attitude toward her. Although she had been meeting with Schroeder, she had not engaged an attorney. A labor lawyer she knew from the Paterson, New Jersey, silk mill workers strike of 1913, Simon H. Pollack, requested a continuance for her, but Hazel insisted on calling the case immediately. Margaret triggered the release of *Family Limitation* and fled to Europe.[28] William Sanger, meanwhile, had returned to New York from Paris, only to become a target for one of Comstock's "sting" operations, recounted in the introduction to this book.

Comstock's agent Bamberger carried a search warrant and proceeded to search William Sanger and the apartment. "He seemed anxious to enter into a discussion of the case," he wrote Margaret, "saying any statement I made would not be used against me. I refused to discuss it, saying that I wished to consult my attorney. He replied that lawyers are expensive and only aggravate the case; and, patting me on the shoulder, said he advised me, like a brother, to plead guilty, and he would recommend to the Court that I would be given a suspended sentence. I refused to entertain any such plea."[29] Comstock also grilled Sanger on Margaret's whereabouts. "He then asked me if you and I were living together or had separated," Sanger wrote. "I flatly told him I would give him no information. He asked me where Mrs. Sanger could be found. I replied that I would not tell him, and that he or any other official of the Government had no right to ask me that.... It was also mentioned that if I would give your whereabouts I would be acquitted. I replied that they would wait until Hell froze over before that would occur."

Comstock and Bamberger took Sanger to a restaurant where the two vigilantes "leisurely ate a meal and kept [Sanger] without communication with his attorney or friends."[30] It was said to be Comstock's practice to delay bringing his detainees to book until it was too late in the day to make bail. During the meal, Comstock again "urged and advised" Sanger to plead guilty, boasting that he had prosecuted some 3,900 odd cases and had been successful in all of them. Comstock warned Sanger that he would get the maximum penalty of $1,000 and one year in prison if he went to trial. Comstock boasted that he "knew the judges ... very well" and said Sanger would get a suspended sentence if Comstock recommended it. When Sanger was finally brought before a magistrate, Comstock entered a guilty plea. Sanger quickly contradicted him. "I do not. I plead not guilty." Bail was fixed at $500, a hearing was scheduled for February 2, and Sanger was sent to the lockup.[31] Gilbert Roe's associate, John M. Scoble, soon arrived at the court with a message asking the magistrate to release Sanger into Roe's custody. "Mr. Sanger has three small children and it would be a great and wholly unnecessary hardship to keep him away from them to-night."[32] Sanger spent the night in jail anyway, and Roe arranged bail the next day.[33]

Comstock's complaint, which was filed in Magistrate's Court on January 19, 1915, the day of William Sanger's arrest, identified the defendant as "John Sanger, whose real first name is unknown." It described *Family Limitation* as "obscene, lewd, lascivious, filthy, indecent and disgusting," in that it "represents and is descriptive of scenes of lewdness and obscenity." Comstock included a complete reprint of the pamphlet, but declined to describe it in detail lest the description "be offensive to the Court." He did say that Sanger advertised in the pamphlet "divers articles, recipes, drugs, and medicines for the prevention of conception," including how to use them and where to get them.[34] That description was quite accurate, as far as it goes. *Family Limitation* is divided into seven sections, several of which focus on contraceptive methods: "Douches and Their Importance," "The Use of the Condom or 'Cots,'" "The Pessary and the Sponge," "Sponges," and "Vaginal Suppositories." And the language is certainly explicit: "Perhaps the most commonest preventive excepting the use of the condom is 'coitus interruptus,' or withdrawal of the penis from the vagina shortly before the action of the semen."[35] But the pamphlet is also filled with Margaret Sanger's social and political views.

> It seems inartistic and sordid to insert a pessary or a suppository in anticipation of the sexual act. But it is far more sordid to find yourself several years later burdened down with half a dozen unwanted children, helpless, starved, shoddily clothed, dragging at your skirt, yourself a dragged out shadow of the woman you once were. . . . It is only the workers who are ignorant of the knowledge of how to prevent bringing children in the world to fill jails and hospitals, factories and mills, insane asylums and premature graves. . . . The working women can use direct action by refusing to supply the market with children to be exploited, by refusing to populate the earth with slaves.

During their post-arrest conversations, William Sanger told Comstock, "You know as well as I do, Mr. Comstock, there's nothing obscene in that pamphlet." To which Comstock replied, "Young man, I have been in this work for twenty years, and that leaflet is the worst thing I have ever seen."[36] In any event, Comstock's complaint was not limited to *Family Limitation*. Comstock charged that Sanger "now has in his possession with intent . . . to commit a public offence, divers and sundry obscene, lewd, lascivious, filthy, indecent and disgusting books, magazines, newspapers, writings, . . . articles and things for advertisements or notices," against the laws of New York, "the people . . . and their dignity."[37]

On February 1, Emma Goldman wrote Roe to advise him that "we are having a Committee meeting here at my place tomorrow at eleven, and will then go to the court with him, so the authorities should know that he doesn't stand alone. I feel that a big fight ought to be made in his case, and in an open way, not by means of hiding and seeking." Goldman asked Roe if he could attend the meeting, but in any event she asked him to call her when he received her letter.[38] The record does not show whether Roe attended the hearing.

City Magistrate Matthew P. Breen presided over the February 2 hearing. Comstock appeared as the complainant; Roe was Sanger's attorney of record, although Scoble, who was "of counsel" to Roe's firm, would conduct the examination. Bamberger testified first and, under direct examination by Comstock, told a slightly more conspiratorial version of Sanger's reaction to "Heller's" visit. "He said, 'Are you from the Government?' I said, 'No sir; you have my card. That shows my business.' He said, 'That is different.' He closed the door and went inside and came out and handed me this book, and said, 'Don't tell anybody where you got this; it might get me into trouble.' I said, 'Any charge?' He said, 'No; you can have it.'"[39]

After Scoble's innocuous cross-examination, Comstock called himself as a witness. He explained that when he arrested Sanger, he stated that Sanger was entitled to an examination before the magistrate or could waive the examination and give bail for trial in the Court of Special Sessions. He also testified that he collected six or seven more copies of *Family Limitation* upon searching Sanger's studio.[40] Scoble moved to dismiss the charges on the ground that William Sanger knew nothing about the pamphlets and had nothing to do with publishing them. Comstock said he made no such claim. When Scoble pointed out that Margaret lived there as well, Comstock interrupted: "Mrs. Sanger is a fugitive from justice."[41]

Magistrate Breen sustained Scoble's demand to strike that last remark from the record but denied his motion to dismiss. Scoble then asked for a brief delay so the bail bond agency could be on hand when and if Sanger was remanded. When court reconvened on February 3, Breen ruled "that the crime [mentioned in the complaint] has been committed and that there is sufficient cause to believe that the within named William Sanger is guilty thereof." Breen set $500 bail and ordered Sanger returned to jail until Scoble arranged for bail.[42] From that point on, the case proceeded along multiple tracks. On the legal track, Roe began to prepare Sanger's defense by moving the case to the Court of General Sessions, where Sanger could get a jury trial. He also began seeking witnesses who would not only bolster Sanger's character but also destroy Comstock's credibility. Behind the scenes, Roe continually prodded Abbott to raise money for Sanger's legal defense.

"While we have spoken of the figure of $500 in the Sanger case," he wrote Abbott on February 4, "I think you ought not to give that as the ultimate amount to be aimed at. If his case should be taken through to the Court of Appeals as it ought to be in case it once starts, $500 would probably not pay printing bills, to say nothing of other disbursements and any pay for services. I think you ought to plan to get all that you can. There is no danger of getting too much. If, by good fortune, enough was raised to more than meet strictly legal expenses, it could be well utilized for publicity and propaganda."[43] Abbott told Roe he would try to raise more. He said he had written all of the Free Speech League directors, asking whether they should—as the league—get into the fight. He also said a meeting was scheduled for the following week in Mabel Dodge's salon.[44] Roe warned him not to make any formal statement at the meeting, at least not so soon. "Meantime, you will find out who will help in the fight, and what the real public sentiment is."[45]

In Abbott's view, $500 or more could be raised, but "laboriously from a great number of people scattered throughout the country." He told Roe that although publicity about the case "until now has been practically nil, yet I have been getting letters and inquiries from all over the country." Recently, however, Max Eastman had written a lead article on the Sanger case in the new issue of *The Masses*. "If this is reprinted in leaflet form and sent throughout the country, with a financial appeal, I think that we can get a lot of small contributions."[46] Eastman's article "Is the Truth Obscene?" had appeared in the March 1915 issue of *The Masses*, which Abbott could have read in early February. In the article, Eastman recounted the Sanger saga and published letters from distraught mothers seeking relief from continuous reproduction. Noting that Gilbert Roe was Sanger's attorney, Eastman declared, "[T]he fight is on." But he pointed out that Sanger had neither wealth nor social connections and requires "the public support of all men and women who believe either in the truth, or in constitutional liberty, to win this case."[47] Abbott reprinted the Eastman article and distributed it along with the Free Speech League's own plea for funds. "More is needed for a campaign of publicity outside of the courts," he wrote. "[S]end as much as you can, and as soon as possible."[48]

On February 15, Sanger's case was called for pleading. Roe was in Albany, but Scoble entered a plea of not guilty to the formal information that was filed. The case was set for trial on March 15.[49] Roe told Abbott the next day, "We must also get up papers immediately to apply for a jury trial, and to have the case transferred to general sessions"; then, with obvious reference to money, he asked Abbott, "How are things coming? We have got to have action from this time forward."[50] Abbott replied that he had sent out thirty of the "manifestos" so far, as well as providing them to everyone who attended the meeting at Mabel Dodge's. Listing the donations he had received to date, including $25 that Emma Goldman had raised at one of her meetings and $20 that Abbott planned to contribute personally, Abbott said he would send the package to another twenty to thirty names. "Some of our best friends have not yet been heard from." He continued to lament the lack of publicity. "Outside of *The Call* and *Mother Earth*, and one paragraph hidden on an inside page of *The Times*, we have had no publicity so far."[51] Roe himself received a letter from Goldman's erstwhile lover, Alexander Berkman, from Denver, where he was avoiding extradition. "I hear you have taken charge of the Sanger case," Berkman wrote. "Hope you'll wallop old man Comstock good and plenty."[52]

Roe acknowledged that Abbott had been doing "excellent work" on the fund-raising front and chided him for making a personal contribution. "It is absurd for anyone to expect you to contribute a dollar. The work you are doing and the time you are giving to the matter, many times exceeds in value the contribution which anyone else will make or be expected to make." However, Roe expressed the fear that Abbott was "going to be disappointed in the financial results. I have never had any confidence in raising money in subscriptions of $5 and $10. Then also, every person who contributes a dollar thinks he is running the lawsuit, or whatever the business is to which he is contributing."[53]

Roe suggested that Abbott select a half dozen or so of the "most substantial persons interested" and ask them to back the litigation. "My idea is virtually to have a few persons underwrite the defense. Then, if they get their money back from many contributors, that does not concern me." Otherwise, he said, "I am inclined to think . . . that I had better drop out and let someone else take it up." In one of his longest letters of the Sanger campaign, Roe revealed several of his frustrations with the case. Reminding Abbott that he provided as much free legal service as he could, Roe told his friend, "just at this time I do not feel that I ought to take on the responsibility of the Sanger case, and do gratuitously the work necessary to be done. I do feel very strongly," he wrote, "that there are so many people with ample means, who have really much more interest in this matter than Sanger has, that they ought to come forward and make the money part of the situation (which is the least) easy."

Roe's unwillingness or inability to handle the case on a pro bono basis likely stemmed from several causes. By 1915, he had become financially overextended. In August, he would write to Eastman, apologizing for his failure to make a $250 contribution to *The Masses* that he had pledged.[54] Then, too, the letter exposes a certain ambivalence about Sanger and his cause. Roe knew well that William and Margaret were separated, that William had not been all that involved in her work, and that, if there were to be a definitive legal breakthrough, it would involve Margaret's prosecution, not William's.[55]

Roe closed his letter to Abbott with an offer. "If you would like to get together a few of the more responsible persons next week, for a frank talk, I will be glad to meet with you, but this should be entirely private, and you should select with care the names of those whom you notify. It is rather important to move quickly, because the application for a jury trial will have to be made very soon, if at all."[56] Four days later, on February 23, the U.S. Supreme Court ruled unanimously against his client, Jay Fox, in "The Nude and the Prudes" case.[57]

Roe did file a motion in the Court of Special Sessions to prosecute the Sanger case further by indictment on March 1, 1915;[58] if granted, Sanger's indictments would have been followed by a jury trial in the higher Court of General Sessions. The motion was accompanied by the affidavit of William Sanger, which recounted the facts of his arrest and subsequent examination and advanced several reasons in support of the motion for a jury trial.[59] Sanger asserted that he had never read *Family Limitation* and had "absolutely nothing to do with its printing, publication or circulation, in any manner whatsoever." He referenced Comstock's boast about knowing the Special Sessions judges "very well" and urged a jury trial "in the interest of fairness and justice." He pointed to Bamberger's "falsehood and gross deception," arguing that a jury should weigh the "testimony of spies engaged in such practices as this." Finally, the question of whether the pamphlet itself was indecent is a question of fact for the jury, he said, and a trial will "present important and difficult questions of law," making precedents for the guidance of courts in the future.

Two days later, Abbott sent Roe a check for $50 and brought him up to date on the publicity campaign. "I have written a brief account of what happened this morning for the *Call*," he wrote, "[the] New York Secular Society has passed resolutions condemning Comstock's action in this matter, and the Liberal Club is to devote next Sunday evening to a discussion of the case."[60] More $50 checks would follow. "Money is coming in nicely & beyond my expectations," Abbott wrote in a note accompanying one of them. "The circular letter & the Max Eastman leaflet are a winning combination."[61] Even the Socialist labor leader Eugene Debs would send five dollars.[62]

On March 4, Special Sessions denied Roe's motion. Roe made arrangements to postpone the trial, from March 15 to April 12,[63] and considered appealing the denial to the Court of General Sessions. Roe knew, and told Abbott, that the appeal would fail. "[Under] the settled practice in this department, the decision of the trial judge denying such motion is always permitted to stand. The primary purpose of such an appeal would be to call attention to the abuse arising from the denial of jury trials and it would of course be considerable work and expense. Do you think the funds in your hands would justify taking this on, with the practical certainty that the order denying us a jury trial would be affirmed or else the appeal dismissed?"[64] Abbott urged the appeal. "I think we should make all we can out of this point. It will appeal to a great many people. Money is still coming in and will doubtless cover the expenses of such an appeal."[65] On March 30, Roe agreed that "the uniform denial of jury trial in this class of cases is one of the most serious things in the whole matter,"[66] and he told Abbott that he was preparing the papers for the appeal. "Of course, I may not and probably will not be successful but you can never tell what you draw in the legal game, until you try."[67] Abbott told Roe he was glad Roe decided to appeal, and sent him a fifth check for $50, "making $250 that I have sent you altogether."[68]

Roe's trial strategy depended, in part, on impeaching Comstock, destroying his credibility as a prosecutor.ABbott was assigned the task of finding witnesses who could testify against him. At one point, he thought *Masses* artists Robert Henri and George Bellows and editor Helen Marot, labor leader Paul Kennaday, publisher Mitchell Kennerley, and others would be willing to testify.[69] But everyone he approached turned him down, saying they didn't know Comstock personally and feared their testimony would be too vague. "I shall be sorry if the plan for impeaching Comstock has to be given up," Abbott wrote. "It would surely arouse wide interest and attention. But I myself feel that the plan would be a failure unless some of the witnesses can give definite instances of Comstock's unreliability."[70]

Roe had urged Abbott to advise prospective witnesses that they did not need personal knowledge, but only needed to testify as to Comstock's reputation.[71] But he seemed to lose heart when Abbott told him that Kennerley (himself a victim of Comstockery) declined to testify on the ground that it was Sanger, not Comstock, on trial.[72] Acknowledging the truth in Kennerley's reply, Roe defended his strategy. "In reality, it ought to be Comstock and not Sanger, who is on trial, and I want to give the trial a turn which will put Comstock on trial."[73] Nevertheless, Roe realized that the refusal of these prominent allies to testify would undermine his strategy. "It is the old story: Radicals are ready to talk but not to fight, and if they must fight, they have no sense of the importance of organization," Roe wrote, with a sense of resignation.

"It looks as though we would have to abandon the idea of impeaching Comstock, although we thereby miss the opportunity of depriving him of most of his power for harm," he told Abbott. "Once thoroughly impeached, he would lose most of his power as a prosecutor, for he always depends in his prosecutions, to a considerable degree, upon his own testimony, and he would be very chary of ever taking the stand after a thorough impeachment. However, I will not attempt it at all unless it can be done right."[74] Instead, he urged Abbott to concentrate on marshaling character witnesses for Sanger. Abbott had been keeping Roe informed about Sanger's increasing impatience with the legal process. "I judge that Sanger, from what he said to me the other day, will be against anything that means further delay," Abbott wrote. "He wants the whole matter settled as soon as possible. His desire is natural enough. But this case is bigger than Sanger personally, and since it is being financed as a result of a public appeal, it should be fought out in the largest way possible."[75] On the matter of character witnesses, Abbott wrote, "Sanger himself is very touchy, and even inclined to be obstructive. . . . He says that he does not want his 'respectability' vouched for, and that he regards it as an insult, rather than otherwise, to be testified to as 'law abiding.'"[76]

Roe was adamant. "On this work Sanger must help. If he is not willing to have this work done, and willing to help get it done, in the best way possible, then I want to know it and retire from the case at this point," Roe insisted. It was his second reference to dropping the case. "I went over this matter with Mr. Sanger thoroughly—I think you were present—and it was understood that this testimony would be offered and he suggested the names of several persons to get. Now it is hard enough work to try a lawsuit, without arguing with the client in order to get him to do what is for his best interests, and if Mr. Sanger will not help on this matter without further discussion, then I want to be let out."[77] On the same day that Roe wrote those words, April 5, Justice Edward Swann of the Court of General Sessions denied his motion to prosecute by indictment before a jury.[78] It is not clear whether the denial prompted Roe's harsh language or merely aggravated his frustration with Sanger, but it surely came as no surprise. In two days, he appealed the order to the New York Supreme Court's Appellate Division.[79] The trial was postponed again until May 10.[80]

Roe's brief reiterated the allegations in the Sanger affidavit and argued that the order was appealable as a "special proceeding," rather than a criminal case. "That the right of trial by jury is a 'substantial' one is not open to question," he wrote, "and it is not rendered insubstantial for the purpose of appeal by the circumstance that there is a discretionary power to refuse it." On the merits, he argued that Sanger had no intention of circulating *Family Limitation*, and if Bamberger said otherwise, "then it is peculiarly for a jury to say whether the testimony of spies and informers shall prevail over that of the plain citizen, whose reputation heretofore has been unsullied." Roe attempted to distinguish "private officers," securing evidence of illegal conduct, and "private spies, entering into a "conspiracy to procure the law to be violated." The difference, he said, should be submitted to a jury. Without naming Margaret Sanger, he also suggested that Comstock was really trying to secure evidence "against someone else." Finally, Roe argued that a jury trial was necessary because of Comstock's boast that he could manipulate the outcome in the Court of Special

Sessions. No matter how fair the justices might be, he said, people in the community will view a conviction there as proof of Comstock's power. "Not only the interests of the defendant, but of the entire community, require a jury trial in this case."[81]

Toward the end of April, Abbott sent Roe another $50 and requested copies of the new appellate brief for himself, Sanger, and other members of the Free Speech League. He also informed Roe about the formation of a new Birth Control League, with Kennaday and Marot as its "most active members."[82] Thanking him for the money, Roe noted a series of articles in *Harper's* on birth control. "This may not be of much use in Sanger's case, but it will be of great value in Mrs. Sanger's case if she ever goes to trial."[83] In fact, Margaret Sanger's case was very much on Abbott's and Roe's minds at the time. On May 1, Abbott wrote to Margaret with a status report on her husband's case. As to her case, Abbott wrote that he found it very difficult to advise her about coming home. "Mr. Roe says that he has no doubt that, if you do return, you will get a long prison sentence. On the other hand, a great deal of propaganda can undoubtedly be made out of your return." Abbott told Margaret about all the publicity and money that had been generated since the cases began. "You will have to decide for yourself whether you want to come back and face the music. A big fight can be made, but you will almost surely have to go to prison."[84]

With no decision from the Appellate Division on William Sanger's request for a jury trial, the trial was postponed until June 18.[85] That month, Abbott told Roe that he had diverted some of the funds collected for the Sanger defense to help Sanger take care of his three children. The older child was sent to stay with Margaret's sister in Buffalo, while the two younger children were taken in at the Ferrer School in Stelton, New Jersey, "though we could ill afford to do it." Abbott said he sent $50 to Margaret but still didn't know when she might return.[86]

As the June 18 trial date approached, still with no word from the Appellate Division, Roe became convinced that there would be another postponement. "The only question in my mind is whether it will go over for a few days, or until fall. The court does not like to try bail cases in summer. My idea is to let the case go over until fall, if we can."[87] The postponement, however, was only for ten days, and Roe thought the case would "doubtless have to be disposed of" then. Roe asked Abbott to arrange a meeting with Sanger, who was working in New Britain, Connecticut, to come back to the city to work on character witnesses. "If he does not come back and you would be willing to do it," he wrote Abbott, "I wish you would call up those character witnesses, a list of which you have, and read them the questions and see if they will testify properly. The questions are somewhat technical, and it is necessary to advise the witnesses in advance just what they will be asked."[88]

Sanger had other ideas. In a handwritten note to Roe, Sanger said, "I have quite decided to cut out the character witnesses—as I don't think they amount to much. Furthermore I am not particularly anxious to convince the court of my respectability. . . . I am just as you are dubious about my getting a jury trial—well we will have to take what the dear darling courts mete out to us." He agreed to meet with Roe a day later than Roe had proposed through Abbott, and went on to express concern that if he drew "two Catholic judges out of three I'm a cooked—article—sure."[89] Roe told Sanger he was "very sorry" about Sanger's decision on character witnesses;[90] then he wrote Abbott, "I think [Sanger] is very foolish. . . . I wish on your own hook, and on the chance of his changing his mind when I talk with him, you would call up the character witnesses we have discussed."[91] But Sanger was adamant. "I don't want any character witnesses," he told Abbott. "I repeat again, for the benefit of those people who dote on respectability, that I don't care a hoot whether or not the courts consider me respectable. If after hearing these witnesses in my behalf they do decide I am respectable, then, by God, there's something rotten in me and the State of Denmark. That's all; so this settles the character witnesses."[92]

Sanger's case was postponed again to July 6, and Roe asked Abbott to set a meeting with Sanger on July 3 to go over this testimony. He also asked Abbott about money. "It is my opinion there will be little chance to raise any money for this trial after it is over," he said.[93] Abbott replied that he expected to send Roe another $50 soon. He agreed that it would be hard to raise money for William Sanger once the trial was over, but he thought hundreds of dollars more could be raised for Margaret. "I think we should push these cases to the limit, and take every appeal possible."[94] Roe decided he would take his family to the mountains for a break on July 15, and he invited the La Follettes to join them.[95] He also wrote to Floyd Wilmot, assistant district attorney, asking that the trial be postponed for another month or until the fall. He justified the request on the ground that he had decided to take his family on vacation, as well as Sanger's need for the income from the architectural work he was doing in Connecticut.[96] The trial was postponed first until July 28[97] and then, because the district attorney also wanted to get away, until late August.[98]

In the meantime, the Appellate Division issued its opinion, again denying William Sanger a jury trial. The opinion was perfunctory. After recounting the procedural posture of Sanger's case, the court pointed out that there was no common-law right of appeal in a criminal case, and that the applicable statutes only permitted appeals from a judgment of conviction. Here, the order denying a jury trial was "an intermediary one," the court said, and therefore not appealable. It might yet be reviewed, but only on appeal from William Sanger's conviction.[99]

Thanking Abbott for sending another $25, Roe instructed him to make a scrapbook of newspaper clippings and anything else dealing with the Sanger case—particularly Comstock's part in it. "Comstock may be out of a job by [the trial]," he wrote, possibly alluding to a tip he had received that Comstock was under investigation, "although I hardly hope for such luck." He also reminded Abbott of a plan Abbott made to collect information about unsuccessful prosecutions that Comstock had attempted in recent years. "You had better make a memorandum of what you get, so that we can refresh our minds when we take up the case in the latter part of August." With that, the Roes headed to Haines Falls in the Catskill Mountains.[100] For his part, Comstock traveled to California to give a speech at the opening session of the World Purity Congress in San Francisco. According to the *New York Times* coverage of the event, Comstock had spoken for about half an hour—boasting of having gradually driven all obscene publications out of New York—when "[p]andemonium broke loose." One man from Albany, New York, and a "local medical student" loudly challenged his handling of the Sanger case.[101] Abbot sent the clipping to Roe, expressing his pleasure at seeing the *Times* finally covering the cases.[102]

Roe had a brief scare when he got word that the trial had been set for August 4, rather than late August, due to what appeared to be a miscommunication within the district attorney's office.[103] It was rescheduled for September 3.[104] On August 30, Abbott wrote to Roe, informing him that Sanger had changed his mind about character witnesses. "I think he has come around to the point of wanting to get off as easily as he can—consistent of course with the straightforward and manly course. But I think he is entirely over the idea of wanting to be a martyr."[105] Apparently not. After Roe once again arranged for a continuance until September 10, so that Sanger's witnesses could return to New York from their own vacations, Sanger and Roe parted company for good. "I beg to advise you that by mutual agreement between Mr. Sanger and myself, I am no longer to act as his attorney," Roe wrote Wilmot on September 7. "Mr. Sanger fully understands that I am not to appear for him upon the adjourned day of the case, and that my relation to the case is terminated."[106]

Nothing in the record indicates exactly why Sanger fired Roe, but it is possible that Roe resisted Sanger's plan to mount no defense to the charges against him, but rather to simply read a lengthy defense of birth control.[107] Nor does the record show whether Roe attended the September 10 trial before Justices McInerney, Herbert, and Salmon. Abbott was in the packed courtroom, along with Alexander Berkman, Amos Pinchot, and other socialist and anarchist activists.[108] In any event, Sanger declined to question Comstock and Bamberger, who testified against him; instead, he asked to read his statement. "I gave the pamphlet," Sanger declared. "I frankly admit it. I admit I broke the law, and yet I claim that in every real sense, it is the law and not I that is on trial here today." Sanger proceeded to describe his entrapment and arrest, but he was cut short by the presiding Justice McInerney. Or, as the *Times* put it, "'Bang,' fell the Justice's gavel." Sanger continued, defending his character, denying that he was a criminal, denying that *Family Limitation* was obscene, and insisting that Comstock offered him a suspended sentence. Again, he was gaveled to silence, and McInerney warned that he would not have "a lot of rigamarole" on the record.

After reviewing the pamphlet and conferring with the other justices, McInerney told Sanger to rise. "Such persons as you who circulate such pamphlets are a menace to society," he scolded. "There are too many now who believe it is a crime to have children. If some of the women who are going around and advocating equal suffrage would go around and advocate women having children they would do a greater service." McInerney told Sanger that although he favored sending Sanger to jail, the judges had decided to fine him. "I sentence you to a fine of $150 or thirty days in the City Prison." Sanger replied, "I will never pay that fine. I would rather be in jail with my conviction than be free at a loss of my manhood and my self-respect." McInerney ordered Sanger taken to the Tombs, and the courtroom erupted with handclapping and shouting. Police assisted the court attendants in moving the spectators into the corridor. There, Abbott told the *Times* that "no law can be right that keeps thousands in ignorance of facts that they ought to know."

Margaret Sanger left Europe in late September[109] and landed in New York on October 5; William Sanger was released from jail four days later.[110] Abbott told Roe that Margaret wanted to go into court, "as Bill did," without a legal defense. "She wants you to act for her in the preliminary legal work. . . . Are you willing to act for her . . . ?" Abbott added that he planned to raise several hundred dollars more from those who had already contributed.[111] Roe expressed surprise that Margaret wanted his help. "Of course I will be glad to assist in every way that I can," he told Abbott, "but there is really little I can do if she does not want any defense made. I would not care to go on the record as her attorney and then have her decide to dispense with her attorney, or at least have it so appear to the public. The members of the Bar might think I had formed a habit of doing that kind of thing."[112]

During the next few months, Margaret discussed her case with several lawyers, including Samuel Untermyer, who had promised Max Eastman that he would defend her without charge.[113] But Margaret proved as intransigent as William had been. "She has wavered between compromise and non-compromise," Abbott told Roe, "between a legal defense and an extra-legal defense, just as William Sanger did." Although she was first inclined to accept Untermyer's offer, Abbott said, "when Mr. Untermyer had nothing better to offer than that she plead guilty, with the understanding that he would do what he could to make things easier for her, she rebelled."[114] Margaret revealed her frustration with lawyers in a letter she sent to friends in England. "I decided to plead my own case without counsel, as the ideas I have sought to promulgate are not within the range of the psychology of men lawyers. I have personally had occasion to see the lamentable results of having questions involving great moral issues subordinated to the legal quibbles in which lawyers so much delight."[115]

In the end, it didn't matter. The authorities dropped the charges against Margaret for the *Woman Rebel* articles on February 18, 1916. She would be tried on other charges in January 1917, represented by her then-current lover, J. J. Goldstein, convicted and sentenced to thirty days in the Workhouse.[116] Anthony Comstock's influence would continue long after his death, but William Sanger's case was his last prosecution. Comstock caught a chill at William Sanger's trial and died a few weeks later.

If Roe's attitude toward birth control—like that of many suffragists—was ambivalent, the free speech aspect of the movement continued to hold his interest. In October 1916, he wrote a scathing letter to New York City police commissioner Arthur M. Woods for the "particularly oppressive and unlawful act" by plain clothes officers in arresting Emma Goldman without a warrant or probable cause. Goldman had been accompanying Bolton Hall from the courthouse following his acquittal on charges of distributing birth control literature a year earlier. Roe was present and personally witnessed the arrest. Goldman had been with Hall at the time of his arrest, but only Hall was arrested. At Hall's trial, the arresting officers testified that both Hall and Goldman had distributed the literature. They denied it, as did other witnesses, and the court dismissed the case, chiding the officers for only arresting Hall if both were guilty. Roe charged that Goldman's arrest after the trial was a response to the court's rebuke. "I call these facts to your attention," Roe wrote, "to the end that you may take such action as this conduct . . . warrants."[117]

"Feminist of Feminists"

Suffrage and birth control were not the only feminist causes that occupied Roe during the prewar years. He had also become involved in the unusual saga of activist Henrietta Rodman, whom Margaret Sanger once called "Feminist of Feminists," in Rodman's struggles with the New York City Board of Education. Rodman was an English teacher and vocational counselor at Wadleigh High School for Girls in Manhattan, but she was also an active participant in the bohemian Greenwich Village scene, its many political clubs and associations, and all manner of feminist and kindred causes.[118] Rodman was also a consummate self-publicist; whether she was speaking on vocational guidance for young women or female teachers' right to marry and have children, Rodman seemed to have little difficulty being heard through the newspapers of the day. Rodman and Gilbert Roe had many common memberships and acquaintances, including the Sangers and, notably, Fola La Follette. In June 1912, for example, Rodman invited Roe to speak at a meeting of the Heretics dinner club on the relation between sex and the state.[119] There was every reason why she should turn to him when she needed legal support. Just such a need arose, for example, when her secret marriage to Herman de Fremery was exposed.[120]

The notion that female teachers should not marry, much less bear children, stems from the legal precept that a woman's labor belongs to her husband, and that women could not serve two masters adequately.[121] Typical was a 1903 opinion of the New York Supreme Court, Appellate Division, upholding as reasonable the dismissal of a teacher upon her marriage under a self-executing bylaw of the Brooklyn school board that read, "Should a female principal, head of department or teacher marry, her place shall thereupon become vacant."[122] The majority opinion held that a wife's principal duties in the home would interfere with her duties at school, while a concurring opinion insisted that a woman had no right to contract her labor once her services belonged to a husband.[123] That decision was ultimately reversed by the Court of Appeals in 1904, but only as to whether the bylaw was self-executing. The highest state court held that the statute under which the bylaw was adopted required an affirmative act by the state board of education, or the borough school board, to remove a teacher, and then only for "gross misconduct, insubordination, neglect of duty, or general inefficiency."[124] It did not rule on whether dismissal for marriage might be enforced under one of those categories.

In 1906, however, an Appellate Division ruling indicated that the principle of dismissal upon marriage was still alive and well. A teacher was married in 1903, before the Court of Appeals decision, and advised by her principal and district superintendent that she would have to resign in accordance with the bylaw. She did but then sought reinstatement after the Court of Appeals decision, claiming duress. Both the trial court and the appellate court held that her resignation was voluntary, and she need not be rehired.[125] In 1909, the city Board of Education adopted a new bylaw providing that "[no] married woman shall be appointed to any teaching or supervising position in the day public schools" unless her husband was incapacitated or had abandoned her.[126] Teachers who were already employed were permitted to marry, provided they reported their marriages to the board, but the new bylaw was interpreted to apply to promotions as well as original appointments. Accordingly, those teachers who did marry after 1909 generally did so in secret to avoid discrimination in assignments and advancement. Rodman was one of the leading instigators of the "silence agreement" among married teachers.

Rodman met Herman de Fremery in 1912 at the Liberal Club, in which Rodman had a leadership role, and they were married on February 17, 1913, in Norwalk, Connecticut. That same year, Rodman spearheaded the relocation of the Liberal Club to Greenwich Village. De Fremery, who later changed his name to Herman Defrem, worked in the forestry department of the American Museum of Natural History. In just over a month after their wedding, the fact of Rodman's marriage was all over the New York newspapers.[127] Rodman took the exposure well, replying "laughingly" to one reporter's inquiry: "Hundreds of us teachers are married in secret and are supposed by the board of education to be single. The favoritism shown single women is responsible for the deception. The board cannot refuse to let a married woman teach but it shows all preferment to single women."[128] When asked by another reporter whether the board might dismiss her for failing to report her marriage, she said she would consult a lawyer before responding to any notice the board might serve.[129]

Indeed, when the *New York Evening Journal* alleged that her new husband had a common-law wife who consented to the marriage and lived with the couple afterward, Rodman swore an affidavit for the board denying the allegations and saying she had "placed the matter in the hands of my lawyer, Gilbert E. Roe, [who] is now preparing to bring suit for libel" against the *Journal*.[130] A few weeks later, she wrote Roe, "I have heard nothing further from [the board] in reference to the *Evening Journal* report, which seems to me to be most desirable. In any case where social hysteria is a possible factor, I like to give the common place of every day living time to work its soothing effect."[131] In the end, nothing came of the libel suit. Roe told Rodman, "I think you are taking the right course to pay no attention to the matter unless you have to. If the School authorities let it pass as they probably will, less harm will be done by ignoring the matter than by getting into Court about it."[132] Rodman had also

The Feminists

asked Roe to speak before a meeting of the Committee on the Civic Service of Women to be held in April. The committee was formed, with Rodman as secretary, to support another married teacher, Katherine Edgell, who had become pregnant and was denied a leave of absence.[133] Roe accepted numerous speaking engagements but did not play an active legal role in that fight, or a similar case involving Bridget Peixotto.[134] Most of the legal work in that campaign was undertaken by a team of lawyers from the Woman Lawyer's Club and its president, Jean H. Norris.[135]

When Rodman finally did provoke the board to action in connection with the issue of teachers bearing children, however, Roe found himself back in the Rodman business. On November 10, 1914, Rodman wrote a viciously sarcastic letter to "The Conning Tower" column in the *New York Tribune*, condemning what she called "mother-baiting," a game whose object was to "kick the mothers out of their positions in the public schools."[136] The reaction to Rodman's letter was swift and serious. New York City school superintendent William Maxwell ordered district superintendent Darwin Bardwell to bring charges of gross misconduct and insubordination against Rodman.[137] When the Board of Education met on November 11, Rodman was suspended, along with another teacher who took two weeks off to deliver a baby.[138] According to the *Tribune*, Rodman and board president Thomas W. Churchill engaged in very heated conversation after the meeting, in which Rodman refused to explain her letter without first talking to her lawyer.

The *Tribune* also editorialized in favor of allowing married teachers to have a leave of absence to have children, a policy that now had the support of the mayor, if not the school board. "The Tribune holds no brief for Miss Rodman, though, like every one else acquainted with the City of New York, it respects her courage and her work. We can conceive of a city getting along very nicely without the directing minds of a Board of Education. We cannot conceive of any successful school system that has not room for a person of Miss Rodman's independence and intelligence."[139] Maxwell apparently changed his mind about suspending Rodman the following day, instructing Bardwell that she could continue to draw her salary until she was tried before the High School Committee of the Board of Education.[140] He also indicated that Rodman might face punishments ranging from reprimand to dismissal. For her part, Rodman said she did not mind the fight. "My great grandfather . . . was a Revolutionary leader, and my grandfather . . . was an Abolitionist. There's fighting blood in me."

Rodman's reprieve was short-lived. By Saturday, November 14, Maxwell reimposed her suspension.[141] Rodman and her lawyer, Jean Norris, decided she should report for duty on Monday and then proceed to the mayor's office to protest if, as expected, she was prevented from teaching.[142] The delegation that visited the mayor on Monday included Rodman's mentor, Charlotte Perkins Gilman, and her friend, Fola La Follette.[143] On Tuesday, Rodman and Norris were "arraigned" before the High School Committee, where she admitted that she wrote the offending letter. The case was referred to Corporation Counsel's Office, which would conduct the "prosecution" at Rodman's public trial.[144] After a postponement to give Rodman more time to prepare her case, the trial date was set for December 15. In addition to Norris, Rodman's legal team included prominent women lawyers Marion Cothren and Inez Milholland-Boissevain.[145] The trial was postponed again until December 22 when Norris withdrew as Rodman's counsel, reportedly because Rodman refused to take her advice to write an apology to the board.[146] Instead, Rodman wrote a strong defense of her actions. "It is not only the right but the duty of citizens to criticize fairly and intelligently the policies and acts of public boards and officials," she wrote.[147]

When the trial finally took place, Rodman was represented by Gilbert Roe and Jacob Bernstein, who argued that the charges against Rodman were undefined. "As the matter stands now, the school board is exercising despotic power over the teaching staff," they charged. "[T]here is no rule on the subject but simply the arbitrary and unrestrained discretion of the board," they charged.[148] Rodman was found guilty of "gross misconduct," although not insubordination, and was suspended until September 1, 1915, with a forfeiture of $1,770 in salary for the period.[149] Seven of the ten board members signed the report, but only one spoke in Rodman's favor.[150] Rodman said she would immediately appeal the decision to the state commissioner of education, John H. Finley, and, if that failed, take the case to court.[151] Rodman had some reason for hope; in January, Finley decided to reinstate Bridget Peixotto, the teacher and mother who had lost her case in the Court of Appeals the previous year.[152]

Other reinstatements followed, as the policy against teachers bearing children was relaxed, but the decision against Rodman, whose suspension was for misconduct, not childbirth, was not reversed. Roe represented Rodman at a hearing in Albany on February 15,[153] but it proved to be fruitless. On June 8, 1915, Finley upheld Rodman's suspension without pay,[154] and on June 23, Rodman was transferred from the Wadleigh High School to the less prestigious Julia Richman High School.[155] Rodman seemed to take the transfer in stride, and she continued to work for the rights of teachers to marry and bear children and for woman suffrage, birth control, and other feminist issues.[156] Roe continued to lobby on Rodman's behalf, asking New York City commissioner of education Ira S. Wile to seek a "material modification" in her sentence. "I would be glad to have an opportunity to appear before the Board and present the matter," he wrote.[157] A strong advocate of birth control, like Rodman, Wile was sympathetic to her cause, and Roe took advantage of that. "I feel very strongly that for the Board to stand out in opposition to the expressed wishes of the Commissioner, is to take a position which will be strongly condemned by the public." He also continued to consult with Rodman on other issues, including birth control. In the spring of 1916, Rodman asked Roe to help recruit prominent physicians in support of an amendment to the penal code to allow physicians to prescribe contraception methods.[158] Roe rejected the recruitment letter Rodman had proposed, sending her another, which he and Schroeder had prepared at Goldman's suggestion. "From the Free Speech point of view," he wrote, "it does not seem to me that it is much of an advance to give the medical trust a monopoly of this information, or rather the right to disseminate it.... I am not willing to back a movement which would stiffen the law against everybody but physicians."[159]

Roe's defense of Rodman was only the beginning of his involvement with New York City teachers. The Teachers Union of New York City was formed in 1916, and Gilbert Roe handled a number of cases for the Union between 1918 and his death in 1929. His name appeared on union letterhead as "counsel," and upon his death, union founder Henry R. Linville sent Roe's wife a glowing tribute. Linville told Gwyneth Roe that her husband was so closely associated with the union—and not just as an attorney in a business relationship—that "we had come to regard him practically as one of our members."[160] Socialists and pacifists, like Linville and the union he led, comprised a substantial portion of Roe's practice, especially during America's gradual slide into World War I. The leading socialist magazine of the era, *The Masses*, represented both groups, and the next chapter begins with Roe's first defense of *The Masses*, editor Max Eastman, and cartoonist Art Young.

Gilbert E. Roe, 1898, in his office at La Follette, Harper, Roe & Zimmerman, Madison. (Wisconsin Historical Society, WHi-30328; photograph attributed to Albert Zimmerman)

Gilbert E. Roe, date unknown. (Wisconsin Historical Society, WHi-32351)

Gwyneth King Roe, ca. 1895. (Wisconsin Historical Society, WHi-32369)

S. S. McClure, date unknown. (Bain Collection, U.S. Library of Congress)

Lincoln Steffens, date unknown. (Bain Collection, U.S. Library of Congress)

Emma Goldman, ca. 1915–20. (Bain Collection, U.S. Library of Congress)

Margaret Sanger, 1922. (U.S. Library of Congress)

Max Eastman, date unknown. (Bain Collection, U.S. Library of Congress)

Upton Sinclair, date unknown. (Bain Collection, U.S. Library of Congress)

"Conscription" by H. J. Glintenkamp, *The Masses*, August 1917. (Tamiment Library, New York University)

Judge Learned Hand, date unknown. (Bain Collection, U.S. Library of Congress)

Gilbert E. Roe (*right*) with Sen. Robert M. La Follette, in 1924 at the U.S. Capitol. (U.S. Library of Congress)

5

The Socialists

[The] right to criticize, disparage, slander and libel that power which [the Associated Press] wields over the course of history ought to be absolutely established in the hands of every citizen of this country.

Max Eastman

I am very happy to be able to announce to my friend, Mr. Roe, that I have at last obtained some documentary evidence, proving definite, deliberate and flagrant suppression of news by the Associated Press.

Upton Sinclair

The Masses

Greenwich Village was the geographical center of New York City's radical culture in the second decade of the twentieth century. And *The Masses* magazine was the intellectual and artistic center of Greenwich Village. Floyd Dell, assistant to editor Max Eastman, described the brief life of the magazine as a "glorious intellectual playtime in which art and ideas, free self-expression and the passion of propaganda, were for one moment happily mated."[1] The magazine was founded in 1911 by Piet Vlag, a socialist immigrant from the Netherlands, with financial support from Rufus Weeks, vice president of the New York Life Insurance Co. William O'Neill called Vlag's magazine "as flat and earnest as the rest of the socialist press, which reached levels of unsurpassed dullness," and by August 1912, it was out of money.[2] Its small editorial staff, including artist John Sloan, cartoonist Art Young, and poet Louis Untermeyer, convened an emergency meeting in September to try to keep the enterprise going.³ Young suggested hiring Eastman, who had left teaching at Columbia University and recently founded the Men's League for Women's Suffrage, as their editor. "You are elected editor of *The Masses*. No pay," they wrote him.⁴

Eastman took over the magazine with a December 1912 issue, apologizing for the three-month lapse and promising his readers a magazine that would "measure up in radical art and freedom of expression" to the foreign satirical journals.⁵ Vowing to remain a "Socialist magazine," Eastman said *The Masses* would be "hospitable to free and spirited expressions of every kind—in fiction, satire, poetry and essay"—without competing in any sense with the "more heavy and academic reviews." Eastman also pledged to avoid internal Socialist Party politics and dogma. "Our appeal will be to the masses, both Socialist and non-Socialist, with entertainment, education, and the livelier kinds of propaganda." To continuously remind Eastman of this promise, radical journalist John Reed suggested that he include a statement of principles in the masthead,⁶ which was done from the February 1913 issue on:

> THIS MAGAZINE IS OWNED AND PUBLISHED CO-OPERATIVELY BY ITS EDITORS. IT HAS NO DIVIDENDS TO PAY, AND NOBODY IS TRYING TO MAKE MONEY OUT OF IT. A REVOLUTIONARY AND NOT A REFORM MAGAZINE; A MAGAZINE WITH A SENSE OF HUMOR AND NO RESPECT FOR THE RESPECTABLE; FRANK, ARROGANT, IMPERTINENT, SEARCHING FOR TRUE CAUSES; A MAGAZINE DIRECTED AGAINST RIGIDITY AND DOGMA WHEREVER IT IS FOUND; PRINTING WHAT IS TOO NAKED OR TRUE FOR A MONEY-MAKING PRESS; A MAGAZINE WHOSE FINAL POLICY IS TO DO AS IT PLEASES AND CONCILIATE NOBODY, NOT EVEN ITS READERS—THERE IS A FIELD FOR THIS PUBLICATION IN AMERICA. HELP US TO FIND IT.⁷

Gilbert Roe and Max Eastman would certainly have crossed paths through the Suffragist movement, possibly also through Henrietta Rodman, who was acquainted with Floyd Dell, or Amos Pinchot, who supplanted Weeks as *The Masses'* principal financier. Roe himself became a small financial supporter of the magazine, though he would come to rely on Pinchot to help him fulfill his commitments. So when Eastman and Young were indicted for criminal libel in November 1913—charged with libeling the Associated Press with an editorial and a cartoon that accused the news agency of distorting the news⁸—Roe was the logical defense attorney.

Roe had his own grievance against AP. On April 12, 1910, Robert La Follette had given a four-hour speech on the history of the merger of the New York,

New Haven and Hartford railroads "as an example of the evils in railroad financing and monopolistic control of transportation."[9] J. P. Morgan was at the "apex of that effort,"[10] and La Follette's speech quoted some abusive language directed at Morgan.[11] The speech was widely reported throughout the country,[12] but the Associated Press version attributed the abusive language to La Follette directly. Roe wrote La Follette that the AP version of the speech was being used to La Follette's very great detriment. "I have heard it referred to many times here," Roe said, "and have been busy trying to correct the false impression which the Associated Press has created wherever I could do so." Roe urged La Follette to demand retractions and offered to take the matter further if necessary. "I have no doubt the report which the Associated Press made of the Morgan affair is libelous and would sustain actions for very heavy damages."[13]

The origin of the 1913 criminal libel case—*The People of the State of New York v. Max Eastman and Arthur Young*—was AP's coverage of the West Virginia coal-mining war of 1912–13. In 1912, United Mine Workers of America members on Paint Creek in Kanawha County, West Virginia, demanded a wage increase to bring their pay up to the level of other workers in the area. Mine operators rejected the demand, and on April 18, the workers began "one of the most violent strikes in the nation's history."[14] The striking Paint Creek miners were joined by miners from Cabin Creek, demanding the right to organize and seeking recognition of their free speech and assembly rights.[15] In response, mine operators brought in guards from the Baldwin-Felts Detective Agency to evict the miners from their company houses, forcing the families into tent colonies. The mine workers, in turn, brought in national labor leaders such as Mary Harris Jones—"Mother Jones"—as well as weapons and ammunition. The conflict escalated, prompting Gov. William E. Glasscock to impose martial law, and military commissions were established to try offenders in the strike areas.[16] Despite the presence of state militia, however, violence remained the order of the day, with mine operators shooting up a tent colony at Holly Creek from an armored train—the "Bull Moose Special"—on February 7, 1913, killing one miner and injuring another. Miners took revenge with an attack on a mine guard encampment at Mucklow, where sixteen lives were lost. Nearly three hundred strikers and their sympathizers were arrested and tried by military courts, including Mother Jones, whose smuggled message to U.S. senator John W. Kern triggered a Senate committee hearing. In April, newly inaugurated governor Henry D. Hatfield issued terms for settlement of the strike, and it finally ended in July 1913.

The Paint Creek strike was vividly recounted in *The Brass Check* by muckraker cum novelist cum socialist agitator Upton Sinclair—who was also one of

Gilbert Roe's erstwhile clients. Sinclair reserved most of his righteous indignation for the Associated Press's reporting of the strike, particularly the "Bull Moose Special" incident, which he compared with testimony presented at Senate committee hearings on the strike. Noting that the armored train carried "two or three dozen men with several boxes of guns," Sinclair quoted at length from a detective who was on the train to show that the first shots were fired from the Gatling gun on board the train.[17] Sinclair contrasted that testimony and similar testimony from other witnesses with several AP dispatches overnight on February 7 and during the following day indicating that it was the "passenger train" that came under fire from the workers' camp. "Such is the news," Sinclair wrote, "and all the news which the Associated Press sent to the public about that exploit of the 'Bull Moose Special' on the night of February 7, 1913." Sinclair also reported that the provost marshal responsible for the military tribunals, John C. Bond, was a close friend of Cal Young, the AP reporter on the ground, and not only shared an office with Young but was his principal, perhaps only, source of information on the strike.[18]

Sinclair published *The Brass Check* in 1919, based largely on materials that Roe had collected in preparation for the libel trial, but the disparity between the AP dispatches and other accounts coming into New York was apparent almost immediately. In an undated statement in Roe's files, Max Eastman noted that articles about the strike appearing in May 1913 issues of the *Independent*, *Collier's*, and *Everybody's* stated or intimated "that the Associated Press was responsible for the suppression of news of the condition of military tyranny . . . that had prevailed in West Virginia for months. Two of these articles stated that the Associated Press correspondent was also the Provost Marshal."[19] Eastman said it occurred to him to write an editorial on that subject "and the methods of the Associated Press monopoly in general" for the July 1913 issue. Eastman's editorial, entitled "The Worst Monopoly," called the Associated Press the "secret reason" why so few people had even heard of the West Virginia strikes and the "military despotism" that accompanied them.[20] Branding AP the "Truth trust," Eastman wrote: "So long as the substance of current history continues to be held in cold storage, adulterated, colored with poisonous intentions, and sold to the highest bidder to suit his private purposes, there is small hope that even the free and the intelligent will take the side of justice in the struggle that is before us."

To accompany the editorial, Eastman said he adapted a cartoon drawn by Art Young months earlier that had already been approved for publication by the editorial staff. The cartoon—entitled "Poisoned at the Source"—pictured a man secretly pouring poison into a reservoir in the dark of night. The reservoir was labeled "The News," and the poison was labeled "Lies," "Suppressed

Facts," "Slander," "Prejudice," and "Hatred of Labor Organization." In the original cartoon, the man was labeled "The Editor," but Eastman had Young change the label to "The Associated Press." Young took it upon himself to change the man's appearance to resemble Frank B. Noyes, president and founder of the Associated Press.

With the cartoon and editorial in hand, William Rand, attorney for the Associated Press, brought John Doe proceedings against *The Masses* in the Municipal Court of New York. Justice Matthew P. Breen dismissed the case, so Rand took the matter to District Attorney Charles S. Whitman, who brought it before a grand jury, which returned an indictment against Eastman and Young for criminal libel.[21] The indictment charged that Eastman and Young, "unlawfully, wickedly and maliciously intending and contriving to injure [the Associated Press] in its ... business and occupation, did unlawfully and maliciously write, print and publish ... a certain false, scandalous, malicious and defamatory libel ... in a certain magazine and periodical called *The Masses*."[22] By his cartoon, the indictment alleged, Art Young meant to assert that AP "intentionally suppressed the truth and distorted and misrepresented the facts in the information ... furnished and supplied by it to the members." Similarly, by his article, Max Eastman meant to assert that AP was willing, for a price, to supply its members "information of such untruthful, biased, and prejudiced nature and so distorted and incomplete as the person paying the money might desire."

Roe obviously showed a copy of the indictment to Theodore Schroeder, whose marginal comments are identified on the file copy by Netha Roe. "This alleges that defs intended to injure but does not allege that the publication resulting from that intention is efficient to that end," Schroeder wrote about the basic charge. "In other words, [the indictment has] not charged that the thing published 'has a tendency to injure.' This 'tendency' is a fact to be found by the jury and must be alleged so. Couldn't have that tendency from the very nature of plaintiff corporation." With regard to the "meaning" that Eastman and Young intended, Schroeder wrote, "The public suspicion and a guilty conscience reads this meaning into the words. No such meaning can be read out of the words."[23]

AP also launched its own counter-publicity, issuing a statement condemning *The Masses* editors and defending AP's integrity. "If these young men had investigated before they spoke, they would never have said what they did," AP wrote; "for if there is a clean thing in the United States it is the Associated Press." AP argued that "no general policy of suppression or distortion" could be carried out without the knowledge of its own reliable journalists, its newspaper members or its competition.[24] In fact, AP had received numerous such complaints from its members about suppressing the news. Sinclair quoted at length from a 1911 Senate investigation in which Robert La Follette questioned Melville E. Stone, AP's general manager, on that precise point:

> SENATOR LA FOLLETTE: Have the members of your association or any member of your association complained that you suppressed important news?
> MR. STONE: Oh, yes, sir, we have had that for years.
> SENATOR LA FOLLETTE: That you have colored news?
> MR. STONE: No, sir, I do not think anybody has ever said that. Well, I don't know about that. We have had complaints on all sides.[25]

Notwithstanding their own publicity, AP officials and lawyers apparently decided they had a better chance of winning if their case were refocused on Frank Noyes as victim, rather than the AP as a whole. In December, the grand jury handed up another indictment, this time alleging that the picture in Young's cartoon was meant to be understood as Frank Noyes and that he was personally libeled. The legal strategy was obvious, but troubling. The new assistant district attorney in charge of the case—Arthur C. Train, appointed to his post on November 6, 1913[26]—planned to dismiss the first indictment and only try Eastman and Young on the second. According to Amos Pinchot, "He contends that upon the trial of the second indictment evidence in regard to suppression and coloring of news by the Associated Press shall be inadmissible, and that the trial shall be limited to the narrow question as to whether Mr. Noyes and the dignity of the people of the County of New York were injured by the publication of this cartoon."[27]

Roe was also concerned about this turn of events. An internal office memorandum asked rhetorically, "Is not proof of the A.P. methods admissible on the Noyes indictment as a matter of principle, since the libel of Noyes is of him in his official capacity. (There must be lots of cases dealing with a somewhat similar situation in civil libel.)"[28] And again, "Noyes having general control of the A.P., as is set out in the indictment, must be held responsible for what it sends out. If the A.P. sends out poisonous reports he must be responsible for them if he has the authority which the indictment imputes to him."

In any event, Eastman and Young were arraigned on December 20, 1913, pleaded not guilty, and were released on $1,000 bail each.[29] Ten days later, Arthur Brisbane, the legendary editor for the Hearst Corporation, whose International News Service competed with the AP, received a letter from someone in *The Masses* camp, urging him to publicize the case. "The A.P. case is no longer a prosecution, but a persecution," the writer said. "They have handed down a second indictment against Max and Art Young, based upon the same editorial and cartoon, this time naming Frank Noyes as the party libeled."[30] The letter also noted that Roe had spoken with new A.D.A. Train, who had formerly been associated with AP attorney William Rand. Train had admitted to Roe that he knew nothing about the case. "The District Attorney is evidently allowing his office to be used, because you remember Rand had charge of the A.P. case before it was brought into the District Attorney's office."

By the beginning of 1914, Roe was operating on several fronts: filing a demurrer to the Noyes indictment in an effort to foil AP's legal strategy, discussing the case with opposing counsel, and interviewing potential witnesses to AP's practices, should they be admissible at trial. The demurrer contended that the facts stated in the indictment, even if true, would not constitute a crime.[31] Specifically, Roe argued that there was no allegation of a publication that exposed Frank Noyes to hatred, contempt, ridicule, or obloquy. Roe pointed out that the indictment failed to state that the picture in "Poisoned at the Source" was a recognizable likeness of Noyes. The accompanying editorial did not explain the picture as referring to Noyes, and there was no allegation in the indictment that anyone who saw the picture understood it to be a representation of Noyes. The demurrer also argued that the indictment was faulty because it lacked any allegation of malice or criminal intent on the part of the defendants, because it charged two separate crimes in printing and editing the magazine, and because it did not carry a plain and concise statement of the act constituting a crime. Roe wrote La Follette on January 30 that he had waited all morning for the demurrer to be called, only to be informed when it was called, that the justice presiding, who had formerly been an assistant district attorney, would not hear it because he had something to do with procuring the indictment.[32] That supposedly put the argument over until early February, but it would be June before that argument actually took place.[33]

The end of January 1914 also found Roe and Rand in conversation about finding some kind of settlement. Eastman and Stone had met on January 28, but neither Roe nor Rand expected much from it. "I was quite as skeptical as yourself of any good results to flow from the meeting yesterday between Mr. Stone and Mr. Eastman," Rand wrote Roe. "If it is still in your mind that the matter in dispute between your clients and the Associated Press is capable of accommodation, I suggest that you and I together could probably go much further along that line without the presence of our respective clients."[34] There was no accommodation.

Roe began taking statements from prospective witnesses on New Year's Day 1914. Thomas Carnes, president of the United Mine Workers of America district that included Paint Creek and Cabin Creek, verified the relationship between AP reporter Cal Young and Provost Marshal John Bond and asserted that Young had never visited or interviewed him during the entire episode. He stated further that AP reports coming out of the territory contained only a limited amount of strike news, omitting "matters of great importance" so that "the true state of affairs was not made known" through Young's reports.[35] The next day, Roe interviewed W. Bruce Reid, a newspaper reporter for the *Charleston Gazette* and the *Kanawha Citizen*. Reid not only reiterated Carnes's statement regarding the relationship between Young and Bond but also added that Young had actually worked for the military at times during the strike and currently worked for the state Public Service Commission. Young himself was "extremely bitter against the miners," Reid said. As to his own experience during the strike, Reid said he was repeatedly asked by those authorities to "suppress certain news and happenings growing out of the strike" and to "distort" the news in favor of the military administration.[36]

Roe collected numerous statements along these lines, and as his investigation proceeded through the winter and early spring of 1914, so too did the publicity campaign generated by *The Masses'* supporters. On March 2, the *New York Times* carried an announcement of a public protest meeting at Cooper Union on March 5 to attack the indictment, with speakers to include the muckraker Lincoln Steffens and feminist Charlotte Perkins Gilman.[37] A poster advertising the meeting was headlined "DANGER! To the Free Press of America."[38] The meeting itself drew between 1,500 and 2,000 protesters and was well covered by the *New York Times* and the *Sun*.[39] The meeting was held under the auspices of the Liberal Club, and Inez Milholland Boissevain chaired it. Amos Pinchot was the first speaker, and he vigorously defended Eastman and Young. "I have had a long acquaintance with the Associated Press," Pinchot said. "I am perfectly willing to stand behind the charge ... that the Associated Press does color and distort the news, that it is not impartial, and that it is a monopolistic corporation not only in constraint of news, but in constraint of truth." Pinchot said the protest should be directed at the district attorney's office for attempting to "muzzle those who would criticize such a monopoly."[40] Steffens urged attendees to boycott all major newspapers for a week, adding that AP would get a shock when it learned what evidence had been gathered to prove the charge that it suppresses and falsifies the news.[41] Outside the hall, police arrested a member of the Industrial Workers of the World when he got up to make a speech. Boissevain noted the irony of such an arrest outside a free speech meeting.[42]

Two days after the Cooper Union meeting, the *Times* editorialized against *The Masses* and, especially, Pinchot's remarks at the meeting. "It is not necessary to say that Mr. Pinchot does not know what he is talking about and to apply unpleasant epithets to him and to his utterance. He is confuted and made ridiculous by the facts of the case."[43] The editorial argued that Pinchot's charges could not be true because AP serves so many newspapers of different shades of opinion. "Mr. Pinchot . . . bears false witness and foolishly butts his head against a rough stone wall. If the assailants of The Associated Press would now and then . . . base their arguments on some other structure than one built up of glaring falsehoods and owlish stupidities, their antics would be more interesting." The *Times* would not carry Pinchot's response, but the *Sun* did a few days later. He defended his remarks by referring to newspaper owners throughout the country who are members of AP and yet are "heartily sympathetic" to the "tumult of protest" against AP "news coloring." He accused the AP of avoiding the issue by securing a second indictment, pertaining solely to Frank Noyes, and called for an investigation that would go deeply into very important questions regarding AP's operations.[44]

Eastman himself addressed a rally at Teutonia Hall in Brooklyn on March 24. Eastman said, "the right to criticize, disparage, slander and libel that power which [AP] wields over the course of history ought to be absolutely established in the hands of every citizen of this country."[45] According to press coverage, his sentiments were echoed by Fola La Follette, who said *The Masses* was on trial for the right of free speech.

To Roe, however, progress on the case itself was slow. "I am 'marking time' here in the case against Art Young and Max Eastman," he wrote La Follette.[46] "Everything is held up awaiting the decision on some questions of law that I have put up to the Court. I expect later to want to take some testimony in Washington, but I cannot do anything more until the Court decides the questions of law that have been raised." Roe's chief procedural concern was whether he could take depositions of witnesses in the first case while the demurrer was pending in the second, and he explained the situation in even greater detail to John O'Hara Cosgrave, Sunday editor of the New York *World*, who helped manage the funds collected for the defense. Roe told Cosgrave that he had been "flooded" with suggestions from all over the country.[47] "I have had man after man high in newspaper circles come to me with information concerning the Associated Press, but pledging me . . . to keep their names a secret." Roe said some were AP members, while others were "in mortal terror of its baleful power and influence. If we are once able to break the power of the Associated Press in the newspaper world," he wrote Cosgrave, "I hope to be relieved from my obligation of secrecy."

In his five-page letter to Cosgrave, Roe revealed several behind-the-scenes maneuvers. For example, he described an offer by lawyer Samuel Untermyer to Max Eastman to use his "intimate acquaintance" with Melville Stone to have the indictments dismissed. Eastman urged Roe to meet with Stone, which he did, but "of course, nothing came of it." Chicago lawyer Walter Fisher also met with Pinchot and Steffens, apparently having heard from Stone that meeting with Roe was a waste of time. Roe said that Stone had proposed to drop the lawsuits if the defendants apologized. Fisher apparently told Pinchot and Steffens that the case should be submitted to arbitration. Roe would have none of it. "Nothing short of taking testimony in the way prescribed by law would serve any useful purpose," he had replied to both propositions. "Under any other procedure it is plain that as soon as our examination approached anything really vital to the Associated Press, that concern on one pretext or another would refuse further information and completely nullify our efforts." Roe briefed Cosgrave on his investigations to date, including sending investigators to West Virginia and carefully comparing AP-sourced newspaper stories to the facts adduced from witnesses. Roe said he was convinced "beyond the possibility of a doubt, that the Associated Press report had been partial, and unfair, and that in many and most glaring instances it had suppressed the news which was favorable to the labor organization."

With this material in hand, Roe then applied for a court order permitting him to take depositions outside the state under the original indictment, beginning with W. H. French, manager of AP's Pittsburgh office, where all of the West Virginia dispatches were received, edited, and retransmitted over the wire. After several adjournments, the matter was finally heard. The district attorney argued that depositions would be useless because they planned to dismiss the first indictment in favor of the second, so Roe demanded immediate dismissal. The prosecution flatly refused. "Of course it would be out of the question to dismiss the first indictment against Eastman before your demurrer to the second had been disposed of," Train told Roe.[48] "Even if your demurrer were sustained I see no reason for dismissing the first indictment, as the defendant might be acquitted on the second indictment, in which event it might be regarded as desirable to try him under the first. The point of my suggestion is that there is no use taking a deposition under an indictment when there is no immediate prospect of that indictment being tried." Nevertheless, the court granted Roe's motion for depositions. At the same time, Roe argued the demurrer to the Noyes indictment, which the court took under advisement.[49]

Despite the favorable ruling on depositions, however, Roe had still not received the actual discovery order when he wrote Cosgrave in April. By then, he was in no hurry. "Since the matter has dragged along so long, it now suits my plans quite well to let it continue in that condition for a little while longer. The trial parts of the Courts adjourn here in June and do not convene until October, and I shall be quite satisfied if the prosecution delays proceeding so that the actual trial cannot be had until October. This will give me several free months to take testimony during the summer." Roe's letter concludes with his speculation that AP had "abandoned all idea of avoiding trial and is making the best preparation it can to meet the issue." Roe said he was not sure how much of the information he had collected—including the "secret connection between the Associated Press and the big financial interests"—would be admissible, especially in a trial on the Noyes indictment only. But he expressed confidence that the information would find its way to the public, if not to a jury. "[It] will show that the evils cannot be eradicated by a mere change in the personnel or its officers, but that a complete change in the organization will be necessary."

In June, Roe received approval to take depositions in the first libel case, and he wrote Eastman the day before reargument was scheduled on the demurrer to the indictment in the second case. "There is no chance of our going to trial in either case until next fall," he wrote. If the demurrer is overruled, "we will then have to plead to the second indictment. . . . I presume Art will also be arrested and he will also have to plead. That is, pleas of not guilty will be entered in both cases."[50] Eastman responded "with gratitude for keeping us out of jail" and asked Roe to keep him apprised of the result of the argument. He asked Roe to find a way to avoid having to appear in court for arraignment on the second indictment and invited Roe and his wife to come out for a weekend in "By-the-Tides" in Provincetown, Massachusetts, where Eastman and his wife, Ida, and their baby were vacationing.[51] Roe, who preferred vacationing in the mountains, declined the invitation;[52] he was not only busy with *The Masses* case, but he was also handling several legal matters for Upton and Mary Craig Sinclair, some business matters involving S. S. McClure[53] and Italian educator Maria Montessori,[54] and keeping up a rigorous schedule of participation in public political discourse.

Roe had previously turned down an invitation to speak at a March dinner meeting of the Intercollegiate Socialist Society on "Freedom of Speech and the Press" because of time constraints. "I have absolutely cut out speech-making for the present because my professional work is so exacting that it takes all my time and energy," he said at the time.[55] He did agree to speak on "Freedom of Speech in Times of War and Industrial Disputes" at a May meeting of that organization[56]—which also featured Art Young of *The Masses* and Frederick Roy Martin of AP, as well as Mother Jones[57]—and eagerly accepted Mabel Dodge's invitation to attend one of her famous salons with John Reed, who had recently returned from covering the Mexican Revolution for the *World*.[58]

With approval to take depositions in *The Masses* case, Roe would become even busier. He met with AP lawyer William Rand on June 24 to receive the records of AP's Pittsburgh office and to depose W. H. French.[59] Sinclair would later write that French "was not satisfied with the bitterly prejudiced reports which his correspondent, Cal Young, and Young's partner, John Bond, sent in to him. He found it necessary to go over their dispatches, and to put in still more poison."[60] Roe told Cosgrave in July that the subpoenaed records amounted to something over 100,000 words, which he was in the process of analyzing.[61] He also asked Cosgrave for money to support his travel to West Virginia and elsewhere to take depositions. "You may send me the balance you have on hand for this purpose. The rest that is promised I shall not need until the time of trial which will not be before October and is likely to be some months later," Roe wrote.

Roe had just received an urgent message from Eastman regarding *The Masses'* precarious financial situation. "I am up against it to find $400 for the *Masses* to keep us going until next October when regular pledges will be renewed and some new ones made up," Eastman wrote.[62] He asked Roe if there was anyone "we can approach with any sob story or blackmailing scheme? This is really a dire situation. Summer is such a hopeless time to touch the pockets of the bourgeoisie, especially when you are trying to have a bourgeois vacation yourself," Eastman wrote from Provincetown. "We have to keep the *Masses* going until the trial or else what is the fun of a trial, so if you think of any way to divert some of the interest in the A.P. matter to an interest in the *Masses* I wish you would tell me." Roe replied that all the funds he could tap were dedicated to litigation expenses and suggested that Eastman call on Amos Pinchot.[63]

Roe turned to Cosgrave: "Have I your permission, out of the money you will now send, to advance [the *Masses*] the $400.00 which will however, be returned and used for the strictly legal purpose to which the entire fund is dedicated? I have just received a letter from the management, saying that unless they can get $400.00 to pay bills which are now pressing, the paper will have to go out of business before the time of trial."[64] Within a few days, Roe also asked Cosgrave for the rest of the litigation fund. "I expect during this month and next to practically complete the preparation of the case for trial, and there will never be a time when money will be more needed for that purpose," he wrote. "I will be glad therefore, if you send me a check for the balance on hand. It will be devoted strictly to the purpose for which it is intended. If I give any help to the publication it will be entirely aside from this, and will not be taken into account in this matter."[65]

Apparently, however, Cosgrave was not willing to let the money be used to fund the magazine itself. The next day, Roe wrote Eastman: "I took up with the representative of our friend here, the question of the use for magazine purposes, of some of the money he had pledged for legal purposes, explaining of course that the money would be paid back to the fund for legal expenses. Our friend's representative is a very good business man and strongly advises against the use of any portion of the money except for legal purposes, and points out what I knew before, that I really had no authority to make this application of the money."[66] Roe expressed his anxiety over whether Eastman could keep the magazine going, and asked if Eastman would be in the city any time soon so they could talk the situation over. Eastman replied with a note apologizing to Roe for being "the cause of your having to explain so much." Eastman told Roe he had seen Pinchot about the money. "I'm sure he can fix it up," Eastman said. "I'll tell him to write you."[67] Pinchot did just that. "I have sent the *Masses* six hundred dollars," Pinchot told Roe. "This is all but $50 of the defense fund. I have also continued my monthly contribution of $100 to *The Masses*. I sincerely hope and believe that we are going to come out of this case with flying colors. Have you heard any intimation of when the case is to be brought to trial?"[68] Eastman also sent Roe the good news. "Pinchot sent us a check of $600.00, and a pledge of $100.00 a month for a year, so you can imagine the joy around here. And congratulate yourself that you are being 'saved' for a while, as you advised."[69]

So, *The Masses* was saved—at least until the following summer—and Roe could continue to prepare for trial, even as he awaited a decision on his demurrer to the Noyes indictment. The war in Europe had begun in August, but it had relatively little effect yet on Roe as long as Wilson remained neutral—as he seemed likely to do. Philip La Follette, Robert's son, and Nellie Dunn, the senator's secretary, were in London, and Roe suggested that even though they seemed to be "well out of the danger zone," it would be a "good plan for them to get back here as soon as they can."[70]

Back in New York, the courts were now in session, but there was no trial that fall or even that winter. In March, Judge William H. Wadhams overruled Roe's demurrer to the Noyes indictment.[71] Wadhams said the indictment sufficiently charged the commission of the crime when it described the libel as malicious, and he added that whether the cartoon sufficiently resembled Noyes was a question of fact for the jury. He further held that the indictment was not procedurally defective, since printing and editing were but two aspects of the same, singular crime, and he summarily rejected Roe's argument that the indictment did not carry a plain and concise statement of the act constituting a crime. The decision to let the Noyes indictment proceed would seem to have cleared the way for exactly the trial that AP wanted. Indeed, Assistant District Attorney Train told Roe that the case would now have to go to trial.[72] But a new, more progressive district attorney, Charles A. Perkins, had been appointed to take

Charles Whitman's place when Whitman was elected governor. Perkins took office on January 1, 1915; soon thereafter, he met with Roe about dismissing the case. Apparently on his own initiative, Train met with Pinchot and Eastman to suggest dismissal. Pinchot wrote to Roe that in Train's view, Perkins was "in a rather embarrassing position about the case and would rather have the indictments gotten rid of without his having to move in the matter."[73]

Roe replied to Pinchot with an update on his meeting with Perkins. "After considerable discussion, and after he had apparently talked with the Associated Press people," Roe wrote, "Perkins and I arrived at the tentative arrangement . . . by which bail was to be discharged at once and, the matter allowed to slumber for a time, and then the indictments would be taken up with a batch of others, and all dismissed together."[74] Subsequently, Roe suggested dismissing the cases immediately lest some new incident revive interest in the matter, which had apparently faded. Perkins rejected that idea but told Roe by telephone that with the bail discharged, "the whole matter could be treated as practically ended." Roe told Pinchot he had not mentioned the discussions with Train. Roe seemed to think that relations between Train and Perkins might be a bit strained, and he asked Pinchot to cut the deal with Train directly.

While the case "slumbered," *The Masses* had to weather another financially difficult summer. Marlen E. Pew, the magazine's business manager, sent Roe a financial statement in May: "I feel that you, who have been providing the sinews of our little war for the life of *The Masses*, should know whether or not there is any success in the undertaking."[75] Pew predicted that *The Masses* could operate without being subsidized if "reasonable" initial capital were provided. In 1914—"a disastrous war year, when publishers . . . suffered severe losses"—the magazine actually increased earnings. Pew expressed the hope that *The Masses* could be self-supporting by the end of the year. Pew told Roe that Pinchot had asked him to collect "guarantees" from contributors during the summer. Roe had promised the magazine $250, and Pew enclosed a statement. In July, Eastman asked Roe to send the money by early August. Otherwise, he said, "the paper will bust. You know the fund was calculated to last just barely—there wasn't a cent over or under. And you and two others are the only ones left to pay up."[76] But by then, Roe was himself too financially embarrassed to pay.

"I am mighty sorry to say that I cannot pay up my $250 to the *Masses* just now," Roe replied.[77] "I have not forgotten my promise, and have been very sorry that I could not make my payments monthly as I had anticipated. I think I was able to send Pinchot one check for $50 on the matter, and that's all." Roe said he had been "suffering the most degraded kind of poverty lately" because of his real estate speculation and promised to "put my obligation in legal form and be able to work it off sometime within the year." Pinchot had the cash and was willing to take Roe's note.[78] Roe sent the note, with thanks, and the promise to "try to work it off in installments as rapidly as I can."[79] He did just that, but was paying well into 1916.[80] By then, Roe had apparently pledged another $300, and Pinchot wrote that "with your generous assistance, the fund of $9,000 to put *The Masses* on a solid business basis, has been successfully raised."[81]

In just over a year, *The Masses* would fail forever, though not for the lack of "a little backing." Roe would again be called upon to represent the magazine—in the most important case of his career—and Eastman and Young would be back in the dock as defendants facing federal criminal charges. But in late 1915, the outlook was rosy. "I am just pulling my old record together in order to be able to present the necessary facts to the Court, showing that we are entitled to have the case against you and Max Eastman dismissed," Roe wrote Art Young. "I will probably make the motion next week."[82] Roe filed his motion on November 26, the day after Thanksgiving, and it was heard on November 30. "When the District Attorney did not move for trial, I moved [for dismissal] in open court . . . and, the District Attorney not opposing, the cases were dismissed."[83] The next day, he would give Young the good news.[84]

Exactly why AP decided to drop the case remains something of a mystery. "For six years I have wondered why it was dropped," Sinclair wrote in *The Brass Check*.[85] "I cannot say now that I know; but I have just met Max Eastman, and heard from his lips the story of a certain eminent corporation lawyer in New York, who on several occasions has 'kicked over the traces' of Big Business. It was his plan to summon the heads of high finance in New York, beginning with Pierpont Morgan, and to question them as to the precise details of their relationship to the Associated Press!" he wrote. "Aren't you sorry that trial didn't come off?" Sinclair did not identify the lawyer in question, but he was probably referring to Samuel Untermyer, who approached Eastman early on with a plan to win the case. Roe saw it differently. In a 1916 letter to Cosgrave, he acknowledged that he did not know what had passed between the district attorney and the AP, but he had no doubt that the testimony taken was submitted to officers of the company.[86] "Nothing but the thoroughness of the preparation and the certainty that the charges made would be proven, in my opinion, brought about the dismissal," he wrote, thanking Cosgrave for enabling him to gather testimony from remote parts of the country. While Roe said he regretted that the case was dismissed instead of tried, "[so] far as the defendants were personally concerned, we accomplished by the dismissal of the case, everything that could have been accomplished by trial."

Eastman and Young must have been pleased with the outcome. In April 1916, *The Masses* carried a two-page cartoon that closely resembled "Poisoned at the Source." In this cartoon, however, a beautiful winged angel labeled "The Associated Press" leans over the reservoir pouring in the contents bottles labeled "Truth," "Pure Motives," "Generous Spirit," "Christian Duty," and "Love of Labor." Caricatures of Eastman and Young are shown kneeling in prayer in the corner of the frame. The cartoon's title: "April Fool."[87]

Upton Sinclair

Upton Sinclair played a number of roles in *The Masses* libel case, from assisting the defense in collecting evidence to chronicling the story much later in *The Brass Check*. At the same time, he was also a Socialist agitator, muckraker extraordinary, and one of Gilbert Roe's most colorful—and aggravating—clients. Roe's legal relationship with Sinclair coincided with and closely paralleled his representation of Eastman and Young, at least before the United States entered World War I. Born in 1878, Sinclair was the youngest of the great muckrakers, greatly influenced by Lincoln Steffens, "whose later friendship Sinclair cherished."[88] Sinclair's biographer, Anthony Arthur, says Sinclair read *McClure's Magazine* in his formative years, including "attacks on civic and corporate corruption," but was then "only a sympathetic observer of the growing progressive movement." He seems to have been converted to socialism by Leonard Abbott, whom he met at the offices of the *Literary Digest* in October 1902. He joined the Socialist Party of America in 1904, founded the Intercollegiate Socialist Society in 1905, and, in 1906, published his most important work: *The Jungle*, a novel attacking the working conditions of the Chicago meatpacking workers.

Gilbert Roe's representation of Upton Sinclair arose from a violent mineworkers dispute, not unlike the strike that prompted his defense of Eastman and Young. In Sinclair's case, the dispute involved a strike by three thousand coal miners in Colorado against the Rockefeller family–owned Colorado Fuel and Iron Company. The strike began in September 1913 and continued until December 1914, but its most dramatic episode was the so-called Ludlow Massacre of April 20, 1914, when troops from the Colorado National Guard and private guards from CFI attacked evicted miners living in a tent colony near Ludlow. The assault was even more deadly than the "Bull Moose Special" incident in West Virginia the previous year. Two women and eleven children died from asphyxiation caused by the soldiers' setting some of the tents on fire; two other children and five strikers also died in the fighting, along with four soldiers.

A week after the Ludlow Massacre, Laura Cannon, wife of the president of the Western Federation of Miners, described the massacre at a Carnegie Hall program that Sinclair attended. Sinclair was outraged, not only by the loss of life, but also by his faulty impression that the newspapers failed to cover the incident, which he attributed to the Rockefeller influence.[89] The next morning, Sinclair and his second wife, Mary Craig Kimbrough Sinclair, or Craig, as she was called, tried to confront John D. Rockefeller Jr. in his office in the Standard Oil Building at 26 Broadway. When they were denied entry, Sinclair left a note saying he planned to "indict" Rockefeller for murder at a meeting of the Liberal Club that evening.[90]

About thirty people attended the meeting, including Steffens and Abbott, both mutual friends of Sinclair and Roe. Members of the club told at least one reporter that the meeting was not an official meeting of the club, but "wholly the work of the Sinclairistas."[91] Over the objection of IWW members in attendance, who urged a more vigorous response, Sinclair and his followers adopted a strategy of peacefully parading down Broadway to Rockefeller's office in complete silence, wearing black crepe arm bands, six at a time, the groups changing each hour, day and night, until the strike was settled.[92] Sinclair told attendees that he originally thought to wait for Rockefeller outside his headquarters, then horsewhip him. Upon his arrest, he planned to go to jail, where he would engage in a hunger strike. Sinclair said he discarded that idea because it included violence—an aversion that distinguished Sinclair from the Wobblies, from the anarchists following Alexander Berkman's assassination model, and from other leftists bent on attacking Rockefeller during that period[93]—but the next day, circumstances resulted in the partial restoration of his original plan, minus the horsewhipping.

Sinclair and four women took the first shift at 10:00 a.m. on April 29; by the time Mary Craig Sinclair—the sixth planned protester—arrived, the five had all been arrested for disorderly conduct.[94] The women arrested with Sinclair were Elizabeth Freeman, a British suffragist; Margorie Remington Charter, a writer and lecturer; Donia Leitner, an artist; and Belle Newman Zilberman, a self-described Daughter of Liberty.[95] When the crowd attracted by the protesters grew to nearly a thousand, two police officers arrested the five and took them to the Old Slip station, where they were charged with disorderly conduct. At least two newspapers sought to capture the moment visually, with a photograph in the *Eagle* and a line drawing in the *Tribune*.[96] Never one to miss an opportunity for publicity, Sinclair railed against Rockefeller's "invisible government" and called for the arrest of the "murderers" in the Standard Oil Building.[97] The five were taken in a police van to the police court at the Tombs, where they were arraigned before Magistrate Charles E. Simms. Sinclair said he did not have a lawyer and would not ask any court to appoint one. He even refused an offer of assistance from IWW lawyer Arthur Caesar. Simms paroled the group until the following day, when he would hold a special hearing in the matter.

Late that afternoon, Sinclair and Abbott—who was president of the Free Speech League at the time—formed what they called the "Free Silence League" and took offices around the corner from Rockefeller's building.[98] The next day, Sinclair reported to court as promised, urging Simms to find that he had broken no law. "My wife is the daughter of a distinguished Southern judge and the cousin of a notable national legislator," Sinclair said. "We did this thing because we had faith in the institutions of our country.... Why is there no lawful way to protest, even as mildly as we tried to, in a peaceable manner according to the law?"[99] Despite the arresting officer's testimony that Sinclair had been a "perfect gentleman,"[100] Simms found Sinclair and the others guilty of disorderly conduct and imposed a fine of $3 or three days in jail. Sinclair and two of the women refused to pay the fine and were duly confined. Joined by Freeman and Leitner, Sinclair started that hunger strike that he initially planned.[101] "I don't care whether they carry me out dead or alive. I won't eat," he declared melodramatically; his hunger strike lasted less than two days.[102] On May 2, Craig paid Sinclair's remaining $1 fine, which enabled him to appeal the sentence and seek restitution.[103] The picketing of Rockefeller—at the office, at his home in Tarrytown, and even at the church where he taught bible class—would continue, with Sinclair keeping his distance from the more violent protesters.[104]

To pursue his appeal, Sinclair—probably encouraged by Abbott and Steffens—retained Gilbert Roe, while Sinclair himself headed for Colorado to research the books he would write on the coal strike.[105] In an article for the May 30 issue of *Appeal to Reason* on the AP's suppression of the truth about the Colorado strike, Sinclair claimed to know Roe "intimately," having discussed with him the need to collect evidence against the AP in *The Masses* case.[106] "I am very happy to be able to announce to my friend, Mr. Roe, that I have at last obtained some documentary evidence, proving definite, deliberate and flagrant suppression of news by the Associated Press," Sinclair wrote. Roe would later tell Max Eastman, who had also traveled to Colorado, that he found Sinclair's article interesting. "It may not be of value as evidence in our case," he wrote, "but it shows the same tracks of the beast which we have learned to recognize."[107]

In any event, on June 5, Roe wrote to Andrew O'Rourke, the stenographer at the magistrate's hearing, asking the cost of the minutes,[108] which he ordered a few days later. He told O'Rourke he needed them right away, since he had to file by June 16 or the court would dismiss the appeal.[109] At the same time, Roe considered Craig Sinclair's request to bring libel suits against newspapers carrying the false AP story on her "arrest." Upton Sinclair later wrote in *The Brass Check* that his wife was informed by lawyers "that she was in a position to collect large damages from the Associated Press, and from every newspaper which had printed the false report. Some thirty suits were filed, but my wife's health did not permit her to go on with them."[110] Well aware of the Sinclairs' penchant for publicity, Roe cautioned Craig to lower her profile. "[You] had better give no interviews and do nothing that will result in our getting further newspaper notoriety," he told her.[111] He also instructed her to begin gathering the clippings of the libelous article they would need to file suit. He also told Craig that it might be helpful if Upton's disorderly conduct decision were reversed on appeal, "or, rather, it might prevent the fact of his conviction being hurtful to us."

The next day, Roe wrote to Upton Sinclair in Colorado to advise him that he and Craig were "contemplating suing all the seven or eight hundred papers receiving the A.P. service." Roe said he would not go into detail regarding her lawsuit. "[We] are merely getting the material together for the present, and you will probably be back here in time to confer about all the features of it before anything is done." He also advised Sinclair that he could not use instances of AP's suppression of the Colorado news in the defense of Eastman and Young, but said "it is good work to get this stuff out and let the public know about it."[112]

A few weeks later, however, Judge Alan McCaskill Kimbrough, Craig's father, told his daughter that he did not approve of the libel cases because they would bring "too much unenviable notoriety."[113] Sinclair conveyed the message by telephone to Roe, who wrote to Craig on June 20. "In view of this attitude of your father, I suggested to Mr. Sinclair that possibly it would be better to wait until we got the result of the appeal that Mr. Sinclair has taken from the judgment convicting him of disorderly conduct. If we should be able to get a reversal which would amount to an adjudication that what Mr. Sinclair did was not unlawful, this would probably change your father's attitude and would be of very great assistance to you in the libel actions." Roe also outlined the approach they might take toward organizing and financing a nationwide attack on the newspapers carrying the false AP story. Roe said he would take the cases on a contingency basis, with any fees for himself coming out of the recovery. They would also have to retain local attorneys around the country, and their fees, like his, would also be conditioned upon the damage awards they received. "On the other hand," he wrote, "you would have to meet the actual disbursements and also provide for the giving of a bond for costs wherever that was required." Roe explained that most defendants would move for a bond to cover the costs of the action; the amount would vary from $100 to $250. In some cases, the local attorneys might be able to arrange this without any indemnification on her part, but not in every case. He proposed a 50 percent contingent fee, which would include his fees and those of most local attorneys, noting that in some special cases, the local lawyer might require another 10 percent. Craig objected to bearing the costs and disbursements in the cases, so Roe had his associate, John Scoble, write her to point out that it would be unlawful and unprofessional for Roe to bear that cost. "[Other] reputable attorneys would also take this position," Scoble said.[114]

But the calculus changed the following week when Judge Thomas C. T. Crain affirmed the Magistrate's Court judgment convicting Sinclair of disorderly conduct.[115] As Roe had not asserted any evidentiary error below, Crain said, the entire case was based on Sinclair's assertion that he lacked "intent to provoke a breach of the peace, or that a breach of the peace might . . . be occasioned" by his "threatening, abusive or insulting behavior."[116] Crain meticulously examined the events of the days preceding Sinclair's arrest, as well as the protest itself. He then translated Sinclair's conduct toward John D. Rockefeller (whom he coyly referred to as "an unidentified Mr. Rockefeller"[117]) as an accusation of "abhorrent and criminal acts. . . . Can it be seriously urged that [Sinclair's] behavior is not insulting to [Mr. Rockefeller]?" Crain asked rhetorically. Crain next turned to the question of intent to breach the peace, or, alternatively, the possibility that a breach might occur because of Sinclair's behavior. On this point, Crain turned Sinclair's own testimony against him. "A recital of the defendant's apprehensions shows that he realized that trouble might result from what he was about to do and subsequently did," Crain said. "His apologies and admissions form a considerable part of his alleged defense. He anticipated that some of his companions at least might lose their self-control." According to Crain, the law provided that anyone who chose to "reprobate the conduct" of another person, in public, without legal justification, where his action might be resented by that person or others in sympathy with him, is liable for behavior "tending to a breach of the peace," even though the conduct itself was peaceable and even courteous. Nor is it justified even if the other person's conduct was reprehensible and deserved reprobation.

"This view does not militate against the right of free speech or against the right of assembly," Crain asserted without explanation, "nor is it primarily for the protection of the one reprobated. Its sanction is the public interest in the enforcement of law and the preservation of order." Crain distinguished the cases Roe had offered to support his position on the grounds that the defendants in one case were peacefully picketing to protect a private interest, that the defendants in another case were petitioning Parliament for redress of grievances, and that defendants in a third case had attracted a crowd for no apparent reason. Sinclair's purposeful, peaceful picketing in support of a public interest "did not come within the principle" of the cases Roe cited. Further, Crain said, the remarks of the magistrate to the effect that Sinclair engaged in no threatening, abusive, or insulting behavior "present no insuperable obstacle" to affirming the conviction. The magistrate's final conclusion was expressed in the judgment—that Sinclair had violated the law.

Roe had been vacationing in the mountains when Crain's decision came down, and that may account for Sinclair's pique when he wrote to Roe on July 15. "Dear Friend Roe," he wrote, "I have been expecting to hear from you before this."[118] Sinclair said he wanted to be sure that Roe filed a timely appeal in his case and asked how much it would cost. "This is the first time that I have ever ventured into the legal jungle," he said, "and I have no idea of what may be the value of the services of a well-known lawyer like yourself." Sinclair expressed concern that Crain's decision would adversely affect the viability of his wife's libel suits and insisted that he would only pursue an appeal in his case if it would help with those suits. "I cannot otherwise afford the luxury," he said, "because I have nearly bankrupted myself in this Colorado fight." As to Craig's lawsuits, Sinclair said her father thought a 50 percent contingency ought to be large enough to get the best lawyers and also justify those lawyers' bearing the cost of the bonds and other risks of loss. Finally, Sinclair suggested starting with a few test cases unless Roe thought the Crain decision could be reversed quickly.

Scoble responded to Sinclair's letter, advising him that the appeal had already been taken, and that Appellate Division would probably hear the case in early October. He also asked Sinclair for $100 on account to help defray expenses.[119] Sinclair agreed to send Roe a check in about ten days,[120] but it still hadn't arrived two months later. "I have had you in mind literally every day," Sinclair wrote to Roe, "and have thought that I would send you a check for $100. But these abominable people who owe me for the *Jungle* moving pictures keep putting me off from week to week. They have done it now for a couple of months. I am going to bring suit against them next week, unless I have received the money."[121]

Early the next year, the Appellate Division affirmed Sinclair's disorderly conduct conviction without opinion.[122] "In view of this decision," Roe told Sinclair, "I am extremely doubtful as to the wisdom of further prosecuting the libel cases. Think it over and we will discuss it the first time you are in the City."[123] Sinclair, meanwhile, had moved about as far away from "the City" as possible. "I still owe you a portion of your bill," he wrote in April 1915 from Gulfport, Miss. "Also I am still hard up, so I hope you won't mind waiting a little." Sinclair wrote that Craig had been "far from well," and they hoped her health would improve in the warmer climate. With regard to the lawsuits, Sinclair said a young lawyer in Gulfport was very eager to take some of Craig's cases and thought there was no doubt of her getting damages in the South. Another lawyer had suggested suing AP itself, rather than the newspapers, and Sinclair asked Roe what the thought of the idea.[124] Roe said he would not take the case on a contingency basis and did not believe Sinclair could afford to pursue such a case on any other basis. As to the money, Roe said, "I deeply sympathize with you and anyone else who is hard up. We all have to do the best we can, and that is what both of us will do in this matter."[125]

The correspondence between Roe and Sinclair would continue for a time, but most of it concerned Sinclair's domestic situation, including a custody battle with his first wife over their son. One might speculate as to how Roe felt about Sinclair, but Netha Roe seemed to have little use for him. In an unaddressed, undated, fragmentary letter from Washington, D.C., where she lived after Gilbert Roe's death, she wrote her correspondent: "If you would 'like to see' Upton Sinclair why don't you call him up and tell him so? He has in my opinion always *loved to be seen*. I would only be afraid you might find another guest like the one you have—coming for a call and remaining endlessly. If I sound as if I didn't like Upton Sinclair, it is probably true."[126] In the coming years, Sinclair would support America's entry into World War I—a position that both Roes would deplore. Notwithstanding, he would go on to enjoy a long literary and activist career, publishing two novels about the Colorado strike, among many others, and founding the California chapter of the American Civil Liberties Union.

Socialist Speech before the War

Roe would continue to represent Socialists of many stripes on speech and press issues, both before and after America entered the war. Many of them ran afoul of the law in opposing the war by word and deed. Such clients ranged from *The Masses*, again, to the New York City Teacher's Union, which he represented from 1918 until his death in 1929. Most of the prewar cases grew out of labor disputes such as the West Virginia and Colorado coal miners' strikes or were otherwise labor-related. The defamation of James Maurer was a case in point. The Maurer case demonstrates once again that Roe viewed the law of libel as both an instrument of persecution—as in the cases of S. S. McClure and Max Eastman—and of retaliation, as in the aborted cases of Henrietta Rodman and Craig Sinclair. Like the latter, Maurer's case ultimately went nowhere, but it is useful in providing an early glimpse of the "loyalty" issue that would come to dominate free speech issues during and after the war.

In 1916, James Hudson Maurer was president of the Pennsylvania Federation of Labor and a Socialist Labor Party member of the Pennsylvania legislature. Maurer was well known in national labor circles for his unsuccessful efforts to abolish the Pennsylvania State Constabulary, the first state police force in the country, established in 1905 following complaints that the National Guard had been ineffective in breaking the anthracite coal miners' strike. At the time, both the labor and socialist movements viewed such state constabularies primarily as a strike-breaking instrument of capital.[127] Maurer's views on the issue were compiled in a book called *The American Cossack*, and he traveled around the country opposing the creation of state constabularies wherever they were proposed. On April 9, 1916, a bill to create a New York State Constabulary was pending in the Assembly, and Maurer was invited to address a weekly Labor Forum meeting at Washington Irving High School in New York City to bolster opposition to enactment. As described by Gilbert Roe, who would briefly represent Maurer, the meeting was quite a spectacle.[128] During his speech, Maurer recounted the funeral of an anthracite miner who died during the strike. The funeral procession, led by a man carrying the American flag, had been interrupted by a detachment of mounted state police officers, who ordered the marchers to disperse. When the officer in charge was shown the miners' permit, "he cursed and growled, 'Well, you get away with it this time, but never again! Anyway, down with the flag! Furl it!'"[129]

The next day, a reporter for the *Sun* wrote that Maurer had shouted, "Down with the Stars and Stripes!" and the *New York Times* reported he had declared, "To hell with the Stars and Stripes!" According to Maurer, "This lying story was flashed across the country, almost every daily between the Atlantic and the Pacific carrying it. It was one of the sensations of the day and for months I was blistered in editorials for what I had not said. I became the favorite horrible example of the super-patriots." Maurer retained Roe to salvage his reputation by demanding retractions and, where necessary, organizing multiple libel suits. In December, Roe demanded and received a retraction from the *Tribune*, which carelessly repeated the allegation after fully vindicating Maurer following the April hearing.[130] In a brief article headlined "Justice for James Maurer," the *Tribune* expressed regret for "the form in which the incident was recalled."[131] Roe sent a copy of the retraction to Carl Beck, the managing director of the Labor Forum, telling Beck he planned to sue the Hearst paper in Chicago.[132]

But the libel cases envisioned by Roe never reached fruition. In April 1919, Maurer brought the episode to an inconclusive close. "I cannot help but feel that the war and the reactionary spirit still prevailing among judges and such as are chosen to act as jurors, makes our case almost a hopeless one," Maurer told Roe.[133] "Had we been able to foresee the war and storm of reaction that came with it, we certainly never would have proceeded as we did. I would, therefore, favor dropping all the cases if it is possible to do so without any expense or in some manner get out of it as gracefully as we can. Should the case come up and we failed to get a verdict, it would be equal to declaring me guilty and, just at this time, I put nothing beyond the average juryman." When Maurer published his autobiography many years later, he would make no mention of the libel suits.

The war, "and storm of reaction that came with it," would come to dominate Gilbert Roe's practice from 1916 on. In May 1915, German U-boats had torpedoed and sunk the RMS *Lusitania*, with the loss of nearly 1,200 lives, including 128 Americans. The sinking would lead directly to Roe's greatest political victory, the successful defense of his life-long friend Robert M. La Follette against those who sought his expulsion from the Senate. And the antiwar advocacy flowing through the art and articles of *The Masses* would lead to Roe's greatest legal defeat, but not before his efforts on the magazine's behalf prompted one of the most important free speech opinions in American legal history.

6

The Pacifists I

I hardly see how it would be safe to say the Lord's Prayer if this bill becomes a law. When we pray that our trespasses might be forgiven us as we forgive those who trespass against us, I think it might be construed that we were praying for the forgiveness of our enemies, the Germans.

Gilbert Roe

Assuming that the power to repress such opinion may rest in Congress in the throes of a struggle for the very existence of the state, its exercise is so contrary to the use and wont of our people that only the clearest expression of such a power justifies the conclusion that it was intended. . . . I am confident that . . . Congress had no such revolutionary purpose in view.

Learned Hand

War and the Espionage Act

The first American troops would land in France on June 25, 1917, but the first casualty of the war—freedom of speech—occurred even before war was declared. On the evening of April 2, legislation aimed at preventing wartime espionage—legislation that had been twice rejected during the past year—was reintroduced by Sen. Charles Culberson (D-Tex.) and Rep. Edwin Webb (D-N.C.). Key provisions of the bill would impose censorship of the press, criminalize interference with military recruitment or causing disaffection in the ranks, and allow the post office to bar dissenting publications from the mails.[1] The significance of the bill was not lost on Gilbert Roe.

"I have heard the rumor that a bill to abridge freedom of speech and of the press has been introduced in Congress," he wrote La Follette, presuming that the bill was thought necessary because of the declaration of war.[2] "There are worse calamities even than war. One of them would be the destruction of free speech and of free press—both of which have already been much restricted even in times of peace." Roe asked La Follette to find out if the rumor were true and, if so, to arrange for him to testify before the appropriate committee as a representative of the Free Speech League. Roe speculated that he only heard about the legislation because of his position with the league. "I do not suppose that there is one person in a million outside of official life who knows that a measure of the sort is under consideration," he wrote. "Unless public hearings are held and some information given to the public about it, we may have our most cherished and fundamental right swept away over night. The forces at work in this country to curtail freedom of speech and of the press will make it very hard to repeal a law now passed after the war is over even though such a measure could get no support at this time except for the war."

In fact, hearings on "Espionage and Interference with Neutrality," H.R. 291, began two days later, and Roe testified on April 12, along with Charles T. Hallinan of the American Union Against Militarism, lawyer Harry Weinberger of the Free Speech League of America, activist social worker Jane Addams, and radical journalist John Reed, among others.[3] Roe focused specifically on the disaffection clause of the bill, which provided that "whoever in time of war shall willfully cause or attempt to cause disaffection in the military or naval forces of the United States, shall be punished by imprisonment for not less than 20 years or for life." The nonmailability clause was apparently not in the copy of the House bill that Roe had when he testified.[4]

Roe began his testimony by pointing out that the Constitution did not provide for any suspension of freedom of speech or the press during wartime; even the suspension of habeas corpus was limited to times of rebellion or invasion, not an offensive on foreign soil. Noting that the Sedition Act of 1798 was far less sweeping than the bill before the committee, he reminded the members that the "indignation with which this legislation was received by the American people . . . swept out of power the administration which passed it."[5] Roe asserted that any speech or publication that causes "disaffection, discontent, disgust, or like feelings in the military," even if truthful, would clearly violate the bill if it became law. "The matter published or spoken may be the truth, and probably the greater the truth the greater the disaffection its dissemination would cause," he said. "Every right to discuss the conduct of the war, the causes which led up to it, and the methods by which it can be terminated are brought under the ban of the proposed statute."

While Roe claimed to express no opinion on the war itself—although he certainly opposed U.S. involvement—he insisted that the people retained the right, if they wished to exercise it, to remove from office those who would continue prosecuting the war against their judgment. "But how is any voter to form an intelligent opinion unless there is the fullest discussion permitted of every phase of the war, its origin, its manner of prosecution, and its manner of termination?" he asked. He cited a *New York Evening Mail* editorial pointing out that the weakness of England and France during the first two years of the war resulted from covering up blunders. "This country," he quoted the *Mail*, "must not pay its blood for silence about blunders . . . because of hysterical and mistaken loyalty of silence when outspoken criticism is needed." Roe tried to answer questions about what conduct the bill covered, although he found it so indefinite that no one could tell what it meant. "Candidly, if you will pardon the statement, I hardly see how it would be safe to say the Lord's Prayer if this bill becomes a law. When we pray that our trespasses might be forgiven us as we forgive those who trespass against us, I think it might be construed that we were praying for the forgiveness of our enemies, the Germans." He urged the committee not to pass this question up to the courts. "It is no more the duty of a court to declare a law unconstitutional than it is the duty of Congress to refrain from passing an unconstitutional law."

During the hearings, Rep. Warren Gard (D-Ohio) redrafted the disaffection provision Roe addressed, but the change was more cosmetic than substantive. "Even modified as suggested," Roe said, "it does not seem to me it helps the situation very much." Ultimately, the provision was amended to read, "[W]hoever, when the United States is at war, shall willfully cause or attempt to cause insubordination, disloyalty, mutiny, or refusal of duty, in the military or naval forces of the United States, or shall willfully obstruct the recruiting or enlistment service of the United States, to the injury of the service or of the United States, shall be punished by a fine of not more than $10,000 or imprisonment for not more than twenty years, or both."[6] If the disaffection clause survived essentially intact, the press censorship clause did not survive at all—although not because of any persuasion from the left. Rather, the opposition came from the mainstream press, toward which Roe was frequently cynical. "It looks as though the newspapers would shoot that [censorship clause] to pieces," Roe wrote La Follette. "They would of course be glad to slip over something against free speech if they could do that without interfering with their right to publish. I think the bill will need to be watched in this particular."[7] Cynical or not, the publishers' opposition was effective.

In language that could have been written by Gilbert Roe himself, the American Newspaper Publishers Association said the censorship provision "strikes at the fundamental rights of the people, not only assailing their freedom of speech but also seeking to deprive them of the means of forming intelligent opinion." Also echoing Roe's earlier testimony, ANPA said "in war especially the press should be free, vigilant, and unfettered."[8] Mainstream newspapers expressed similar hostility,[9] and the only press support for the clause came from the ethnic and foreign language press, which saw censorship as a shield against accusations of disloyalty.[10] On May 31, over Wilson's very strong objection, the House voted 184-144 to strip the censorship clause from the bill.[11]

Although Roe was busy gathering materials for La Follette to oppose legislation funding the war and raising an army through conscription,[12] he was sufficiently aware of the Espionage Act's progress to recognize that the nonmailability clause was the most "dangerous" portion of the bill.[13] Specifically, Roe pointed out that the provision was not temporary, but would last forever unless repealed. "No one can appeal to the Courts from a decision of the Postoffice Inspector who may declare anything to be anarchistic or treasonable or seditious that he pleases," Roe wrote, speaking practically if not literally. "I have been through this with other publications which the Post Office officials suppressed on the ground that they were obnoxious to other portions of the Statute and I know what a tremendous instrument of tyranny this rather innocent looking provision of the bill will become." Because there was no powerful counter-constituency like the newspaper publishers, however, the nonmailability provision remained part of the bill when it was enacted on June 15, 1917. Section 1 declared that no material violating any provision of the act could be delivered by the mail. Section 2 declared nonmailable any matter advocating treason, insurrection, or forcible resistance to the law. And Section 3 imposed fines of $5,000 or imprisonment for up to five years or both.[14]

Shortly after the law was enacted, Roe wrote to Roger Baldwin of the American Union Against Militarism, presciently predicting that before the question of the mailability of any material could be decided by the courts, "the work desired will be done and [the] publisher ruined."[15] Indeed, Postmaster General Albert Sidney Burleson of Texas "began to ban socialist publications from the mails even before the Act had passed, and continued to do so at an accelerating pace thereafter."[16] The day after enactment, Burleson secretly directed local postmasters to keep a "close watch on unsealed matter, newspapers, etc., calculated . . . to cause insubordination, disloyalty, mutiny, or refusal of duty in the military or naval service, or to obstruct the recruiting, draft or enlistment services . . . or otherwise to embarrass or hamper the Government in conducting the war."[17] Copies of suspect publications were to be sent to Washington for instructions. Within a month, about fifteen major publications, most of them socialist, were excluded from the mails. Among them were the *International Socialist Review*, *Appeal to Reason*, *American Socialist*, the *Milwaukee Leader*, and, most famously, *The Masses*.

Masses Publishing Co. v. Patten

At the very beginning of July 1917, in the normal course of business, the Ricker News Co. delivered hundreds of copies of the August issue of *The Masses* intended for nationwide circulation to the post office in New York City.[18] They were wrapped as usual for second-class delivery, and the proper postage was paid.[19] Following the instructions of the postmaster general, the postmaster at New York City, Thomas G. Patten, sent a copy of the magazine to Washington with a request for instructions. William H. Lamar, solicitor for the Post Office Department, received the request on or about July 3.[20] A day or two later, Ricker informed Merrill Rogers, the magazine's business manager, that the magazines would not be permitted to go through the mail. Rogers immediately telephoned Frederick G. Mulker, superintendent of second-class matter at the New York post office, to verify Ricker's report. Mulker verified that the magazine had been held up pending receipt of instructions from the solicitor of the Post Office Department in Washington.[21]

Shortly thereafter, Rogers received a telephone call from Mulker, to the effect that the magazines would be held as nonmailable under the Espionage Act.[22] On or about July 5, Rogers received a letter from Patten confirming the information in the telephone call that "according to advice from the Solicitor for the Post Office Department, the August 1917 issue of 'The Masses' is nonmailable under the Act of June 15, 1917." There was no further explanation.[23] Rogers immediately traveled to Washington to meet with Lamar and to determine what portions of the issue were regarded as objectionable. Rogers offered to remove those portions from the magazine, but Lamar refused to specify what portions had triggered the decision or what provisions of the law were being enforced. Instead, Lamar said the whole tone and tenor of the magazine constituted a violation of the act. Later, the government would reveal that in reaching his decision the postmaster had considered not only the August issue, but also the June and July issues of *The Masses* and the June issue of *Mother Earth* magazine,[24] published by Emma Goldman and Alexander Berkman—then on trial in New York City for conspiracy to violate the selective service law.[25] The additional materials were reviewed to show a "persistent and continuing policy in violation of the purposes and intent of the . . . Conscription and Espionage

Acts," as well as to appreciate "the interpretation that would be placed [on the offending articles and cartoons] by habitual readers and subscribers."[26] Goldman and Berkman were convicted on July 9.[27]

On July 12, Gilbert Roe filed a bill of complaint against Patten in U.S. District Court for the Southern District of New York. The complaint asserted that mail delivery was "absolutely necessary to the . . . continued publication and circulation" of *The Masses*[28] and that the magazines held up by the Post Office were, in all respects, mailable under the law. Roe complained that the magazine's officers had never been given an opportunity to be heard on the issue of mailability and that the Post Office's refusal to mail the magazines, if continued, would completely ruin the business. Accordingly, he said, the court should enjoin the Post Office from treating the magazines as nonmailable and command it to transmit them through the mail in the usual way. To the great, if short-lived, benefit of *The Masses*, the case was assigned to District Judge Learned Hand, the brilliant young jurist with whom Roe had corresponded when Hand lost an election to become chief judge of the New York Court of Appeals on the Bull Moose ticket in 1913. In a previous speech-related case, Hand had sharply criticized as too restrictive the prevailing common-law rule on obscenity, although he felt bound by precedent to follow it.[29] American courts began to relax that rule in the 1930s,[30] but it was not until 1957 that the U.S. Supreme Court formally abandoned it.[31] That would not be the last time that Hand's insights on freedom of speech would be more influential decades later than contemporaneously.

Responding to Roe's complaint, Hand ordered Patten to appear in court on July 16 to show cause why the injunction Roe requested should not be issued.[32] When that day arrived, however, he adjourned the hearing until July 21, a Saturday, at the request of Patten's attorney, Earl B. Barnes.[33] Roe objected strenuously to the postponement, arguing that the delay cost the financially strapped magazine $100 a day, but Barnes prevailed on the ground that he needed time to study previous issues of the magazine to prove that its obstruction of military recruiting was deliberate. "The government got it over on me," Roe told La Follette.[34]

That same day, a high-profile committee of socialists and their representatives, alarmed by the assault on socialist publications, met with the postmaster general and the Department of Justice in Washington, not only to protest the suppression campaign but also to try to identify the criteria for mailability under the act. The delegation was headed by socialist lawyer Morris Hillquit and included socialist leader Seymour Stedman, lawyers Amos Pinchot and Clarence S. Darrow, socialist editor Thomas Hickey, antiwar activist Roger N.

Baldwin, and Frank P. Walsh, former chairman of the Industrial Relations Commission.[35] The trip would prove futile. "Mr. Burleson received us very pleasantly," Hillquit reported, "but he did not seem inclined to recognize the validity of our point of view. . . . He promised to give our representations general consideration, but declined to give us any definite guide for future conduct, leaving the question of mailability to be decided by himself or some one appointed by him in the case of each issue of each publication." Hillquit said the committee found a more sympathetic ear at Justice, but "unfortunately, the Department of Justice has no jurisdiction in the matter of closing the mails to publications."[36] A private report to La Follette was more direct, charging "that they had been given an ultimatum to 'Cut-out war criticism or stay out of the mails.'"[37] Walsh was so angry that he wrote to Burleson, denouncing the "ultra-bureaucratic method adopted by you for suppressing newspapers."[38] When Walsh complained that anyone at the Post Office could apparently destroy a business on a whim, Burleson responded that he assumed responsibility for any action taken by his subordinates and that Walsh's letter was both impertinent and offensive. Burleson later recalled threatening to resign when Wilson suggested he let the socialists "blow off steam." Wilson deferred to his postmaster. Wilson adopted a similar position when Eastman sent a letter of protest directly to the president.

Roe and Barnes met in Hand's chambers on Saturday morning, July 21; the argument lasted from about 10 a.m. to 5 p.m.[39] Roe began by pointing out that the publishers had been unable to learn what might be objectionable to the Post Office Department and offered to withdraw anything shown to be illegal.[40] Barnes then submitted affidavits from Burleson and Lamar, prepared two days earlier, setting out in detail and for the first time exactly what prompted the nonmailability order.[41] Specifically, Burleson's affidavit listed four cartoons— "Liberty Bell," "Conscription," "Making the World Safe for Capitalism," and "Congress and Big Business"—and four articles—"A Question," "A Tribute," "Conscientious Objectors," and "Friends of American Freedom"—as violating the Espionage Act. The affidavit also listed items from the June and July issues of *The Masses* and the June issue of *Mother Earth* to assist in interpreting the offending cartoons and articles.[42]

"Conscription," by Henry J. Glintenkamp, depicted three naked figures bound to a cannon, with a young man labeled "Youth" bent backward over the muzzle, a woman labeled "Democracy" tied to one wheel, and a man labeled "Labor" on the carriage. In the foreground, a woman on her knees representing "Motherhood" appeared to be wailing over the body of a dead child who lay before her.[43] "Liberty Bell," also by Glintenkamp, showed that iconic symbol breaking apart. "Making the World Safe for Capitalism," by Boardman

Robinson, was a two-page spread, showing a Russian worker concentrating on "Plans for a Genuine Democracy" while being threatened on one side by figures representing a militaristic Japan and the English symbol John Bull and on the other by figures representing Americans Elihu Root and Charles Edward Russell of the Root Commission, dispatched to Russia between the two revolutions of 1917 in hopes of keeping the Kerensky government in the war. "Congress and Big Business," by Art Young, sometimes called "War Plans," showed a lonely figure representing Congress seeking access to a room where businessmen were poring over a map labeled "War Plans." Congress asked: "Excuse me, gentlemen—where do I come in?" Big Business responded: "Run along now!—We got through with you when you declared war for us." "A Question" was an essay by Max Eastman that asked how many people admired the "self-reliance and sacrifice of those who were resisting the conscription law," and how many agreed with the American press that characterizes resisters as "slackers." "A Tribute" was a poem by Josephine Bell that paid homage to Emma Goldman and Alexander Berkman, "in prison tonight." "Conscientious Objectors" sympathetically introduced a number of letters from conscientious objectors in English prisons compiled by Floyd Dell, while "Friends of American Freedom" was an unsigned essay soliciting contributions for the defense of Goldman and Berkman.[44]

Lamar's affidavit said Judge Advocate General Enoch Crowder had expressed the opinion that these items in the magazine would "cause insubordination, disloyalty, mutiny and refusal of duty in the naval and military forces of the United States and would obstruct the recruiting and enlistment service." Barnes added that the cartoon "Making the World Safe for Capitalism," lampooning the Root mission to Russia, would interfere with the successful conduct of the war.[45] Hand asked whether that same argument might be applied to efforts to repeal conscription or other laws, or whether any political agitation for cessation of the war might not be banned on the same charge. Barnes replied that, in passing the Espionage Act, Congress intended to ban from the mails anything that could obstruct the war effort, not merely treasonable matter.

Roe challenged the constitutionality of the nonmailability provisions of the Espionage Act, but Hand pointed to precedent holding that the mails were always considered a privilege, which Congress, on occasion, could take away.[46] Roe also urged that the magazine had not violated the law, but was merely expressing opinions.[47] Hand said he found nothing in the cartoons to support the claim of nonmailability. "They did not go beyond the argument against conscription and the horrors of war," he said.[48] Roe argued that a publication could not be condemned as unmailable on the basis of material that would not make its publishers criminally liable. As long as *The Masses* did not commit any overt act in violation of the law and confined itself to expressions of opinion, it could not be considered in violation of the act and, therefore, could not be unmailable. Judge Hand agreed, saying the government could not make a distinction between matter that was unmailable, but not indictable, and matter that was indictable under the act. "You cannot expand the meaning of the statute to apply to mailability and contract it as applied to indictability," Hand reportedly said. "You cannot play fast and loose with it. That violates all idea of law and its intent." Otherwise, Hand reserved judgment and brought the argument to an end.

On Monday, Eastman filed an affidavit pointing out that the June and July issues of *The Masses* were published and mailed before the Espionage Act was enacted, and that he never read the *Mother Earth* issue in question.[49] The next day, Roe submitted an amendment to his complaint, alleging that the Espionage Act was itself unconstitutional, depriving his clients of due process of law and violating their First Amendment freedoms of speech and press.[50] Neither argument seems to have made any difference, because on Tuesday, July 24, Judge Hand filed his opinion in *The Masses* case, holding that the Espionage Act's nonmailability provisions could only be enforced against publications that directly advocated violating the law.[51] His order granting a preliminary injunction was filed on Thursday.[52]

Hand began his opinion by asking whether the words and pictures of the banned magazine, interpreted as broadly as permissible, must necessarily violate the Espionage Act. If so, he said, the postmaster's decision must stand. Hand rejected the notion that the power of Congress to do anything required during times of war—including restricting personal rights such as freedom of speech—was at issue in this case. "Here is presented solely the question of how far Congress after much discussion has up to the present time seen fit to exercise [such] a power." If Congress left any necessary, if repressive, measures out of the Espionage Act, it was up to Congress to deal with that.[53] Hand conceded the government's argument that the cartoons and articles at issue may have the effect of interfering with the success of the military by enervating public opinion at home and encouraging the success of the enemy. They were not, however, covered by the provision of the act pertaining to false statements of fact, he said, as they were all "within the range of opinion and criticism" and "believed to be true by the speaker." Whether the criticism is temperate reasoning or indecent invective is the speaker's choice "in countries dependent upon the free expression of opinion as the ultimate source of authority."

Hand noted that the government also relied on a provision of the act that prohibited "willfully causing insubordination, disloyalty, mutiny, or refusal of duty." Here, too, Hand conceded that men who believe that the war is unjust may be more prone to insubordination than men who have faith in the cause. "Yet to interpret the word 'cause' so broadly would, as before, involve necessarily as a consequence the suppression of all hostile criticism," he said. "Assuming that the power to repress such opinion may rest in Congress in the throes of a struggle for the very existence of the state, its exercise is so contrary to the use and wont of our people that only the clearest expression of such a power justifies the conclusion that it was intended." He concluded that the language of the statute did not support the government's position regarding the suppression of the free utterance of abuse and criticism of the existing law, or of the policies of the war. Of course, that begged the question of what Congress thought it was prohibiting when it passed the law. Hand's answer: Congress, in adopting the Espionage Act, meant only to prohibit advising or counseling others to violate the law as it stands, that is, to urge that it is their duty or interest to break the law.

> Political agitation, by the passions it arouses or the convictions it engenders, may in fact stimulate men to the violation of law. Detestation of existing policies is easily transformed into forcible resistance of the authority which puts them in execution, and it would be folly to disregard the causal relation between the two. Yet to assimilate agitation, legitimate as such, with direct incitement to violent resistance, is to disregard the tolerance of all methods of political agitation which in normal times is a safeguard of free government.
>
> The distinction is not a scholastic subterfuge, but a hard-bought acquisition in the fight for freedom, and the purpose to disregard it must be evident when the power exists. If one stops short of urging upon others that it is their duty or their interest to resist the law, it seems to me one should not be held to have attempted to cause its violation. If that be not the test, I can see no escape from the conclusion that under this section every political agitation which can be shown to be apt to create a seditious temper is illegal. I am confident that by such language Congress had no such revolutionary purpose in view.

Applying his view of the law to the facts of the case, Hand said none of the language and none of the cartoons in the August issue of *The Masses* "can be thought to directly counsel or advise insubordination or mutiny." As to the third provision on which the government relied, prohibiting willful obstruction of recruiting or enlisting services, Hand said he disagreed with Roe's argument that the provision refers only to acts other than words and that the obstruction must be successful. But he did limit the scope of the provision to "direct advocacy of resistance to the recruiting and enlistment service." Again, neither the cartoons nor the articles met Hand's test of direct advocacy. Of the cartoons, he said,

"Conscription" comes closest to meeting his test, but "the most that can be said of that is that it may breed such animosity to the draft as will promote resistance and strengthen the determination of those disposed to be recalcitrant." But there is no intimation that the resisting of the draft is either one's duty or in one's interest. Likewise, the articles praising Goldman and Berkman and draft resisters, interpreted "in the most hostile sense," only go so far as to say: "These men and women are heroes and worthy of a freeman's admiration. We approve their conduct; we will help to secure them their legal rights. They are working for the betterment of mankind through their obdurate consciences." Such words, Hand said, contain "not the least implied intimation . . . that others are under a duty to follow" these subjects of admiration. "I cannot see how the passages can be said to fall within the law," he wrote. Hand reiterated his position during the argument—and Roe's position—that the question in this case was indistinguishable from a motion to dismiss an indictment. If the issue was nonmailable, then the editors committed a crime in publishing it. "I cannot think that upon such language any [guilty] verdict would stand," he concluded.

Hand then turned to the question of the magazine's "general tenor and animus [as] subversive to authority and seditious in effect" as evidenced by the introduction of materials from the June and July issues of *The Masses* and from *Mother Earth*. "I cannot accept this test under the law as it stands at present," Hand said. "The tradition of English-speaking freedom has depended in no small part upon the merely procedural requirement that the state point with exactness to just that conduct which violates the law." While Hand conceded that Congress might be able to establish a broader censorship of the press under the war power, "it has not as yet chosen to create one."

Hand's order granting the temporary injunction against the postmaster and ordering the magazine transmitted through the mails "without delay" was dated July 26, two days after the decision became known.[54] During that brief period, the company pulled back the copies sent to the Post Office so the edition could be delivered by alternate means.[55] On the same day the order was issued, U.S. Attorney Francis G. Caffey filed an Assignment of Error listing grounds on which he would rely in his appeal from Hand's decree. In all, there were seven alleged errors, although essentially all of them went directly to the bottom line: Hand was wrong in finding for the magazine under every provision of the Espionage Act raised by government and wrong in granting the injunction.[56] A hearing date on the appeal was originally set for August 23, 1917,[57] but the government was not about to wait that long. On July 26, the postmaster secured an order from Second Circuit Judge Charles M. Hough, who had ruled against Roe in *Philipp v. S. S. McClure* in 1908 as a district court judge, staying Hand's order and setting a hearing for August 2, at Windsor, Vermont, near Hough's country home in Hanover, New Hampshire. "It is easy to understand why this order is made returnable in the most remote point in this district," Roe wrote La Follette, "and why Hough was selected. 'The Masses' are game, however, and I expect to be in Windsor, Vt., a week from today if the trains run and 'The Masses' can raise carfare."[58]

On a personal note, Roe told La Follette that Netha was away for a few days, "looking for some place where we can send the children out of this heat here for a couple of weeks, and still have them near." Roe said he had hoped to spend some time in Washington to work on La Follette's latest legislative initiative, but "[this] Windsor business has put me a good deal up in the air." Having been defeated on both the Espionage Act and the Conscription Act, La Follette was now working on the War Revenue bill to insure that the $2 billion it would raise to finance the war came largely from surplus incomes and war profits. Despite the Windsor interruption, Roe spent a good deal of time on the bill. "Night after night [Roe and La Follette] returned to the office, staying until two o'clock in the morning, drafting amendments, working with experts from the Treasury Department assigned at Bob's request, and assembling data to be used on the Senate floor."[59]

Roe did make it to Windsor, and, again, the argument lasted all day. "The solicitor for the Department [Lamar] was there in person," Roe wrote La Follette. "I have little doubt of the result but at least I raised up a few difficulties which I think they had not anticipated, and made them look rather glum. Anyway, I have a plan blocked out which will keep the *Masses* going, anyway, and, I hope, increase its readers. They are running off more copies this month than ever before."[60] Roe's "plan" apparently included several new initiatives. On August 3, Merrill Rogers personally delivered two copies of that September issue of *The Masses* to the Post Office with the request that they be forwarded to Washington to determine their mailability.[61] Meanwhile, newsboys were hawking copies on the streets, reportedly shouting, "Get your latest issue of *The Masses*, suppressed by the Post Office Department."[62] Additional copies were shipped by express to about three hundred cities and towns, where copies were distributed by news dealers. In addition, letters were sent out to all subscribers urging them to fight the ban. Despite Hand's order, the letters said, "the post office is still exercising bureaucratic powers. We are going to fight this straight through to the Supreme Court. We are not going to swerve one hair's breadth in our policy. We are going to establish, [once and] for all whether free speech in America is a reality or a grim joke." The letter went on to appeal to every subscriber to contact local news dealers and request them to order the magazine in lots of at least ten copies, the smallest number that could be sent economically by express.

On August 6, Hough filed his opinion granting the government's motion to stay Hand's order.[63] The opinion began with Hough acknowledging that his opinion would be, and should be, based on the facts as found by the lower court. "And by facts, I mean, not only facts physical, phenomena seen or heard, but mental conditions or intents." Hough also conceded that the company still had a legally cognizable case, even though the issues in question had already been distributed by other means. On the other hand, the failure to issue a stay in the matter would render any appeal by the government moot. Hough summarized Hand's findings of fact, his test of law, and his conclusion that none of the words or pictures raised by the Post Office Department met the test of "urging upon others that it is their duty or interest to resist the law." The questions before him on this motion, then, were "(1) Is such view of the law correct? (2) Is it so clearly correct that the courts should interfere?" As to the second inquiry, Hough said the courts should not interfere with an executive department in interpreting law that affected it except in the clearest cases, and as to the first, "it is at least arguable whether there can be any more direct incitement to action than to hold up to admiration those who do act." Hough also pointed out that the postal service was not a common carrier but rather was pursuing a high governmental duty. "[It] is at least arguable whether any constitutional government can be judicially compelled to assist in the dissemination and distribution of something which proclaims itself 'revolutionary,' which exists, not to reform, but to destroy, the rule of any party, clique, or faction that could even give lip service to the Constitution of the United States." With that declaration, Hough extended his stay of Hand's order, provided the government post a $10,000 bond to cover any damages that might be awarded the company on appeal.[64]

The same day, August 6, the company delivered another thirteen copies of the September issue to the Post Office and paid second-class postage for their delivery. At the same time, however, Postmaster Patten received instructions from Lamar in Washington to hold any copies of the September issue until further advised. Rogers was informed of those instructions on August 7.[65] The Post Office Department then issued the company an order to show cause why its second-class mailing privilege should not be revoked altogether. The cynical ground for revocation? Since the August issue was not mailed, *The Masses* was no longer being mailed in the regular course of business and was therefore no longer eligible as second-class matter. The order set a hearing on the matter for August 14. Roe argued the case again, in Washington, pointing out that Judge

Hand had ruled that the August issue had been "illegally and wrongfully" barred from the mails, and that the Post Office Department had no right to take advantage of its own wrongful and illegal act to deny the magazine its second-class privilege. He cited a letter from Burleson to Chairman John A. Moon of the House Committee on Post Office and Post Roads declaring that "any publisher who may question the validity of the rulings of the Postoffice Department" has the right of judicial review. "That can only mean that a publisher has the protection of the courts against illegal rulings of the department," Roe said. "But this proposal to bar 'The Masses' from the second class privileges is a plain violation of the assurance given to the public by the Postmaster General that no publisher is wholly at the mercy of the department."[66]

The hearing ended with the third assistant postmaster taking the case under advisement, but the very next day, August 15, Patten received letters from both Lamar and Burleson formally revoking *The Masses'* second-class mailing privileges;[67] Patten so informed the company on August 16. The magazine sent representatives to Hough, who reportedly called Burleson's order "a rather poor joke," but did nothing about it.[68] Roe again moved for an injunction in the U.S. district court to block the action,[69] arguing that Hough's stay had been predicated on his opinion that "any wrong suffered by [The Masses Publishing Co.] can be wholly redressed by damages, apparently (only) measured by the expense of the different transportation arrangements now confessedly perfected."[70] Roe said Hough would have ended the stay had he known that the Post Office planned to attack the magazine's second-class privileges, and he asked the court to require the Post Office Department to order the September issue of the magazine mailed immediately. In reply, Patten submitted a deposition from his superintendent of second-class matter, Frederick Mulker, listing the addressees of the thirteen copies of the magazine on deposit at the Post Office and noting that no instructions had been received from Washington on their mailability.[71] As to the claim that failure to mail those thirteen copies would result in irreparable damages, Mulker quoted an interview that Merrill Rogers gave the *New York Tribune* on August 17. Calling the revocation of second-class privileges a "technical trick to ruin us," Rogers said the magazine would continue to be mailed regularly, at the first-class postage rate if necessary.[72]

This time, Judge Augustus Hand, Learned Hand's cousin, heard Roe's motion for an injunction. "I have spent most of today trying to save the wreck of the second 'Masses' case," Roe wrote La Follette on August 24, "and doubt if I have done it."[73] He was certainly right about that; Hand would come down foursquare for the government on September 12. "The August issue of the

Masses was filled with glorification of those who refused to enlist and violated the law, and the September issue contained similar matter in diluted form," he wrote in a four-page unpublished opinion.[74] "In September, the editor adopted a somewhat milder and less pronounced tone than in August, but continued to hold up violators of the conscription act to admiration and to say what he thought he safely could to promote opposition to the war and to undermine the successful conduct of it." On the technical issue of second-class privileges, Hand asserted that the "position of the Postmaster General that the privilege might be revoked because a magazine which published unlawful matter in some of its issues was not regularly issued within the meaning of the statute seems not unreasonable. That which must be regularly issued is a lawful magazine. If the publication contains matter in violation of law, it ceases to be a mailable publication at all, and hence can lay no claim to regularity of issue. It was for this reason that the *Masses* was held by the Department not to be regularly issued and not for the absurd reason suggested at the argument that transmission had been interrupted by the stay of Judge Hough. A more important ground of revocation than regularity of publication was the illegality of matter contained in recent issues."[75]

In this conclusion, Hand echoed a report that Burleson had provided the Senate on August 22, in which the postmaster denounced the magazine as a leader in organized propaganda to discourage enlistments, prevent subscriptions to the Liberty Loan, and obstruct the draft act.[76] As submitted to Chairman John H. Bankhead (D-Ala.) of the Senate Committee on Post Offices and Post Roads, in response to a Senate resolution of inquiry sponsored by Sen. Thomas Hardwick (D-Ga.), Burleson's report said in the case of *The Masses* and other publications covered by the Harwick resolution, "not only have the particular issues which have been declared to be nonmailable but various other issues of the publication have been taken into consideration in determining their right to the second-class privilege, so that the final action was necessarily based principally on other and very much broader grounds than the break in the continuity of the publication."[77]

At the time Augustus Hand's decision came down, *The Masses* was also facing a threat from the American Defense Society to have the magazine excluded from the New York public libraries.[78] "Since the Postoffice Department has found 'The Masses' too unpatriotic to be sent through the mails, it seems improper that it should be available in the reading rooms of the public libraries," the society's chairman, Richard M. Hurd, declared September 11. "There is no place in America to-day for any literature that cloaks itself in the garb of the enemy. The publishers of such papers are standing close to the treason zone. They have been quietly 'getting over' editorials that are not only false, but are misrepresentative of the aims of the Administration. They serve to incite sedition and treason."

Desperate, Eastman wrote directly to Wilson asking him to review Burleson's actions.[79] Wilson wrote back on September 18: "I think that a time of war must be regarded as wholly exceptional and that it is legitimate to regard things which would in ordinary circumstances be innocent as very dangerous to the public welfare. . . . I can only say that a line must be drawn and that we are trying—it may be clumsily, but genuinely—to draw it without favor or prejudice."[80] Eastman commented on the president's response. "I think the Government is making a grievous mistake in discouraging the popular discussion of the war aims and peace terms," he said. "This is an impractical way to conduct a war for democracy. It is important that when peace is made it should be made not only with the German people, but by the American people. And this will not happen unless the terms of peace are fully and freely discussed beforehand by everybody."[81]

Toward the end of September, Roe spotted yet another existential threat to the magazine. "I notice by the newspapers that they have a Bill in the Senate, I think it has been added as a rider to some other bill, by which it is not only going to be unlawful to publish papers in foreign languages but it is also going to be unlawful to transport via express the magazines which have heretofore been shut out of the mails by the Postmaster," he wrote La Follette's private secretary, John Hannan. "I wish you would get hold of the Bill. . . . I would certainly like to be heard on it. The 'Express' feature of the Bill certainly does put us out of business if it passes."[82] It did pass. On October 6, Congress enacted the bill—known as the Trading with the Enemy Act—that threatened to cut off the last distribution channels remaining for *The Masses*. Specifically, Section 19 of the act, which dealt primarily with regulations governing foreign-language publications, also made it "unlawful for any person, firm, corporation, or association, to transport, carry, or otherwise publish or distribute any matter which is made nonmailable" by the Espionage Act.[83]

On the same day, Burleson finally outlined what could and could not be sent through the mail. "There is a limit. And that limit is reached when it begins to say that this government got into the war wrong, that it is in it for the wrong purpose, or anything that will impugn the motives of the Government for going into war," he said.[84] "They cannot say that this government is a tool of Wall Street or the munitions makers. That kind of thing makes for insubordination in the army and navy and breeds a spirit of disloyalty through the country. It is a false statement, a lie, and it will not be permitted. And nothing can be said exciting people to resist the laws. There can be no campaign against conscription and the Draft Law, nothing that will interfere with enlistments or the raising of an army. There can be nothing said to hamper and obstruct the Government in the prosecution of the war." Department solicitor Lamar added, "You know I am not working in the dark on this censorship thing. I know exactly what I am after. I am after three things and only three things—pro germanism, pacificism, and high browism."[85]

Eastman wrote to Burleson, promising to abide by the regulations and refrain from publishing any matter detrimental to the interests of the United States in its prosecution of the war.[86] He reserved only the right to criticize, as far as it does not give aid to the enemy, and to discuss the demand for peace with freedom of seas, peoples and markets, world unions, and disarmament. Nothing changed; everything would now depend on the decision of the U.S. Court of Appeals for the Second Circuit.

The government's brief for the Second Circuit, submitted on September 16 by Francis G. Caffey, U.S. Attorney for the Southern District of New York, argued that Learned Hand's decision was in error when it declared the August issue of *The Masses* to be mailable, when it disturbed the postmaster general's decision that it was not mailable, and when it granted an injunction, irrespective of the publisher's legal rights.[87] Following a detailed analysis of the Espionage Act, Caffey asserted that the courts had no business interfering with mailability decisions of the postmaster general "unless it appears that he has overstepped his authority or that his action was clearly wrong." To show that the postmaster was *not* wrong as to mailability, Caffey dissected each of the cartoons and texts on which Hand ruled to find that they satisfied the requirements of the Espionage Act, particularly in "attempting to cause" disaffection in the military. Caffey took direct aim at Hand's holding that the law required a publisher to "directly advocate resistance" to the law before being found in violation. "[No] possessor of a free soul fed and nourished upon the seditious diet of the June and July 'Masses' could accept the article on conscientious objectors in the August issue without feeling that it was his duty as such to suffer any punishment rather than obey the Conscription Act." Caffey also found ammunition in Judge Hough's language to the effect that holding violators up to admiration was tantamount to direct incitement, and added even more damning language from another nonmailability case involving the Georgia-based *Jeffersonian*. "Had the Postmaster General longer permitted the use of the great postal system which he controls for the consumption of such poison," wrote U.S. District Court Judge Emory Speer in that case, "it would have been to forego the opportunity to serve his country afforded by his lofty station."

On the second point of his argument—that Hand erred in disturbing the postmaster general's determination that the issue was not mailable—Caffey relied largely on precedent to the effect that, when Congress has entrusted a question of fact, or even a mixed question of fact and law, to the head of a department, the executive's decision "will carry with it a strong presumption of its correctness and the courts will not ordinarily review it." Finding in Hand's own opinion substantial evidence that the postmaster general's position was at least arguable, Caffey concluded that Hand simply "overlooked the well established limitations upon the courts in reviewing the determination of the Postmaster General."

Finally, to show that the injunction was issued in error even if the publisher's rights were violated by the postmaster general's order, Caffey argued that a mandatory injunction to mail the August issue—rather than an injunction that merely preserved the status quo until the case could be heard—was an extraordinary remedy "not to be granted except in the clearest case of a violation of legal rights under circumstances of immediate impending irreparable injury and after careful consideration of the interests of the public as well as those of the parties to the action." In this case, Caffey charged, the injunction was in disregard of the public interest and contrary to public policy; the plaintiff did not come into court with "clean hands" as required for an equitable remedy; and insufficient facts were offered to show immediate impending irreparable injury if the injunction were not issued. Caffey noted that public interest issue had not been raised below, but if it had been, he insisted the outcome would have been other than it was. As to "clean hands," Caffey referred to *The Masses'* claim to be a "revolutionary" magazine: "Compared to this complainant," he quipped, "the historic highwayman who sought in a Court of Equity to obtain an accounting from the partner of his crimes was a petitioner of modest and unassuming disposition." With no facts to show irreparable injury, Hand's order should be reversed, Caffey concluded.

Roe's brief for *The Masses*, filed October 1, sought to separate the violation the magazine allegedly committed—"willfully attempting to cause insubordination, disloyalty, mutiny or refusal of duty" in the military, in Section 3 of Title I of the Espionage Act—from the nonmailability provision in Section 1 of Title XII of the Act. Although the latter referred to matter in violation of any provision of the act, Roe argued that Title I violations were solely focused on espionage and could not relate to "public discussions, expressions of opinion, or to criticism or condemnation of the government, its policies or its laws."[88] Otherwise, Roe said, nonmailability was limited to matter "advocating or urging treason, insurrection, or forcible resistance" under Section 2 of Title XII—none of which were alleged against *The Masses*. Following an overlong and largely unhelpful discussion of antiwar criticism during the Mexican and Boer Wars, Roe turned to the offending text and cartoons from the August issue. Before commenting on each, Roe noted that *The Masses* was in no way pro-German and that it rarely if ever circulated among military members. Roe defended each item, ultimately relying on an opinion in *United States v. Baker*,[89] which acquitted individuals who circulated directly to soldiers literature "which went much further than anything in *The Masses* in its opposition to the draft law and the present war policy."[90]

In the last seven pages of his fifty-eight-page brief, Roe asserted four arguments, the first three of which were implicit in the rest of the brief: "There is nothing in the August issue of *The Masses* that by any possibility can be construed as an advocacy of 'treason, insurrection or forcible resistance to any law of the United States.' There was no evidence before the postmaster of any violation of Section 3 of Title I of the Espionage Act. [And the] defendant postmaster had no authority, under Section 3, Title I, to exclude the entire magazine because he claimed certain articles in it to be unmailable," particularly where the publisher had expressed the willingness to remove any offending material. The final point took just a over a page in the brief: "The Espionage Act, if construed as the Post Office Department construes it, plainly violates the First and Fifth Amendments to the Federal Constitution." Roe cited five cases to support this bare constitutional conclusion that the Act would violate both freedom of the press and due process of law if the government's construction were accurate. There was no analysis or argument on either issue, but, Roe concluded, "this brief is already much too long." In all probability, it would have made no difference in the outcome.

Roe argued *The Masses* case before Circuit Judges Henry G. Ward and Henry W. Rogers and District Judge Julius M. Mayer on October 8.[91] Their decision came less than a month later. In an opinion written by Rogers and joined by Mayer, reversing Learned Hand's injunction, the court made short work of Roe's arguments. "It is the clear intent of title 12 to close the United States mails to any letters or literature in furtherance of any acts prohibited under the other titles of the statute."[92] There would be no de-linking of the espionage title from the mailability title. The opinion answered Roe's First Amendment argument with considerably more discussion than Roe accorded it, but it largely came down to the court's Blackstonian view of the amendment—that freedom of the press consists "in laying no previous restraint upon publications, and not in freedom from censure for criminal matter when published."[93] The court found no prior restraint in the Espionage Act, and no restraint afterward beyond the mailability restrictions. "Liberty of circulating may be essential to freedom of the press, but liberty of circulating through the mails is not, so long as its transportation in any other way as merchandise is not forbidden."[94] The restrictions on alternate means of distribution imposed by the new Trading with the Enemy Act were never raised below, and the court did not address them.

As to Roe's perfunctory Fifth Amendment due process claim, the court cited precedent for the proposition that "due process of law does not necessarily require the interference of the judicial power" and held the Espionage Act constitutional "in so far as it excludes from the mails certain matter declared to be unmailable." As to who makes that declaration, the court held that, where, as here, "the Postmaster General has been authorized . . . to determine whether a particular publication is nonmailable under the law . . . his decision must be regarded as conclusive by the courts, unless it appears that it is clearly wrong." Accordingly, the court once again examined each of the items in the August issue to determine whether the postmaster general was "clearly wrong" about any of them. Considering the "natural and reasonable effect of the publication," only the cartoon "Liberty Bell" survived that test. Finally, the court confronted Hand's opinion that where "one stops short of urging upon others that it is their duty or their interest to resist the law," no violation of the act occurred. "This court does not agree that such is the law." Instead, the court agreed with Judge Hough's view that "to hold up to admiration those who do act" to violate the law constitutes a sufficiently direct incitement to action by the reader. Judge Ward's brief concurrence emphasized the finality of the postmaster general's decision, "whether we agree with him or not," and suggested a bit more breathing room for honest opinion. In the end, though, he agreed that certain of the items in the August issue could have been intended to obstruct recruitment. The court made no mention of Eastman's offer to edit those items out of the August issue.

The defeat was total, and the repercussions were devastating. The day after the decision was filed, Caffey announced that publishers of materials found to be in violation of the Espionage Act could face imminent prosecution unless they took steps at once to comply with the law.[95] On November 19, the federal grand jury indicted seven members of *The Masses* staff and contributors—Eastman, Dell, Rogers, Young, cartoonist Glintenkamp, writer Reed, and bookstore manager Bell—for violating the Espionage Act and conspiracy. Two other indictments for attempting to use the mails for nonmailable material were returned against Masses Publishing Co. and Rogers as business manager. Judge Julius Mayer, who had served on the Second Circuit panel, issued the arrest warrants.⁹⁶ Eastman, Dell, Rogers, and Young entered not-guilty pleas and were released on bond to the custody of their new lawyer, Morris Hillquit.⁹⁷ Bell, whose "A Tribute" was her first published poem, also entered a plea of not guilty and was released on bond.⁹⁸ Reed was still in Europe, trying to return to the United States from Russia, where he had been covering the revolution and working for the Comintern, and Glintenkamp was said to be somewhere in New Jersey when the indictments were handed up.⁹⁹

Immediately following the Second Circuit decision, newspaper and magazine distributors cut off service to *The Masses* and other radical publications in anticipation of the government's enforcement of the Trading with the Enemy Act, which criminalized the handling of publications declared nonmailable.¹⁰⁰ The November-December issue of *The Masses* had just come off the press and had nowhere to go. On December 7, the editors threw in the towel at a party at Tammany Hall. "There is no room in the United States at this time for a free magazine," said a statement issued by Eastman, Dell, Rogers, and Young. "The Masses has made every effort consistent with the intellectual and artistic liberty which is its being to secure from the United States government the privilege of distribution. If we were a hard working, self-supporting paper we could perhaps find means to exist without consent of the government. But being what we are, a luxury like truth and beauty, a child of play and energetic idleness, it is financially impossible for us to survive this organized hostility," they wrote. "To those thirty thousand friends who bought us and read us and believed in us every month, we say farewell until a happier time. We do this with a smile, because between us it is only a proof and an authentication of certain prophetic things we have been saying."¹⁰¹

There was yet one more casualty from this struggle: Judge Learned Hand was passed over for a seat on the U.S. Court of Appeals for the Second Circuit.¹⁰² Hand had known Max Eastman slightly through his wife, Frances, also an ardent suffragist. In 1916, Eastman had asked for Hand's help when Ward & Gow—the distributor of magazines to newsstands in New York City subway stations—refused to distribute *The Masses* because of an allegedly blasphemous poem comparing the Virgin Mary to an unwed mother. Eastman asked Hand to write a letter on the magazine's behalf to a legislative committee holding hearings on the ban. It would be, he said, "the favor of a lifetime." Hand responded that he did not agree with Eastman's ideology, preferring another way, but that "does not blind me to the wisdom of giving you the chance to persuade men of yours." Good or bad, Hand said, yours is a way of "getting men to think and feel about those things in which it is most important that they should think and feel. I can conceive of no possible defense for excluding you except either that such matters must not be discussed, or that they must be discussed only in a way which accords with the common standards of taste. One alternative is tyrannous absolutism, the other, tyrannous priggism." Despite Hand's defense, the ban remained in force. When *The Masses'* 1917 case was assigned to him, Hand told Frances that he found nothing illegal in the magazine's content. "I should think that in fairness I should be obliged to protect them," he said. But he also recognized the danger to his career. If his decision went against the government, he wrote, "then whoop-la your little man is in the mud." Still, he said, "I must do the right as I see it. . . . There are times when the old bunk about an independent and fearless judiciary means a good deal. This is one of them, and if I have limitations of judgment, I may have to suffer for it, but I want to be sure that these are the only limitations and that I have none of character."

In the months following the Second Circuit decision, Judge Augustus Hand would preside over the first trial of *The Masses'* staff and contributors. He dismissed all counts of the indictment against Josephine Bell and the conspiracy counts against everyone else.[103] He left the charge of obstructing recruiting and enlistment to the jury, which could not reach a unanimous decision. Hand declared a mistrial. A second trial commenced after Judge Learned Hand refused to quash the remaining indictments. This time, the defendants—including John Reed—were represented by Seymour Stedman, Charles Recht, and Walter Nelles and tried before Judge Martin Manton. Again, the jury deadlocked; they were discharged on October 5, 1918, and the government declined to prosecute further. *The Masses'* ordeal was over, but the magazine was dead. Gilbert Roe played no role in the criminal trials, although he did serve as a resource for Hillquit. Roe had dedicated countless hours to the cause of *The Masses* and its editors, before and during the war, with little prospect of remuneration. There is nothing in the record to show that his services were either sought or rejected following the Second Circuit opinion. In fact, Roe was working "under high pressure" on a private lawsuit involving more than a million dollars during December 1917.[104]

7

The Pacifists II

> [It] is extremely dangerous to exercise the constitutional right of free speech in a country fighting to make democracy safe for the world. . . . I would rather a thousand times be a free soul in jail than a sycophant or coward on the streets.
>
> Eugene Debs

> For the first time in all our history . . . the federal government has virtually silenced all critical or hostile discussion of war policies. . . . It is that fact which calls upon this court to re-establish the faith of the people of this country in their constitution and its guarantees of free speech and free press.
>
> Gilbert Roe

The La Follette Expulsion Case

"Probably you know that I decided last moment to go with Bob to St. Paul. . . . The St. Paul and Toledo meetings were wonderful beyond imagination and description. They satisfied me as nothing other than the experiences of being there could—how the American people—the working people and the farmers are thinking and feeling."[1] At the time she wrote this letter to Netha Roe, Belle Case La Follette could not have known that Robert La Follette's St. Paul speech of September 20, 1917, would begin one of the most difficult chapters in their personal and political lives. With *The Masses* cases behind him, Gilbert Roe would spend more and more of his time in Washington when his dearest friend needed him most.[2]

The personal vilification of Robert La Follette for his opposition to World War I began even before the United States entered the war. At least as early as the La Follette–led filibuster that resulted in the defeat of the Armed Ship bill in early March 1917 and President Wilson's angry reaction to it, La Follette became the target of editorial writers and political cartoonists throughout the country, not to mention his own Senate colleagues. Among the epithets used to describe La Follette and his handful of allies: wretches, knaves, delinquents, dastards, perverts, unsocialized creatures, and, most frequently, traitors.[3] When the *New York Telegram* depicted the ghost of Benedict Arnold gazing at La Follette and four other senators in a cartoon entitled "And They Called Me Traitor," Roe responded angrily: "I am enclosing a cartoon from the *Evening Telegram*, which is the most atrocious libel I ever saw," he wrote. "I never yet have advised the bringing of a libel suit, but it seems to me that it might be a wholesome thing to do in this case. I also enclose an editorial from the New York *Times* this morning, which, while not as extreme as that of some that have been published, you will notice refers to 'the eleven Senators who conspired against their country.'"[4]

Following the president's request for declaration of war, La Follette came in for additional rounds of vicious personal attacks when he voted against the declaration resolution,[5] when he challenged the president's War Revenue bill,[6] and, again, when he introduced a resolution calling for a declaration of war objectives that would ultimately lead to an early and lasting peace. The latter, which Roe helped to craft, drew the ire of Sen. Atlee Pomerene (D-Ohio), who would become La Follette's principal nemesis over the next year or so, and the first to talk of expelling La Follette from the Senate.

The event that actually triggered expulsion proceedings, however, was a speech that La Follette gave in St. Paul on September 20, 1917, in response to an invitation from the Nonpartisan League to discuss the high cost of living. There, to a mostly supportive audience of farmers and workers, La Follette spoke extemporaneously about his opposition to the war. "I don't mean to say that we hadn't suffered grievances [against Germany].... They had interfered with the right of American citizens to travel upon the high seas—on ships loaded with munitions for Great Britain." To both heckles and cheers, he continued: "I say this, that the comparatively small privilege of the right of an American citizen to ride on a munition-loaded ship, flying a foreign flag, is too small to involve this Government in the loss of millions and millions of lives." Pressed to address the *Lusitania* specifically, La Follette added: "Four days before the *Lusitania* sailed, President Wilson was warned in person by Secretary of State Bryan, that the *Lusitania* had six million rounds of ammunition on board, besides explosives; and that the passengers who proposed to sail on that small vessel were sailing in violation of a statute in this country. . . . And Secretary Bryan appealed to President Wilson to stop passengers from sailing on the *Lusitania*."

The audience reaction was very positive, which accounts for Belle's high spirits, but an overnight dispatch from the Associated Press reported La Follette as saying "We had no grievance against Germany" and defending the sinking of the *Lusitania*. Theodore Roosevelt called for La Follette's expulsion from the Senate, as did Nicholas Murray Butler, president of Columbia University. La Follette found a more supportive audience in Toledo, where he tried to correct the record regarding his St. Paul speech, but the damage had already been done. On September 29, 1917, the Senate received a resolution from the Minnesota Public Safety Commission petitioning for La Follette's expulsion on the ground that his St. Paul speech was "disloyal and seditious . . . giving aid and comfort to our enemies and hindering the Government in the conduct of the war."[7] It was one petition among many, but it became the focal point for the Senate's deliberations on expulsion.

The resolution had been introduced by Sen. Frank B. Kellogg (R-Minn.) and was referred to the Committee on Privileges and Elections on which Kellogg sat.[8] Kellogg asked the State Department for information concerning Bryan's alleged conversation with the president regarding the *Lusitania*, prompting Bryan—who had resigned in June 1915, shortly after the sinking—to telephone La Follette to say he would publicly deny any such conversation. The State Department also denied any such conversation. On October 5, the committee appointed a subcommittee to investigate the facts in La Follette's speech. The subcommittee was chaired by full committee chairman Atlee Pomerene and included Thomas J. Walsh (D-Montana), Ollie M. James (D-Kentucky), William P. Dillingham (R-Vermont), and Albert B. Fall (R-New Mexico).[9] On October 6, the last day of the first session of the 65th Congress, La Follette gave a three-hour speech defending his position, which was followed by speeches denouncing La Follette from Sens. Kellogg, Fall, and Joseph T. Robinson (D-Ark.).

Gilbert Roe had spent most of his time in Washington during early October, putting together La Follette's defense strategy in the Senate and also considering when and how to file libel suits against the newspapers that had misrepresented the St. Paul speech.[10] The first task was to obtain an accurate copy of the speech itself from the official stenographer on the scene and to provide it to the subcommittee. A certified copy of the speech was transmitted to the subcommittee on October 11, along with a cover letter from La Follette asking to be heard in person and by counsel if any portion of the speech were challenged.[11] Pomerene acknowledged receipt the next day and invited La Follette to attend the next meeting of the committee on October 16 where he could attest to the accuracy of his statements. La Follette—and Roe, who was deeply involved in drafting this correspondence—responded that the procedure Pomerene suggested was "most extraordinary and wholly unprecedented," in that La Follette was expected to support the accuracy of facts presented in his speech which Pomerene had not identified as having been challenged, nor by whom or in what manner. He specifically asked, as a condition of his appearing on October 16, to be told which statements were challenged as inaccurate, to be given any evidence gathered by the subcommittee, and to be accorded the right of cross-examination.

Pomerene acceded to all of the procedural demands, but insisted that the committee had not challenged any of the facts in the speech; rather, he said, the subcommittee wanted La Follette to provide his sources for all of them. When the subcommittee convened the following day, La Follette delivered a written statement—"all the statement that I deem it proper or necessary for me to make at this time"—bid the committee "good morning," and left. In his written statement, La Follette reasserted his position that he would defend the accuracy of any statement challenged by adverse evidence, but not before the committee advised him of any such challenge and made any such evidence available to him. The committee went into executive session and then adjourned until November 26.

On October 26, La Follette wrote Pomerene requesting a list of witnesses expected to appear at the November 26 hearing, as well as a list of documents the subcommittee planned to consider.[12] Pomerene's response on November 5 assured La Follette that he would have an opportunity to cross-examine witnesses and examine documents before any decisions were made, but it was evasive as to La Follette's request for specific information as to what facts would be at issue. Based on newspaper accounts, however, La Follette and Roe had already assumed that La Follette's assertion that the *Lusitania* was carrying munitions bound for England would be high on any list the subcommittee might produce.[13] Accordingly, they set out to collect hard evidence of that fact, apart from rumors published in the newspapers at the time, but they were denied official records by the State Department. Roe then arranged for La Follette to meet with Dudley Field Malone, the Collector of the Port of New York, who had written a report based on the ship's manifest. The meeting took place on November 4 at the apartment of La Follette's daughter, Fola, and son-in-law, George Middleton, and Malone promised to provide a copy of his report, which showed that the ship carried thousands of cases of ammunition to England.

In any event, the November 26 hearing was postponed until January 8, in the next session of Congress; in fact, it was postponed several more times and would not begin until May 21, 1918.[14] Various reasons have been cited for the delay, including Bryan's reluctance to testify under oath, Wilson's desire to prevent La Follette from becoming a martyr,[15] and the persistence of Bob Jr.'s severe lung infection. Roe saw the latter reason as an attempt to put the burden of the delay on La Follette. "This, of course, is a damn fraud," he wrote John Hannan, La Follette's private secretary. On Roe's instructions, Hannan wrote Pomerene that the Senator was ready to proceed eight weeks before his son's illness and never requested a delay.

During the six months between the first scheduled hearing and the actual hearing, La Follette and Roe continued to collect information that might be useful to their cause, and Roe set about preparing a brief in support of La Follette to submit to the subcommittee. But several other matters also required Roe's attention, including preparing for the final phases of the *Flagg* case, consulting with Morris Hillquit in *The Masses* criminal cases,[16] and advising La Follette's Madison attorneys, Crownhart & Wylie, regarding the several libel cases they filed on the senator's behalf.

By the spring of 1918, it appeared that the expulsion hearings would finally proceed, but the focus had shifted from the subcommittee's investigation into the factual accuracy of the St. Paul speech to the full committee's inquiry into the general charge of disloyalty. On April 24, Roe wrote to Pomerene asserting that "the charges of the Minnesota Commission on Public Safety present nothing for the consideration of the Senate or your Committee" and asking to be heard on a motion to dismiss any charges against La Follette.[17] On May 9, Roe sent another letter to Pomerene, reiterating his call for a hearing at the earliest possible date, whether or not La Follette was able to attend personally on account of his son's illness.[18] Roe sent yet a third letter to Pomerene on May 13, after reading in the newspapers that the committee would meet on the fifteenth "to dispose" of the charges. Again, Roe asked to be heard, and again, he asserted the argument that the primary issue before the committee was whether La Follette had a right to make the St. Paul speech; and if he did, the charge of disloyalty must be dismissed.[19] The committee met on May 15 and decided to schedule a meeting to hear Roe at the earliest mutually convenient time.[20] That proved to be May 21, although Bob Jr.'s condition prevented La Follette from attending. Roe had submitted copies of a brief he prepared for each member that argued that La Follette's speech afforded no reason for expulsion, and, therefore, there was nothing in the Minnesota report for the Senate to consider.[21]

When the committee convened on May 21, Roe reframed the question in his opening statement: "whether this speech made at that time and under those circumstances is such evidence of disloyalty—that is the charge—as to justify a Senator or Senators in saying on their oath and their conscience and under the Constitution that the Senator making it is unfit to be a Member of the United States Senate." Roe led the committee through a long series of expulsion precedents, which, he said, led to the conclusion that, if a senator "believes that the war is wrong, he is at liberty to say so under the Constitution." Roe pointed out that although La Follette opposed going to war and conscription, "yet, the country having declared war, he has simply taken the position that he recognizes that as the will of the Government lawfully expressed." Out of approximately sixty war measures enacted since that time, Roe said, La Follette opposed only one. Compared to analogous historical examples, he has taken a much more moderate position, "which is absolutely . . . beyond the possibility of criticism if any individual opinion, if any freedom of opinion and action is to remain." Roe next took the committee through a lengthy, line-by-line analysis of the St. Paul speech itself, then submitted his brief for the record as the first day of the hearing came to a close. The hearing reopened on May 23, with a discussion of a Memorandum of Information, a collection of precedents in Espionage Act cases compiled by the Justice Department at the committee's request.[22] Neither Roe nor La Follette had ever seen the compilation; it came to Roe's attention only because a senator had been reading from it during the first day of the hearing.[23]

In his substantive testimony, Roe addressed the most controversial aspects of La Follette's speech. First, he took on the distortion of La Follette's statement: "I was not in favor of beginning the war. I don't mean to say that we hadn't suffered grievances. We had. Serious grievances. We had cause for complaint." Every Associated Press account of that statement, Roe said, was rendered: "I was not in favor of beginning the war. We had no grievance." On the critical passage regarding the *Lusitania*, Roe quoted La Follette as saying that the American rights infringed by the sinking included the "right of some person to ride upon a munition-laden vessel in violation of an American statute that no vessel that carries explosives shall carry passengers." The members debated whether the Passenger Act referenced here prevented passenger ships from carrying explosives, or munitions ships from carrying passengers, and whether La Follette intended to say the sinking was the sole cause of the war. Roe denied the latter, but conceded that La Follette may have used "loose language" in describing the statute. In any event, he said, it never occurred to him that La Follette meant to impugn the administration's failure to stop the ship or the passengers as had been requested by Secretary Bryan.

The focus of debate shifted briefly to the Senate's power to punish or expel La Follette. Roe maintained that the Constitution provided no power to censure the senator for anything that did not involve "disorderly behavior," but that the Senate's power to expel was unlimited. After making that point, Roe told Chairman Pomerene that he had finished the outline of his argument. "I hardly need invite questions, because I know they will be asked me anyhow," he said.

They were, indeed, but broke no new ground, and the hearing adjourned at 6:10 p.m., with Roe being given an opportunity to submit a reply brief. Roe's reply brief, which was submitted June 6 and incorporated into the hearing record, began by discussing the Memorandum of Information that—"through an oversight," he said charitably—was never sent to La Follette or to himself. Roe said the collection of Espionage Act precedents was unhelpful, even misleading, since the issue before the committee had nothing to do with violating the Espionage Act. He also argued that congressional precedents and definitions of treason, included in what he called "the pamphlet," were just as irrelevant. "This entire case against Senator La Follette is a case of 'much ado about nothing,'" Roe concluded.

Appended to Roe's reply brief, and to the hearing record as well, was a letter from Frederick Roy Martin, assistant general manager of the Associated Press. Dated May 23, the letter claimed to have first learned of the misquotation from the hearings. The story was written by a reporter for the *St. Paul Pioneer Press*, the letter said, but the error was introduced by careless editing. "The error was regrettable and the Associated Press seizes the first opportunity to do justice to Senator La Follette." The hearings, including the Associated Press's error, were widely reported in the press. An editorial in the *New York Evening Post* said the misquotation had done irreparable injury to La Follette. "Whether this was done maliciously or accidentally will probably never be known," the paper said. "No amount of apology can undo it."[24] There was no further action on La Follette's expulsion throughout the summer and fall, but the November elections brought the matter to a head. The new Senate included 49 Republicans and 47 Democrats; one Republican vote could determine which party would organize and effectively run the Senate. In the end, the committee voted 9–2 to dismiss, with Pomerene and Walsh dissenting. On January 16, 1919, the Senate voted 50–21 in favor of the committee report dismissing the charges.

The Debs Case

About a month after Gilbert Roe testified against La Follette's expulsion, another antiwar politician gave a public address that proved even more problematic than La Follette's speech in St. Paul. Eugene V. Debs, labor leader and perennial socialist presidential candidate, addressed a Canton, Ohio, audience on June 16, 1918, primarily on the subject of socialism. But Debs's comments on the war and the draft ran afoul of the Espionage Act as interpreted in those days. His subsequent conviction was appealed to the U.S. Supreme Court.[25] The decision in *Debs* was one of the first four Espionage Act decisions to reach the high court and helped set the stage for a complete—if gradual—reappraisal of the First Amendment. Gilbert Roe was not an original member of the defense team, but his amicus curiae or friend-of-the-court brief certainly contributed to that reappraisal. It was so compelling that the government felt obliged to submit a reply brief solely to address Roe's constitutional argument. Debs lost his case, but the quartet of cases—*Schenck*,[26] *Sugarman*,[27] *Frohwerk*,[28] and *Debs*—became the bridge between old and dramatically new First Amendment doctrines.

Born in 1855, Debs began his union career as a railroad worker, advancing to become secretary-treasurer of the Brotherhood of Locomotive Firemen in the early 1880s.[29] In the beginning, Debs was relatively conservative in orientation, tending to favor the traditional craft union concept of the American Federation of Labor over the burgeoning industrial union movement. Several failed strikes in the late 1880s prompted him to move to the left in his thinking, and in 1893, he became president of a new American Railway Union, which was both more inclusive and more confrontational than the brotherhoods had been. Debs rose to national prominence in the aftermath of the ARU's strike and boycott against the Pullman Palace Car Company, for which Debs was ultimately convicted of contempt for violating a federal court order.[30] In prison, Debs completed his conversion to socialism.[31] Indeed, Max Eastman would later call him the "spiritual chief and hero" of American socialism.[32] Debs was one of the founding members of the Industrial Workers of the World in 1905, but he later split with the IWW and Big Bill Haywood over its more anarchistic tendencies and cast his lot with the so-called parliamentary socialists such as Morris Hillquit and Victor Berger.[33]

Debs delivered his 1918 Canton speech to the Ohio Socialist Convention, and he opened with a warning about speaking freely that, in retrospect, rings prophetic: "[It] is extremely dangerous to exercise the constitutional right of free speech in a country fighting to make democracy safe in the world," Debs said. "I realize in speaking to you this afternoon that there are certain limitations placed on the right of free speech. I must be extremely careful, prudent, as to what I say, and even more careful and prudent as to how I say it."[34] However cautious Debs might have been, he was not cautious enough. Among other things, he spoke admiringly of "loyal comrades" Charles E. Ruthenberg, Alfred Wagenknecht, and Charles Baker, who were serving time for violations of the

The Pacifists II

Selective Draft Law,[35] of Kate Richards O'Hare, convicted of violating the Espionage Act by obstructing the enlistment service,[36] and of Rose Pastor Stokes, also convicted of violating the Espionage Act for attempting to cause insubordination in the military.[37] "I want to say that if Rose Pastor Stokes is guilty, so am I," Debs declaimed. "If she is sent to the penitentiary for ten years, so ought I."[38]

If *The Masses* case proved anything, it was that, as interpreted by the government and most courts, praising antiwar activists was tantamount to inciting listeners to emulate their crimes, and Debs was duly indicted. His trial began on September 9, 1918, in the federal courthouse in Cleveland. When the prosecution finished its case, the defense rested, and Debs addressed the jury. He admitted giving the Canton speech, and he admitted expressing "my perfect sympathy" for his imprisoned comrades. His sole purpose, he said, was to "educate the people to understand something about the social system in which we live, and to prepare them to change this system by perfectly peaceable and orderly means into what I, as a Socialist, conceive to be a real democracy." In his wide-ranging speech, Debs reminded the jury of the plain language of the First Amendment, then left his fate in their hands. "What you may choose to do to me will be of small consequence after all. I am not on trial here. . . . American institutions are on trial here before a court of American citizens. The future will tell." The jury found Debs guilty, and following another long speech by Debs, the judge sentenced him to ten years in prison.

Debs's legal team was headed by Seymour Stedman, who would later be the Socialist Party vice-presidential candidate, assisted by William Cunnea.[39] Two lawyers who worked on the *Ruthenberg* case, Joseph Sharts and Morris H. Wolf, were also on board, as was Morris Hillquit, socialist lawyer and political figure, for a time. For the appeal to the U.S. Supreme Court, Isaac E. Ferguson helped with the main brief, and Gilbert Roe entered as amicus curiae. Stedman's brief asserted all of the technical errors one would expect: that the indictment failed to state a crime, that certain evidence was improperly admitted, that the jury instructions were flawed. But it also advanced a First Amendment argument that paralleled and reinforced Debs's speech to the jury. The brief put the issue squarely before the court: "What degree of tolerance of minority sentiments is to be read out of or into the American Bill of Rights in the year 1919 by the court of last resort?"[40] The brief argued that, of all published decisions under the Espionage Act, only Learned Hand's opinion in *Masses* could be reconciled with the First Amendment. In all other cases, "the trial and Circuit appellate judges have easily swept it aside."

Stedman went on to discuss the Hand opinion in *Masses* at great length and, taking the Second Circuit's opinion into account, fashioned an "unsatisfactory" but workable rule that only a "purposeful urging, by direct or indirect means, of insubordination or refusal of duty in the military service, or purposeful obstruction, by like means, of the recruiting service" can constitute a violation of the Espionage Act. "Search this speech through from first to last, and what is there in it that may be read as an incitement or encouragement toward dereliction of military or civic duty in relation to the war?" he demanded, ultimately finding "not one syllable" meeting that test. Instead, he said, the government's case was based solely on a notion of a criminal "intent derivable in law," based on no evidence whatsoever, from the "reasonable and natural consequences" of the Canton speech. "Freedom of speech, as enunciated by the First Amendment, must be declared in the broad terms of its universal understanding as the primary condition of human progress," Stedman's brief concluded. "No precision of judicial logic will give credence to any other reading of the First Amendment."

In his amicus brief, Roe explained that he was representing Louis B. Nagler before the Supreme Court. Since *Debs* would be argued before *Nagler*, Roe sought and received authority to enter as a friend of the court. "Because of my interest in other litigation involving the same questions as those involved in [*Debs*]," he said, "I am particularly desirous of having called to the attention of this Court those authorities and suggestions which seem to me to bear upon the questions decided."[41] Roe's brief purposefully avoided any discussion of error specific to the Debs case—in fact, the brief was initially drafted for a different case altogether—but it does meticulously dissect the Espionage Act to show that most of the courts hearing cases under the act have misconstrued it. "The most that any jury or any judge can say about any language of a speech or article in the absence of any evidence that it produced a particular effect, is that it would have a tendency to produce the results complained of, and that is the manner in which the instructions have been given in most of the cases prosecuted under . . . the Espionage Law."

The rest of the brief was devoted to the First Amendment analysis, beginning with the assertion that the act was unconstitutional "if construed and applied so as to punish any individual for speaking or publishing his opinions on any measures of the government." Roe argued that the Bill of Rights generally, and the First Amendment in particular, were designed to limit all other powers of government, including the power to make war. "[If], for example, an army cannot be raised without abridging freedom of the press, the army will not be raised, and an army ought not to be raised unless it can be done in spite of every reason that can be urged against it," Roe declared. "Clearly, freedom of speech and of the press meant to the Fathers of the Constitution the right to discuss every act of the government, whether to praise, condemn or threaten," Roe argued. "For the first time in all our history, this constitutional right has been denied and the federal government has virtually silenced all critical or hostile discussion of war policies.... It is that fact which calls upon this court to re-establish the faith of the people of this country in their constitution and its guarantees of free speech and free press."

The government was represented by John Lord O'Brian and Alfred Bettman, both appointed special assistants to the attorney general for Espionage Act cases. Their principal brief rebutted each of the "errors" cited in Stedman's brief and then made a First Amendment argument that freedom of speech was not absolute and that intentional incitement to violation of law and deliberate obstruction of raising armies were not protected.[42] The government's reply to Roe's brief rejected the notion that Debs was prosecuted for hostile criticism of the war. "He was prosecuted for a willful and deliberate attempt to obstruct the execution of a Government policy, namely, to obstruct the process of raising an army, unprotected by any definition of free speech," the brief said.[43] The brief rebutted, point by point, Roe's historical analysis, rejecting in particular his assertion that the Bill of Rights was adopted to destroy British tyranny rather than to perpetuate it. "This court . . . has repeatedly stated that the early amendments of the Constitution were designed to preserve certain liberties, which had been won and become fixed in the Constitution of England."[44]

Oral arguments in the case were heard on January 27 and 28, 1919; La Follette wrote his family on the last day of argument that Roe's brief was "exceptionally fine and '*must make an impression on the Court*—if there is anything there left to impress.'"[45] Apparently, the court was not impressed at all. When the decision was issued on March 10, Debs's conviction was affirmed by a unanimous court. Justice Holmes wrote the short opinion, resolving the case on the ground that the trial court's evidentiary decisions were correct. The First Amendment question had been "disposed of" in Holmes's opinion in *Schenck*, decided a week earlier.[46] Charles T. Schenck had been general secretary of the Socialist Party before he was convicted of distributing a circular calculated to cause insubordination in the military and obstruction of the enlistment service.[47] Schenck had admitted that a jury might rule against them on a "bad tendency" instruction. But he argued that, even so, his writings were nevertheless protected by the First Amendment. Holmes conceded that, Blackstone notwithstanding, the First Amendment does more than prohibit prior restraints. He was even willing to concede that, "in many places and in ordinary times," the defendants' speech might have been so protected. "But the . . . most stringent protection of free speech would not protect a man in falsely shouting fire in a theatre and causing a panic," he wrote. "It does not even protect a man from an injunction against uttering words that may have all the effect of force."

> The question in every case is whether the words used are used in such circumstances and are of such a nature as to create a clear and present danger that they will bring about the substantive evils that Congress has a right to prevent.... When a nation is at war many things that might be said in a time of peace are such a hindrance to its effort that their utterance will not endure so long as men fight and that no Court could regard them as protected by any constitutional right.

Although this "clear and present danger" test would come to have a far more protective meaning than the "bad tendency" test, that had not happened yet. According to Holmes, if the tendency of the act of speaking or circulating a paper, and the intent with which it is done, are the same, "we perceive no ground for saying that success alone warrants making the act a crime." Debs was imprisoned in the federal penitentiary in Atlanta, where he ran as the Socialist Party candidate for president in 1920. In 1921, President Harding commuted his sentence. He died in 1926.

As to the other two decisions in this famous quartet, the *Sugarman* opinion was written by Justice Brandeis and published the same day as *Schenck*. It affirmed the conviction of Abraham L. Sugarman for an antiwar address at a socialist meeting in Minnesota.[48] Jacob Frohwerk was a writer for a German language newspaper, the *Missouri StaatsZeitung*, and was convicted of publishing a dozen articles in violation of the Espionage Act.[49] Again, the court affirmed the conviction. And again, Holmes deferred to his decision in *Schenck* to dispose of any constitutional issue. Although Holmes would gradually adopt a more protective interpretation of the First Amendment, he would never renounce his decisions in the first Espionage Act cases to reach the Supreme Court.[50] Roe, however, thought those decisions set back the First Amendment two centuries,[51] and he continued to attack the Espionage Act, in his writing and in the courtroom, through the early 1920s.

The Stephens Case

Roe could not have known the outcome of the *Debs* case when he wrote "The Espionage Law" for the March 1919 issue of *Pearson's Magazine*, but the short article closely tracked his *Debs* brief in laying out the historical and practical reasons why the law was unconstitutional.[52] Asserting that "public opinion is looked to in this country to shape political policies," Roe said, there is "every reason, therefore, to allow the freest and fullest discussion of every matter connected with the war." As a result of the Espionage Law, however, "[w]e are now reaping the first bitter fruits of the policy which has suppressed free speech and free discussion of war issues." In particular, Roe condemned the suppression of any criticism of how the war was financed. "Anyone who wishes to discuss the proper financing of the present war runs a risk of being prosecuted for violation of the Espionage Law, since his argument may possibly discourage the purchase of Liberty Bonds." Indeed, one of Roe's clients had found himself in exactly that predicament just a year earlier. For Frank Stephens, however, the outcome was better than for most Espionage Act defendants.

Stephens was a prominent Philadelphia sculptor who had been a protégé of Thomas Eakins at the Pennsylvania Academy of Fine Arts, until that relationship ended with Stephens alleging that Eakins had committed sexual misconduct with his students—including Stephens's sister. In 1900, Stephens and architect Will Price founded the utopian community of Arden, Delaware, based on the principles of socialist Henry George, who believed that a single tax on land, rather than on labor, would yield the most equitable distribution of wealth. Upton Sinclair, Scott Nearing, and other prominent socialists lived in Arden from time to time.[53] On April 16, 1918, Stephens allegedly confronted a Liberty Bond seller named Mabel F. Van Trump, calling her a "murderer," along with anyone else who sold the bonds. "[You] are sending our soldiers abroad to be murdered," he reportedly said. "[No] lady would be out on such an errand as you." The following month, a federal grand jury in Delaware indicted Stephens for violating the Espionage Act in that his outburst was "willfully made by him with intent to interfere with the operation and success of the military and naval forces of the United States."[54]

The record does not show how Gilbert Roe came to represent Stephens, along with his local lawyer, Phillip L. Garrett. But Roe had many acquaintances in the single tax movement, including Free Speech League colleague Bolton Hall, and Upton Sinclair had lived in Arden from 1910 to 1912.[55] In any event, two weeks after the indictment was handed up, Roe filed a demurrer on Stephens's behalf, charging that the indictment was insufficient for failing to specify any facts that might constitute a crime under the Espionage Act and, in any case, the act was unconstitutional under the First, Fifth, and Sixth Amendments to the Constitution.[56] On June 10, Circuit Judge Victor B. Woolley overruled the demurrer, and the *Stephens* case went to trial on June 20. According to a contemporaneous account,[57] Roe asked Stephens whether he had any intention, by his conversation, of interfering with the operation of the military forces of our country. "None whatever," Stephens answered, asserting that he had many close friends who purchased the bonds and never tried to discourage them. He also denied that he had advised his son Donald not to register for the draft. A leader in the People's Council of America for Democracy and Peace, Stephens did assert his own conscientious objection to war: "I am a pacifist; a peace maker; one who stands for peace." In charging the jury, Judge Woolley rejected Roe's argument that the type of speech punishable under the Espionage Act was protected by the Constitution and said jurors need not concern themselves with that question. "The main questions for you to consider are, whether the words attributed to the accused were said by him, and if so, whether they were said in violation of the statute." Woolley told the jury that if the words constituted nothing more than opinion they should find Stephens not guilty. After several hours of deliberation, that is exactly what they did.

The following month, Stephens wrote to Netha Roe. "So far as I am concerned, it was worth all the experience cost me to become acquainted as I did with your husband," he said. "Truly I think him very wonderful, his handling of the case admirable beyond praise."[58] Stephens told Netha he believed his case was "of great importance with reference to similar prosecutions, and your husband has done a great work against great odds with the certainty of much greater results than are concerned with my being in prison or not."

The Nagler Case

Roe handled a number of Espionage Act and related cases throughout 1918–20. Some required trial work, like the Stephens case, including one court martial at Camp Dix, New Jersey.[59] Much of the work involved negotiating with the government, as in a series of letters between Roe and the U.S. Army seeking a reduction in the sentence of Amerigo V. Alexander, a socialist convicted by court martial.[60] Roe also handled the appeals in cases tried elsewhere, including two that reached the U.S. Supreme Court.

Before entering politics, Louis B. Nagler had been a farmer, schoolteacher, and newspaper publisher. In 1905 he began working as a journal clerk for the Wisconsin State Assembly and, two years later, became chief clerk in the office of the Secretary of State. He served as assistant secretary of state for Wisconsin for six years in the McGovern and Philipp administrations. And he claimed Robert La Follette as a personal friend.[61] On November 14, 1917, while in office, Nagler was approached for a contribution to the YMCA. Years earlier, Nagler's wife had been denied the use of a YMCA auditorium for her liberal debating

The Pacifists II

association while at the University of Minnesota, and Nagler told the solicitors, Paul E. Stark and S. T. Walker, that he "had a prejudice against the YMCA, had never contributed, and could not do it." According to subsequent grand jury findings, Nagler's response was a little more colorful: "I am through contributing to your private graft. . . . No, I do not believe in the work of the Y.M.C.A. or the Red Cross, for I believe they are nothing but a bunch of grafters."[62] On November 19, the last day of the YMCA fund-raising drive, Nagler was again approached, this time by Cyril Marks and Charles H. Thompson. Again, Nagler refused, and, according to the grand jury, "planting his fist on the table and his face coloring with anger, he said I won't give you a cent. The Y.M.C.A., the Y.W.C.A. and the Red Cross [are] a bunch of grafters. Not over ten to fifteen percent of the money collected goes to the soldiers. . . . Who is running this war? A bunch of capitalists composed of the steel trust and munitions makers." Nagler would later deny that he made the more incendiary of these remarks, and he asserted that the solicitors went out of their way to insult La Follette, whose picture was on Nagler's desk.[63] In any event, a federal grand jury in Madison believed Nagler's accusers and handed up an indictment on December 8, 1917, charging Nagler with making false statements with the intent to interfere with the YMCA and Red Cross in collecting the funds necessary to support the war effort. That, the grand jury charged, was tantamount to interfering with the American military and a violation of the Espionage Act.[64]

As befits a friend of La Follette, Nagler was represented at trial by Crownhart & Wylie, with Burr Jones of counsel. U.S. Attorney Albert C. Wolfe represented the government, along with special assistant attorney general B. R. Goggins. After an extended delay, Crownhart & Wylie filed a motion to quash the indictment on July 23, 1918, arguing principally that nothing Nagler might have said about the YMCA or the Red Cross could be construed as referring to "the military or naval forces of the United States,"[65] notwithstanding various proclamations and executive orders introduced by the government to show the contrary.[66] They also argued that Nagler's words regarding those organizations "were not reasonably adapted" to interfere with military operations. Two days later, Acting District Judge Evan A. Evans denied the motion,[67] holding that the term "military or naval forces" could not "fairly be defined or construed so as to exclude either the Red Cross or the YMCA." Clearly miscalculating the temper of the times, Crownhart & Wylie had argued that if the YMCA and the Red Cross were deemed "military or naval forces" then any false statement spoken with bad intent against the Knights of Columbus, the Salvation Army, or the Jewish Relief organization would be a violation of the Espionage Act. Evans agreed, finding all of those organizations part of the war effort.

Nagler was found guilty and sentenced to thirty months in the federal penitentiary at Leavenworth, Kansas.[68] On November 15, 1918, Crownhart & Wylie filed an application for a writ of error in the U.S. Supreme Court, noting sixty points of error below.[69] Gilbert Roe would take over from there. Whether the result of Roe's negotiating skills, increasing distance from the war itself, or an uncharacteristic outbreak of common sense in Washington, Solicitor General William L. Frierson confessed error on the part of the government, and Nagler's conviction was reversed on October 20, 1920.[70]

The O'Connell Case

If the La Follette expulsion hearing was more political theater than serious loyalty trial, and the *Debs, Stephens*, and *Nagler* cases seemed egregiously contrived, even by wartime standards, the *O'Connell* case that Roe took to the Supreme Court involved a very real conspiracy. Despite Roe's eleventh-hour efforts, the outcome was serious prison time for its leader.

On the evening of August 8, 1917, San Francisco attorney Daniel O'Connell, founder of American Patriots, a newly formed organization dedicated to resisting the draft, was arrested while attending a political meeting. A federal marshal told O'Connell he was under arrest on federal conspiracy charges and handed him a warrant listing more than a dozen alleged co-conspirators.[71] O'Connell took the rostrum and read the charges to the audience, which responded with "cheers, hisses, catcalls and shouts of derision." As he was being escorted out of the hall, O'Connell exclaimed, "This doesn't bother us at all. We will meet the issue and I will be back at the meeting tonight." Actually, O'Connell spent most of the night raising the $10,000 bail that had been set.

According to an indictment handed up by the federal grand jury on September 7, the alleged conspirators—O'Connell, David J. Smith, Herman R. Smith, Carl J. F. Wacher, Thomas Carey, E. R. Hoffman, and William C. Mengendoth—feloniously conspired to obstruct the recruiting and enlistment services of the United States in violation of the Espionage Act.[72] O'Connell and the Smiths, moreover, were charged with incorporating American Patriots for that purpose, circulating a document entitled "Legal Opinion and Advice on the Conscription Law to American Patriots." A second count charged all of the defendants with inducing six named men, and others unnamed, to make false statements as to their eligibility and fitness for the draft in violation of the Conscription Act.

O'Connell opted to represent himself and his fellow defendants, filing a demurrer to the indictment on September 11.[73] The following day, District Judge William C. Van Fleet overruled the demurrer, the defendants pleaded not guilty to the charges, and the jury was selected.[74] On September 13, the trial began in earnest, with Assistant U.S. Attorney Annette Adams asking the jury to "whip this crowd with the lash of justice in order that it may go to the ends of this land of ours that we are a free people fighting a just war."[75] O'Connell then spoke for three hours, declaring that free press and free speech were gone and that Daniel Webster would rise out of his grave if he could see the manner in which the federal Constitution was being violated day after day.

The trial ended on September 25, when O'Connell declined to take the stand on his own behalf. Van Fleet's charge to the jury responded to O'Connell's free speech argument: "Free speech . . . does not extend to the privilege of doing or saying that . . . which is calculated or intended to excite in the public mind opposition to a law or measure to an extent that it will prevent or obstruct the execution by those whose duty it is to carry it into effect."[76] Van Fleet also made sure the jury understood that the limitations on free speech applied to lawyers as much as anyone else. Van Fleet gave the case to the jury at 5:27 p.m., and they returned at 6:35 p.m. with a verdict of guilty for all defendants, although the form on which the verdict was submitted was left blank as to which counts the verdict applied.[77] Van Fleet entered judgment on September 29, sentencing O'Connell to seven years' imprisonment in the U.S. Penitentiary at McNeil Island, Washington.[78]

Gilbert Roe joined O'Connell's defense team for the appeal to the Supreme Court. O'Connell's own brief ran 243 pages and covered every argument raised in the bill of exceptions, including the unconstitutionality of the Conscription Act and the Espionage Act.[79] Roe signed onto that brief but also filed his own brief on January 2, 1920.[80] Roe's brief was only 83 pages long and dealt with defects in the verdict, admission of evidence, and jury charge, as well as arguing that the government failed to prove the conspiracy charged. Roe also submitted a reply brief defending the procedural validity of O'Connell's bill of exceptions on April 16.[81] Roe argued the case on April 23 and 26; less than a month later, Justice James C. McReynolds delivered the opinion of the court affirming the convictions.[82] McReynolds held that much of the voluminous record in the case was not properly before the court because of delays in the court below. Of the remaining assignments of error, he said, only four required special notice. The constitutionality of the two statutes at issue had been decided affirmatively by previous decisions of the court, he wrote, as had the question of whether "inducement and persuasion" to obstruct recruiting constituted a sufficient basis for criminal conspiracy. The defective jury form was harmless error, and the defendants did not have to be government officials to violate the Conscription Act. "We find no adequate cause for interfering with the judgment of the court below."

O'Connell's troubles did not end with the U.S. Supreme Court decision. On December 28, 1920, he was disbarred by the California Supreme Court on the ground that he had been convicted of a "felony or misdemeanor involving moral turpitude."[83] Since the record of conviction was deemed conclusive in such cases, the only issue before the court was the question of moral turpitude. "It seems to us that it would, indeed, be a narrow and restricted definition of the term that does not include such an offense," the per curiam opinion stated, as "having willfully engaged in a conspiracy having for its definite purpose the obstruction, while the United States was at war, of the recruiting or enlistment service of the United States."

For Gilbert Roe, the representation of sundry antiwar activists, draft resisters, and conscientious objectors must have seemed a thankless task. Apart from Learned Hand's opinion in *Masses Publishing Co. v. Patten*, the Espionage Act cases that occupied so much of his time from 1917 to 1920 brought little money and even less glory. A decade later, however, his contribution would be remembered by another veteran of those battles, Roger Baldwin, a conscientious objector and early member of the American Union Against Militarism. Baldwin would go on to become founder and executive director of the American Civil Liberties Union, a position he held in 1930 when he wrote to Netha Roe that Gilbert "was one man we could always turn to with a sure sense that he would understand and respond with an uncompromising stand on principle. . . . [He] embodied the very best of the old American tradition of defending the rights not only of those with whom he agreed, but particularly of those with whom he totally disagreed.[84]

While Roe maintained his relationship with Baldwin's civil liberties organizations for the rest of his life, the same could not be said of Theodore Schroeder. Indeed, Rabban has attributed the disintegration of the Free Speech League to Schroeder's changing focus from free speech to psychoanalysis and to philosophical differences between Schroeder and Baldwin.[85] Roe would have one more significant Espionage Act case, but it had more to do with violent revolution than with pacifism. Roe's representation of Agnes Smedley in a case involving radical Indian nationalism reflected dramatic changes in the American Left following the Russian Revolution and the growing threat to freedom of speech from the American reaction to Soviet communism.

8

The Communists

> Nothing that I used to think could stand in the face of that Russian experience. . . . The wreck of my political philosophy in the war and the revolution and the threads of the new, and better, conceptions which lay mangled but traceable in the debris.
>
> Lincoln Steffens

> Too often patriotism . . . is confused with militarism; "Loyalty" is confused with intolerance and persecution. We are already reaping some of the terrible consequences resulting from whipping up this spirit of intolerance in the cases of lynching, mob violence and outrages taking place all over the country.
>
> Gilbert Roe

It would be difficult, if not impossible, to overstate the impact that the Bolshevik revolution of November 1917 had on the political and legal environment in which Gilbert Roe practiced civil liberties law. "The impact of the Bolshevik Revolution on the American left wing was stunning," according to historian Theodore Draper. "It was as if some left-wing Socialists had gone to sleep and had awakened as Communists. The Bolshevik Revolution had a dazzling, dreamlike quality."[1] To be sure, the socialists had been divided over the war even before the revolution. For example, Upton Sinclair, who had denounced war in 1907, declaring that "under no circumstances will we be led out to slaughter our fellow-men," had, by 1916, come to see Germany as a threat to civilization and was calling on the country to join "the final struggle on behalf of Democracy."[2] Sinclair fully supported Wilson's war effort, even in the face of death threats. But Sinclair was among a small minority of like-minded socialists, and he resigned from the American Socialist Party in July 1917, a few months after the party declared the war "a crime against the people of the United States" at an emergency convention in St. Louis.[3]

The war had also divided the labor movement, with one-time pacifist Samuel Gompers leading the American Federation of Labor on March 12, 1917, to pledge support for the war in return for government guarantees on organizing, collective bargaining, wages, and working conditions. The pledge was adopted unanimously, but some unions, like the United Mine Workers, had refused to attend, and the Seamen's Union's Andrew Furuseth—who had worked closely with La Follette and Roe on the Seamen's Act to provide better working conditions for sailors[4]—warned Gompers that he was destroying "your forty years of work for labor."[5] Indeed, the months before the November revolution saw the labor movement split between Gompers's pro-war American Alliance for Labor and Democracy and the antiwar socialist People's Council of America for Democracy and Peace, each vying for the support of the American worker.

The success of the Bolsheviks in November both exhilarated the Left and, very soon, exacerbated its internal conflicts and external, existential threats. In Gilbert Roe's immediate social circle, the Bolshevik cause would be warmly embraced by Lincoln Steffens and actively advanced by Jack Reed. It would also bring him a new and historically important client in Agnes Smedley. And it would provoke a reinvigorated "Red Scare" that would keep him busy for years defending its victims—particularly members of the New York City Teachers Union, which would itself be riven by the communist movement.

Steffens, who was among the first to introduce Roe to the bohemians of Greenwich Village, had been quite comfortable with the first Russian Revolution. "What I have seen in Russia is great," he wrote Netha Roe on a postcard from Japan in the spring of 1917.[6] The second revolution, however, "seemed to me to require a complete change of mind. . . . Nothing that I used to think could stand in the face of that Russian experience. . . . The wreck of my political philosophy in the war and the revolution and the threads of the new, and better, conceptions which lay mangled but traceable in the debris."[7] In his writings and lectures, Steffens assumed the role of explaining the evolving Russian phenomenon, reconciling it with President Wilson's plans for peace and, as time went on, contrasting it with nascent fascism. In 1933, more than three years after Gilbert Roe's death, Steffens wrote Netha, "How I would like to sit down and talk it all over with Gil! He'd understand, I know. He'd see the difference between Stalin and Hitler, between Stalin and Mussolini. But then you would, too."[8]

If Steffens experienced Bolshevism from a physical and philosophical distance, Jack Reed could not have been closer. The author of the iconic *Ten Days That Shook the World* was one of Steffens's closest friends, but he showed none of the old progressive's ambivalence. In fact, Steffens's biographer, Justin Kaplan, claims Reed thought Steffens "had been left behind by history; for all his revolutionary sympathies, Steffens remained only a rebel, a liberal gripped by the deadly habit of seeing both sides of the issue and therefore unable to commit himself in action."[9] And he quotes Reed as asking Steffens at their final meeting, "Why don't you join us? We are trying to do what you used to talk and write about."

John Silas Reed settled in Greenwich Village in 1911 after graduating from Harvard University. His closest acquaintances—Steffens, Max Eastman, and Mabel Dodge—would connect him with Gilbert Roe in many different ways, although not, strictly speaking, as a client. Of course, Reed was a prominent member of *The Masses* staff, but he was not personally named in the Associated Press libel suit and spent the Post Office litigation abroad. He was named in the criminal indictments, but Roe was not directly involved in that defense. If Reed and Roe had not met earlier, they certainly crossed paths during the various activities surrounding the Paterson strike. Reed visited Paterson several days after hearing strike leader Bill Haywood at one of Mabel Dodge's salons. Reed got himself arrested and spent a few days in jail, and then returned to New York to write about the experience in *The Masses* and coordinate a pageant at Madison Square Garden to support the workers in Paterson.[10] Roe represented Reed's friend, Frederick Sumner Boyd, and both signed Boyd's clemency petition. In any event, by early 1914, Roe was referring to him as Jack.[11]

In late 1913, Reed set out for Mexico to report on the revolution for *Metropolitan Magazine*.[12] From Pancho Villa's headquarters in Chihuahua, Reed wrote to Roe, who was then in the process of collecting intelligence on Associated Press practices for his defense of Max Eastman and Art Young: "The present A.P. correspondent here (Chihuahua) is the representative in Chihuahua of all the big mining companies here. . . . They are all for intervention, and so is he, personally. . . . Don't tell where you got this—yet."[13] When Reed returned in April 1914, Reed's mistress, Mabel Dodge, invited Roe—who was now handling her divorce and property settlement[14]—to attend a salon with Netha. "I was surprised and pleased to get your note saying that Jack Reed would be here Tuesday evening," Roe wrote to Dodge. "I supposed that he was in Mexico with Villa. Indeed, I had just finished reading a special dispatch from him in the *N.Y. World*, before I opened your letter. I am more than pleased to know that he is safely back. We will surely come if we can Tuesday night."[15]

By the end of the month, Reed was on the road again, this time accompanying Max Eastman to cover the Colorado coal miners' strike and the Ludlow Massacre.[16] During much of 1914 and 1915, Reed covered the war in Europe, from England and France to the Balkans and Russia, with a few months in early 1915 spent in New York writing. Somehow, he found time to help edit some of Netha Roe's poetry,[17] telling Netha he was sailing to Italy and then on to Russia, "but I shall see you surely when I come back in the summer."[18] Reed returned to New York in late 1915. His affair with Mabel Dodge was over, and he fell in love with Louise Bryant on one of his trips to visit his mother in Portland.[19] Reed spent 1916 writing, covering the political conventions, and sorting out his complicated love life. The following year, however, brought the lowest point—America's entering the war and repressing dissent at home, including the destruction of *The Masses*, Reed's principal outlet—and the highest point of his career—the Russian Revolution. Reed and Bryant set out for Russia in August, with credentials from the *Call* and money from socialist supporters. Netha Roe recalled sharing a box with Reed at the theater on the night before his departure.[20]

There is no record of any correspondence between Reed and either Gilbert or Gwyneth Roe after Reed joined the Comintern, and, of course, Roe's own politics were never that far left. But one of Roe's Espionage Act clients would become a highly regarded Comintern operative and Soviet spy. Agnes Smedley would remember Roe fondly, long after his death, and continue to correspond with Netha Roe—though it is not certain that either Roe knew all the details of Smedley's professional affiliations.

The Smedley Case

Agnes Smedley was one of Gilbert Roe's most interesting and enigmatic clients—and that's saying something. Her principal biographers disagree utterly as to her affiliation with the Comintern or even the Communist Party. Janice and Stephen MacKinnon wrote in 1988 that Smedley "shared the anti-imperialist goals of the Comintern and consciously cultivated friendships with leftists . . . whom she undoubtedly knew were Comintern representatives, but a Comintern or Communist Party member she was not."[21] They pointed out, "For the rest of her life, Smedley had to face allegations—originating in Shanghai with British intelligence in the early 1930s—that she was a Comintern agent." Writing in 2005, well after the fall of the Soviet Union and with a wealth of Comintern and other archives at her disposal, Ruth Price had set out to disprove those allegations, but found that, if anything, they were understated. "The real Agnes, I came to realize, was a master of deception, a skilled poseur who had prevailed on powerful friends like Roger Baldwin and Margaret Sanger to defend her as an innocent victim of wartime hysteria."[22] One of those friends was Gilbert Roe, who would probably not have known that she was, in Price's words, "guilty as hell" of the charges against her.[23]

Agnes Smedley was born in 1892 near Osgood, Missouri, but moved to the coal-mining town of Trinidad, Colorado, in 1901, where her father served as a teamster for Rockefeller's Colorado Fuel and Iron Co.[24] When the United Mine Workers sent Mary "Mother" Jones to Trinidad in 1903 to organize the miners, CF&I ruthlessly put down the insurrection Jones instigated. But Smedley had found a role model in Mother Jones—"the first female to suggest an alternative image of womanhood in which it was acceptable and even admirable to resist with all the force of one's being the unjust circumstances that robbed people of freedom and opportunity." In 1910, Smedley left Colorado, drifting from Phoenix to San Francisco to San Diego with a socialist companion from Greenwich Village named Thorberg Brundin. Brundin would marry Marxist lawyer Robert Haberman, while Smedly would marry Brundin's brother Ernest.

At Berkeley, Smedley became attracted to the Indian nationalist movement and, by 1914, had joined the Hindustan Ghadr Party, organized by Har Dayal, which sought to instigate a mutiny against the British in India and, ultimately, overthrow colonial rule there. In early 1915, however, the British crushed the group's efforts to provoke an armed uprising in the Punjab. With the financial support of the German Foreign Office, Har Dayal formed another organization to begin funncling men and weaponry from the United States to India. Smedley secretly became involved in that effort during the summer of 1915. In early 1916, Smedley also met Upton Sinclair, who was giving a series of lectures in San Diego, and worked with him to establish a chapter of his Intercollegiate Socialist Society. That summer, however, she left her husband and returned to San Francisco, where Bhagwan Singh, with German support, had taken control of the Ghadr movement. The Berlin India Committee, which coordinated the funding for anti-British revolutionary movements in India, had established a base in New York City, and Smedley offered to relocate there. On New Year's Eve, 1916, Smedley left California for Greenwich Village.

In New York, Smedley lived with Thor Brundin and her husband Robert Haberman, who introduced her to Henrietta Rodman and the rest of the Village's bohemian society. She also joined the Civic Club, where she met Lajpat Rai, a leading Indian reformer, and began working with him. But Smedley was much closer politically to more extreme Indian nationalists, particularly

Sailendra Nath Ghose, who had recently arrived in New York with instructions to improve communications between revolutionaries in the United States and Bengal. Smedley was also attracted to Margaret Sanger's birth control movement, beginning as a street-corner advocate and ultimately moving to the staff of Sanger's *Birth Control Review*.

As U.S. entry into the war approached, the British increased pressure on American authorities to crack down on the German-supported Indian independence movements. By May 1917, most of the Indian revolutionaries were in jail or under surveillance. M. N. Roy, Ghose's mentor and Smedley's one-time sexual partner, seized the leadership of the independence movement and moved its headquarters to Mexico City. Ghose asked Agnes to stay behind and act as a secret "communications center" for the movement. She agreed, at the expense of her relationship with the moderate Lajpat Rai, and began covertly overseeing the publication and distribution of anti-Allied propaganda, moving from one apartment to another to avoid detection. Ghose returned to San Francisco at the behest of Tarak Nath Das, an American citizen and author of the most virulent propaganda, who implemented a plan to pose, with Ghose and Bhagwan Singh, as members of a fictitious Indian Nationalist Party and to seek recognition as diplomats. Both Das and Singh were under indictment in San Francisco and awaiting trial, but Ghose was free to travel to New York, where Smedley handled the "diplomatic" correspondence under the name Marie Rogers. When the conspirators attempted to contact Soviet foreign minister Leon Trotsky to secure support for the Indian defendants in San Francisco, some of the relevant correspondence was intercepted and Smedley's participation was exposed. On March 15, 1918, Naval Intelligence agents took Smedley to the Delancey Street jail for questioning and searched her apartment for evidence without a warrant.

On March 18, she was formally arrested and charged with violating the Espionage Act for conspiracy to falsely represent herself as an official of the Indian Nationalist Party and also a local ordinance prohibiting the distribution of birth control information.[25] Ghose was apprehended the following day while he was trying to visit Smedley, and Das was picked up in San Francisco a few days later.[26] Bail was set at $25,000 for Ghose and $10,000 for Smedley, and both were taken to the Tombs. In late April, a trial jury in San Francisco sentenced Das and Singh to prison. On April 1, a federal grand jury in New York indicted Smedley, Ghose, Das, Singh, and Jadu Gopal Mukerjee for violating the Espionage Act.[27] Sanger and pacifist minister John Haynes Holmes, who would become a cofounder of the ACLU, raised the $10,000 for Smedley's bail, and Gilbert Roe agreed to take her case "for whatever the defendants could afford to pay."[28] Smedley was delighted to be represented by Roe and another lawyer, Charles Recht, who were "American in every respect . . . with American sympathies" in the war. For his part, Roe told civil liberties lawyer Walter Nelles, that Smedley would receive "as good a defense as if she had been a real criminal, and a rich one at that."[29]

Smedley and Ghose pleaded not guilty on April 3,[30] and Recht filed a demurrer on April 9.[31] The demurrer was argued and overruled on April 25.[32] That date had been set for trial, but the trial never took place. Smedley was released on May 7 into Roe's custody, after eight weeks in jail, and moved in with Rodman.[33] Sanger threw a party to celebrate her release and raise money for Ghose.[34] An "Agnes Smedley Defense Fund," whose officers included Rodman's husband, Herman Defrem, was organized to raise funds for the defense.[35] On June 11, a federal grand jury in San Francisco returned an indictment, charging Smedley and Ghose, along with Das and several others (including the fictional head of the fictional Indian National Party, Pulin Behari Bose), with conspiring to violate the Espionage Act through their fraudulent representations and distribution of anti-Allied propaganda.[36] The West Coast indictment was certified on July 11,[37] and on August 8, Robert P. Stephenson, assistant U.S. attorney in Manhattan, filed a complaint seeking the removal of Smedley and Ghose to the Northern District of California for trial on the charges alleged in that indictment.[38]

Back in New York, Recht petitioned the District Court for return of all the materials taken on March 15 by federal agents.[39] Attached to the petition was a list of forty-three items, naming books, manuscripts, pamphlets, newspaper clippings, and letters, including a carbon copy of the letter to Trotsky. In response to that petition, U.S. District Judge J. M. Mayer issued an order on August 29, requiring U.S. Attorney Frances Caffey to appear on September 5, at 10:30, to show cause why the petition should not be granted.[40] That hearing was postponed until September 19[41]—perhaps because matters were heating up on the San Francisco indictment—and the legal fight for the return of her personal property would last until May 1920.[42]

Although the San Francisco indictment was handed up in July, no effort was made to arrest Smedley and Ghose until October 14, even though the authorities knew where they were living.[43] On that date, Smedley and Ghose appeared before Commissioner Samuel M. Hitchcock, where bail was again imposed at $25,000 for Ghose and $10,000 for Smedley. Again, Smedley was released to Roe's custody, but Ghose remained in jail. When the proceedings reconvened on October 17, Roe duly identified the defendants as the persons named in the indictment (although he did not admit to the various aliases listed for Smedley). But he objected to the presentation of the indictment as incompetent and failing to state facts tending to show the commission of a crime. Hitchcock overruled the objection. Roe then moved to dismiss the proceedings altogether on the ground that there were no facts warranting their incarceration. Hitchcock dismissed the motion and adjourned the hearing until October 22.

When the hearing reconvened, Roe renewed the motions to dismiss, this time adding the ground that Hitchcock lacked jurisdiction. Hitchcock gave Roe until October 24 to submit a memorandum stating his objections to the indictment, and scheduled a further hearing on October 25 to consider it. That hearing was postponed until October 28, when Hitchcock again denied Roe's motions. The next day, Roe petitioned for a writ of habeas corpus, restating all of the grounds cited in his previous motions and adding two others: that if any crime were committed, it was triable in New York, not California, and that the continued detention of Smedley and Ghose violated the Fourth, Fifth, Sixth, and Fourteenth Amendments to the Constitution. The same day, Hitchcock ordered Smedley back to jail in the custody of Thomas D. McCarthy, U.S. Marshal, and ordered them to appear before Judge Augustus Hand on October 31 for disposition of the habeas petition.[44] On November 12, Hand ruled that the indictment was sufficient to hold Smedley and Ghose, and he dismissed the habeas petition.[45] Roe immediately petitioned the court for an order allowing them to appeal Hand's ruling to the U.S. Supreme Court on the constitutional questions, and on November 15, Hand agreed, staying all further proceedings involving the removal until that appeal could be heard. He also set supersedeas bonds of $1,000 for Smedley and $5,000 for Ghose and ordered Roe to have the case docketed at the U.S. Supreme Court by November 25.[46] Rodman and Charles H. Ingersoll posted the bond that very day, and Smedley was free once again.[47]

As to the New York indictments, Roe wrote to Caffey and Stephenson on November 18, requesting that Smedley and Ghose either be tried immediately or the indictments dismissed. "Is there any reason why the indictments here against Smedley and Ghose should not either be brought to trial at once or dismissed?" he wrote. "The bond of $25,000. required of Ghose is, in view of his destitute and friendless condition, practically prohibitive and it seems to me in every way wrong that a man should have been confined in the Tombs here for nine or ten months and no effort made to bring him to trial."[48] When neither trial nor dismissal was forthcoming, Roe and Recht filed a formal petition on December 10 to dismiss the indictments against Smedley and Ghose for violation of their Sixth Amendment right to a speedy trial. Judge Learned Hand issued an order requiring Caffey to appear on December 13 and show cause why the petition should not be granted. Following that hearing, Hand ordered the indictments dismissed and Smedley's bond discharged.[49] But it would be June 5, 1923, before the U.S. Attorney would formally decline to prosecute the others indicted with Smedley and Ghose more than five years earlier.[50]

Although Smedley resumed her position as associate editor of Sanger's *Birth Control Review*, she was much more committed to the Indian independence movement. The National Civil Liberties Bureau, headed by Roger Baldwin, whom Smedley had met in the Tombs, agreed to subsidize her legal fees as Roe continued to fight the San Francisco indictments. Freed from that concern, Smedley formed the Hindu Defense Fund in January 1919, persuading Sanger, Socialist Party leader Norman Thomas, and others to help her raise money to defend revolutionaries headed for jail or deportation.[51] Despite some fundraising success, Smedley was increasingly disillusioned and sought a larger role in the movement. She would find it in her relationship with Virendranath Chattopadhyaya, or Chatto, a member of the Berlin India Committee, with ties to the Soviet Union. While Roe tried to emphasize her affiliation with moderates like Lajpat Rai, at least in his correspondence with prosecutors involved in her continuing legal saga on the West Coast, federal agents discovered evidence of her more revolutionary connections by breaking into Roe's office in January 1919 and conducting a "discreet investigation" of his client.[52]

In early March, the Soviet Union launched the Comintern to support revolutionary movements throughout the world. To position himself as the leader of India's revolutionary movement, and perhaps obtain Comintern funding, Chatto encouraged Smedley to organize an American-based propaganda service, Friends of Freedom for India, which she did on March 6. FFI operated from an office in the socialist-oriented Rand School of Social Science, with University of Chicago professor Robert Morss Lovett as its president.[53] Baldwin agreed to serve on the executive committee; Gilbert Roe and Frank Walsh were named legal advisers. Roe also served as a member of the FFI National Council, which included Upton Sinclair, Norman Thomas, Herman Defrem, and W. E. B. Du Bois, among others.[54] Smedley was listed fourth among the officers, as general secretary; Chatto was never formally associated with the organization, and few, if any, of FFI's well-known supporters knew of his existence or his Comintern ties.[55]

Also in March, Alexander C. King, the U.S. solicitor general, along with John Lord O'Brian, the special assistant for Espionage Act cases, filed a motion in the Supreme Court to dismiss the appeal on the ground that the constitutional questions raised "have been foreclosed by prior decisions of this Court and are so wanting in merit as to be frivolous."[56] In the alternative, King said, the court should affirm Hand's ruling because the questions raised had already been resolved by the court and the appeal was manifestly a delaying tactic. After paraphrasing Roe's assignment of error, King argued that it was utterly without merit and that the appeal should be dismissed. King attacked Roe's primary argument, that the West Coast indictment was factually insufficient to support probable cause; King argued that a grand jury indictment was itself sufficient in cases like this one, especially where Roe had introduced no evidence to overcome the existence of probable cause. King argued further that any technical defects in the indictment, if there were any at all, could not be raised in either a removal or a habeas proceeding but must be left for the trial judge's determination. Finally, King rejected Roe's jurisdictional and constitutional arguments.

In responding that King's motion should be denied, Roe characterized Hand's assessment of the counts in the indictment as "good as to the second count, doubtful as to the first, and probably bad as to the third."[57] The government seems to be arguing, Roe said, that "any indictment—whether good or bad, is sufficient in the absence of any other evidence, to require [holding] the accused for removal." Specifically, he argued that the Espionage Act simply did not cover the kind of conspiracy alleged in the indictment, that the indictment did not comply with New York law requiring a full statement of facts, and the propaganda charge failed to specify what parts of its content were unlawful.

Roe continued to work for the dismissal of the San Francisco indictments against Smedley and Ghose, writing Attorney General Mitchell Palmer in October, "A mistaken patriotism, or a too fervent attachment to the cause of the oppressed people of other countries, is not an offense that we ordinarily have any reason to prosecute in time of peace." Assistant Attorney General Robert P. Stewart agreed, telling Palmer the charges seemed to be of a "manifestly political character and so subversive of the political ideals of this Government, and the spirit of its laws, [that] the United States should not be a party to further pressing this case." Solicitor General King also signed on to Roe's argument, suggesting that the case "probably sprang out of the close relations between this Government and the English Government, and the supposed connection of these defendants with the effort to raise disturbances in India under German instigation." On November 26, 1919—one day after the conclusion of a series of raids to arrest radicals—Palmer informed Roe that the San Francisco indictments had been dismissed.[58] Roe then moved to have the U.S. Supreme Court appeal dismissed, which was done on December 11.[59]

Through FFI, however, Roe was still assisting in the representation of Gopal Singh, a young Indian revolutionary in San Francisco, who had been convicted of violating American neutrality in April 1918 and sentenced to a year and a day at McNeil Island Prison. On February 10, 1919, thirteen days before the expiration of his sentence, he was notified of his imminent deportation for crimes involving moral turpitude.[60] Singh was still awaiting deportation in December 1919, when he received a letter from Smedley. "I feel a lessening in the tension of our friends," she wrote; "they say the Hindus will not be deported. I think that [idea] is dangerous . . . born of desire. I have been talking with Mr. Roe, your attorney here, and he tells us that we must keep up the fight without fail. He is in Washington often and he feels that we need more support than we have been able to muster."[61] Indeed, a second round of Palmer raids would begin only a few weeks later, on January 2, 1920, with the arrest of thousands of aliens and other radicals over the next five months.

On February 28, 1920, Roe spoke at an FFI dinner on "The Menace of English Imperialism," with Republic of Ireland president Eamon De Valera as the featured speaker.[62] By the end of the year, FFI was ready to hold a national convention. A fund-raising letter on November 2, 1920, asked for $10,000 to support the convention, to be held at the McAlpin Hotel in New York City on December 5.[63] Gilbert Roe was prominently featured on the letterhead. But within two weeks, Smedley embarked for Europe, working without a passport as a stewardess aboard a Polish freighter.[64]

Roe continued to serve as Smedley's pro bono lawyer throughout the 1920s. In 1925, for example, while she was living in Germany, Smedley asked Roe to help her find an American publisher for her autobiographical novel *Daughter of Earth*.[65] He successfully negotiated a publishing contract with Coward-McCann in late June 1928, and the book was published the following year.[66] In October 1928, Smedley received a visa for China, thus launching a new career chapter that would encompass journalist, birth control advocate, Comintern propagandist, Soviet espionage agent, and confidante of the ultimately triumphant Chinese Communist Party and its leaders. Although it is clear that Gilbert Roe sympathized with Smedley's anti-imperialist aspirations, it is uncertain whether he knew how deeply Smedley was involved in German and later Soviet intrigues. In two letters she wrote him in the months before his death, Smedley certainly expressed sympathy for China's poor, revulsion at the death and destruction caused by China's civil war, enthusiasm for the revolutionary spirit of the students she encountered at Shanghai's Fudan University, and contempt for the British Secret Service and their American helpers.[67] But she also wrote that she told American authorities she had never sworn allegiance to any other government, and Roe had no reason to suspect otherwise.

Disloyalty in New York

The virulent reaction that the birth of communism provoked in the United States accounted for most of the civil liberties cases Roe took on during the last dozen years of his career. The socialist-oriented community in which Roe worked had always been viewed with suspicion by mainstream America, as much for its ethnicities as for its ideologies. But that suspicion increasingly turned to fear after the revolution in Russia, and fear was an emotion that could be exploited for political advantage, to break unions, or simply to build reputations. Roe found himself defending, not just nascent communists such as Agnes Smedley, but completely innocent socialists and others accused of disloyalty in the Red Scare of the late teens and early twenties. In many instances, the anti-communist persecution that followed the Bolshevik revolution was merely a continuation and escalation of long-standing anti-labor sentiments and wartime suspicions of disloyalty, particularly directed against Jews and other recent immigrants. Among Gilbert Roe's clients, there was no better illustration than the three New York City schoolteachers who were dismissed for disloyalty in 1917.

Thomas Mufson, A. Henry Schneer, and Samuel D. Schmalhausen, teachers at New York City's DeWitt Clinton High School, were members of the year-old New York City Teachers Union when they were singled out as examples by the school system and the Board of Education in the fall of 1917. All three had participated in an aborted strike against the decision by Associate Superintendent John L. Tildsley to lengthen the school day, and all three had voted for a resolution of the Teachers Council condemning school board vice president John Whalen's threat to close down the schools if the strike continued.[68] And all three were Jews. All three were suspended, pending a short "trial" that began on December 3, 1917; six other teachers who had been involved with the so-called Whalen Resolution were transferred.

The case was styled as "In the Matter [of] The Charges of Conduct Unbecoming a Teacher, Preferred by Associate Superintendent Tildsley against Thomas Mufson, A. Henry Schneer and Samuel D. Schmalhausen, teachers in the DeWitt Clinton High School."[69] It was tried before the Committee on High Schools and Training Schools, Department of Education of the City of New York, with Whalen himself presiding. Although all three teachers had been questioned extensively regarding their participation in the Whalen Resolution, board president William G. Wilcox had insisted that the teachers were not being charged with disloyalty.[70] New York attorney Herbert C. Smyth, whose most famous case would be the Gloria Vanderbilt custody trial of 1934, represented the teachers; Charles McIntyre and William E. C. Mayer, both assistant corporation counsel, represented the Board of Education.[71]

The evidence presented against Schmalhausen, an English teacher, showed that, on October 22, 1917, he had assigned his students to write an open letter to the president. Ellen E. Garrigues, head of the English department, described the assignment: "Write a very frank letter to Woodrow Wilson commenting within the limits of your knowledge upon his conduct of the war against the German Government." Garrigues testified that the principal, Dr. Francis Paul, thought the assignment was treasonable and sent her to Schmalhausen's classroom to collect all the papers.[72] One of the papers, written by a student named Hyman Herman, was particularly hostile, bordering on rabid, and she pointed it out to Paul. "Now I've got him," she said Paul exclaimed, but Whalen declared the whole topic of animus irrelevant. Smyth protested in vain that it went to prove that the genesis of the charges was the Whalen Resolution.[73]

The hearing on Schmalhausen concluded around 9 p.m. on December 3, and Whalen called Mufson's case. As the board's first witness McIntyre called Tildsley, who testified that, in an interview with Mufson—also an English teacher—on November 5, he asked a hypothetical question: would Mufson intervene in a classroom discussion of whether the United States would be better off under its present system or under anarchy—if those favoring anarchy were the better debaters and were prevailing. According to Tildsley, Mufson said no, but also that he would not have such a debate in his class. Tildsley also said Mufson would not intervene in a discussion where those favoring an early peace were getting the better of those favoring the sale of Liberty Bonds. Tildsley testified that, by remaining neutral, Mufson implied that he opposed cooperating with the war effort, even though he denied it. At 10 p.m., the committee called the case against A. Henry Schneer, a mathematics teacher. Again, Tildsley was the board's first witness, and he cited two grounds for discharging Schneer. First, in conversations that Tildsley had with Schneer, Schneer allegedly said he would not permit someone wearing a military uniform to address his students and did not favor military training for students. Secondly, Schneer had prepared a literary bibliography, "A Brief Guide to Contemporary Literature," with individual works characterized using romantic or mildly sexual references, and had it placed in the school bookstore.

Even before the Board of Education met to determine the fate of the teachers, public interest in their cases ran high. Renowned professors John Dewey and Charles A. Beard condemned the suspensions at a public meeting sponsored by the Teachers Union. Beard found "no little anti-Semitic feeling in the case." Dewey said that after studying the transcript of the teachers' trial, he was convinced that no court of law would consider such a case. "I don't know what this is called in 1917," Dewey said, "but in the old days it used to be called the inquisition."[74] All three teachers were dismissed at a meeting of the Board of Education on December 19, 1917, but not until after a heated debate that saw one member call the trials "a most pitiable travesty of a trial that I have ever witnessed in my long career."[75] Technically, the ground for dismissal was "holding views subversive of discipline and of undermining good citizenship." But one board member called it simply a lynching. The Teachers Union wasted little time planning an appeal to the state's Commissioner of Education John H. Finley,[76] and Gilbert Roe was chosen to lead the fight.

In his brief on behalf of the teachers, Roe argued that the trial had been based on a misunderstanding of the law, namely that the teachers had somehow lost the security of position that the law had guaranteed and that they held their positions at the board's discretion. "This error appears from the character of the charges filed," Roe said, "and from the conduct of the case."[77] Roe pointed out that the law, as it stood after the Henrietta Rodman case, gave the board unfettered "disciplinary power over every act of a teacher that might impair her usefulness as a teacher or affect the administration of the school system." That was changed, Roe said, by the Act of June 8, 1917, which provided that "charges might be preferred against a teacher for gross misconduct, insubordination, neglect of duty or general inefficiency, and that as a result of trial on those charges, the teacher might be either fined, suspended for a fixed time without pay, or dismissed." The primary purpose of this provision was to "secure the teacher against discharge by the Board for any cause except that which the legislature prescribed."

In this case, Roe said, there is no charge that any of the three teachers were incompetent or had failed in good behavior. Schmalhausen, for example, was charged with "conduct unbecoming a teacher," but there is no provision in the statute that authorizes dismissal for conduct the board might consider unbecoming. "What conduct is 'unbecoming a teacher'?" Roe asked. A certain style of dress? Going to dances? Holding unorthodox views on any subject? The effect of such an interpretation would be to "absolutely destroy the right of the teacher to be secure in his position during competency and good conduct," he declared. Following a more technical argument as to why the committee lacked jurisdiction to conduct the trial, Roe closed with a remarkably personal appeal: "I yield to no one in the exacting demands I make for loyalty and patriotism on the part of the teachers charged with the duty of educating the children of our public schools," Roe said. "My own children are among the number receiving their instruction from such teachers today. Too often patriotism, however, is confused with militarism; 'Loyalty' is confused with intolerance and persecution. We are already reaping some of the terrible consequences resulting from whipping up this spirit of intolerance in the cases of lynching, mob violence and outrages taking place all over the country, which can only discredit us in the eyes of rational people everywhere and which will discredit our cause throughout the world."

The appeal was formally filed on January 19, 1918,[78] but the decision was not announced until November. Acting Commissioner Thomas E. Finegan upheld the board in every respect and dismissed the appeal.[79] Commenting on his decision, Finegan said that following the declaration of war, a teacher in the public school system "will not be permitted to hide behind any claim of privilege when a question affecting his loyalty to the Government is concerned. He must come out in the open and cheerfully and unhesitatingly stand up and make known to the entire community in which he is employed that he is giving his unquestioned support to the President and to the Government in the prosecution of this war, and if he refuses to give such assurance he shall not be permitted to discharge the high office of teacher in an American public school system."

There were other dismissals based on disloyalty in wartime. Mary E. MacDowell, a Latin teacher at Manual Training High School in Brooklyn, was dismissed in June 1918 for failing to support the war effort through the sale of thrift stamps. The board rejected her defense that war was contrary to her religious beliefs as a Quaker. And Berlin-born Gertrude Pinol, a German teacher at Manual, refused to renounce the love she felt for her native culture and language, even though she also loved America. Pinol was also dismissed in June 1918.[80] While the 1917 and 1918 cases were ostensibly grounded in the establishment's hostility to antiwar sentiments—real or imagined—they set a precedent that would be easily applied to the growing fear of communist subversion—a fear fed, too, by long-standing anti-labor, anti-immigrant, and anti-Semitic biases. Indeed, by January 1918, the DeWitt Clinton teachers had aligned themselves with militant socialists, addressing a mass meeting sponsored by the "East Harlem agitation committee of the Socialist party." The committee denounced the school board in a resolution calling for a halt to the "inquisitions" that were "demoralizing" the public schools.[81] So it was no surprise that within two months of the Finegan decision, the board turned its guns on another Jewish teacher—this time for his failure to denounce Bolshevism.

Benjamin Glassberg was a teacher of history at Commercial High School in Brooklyn when he was notified, on January 16, 1919, that he was charged with conduct unbecoming a teacher and suspended without pay from further service. The notice, signed by Associate Superintendent John Tildsley, said a copy of the charges would be served with a notice to appear for trial.[82] This time, the Teachers Union retained Gilbert Roe to defend Glassberg at the very beginning of the proceedings.[83] The official charges against Glassberg were not released until March 7, but the allegations began appearing in the newspapers as soon as the suspension was made public in January. Twelve students reportedly signed a statement asserting that Glassberg had devoted half of his history lecture on January 14 to a discussion of Bolshevism, about which he made several favorable statements. Defending himself at a January 17 meeting of the Teachers Union, Glassberg said he had been asked whether he thought Lenin and Trotsky were German spies. "I replied that I didn't think so, and quoted from several noted Bolshevists. I was trapped by the questions asked, which I had to answer as I did or lie, and I didn't choose to lie." He also implied that he had been set up by Principal Gilbert Raynor's selection of non-Jewish witnesses against him.[84]

When no specific charges were filed in January or February, Roe went to court for a writ of mandamus compelling the service of charges. "Never before, in all the history of the Board of Education," Roe said, has it been necessary to apply to the courts in such circumstances. Shortly thereafter, the charges were served and a trial set for March 19. "That the intervening weeks were quite fully occupied in coaching the boys who were to be used as witnesses against Mr. Glassberg explains the delay," Roe said, "but certainly fails to excuse it."[85] The specific charges against Glassberg were divided into two specifications. In the first, Glassberg was charged with telling his class that the United States government was "systematically suppressing true reports about the Russian Bolsheviki," and that if the truth were known, it would show that the "Bolsheviki are not so bad as most people think."[86] Glassberg also allegedly said American Red Cross workers returning from Europe were being prevented from telling the truth about the Bolsheviks, that Lenin and Trotsky had brought about the end of the war through their representatives in Berlin, and that he, Glassberg, was not permitted to tell the truth to his students. In the second specification, the board charged that Glassberg had suggested that it might be right, "in a sense," to fly the red flag above the American flag, without further explanation.

Assistant Corporation Counsel Edward Mayer opened his case with the testimony of Edgar Grimmel and Martin Carroll, two of the boys who signed the statement of charges against Glassberg. The boys testified that Glassberg did, in fact, utter most of the statements charged in the first count, and Mayer elicited the implication that Glassberg's words weakened the allegiance of the students and caused them to think better of Bolshevism.[87] Another student,

George John Mack, testified that Glassberg had made the remark about the red flag alleged in the second count.[88] In all, Mayer called eight of Glassberg's students.[89]

Roe opened the defense case on April 4 with the testimony of Col. Raymond Robins of the American Red Cross, who had recently appeared before a Senate committee investigating Bolshevism in the United States. Robins testified that although Lenin and Trotsky never pretended any affection for the United States or the Allies, almost everything they did indirectly favored the Allies.[90] Later, Roe called eight other Commercial High School students to contradict the testimony of Grimmel, Carroll, and Mack. When Roe sought to call every one of the twenty-seven students in Glassberg's class who had not already been called, however, Mayer objected, and the parties finally reached an unusual stipulation providing that each of the remaining members of the class would deny the truth of every charge made against Glassberg.[91]

Taking the stand on his own behalf, Glassberg accepted the stipulation as to the first specification and then denied the red flag allegation in the second.[92] Following Glassberg's statement, Mayer asked him, in effect, whether he was a socialist. Roe objected to the question on the ground that, even if he were, and Roe thought he was, there was no charge against him for that.[93] Roe was overruled, but Glassberg still refused to answer the question directly. Glassberg did admit to lecturing at the Rand School of Social Science and to being a member of the board of the *Call* daily newspaper, both socialist institutions. He also admitted to teaching in socialist-operated Sunday Schools and to signing a letter in the *Call* that demanded a reorganization of the Socialist Party of America and condemned "moderate Socialists" and "social patriots."[94]

Roe concluded his presentation of evidence by calling a number of character witnesses and submitting the record of Glassberg's perfect teaching assessments.[95] In his closing argument and brief, Roe emphasized that the charges were framed to leave the impression that Glassberg essentially prefaced a lecture to his class with the statement that because he was a public school teacher, he could not tell the truth about Bolshevism, but that he would do so nevertheless. In fact, all of Glassberg's remarks that day were impromptu responses to student questions, Roe said. Not only are the specifications so framed to give a generally false impression, Roe said, but "each and every one of them is false."[96] Roe also pointed to evidence in the record indicating that the city's witnesses had been handpicked on religious grounds. Of the forty-three students in Glassberg's class, about three-fourths were Jewish. Yet only two or three of the students considered as witnesses for the city were Jewish, and none of them was called to testify.

Once again, Roe's conclusion was personal and powerful: "I only care to say that no one will go further than we on this side of the table in promoting Americanism in our public schools," Roe said. "But Americanism as I understand it means toleration and investigation, not bigotry and dogmatic assertion. It means the right to investigate and to know whatever there is to be known of the political, social and economic conditions in this country and in the world. Americanism is not so tender a plant that it needs to be shielded from criticism, however severe, or from comparison with any other political creed or policy."

Neither the favorable stipulation nor Roe's eloquent argument was sufficient to save Benjamin Glassberg's job. On May 27, newspapers were reporting that Glassberg had been found guilty by the committee that tried him,[97] and that verdict was presented at a meeting of the whole Board of Education the next day.[98] Both the *Times* and the *Tribune* identified Glassberg as a socialist and a member of the Teachers Union; both also noted that he was represented by Gilbert Roe, further identified as counsel to the union. Glassberg immediately announced his intent to appeal to the State Commissioner of Education.[99] Glassberg also said that "a great mass meeting" would be held soon in Brooklyn for the benefit of Commercial High School parents. "Gilbert E. Roe, representative of organized labor, and myself will outline to the parents the causes involved in my dismissal," Glassberg said, "and the necessity of restoring the control of the schools into the hands of the people." That meeting was held at the Brownsville Labor Lyceum on June 11, 1919; Glassberg, Roe, and James P. Boyle of the Bookkeepers' and Stenographers' Union addressed about five hundred supporters.[100]

As promised, Roe appealed the case to the state commissioner of education, John H. Finley, who scheduled a hearing for November 28.[101] The appeal was actually heard by Deputy Commissioner Frank B. Gilbert,[102] but it went for naught. In an undated memorandum, Roe wrote, "The case is still undecided. That is now about three years ago. In the meantime, Mr. Glassberg remains out of the schools."[103] Finally, on August 11, 1925, nearly five years after the appeal was filed, Gilbert published a decision dismissing the appeal.[104] Gilbert explained the delay in issuing the opinion on his belief that the publicity surrounding an unfavorable appellate opinion might adversely affect Glassberg in the new job he had obtained following his trial. But when Glassberg sought reinstatement in 1923, and the board again denied him, it became necessary to dispose of the appeal. Gilbert acknowledged that the evidence against Glassberg was not conclusive, but said it was sufficient to sustain the board's ruling.

Glassberg had indeed moved on to engage in ultra-left politics and publishing, joining Rand colleague Alexander L. Trachtenberg and others in forming the Committee for the Third International or Workers' Council, which advocated immediate revolution.[105] By 1923, however, he seemed to have recanted his more radical views as he sought reinstatement to the public schools.[106] Ultimately, Glassberg moved to Milwaukee to become executive director of Federated Jewish Charities there. In January 1927, he wrote to Roe complimenting Roe's son Jack on winning the University of Wisconsin's oratorical contest. "You may recall that it is now nine years since I had the pleasure of having you as my counsel in that very interesting case with the New York Board of Education. It was worthwhile going through with it to have you in that capacity."[107] Roe wrote back, "We are still making the old fight for the teachers here. They are not now discharging Progressive teachers, but are trying to discourage them by denying them the promotion to which they are entitled on their record. We just put Lefkowitz through here the first of the year, and got him his promotion. We are now taking up the cause of Miss Hardy, one of the women teachers."[108] Abraham Lefkowitz and Ruth Gillette Hardy had been at the top of their promotion lists for department head and principal, respectively; both eventually received their promotions.[109]

After Roe's death, Glassberg wrote Netha, "The United States could ill afford to lose so gentle and so noble a man. For several months during 1919, I was in almost daily contact with Mr. Roe. It was my first intimate contact with one of America's progressive leaders, one who was ready to do battle for the maintenance of our Constitutional liberties, no matter how unpopular such an attitude might be at the moment. My admiration and love for Mr. Roe which I then conceived will always be for me a most cherished recollection."[110]

Roe took on a number of other individual cases for the Teachers Union after Glassberg, including the case of Sarah Hyams, a teacher of cooking in the public schools. Hyams had signed an application card for membership in the left-wing section of the Socialist Party and then later professed ignorance of the party's purpose. The case against her was initiated by Superintendent of Schools William L. Ettinger in March 1921, who charged her with "holding political views which unfit her properly to perform her obligations as a teacher." Ettinger recommended a trial to determine the issue of her fitness to remain a teacher.[111] The trial was held on December 13, 1921, and on February 16, 1922, Roe received a letter from the Board of Education transmitting a resolution adopted the previous week directing Ettinger to "severely reprimand Miss Sarah Hyams" and ordering that further action in her case be withheld during her good behavior.[112]

Roe's most important service to the Teachers Union may have been his assistance in the campaign to repeal the infamous Lusk Laws. In 1919 the New

York legislature established a Joint Legislative Committee to Investigate Seditious Activities, which became known as the Lusk Committee after its chairman, Sen. Clayton R. Lusk.[113] Among other things, the report submitted to the legislature in 1920 recommended that every teacher be required to obtain a certificate of qualification from the commissioner of education. "Such certificates shall state that the teacher," Lusk recommended, "is a person of good moral character and that he has shown satisfactorily that he is loyal and obedient to the government of this state and of the United States."

The legislature adopted the Lusk recommendation, but Gov. Alfred E. Smith, a Democrat, vetoed the bill. In 1921, however, Smith was replaced by Gov. Nathan L. Miller, a Republican, who signed the Lusk Laws passed again by the legislature. According to historian Howard K. Beale, "The passage of the Lusk Laws led to an orgy of investigation and persecution. Principals were instructed to report on the loyalty of every teacher. A committee of five [the Advisory Council] was set up in New York City to pass upon cases of suspected 'disloyalty.'"[114]

The Teachers Union led the opposition to the Lusk Laws and was itself branded as disloyal. The official Teachers Council declared that the state "would be justified in punishing by dismissal from service any person who, while holding a position in the public schools, persists in remaining or becoming a member of this un-American organization."[115] Representing the union, Roe challenged the right of the Advisory Council to administer the Lusk Laws and to inquire into the loyalty and morality of teachers. "The Union holds that the order is not only a denial of civil liberty," Roe wrote, "but that it is also an act establishing a policy of espionage in the educational system of the entire state."[116] Later the union called Roe's challenge effective, resulting in "the public condemnation of the Lusk laws and their ultimate repeal in April 1923."[117] Alfred Smith, now governor again, signed the repeal legislation.[118]

Of course, teachers were not the only ones who suffered from the postwar Red Scare. Beginning on November 7, 1919, the anniversary of the Bolshevik revolution, several hundred home-grown and alien leftists of every variety were swept up in the so-called Palmer raids, named for Attorney General Mitchell Palmer and supported by the up-and-coming J. Edgar Hoover, newly appointed to head the Bureau of Investigation's General Intelligence Division within the Justice Department. The next series of raids, beginning in January 1920 and lasting about six weeks, saw some four thousand anarchists, socialists, and communists arrested in thirty-three cities, with a view toward mass deportations.[119] Among those caught up in the Red Scare were five Socialist Party members elected to the New York State Assembly. On January 7, 1920, all five—two from Manhattan, two from Queens, and one from Brooklyn—were called to the well of the House by Speaker Thaddeus C. Sweet and charged with membership in an organization, the Socialist Party, whose ideals were inimical to the U.S. government. The Republican-controlled Assembly passed a resolution temporarily suspending their membership in that body pending an investigation by the Judiciary Committee.[120] Not coincidentally, the five were known to oppose increased funding for the Lusk Committee, expected to be requested during the session.[121]

The Judiciary Committee set the hearing to begin on January 20. Despite his illness, Morris Hillquit, socialist lawyer and politician, was chosen to lead the defense team.[122] Other members of the team were S. John Block, counsel for the Socialist Party in New York City, former assemblyman William Karlin, noted labor lawyer Seymour Stedman, civil liberties lawyer Walter Nelles, and Gilbert Roe. Also participating on the defense team were two of the ousted assemblymen, Charles Solomon of Brooklyn and Samuel Orr of the Bronx.[123] The defense team's formal answer to the charges argued that the five ousted assemblymen were duly elected and qualified to hold office, and the Assembly and its Judiciary Committee had no jurisdiction to inquire into whether they possessed qualifications other than those prescribed by law. The resolution of January 7, denying them seats pending investigation, was illegal and void, the brief said. Further, the five denied every charged contained in the resolution, except for their affiliation with the Socialist Party, a lawful and legitimate political party. Finally, the brief argued, the investigation had been instituted lawlessly, in bad faith, and with malice, by a conspiracy among certain members of the Assembly.[124]

Testimony during the Judiciary Committee hearings—often referred to as a "trial" in the press—dragged on through the rest of January and all of February. Writing for *La Follette's Magazine*, Roe asserted that "not one single fact was produced with regard to the Socialist party that has not been known for years and that has not been the principal business of the Socialist party to make public by every means in its power." Roe would only concede that "there was some flimsy and unreliable evidence offered to show intemperate speeches on the part of some of the five Assemblymen."[125] Testimony ended February 27; three of the five defendants had taken the stand on their own behalf.[126] Closing arguments took place in early March, and briefs were submitted later that month. Martin Conboy, counsel to the committee, closed for the prosecution with a vicious denunciation of the socialists as traitors. "The Socialist party of America is not a loyal organization disgraced occasionally by the traitorous act of a member," Conboy said, "but a disloyal party composed of perpetual traitors."[127] Hillquit and Stedman focused their arguments on the unwarranted power exercised by the committee; Stedman compared the Assembly to the czar.[128]

The Judiciary Committee issued a majority report on March 30, calling for expulsion of the five socialists on the grounds that they were disloyal to the United States and the state of New York, affiliated with the disloyal Socialist Party, and intent upon the overthrow of the government by force. The majority report, signed by seven of the thirteen members of the Committee, also called for new legislation denying the Socialist Party the status of a political party. Five other members, who filed four separate minority reports, called for reseating the ousted socialists on the ground that the Assembly lacked legal authority to disqualify them on the charges presented.[129] Debate on the expulsion recommendation began the following day and lasted into the early morning hours of April 1. The date was significant—and the length of debate shrewdly calculated—because New York election law precluded any special election to fill vacancies arising after March 31.[130] After twenty-two hours of debate and maneuvering, the Assembly voted to expel all five socialists by margins of 70 percent to 80 percent.[131] Roe decried the cynical delay of the vote. "That the expelled men would be immediately reelected by a greatly increased vote if a special election had been called is admitted by Republicans and Democrats alike," he wrote. "Therefore, the five members were treated as being in their seats so that no vacancy occurred until after the time when a special election could be called."[132]

Despite his initial determination that he lacked the authority to call a special election,[133] Gov. Alfred Smith found an exception in the law that provided for special elections whenever they were made necessary by the governor's calling a special session of the legislature. Smith did just that and called for elections to fill any vacancies on September 16.[134] As Roe had predicted, all five Socialists were re-elected.[135] When the Assembly convened for the special session, however, it again voted to oust three of the socialists; the other two were seated but resigned in protest. The Assembly cheered their resignations.[136] It was over, except for this postscript. In a note to Roe following the proceedings, Morris Hillquit wrote: "In the strenuous and business like atmosphere of our work in Albany I have had no opportunity to tell you how much I appreciated your cooperation and how much I enjoyed your genial, cheerful companionship. I think I shall always remember it with joy and affection."[137]

9

Winding Down

> Today the actual ruler of the American people is the Supreme Court of the United States. The law is what the courts say it is, not what the people through Congress enact.
>
> Gilbert Roe
>
> This was the last day I dared trust that Gilbert would get well. N.
>
> Gwyneth King Roe

Postwar Life, Work, and Politics

The war years, of course, represented the pinnacle of Gilbert Roe's career as a free speech advocate, but his postwar life remained personally rich and professionally rewarding. In early 1919, the Roes would move from their suburban retreat back to the Upper West Side at 498 West End Avenue,[1] near where Gilbert and Netha began their life together in New York. According to a series of family newsletters written in 1920 and 1921 by thirteen-year-old Jack Roe, the family took every advantage of returning to the city. Busy as he was in 1920, Roe somehow found the time to take his family to numerous movies, plays, and lectures, an aeronautical exposition,[2] and, more than once, to Atlantic City.[3] The Roes dined out occasionally but more often invited guests to the apartment. Visiting King and La Follette family members were frequent guests, as were close friends and political allies.[4] According to Jack, at least some of the food the Roes served in Manhattan came from a 150-acre working farm at Wappinger's Falls, in Dutchess County near Poughkeepsie, that Roe had purchased—to Netha's surprise. "Knowing the deep dislike Gilbert had for farm life (he always said his incentive for studying law was to insure his getting away from the farm), it was hard for me to believe he was serious when he suggested we scour the country to find a farm 'for the kids' sake,'" Netha wrote in her draft autobiography.[5]

The family loved spending weekends and school vacations at the farm. "At the time of going to print, the Editor's school is about to finish its present term and merge into a vacation of two weeks," Jack wrote in March 1920. "As soon as this glorious event takes place, the family will pull up stakes and run for the farm *quam celerrime*."[6] The farm was actually operated by a family named Bates, who cared for the livestock and vegetable gardens and, especially, the car—a Ford—which Jack got to drive when they visited. "Janet and Gwyneth Roe have been weeding the cornpatch," Jack wrote in June 1920. "Jack Roe, popular good-looking Wisconsin man, is working in the hayfield. . . . He is getting a glowing tan color that makes one feel good to look at him."[7] But no one loved the farm more than Netha. "I want to tell you why I love the farm," Netha wrote around 1919. "Of course 1st for its Beauty—I may imagine more than exists—for there is no grandeur about it, no magnificent wide outlooks from it but there are wonderful trees, sunny slopes—beauty everywhere you look, night as well as day—so a great hunger is satisfied." She went on to describe many more attributes, including the farm's remoteness, closing: "In town I think & stop breathing. On the farm, I breathe & stop thinking."[8]

Gilbert Roe also traveled regularly to Washington, sometimes with the family, more often without. Jack reported in March 1920 that "The entire Roe family had the extreme pleasure of visiting Washington" for the Harding inauguration.[9] A month later, he wrote, "Mr. and Mrs. G. E. Roe expect to go to Washington in the near future. . . . Mr. Roe is to try a case in the Supreme Court and Mrs. Roe is to visit the La Follettes."[10] Roe would have been arguing the *Nagler*[11] case then, but as the Red Scare gradually died down, so did Roe's free speech–related practice.

Roe did have three non-speech-related cases that led to reported decisions between 1921 and 1923.[12] But much of his time in 1922 and 1923 was taken up by his duties as counsel to a subcommittee of Sen. Robert La Follette's Senate Committee on Manufactures. The subcommittee was formed to investigate the high cost of gasoline and other petroleum products from 1920 to 1922, pursuant to a resolution introduced by La Follette and passed on June 5, 1922.[13] Roe's investigation was launched to support another investigation into the leasing of naval oil reserves by the Senate Committee on Public Lands, also pursuant to a La Follette resolution.[14] Ultimately, the parallel investigations led to the exposure of the notorious Teapot Dome scandal.

The Campaign of 1924

The Teapot Dome scandal made mainstream Republicans seem very vulnerable in the 1924 presidential election,[15] and Roe all but abandoned his law practice to work full-time on Robert La Follette's final run for the presidency.[16] In 1924, progressive legislators had formed a "cohesive voting block" in Congress but had little hope of nominating a progressive presidential candidate.[17] As expected, the Republicans nominated Calvin Coolidge in early June,[18] while the Democrats chose John W. Davis, a West Virginia conservative, on the 103rd ballot in July.[19] When a La Follette for President Committee, including Gilbert Roe, delivered two hundred thousand petitions calling on La Follette to run, he agreed to run as an independent.[20] Both La Follette and Roe hoped that La Follette's independent candidacy, if successful, would ultimately lead to a new Progressive Party that would carry on the cause in subsequent elections. "If it is possible to secure harmonious action of all the forces which desire to support you," Roe had written in June, "your election is quite possible, indeed probable, but at all events you will have brought into existence a political party which would advance the policies you labored so hard for long after you and all the rest of us have passed out of the picture."[21] Roe's unusually long letter set out the strategy that La Follette would follow throughout the campaign. La Follette did win the support of the Conference for Progressive Political Action, including such luminaries as Fiorello La Guardia, John Dewey, and Louis Brandeis, and the Socialist Party of America, including Eugene Debs, Morris Hillquit, and Victor Berger.[22] Surprisingly, he also received the endorsement of the American Federation of Labor.[23]

La Follette chose progressive Democratic senator Burton K. Wheeler of Montana as his running mate. Roe became La Follette's eastern regional campaign director,[24] and he spent very little time on anything else.[25] But Roe's influence on the campaign went far beyond lining up votes in the East. For example, a campaign statement on the courts was almost certainly written or vetted by Roe,[26] author of *Our Judicial Oligarchy* so many years earlier. "Today the actual ruler of the American people is the Supreme Court of the United States," it began. "The law is what the courts say it is, not what the people through Congress enact."[27] The statement listed examples of the fifty-five cases in which the Supreme Court had declared the most progressive acts of Congress unconstitutional—cases dealing with income tax, labor unions, employer liability, child labor, election regulation, gambling, and minimum wages. "The time has come to face this judicial usurpation squarely," the statement continued.

"Federal judges must be made responsive to the basic principle of the government." Specifically, the statement called for a constitutional amendment providing that no inferior court be empowered to set aside an enacted law on the ground of unconstitutionality. And if the Supreme Court should strike down any law as unconstitutional, based on "the political, social or economic theories of the judges, the Congress may, by re-enacting it, establish it as the law of the land." The statement also called for a constitutional amendment to provide for the election of all federal judges "without party designation, for fixed terms not exceeding ten years, by direct vote of the people."

By all accounts, Roe worked tirelessly on the campaign. "What sacrifices Gilbert is making," Belle La Follette wrote Netha in August, "and how hard for you to have him away! Surely all this unselfish expenditure of energy must have some good result."[28] Wheeler campaigned vigorously in the West, while La Follette, ailing and tired, largely confined his activities to the Northeast and Midwest.[29] Even so, the candidate thought his prospects were good late in October. In a telegram to Roe, La Follette said he had advised Wheeler that they could win the West "if state and local organizations put on full steam from now until polls close. Prairie states are aflame with progressive sentiment from Mississippi to Rockies. Every advice I have received from Pacific Coast and Rocky Mountain states confirms your assurance of success there. . . . The election is ours if we carry progressive states east of the Mississippi with large electoral votes. . . . I am convinced that victory is at hand."[30]

Of course, it was not to be. Coolidge won more than 15 million votes, compared to more than 8 million for Davis, and just under 5 million for La Follette. Only Wisconsin voted for La Follette in the electoral college.[31] Publicly, La Follette took the election results with characteristic swagger. "The Progressives will not be dismayed by this result," he declared. "We have just begun to fight."[32] In fact, there would not be much time left to fight. In early April 1925, Gilbert and Netha Roe, along with Janet and Gwyneth (Jack was now at the University of Wisconsin), visited the La Follettes in Washington, where the senator took the Roe children on an excursion to Mount Vernon. By the end of the month, however, his health had taken a turn for the worse and continued to deteriorate through May and June.[33] Robert La Follette died of a heart attack in the early afternoon of June 18.[34] Roe accompanied the La Follette family as they escorted the coffin by train from Washington to Madison. Later that year, Roe would write a tribute to his friend for the January 1926 issue of *La Follette's Magazine*, which Belle had taken on,[35] followed by an article entitled "Reminiscences of Ten Years Association with Mr. La Follette in the Practice of Law," which appeared in the magazine in July 1926.[36] Just months before his own

Winding Down

death in 1929, Roe would write a chapter, "Senator La Follette and the World War," for Belle and Fola's two-volume biography,[37] deliver a lengthy memorial address before the Dane County Bar Association,[38] and speak at the unveiling of a statue of La Follette in Statuary Hall in the United States Capitol.[39]

The Final Years

In the spring of 1926, with the girls in boarding school and Jack at the University of Wisconsin,[40] Roe decided to move house again, this time downtown, to the John Alden apartments at 44 West 10th Street.[41] "Now we have found the perfect apartment," Netha wrote. "Being half way between 5th and 6th Avenues, we were at the edge of Greenwich Village without being in it; on the fringe of Fifth Avenue without being of it. . . . It was nearer the office than Gilbert had ever been. It gave a choice of subway or elevated. Even a cab might be considered in unusual need."[42]

Roe continued the general practice of law, representing, among other clients, several American citizens who had been awarded compensation by the Mixed Claims Commission for losses sustained at German hands. In November 1926, he testified before the House Committee on Ways and Means on proposed legislation calling on the United States to pay those claims until Germany was in a position to reimburse the Treasury.[43] Roe pointed out that there were "thousands of American claimants whose claims are not in dispute who absolutely are suffering for the want of this money." Roe argued that "the property which the United States has in its hands of German nationals be held until Germany makes suitable provision for the payment of these claims," with the United States acting as trustee for the property. Congress could then appropriate the funds needed to pay all the American claims. "I do not believe the United States will ever lose a dollar by doing that," he said. "I think it has appeared that Germany is one country that is going to pay its debts, and I think we will get our money from Germany before we will get some other money we have advanced to other countries." Roe did not name his clients in the testimony, but his 1928 office accounts show a damage award of more than $77,000 received for the "German claim," with nearly $26,000 each paid to Ellen and Erna Ross.[44] Roe retained a similar amount for the practice.[45]

Roe drew a small monthly retainer from the Teachers Union and a much larger one from the New York Oil Co. His office accounts even show $100 received for a consultation with architect Frank Lloyd Wright in 1927. Netha wrote to her sister that Gilbert had taken a call from "the Wisconsin architect

Wright who designed the only building in Tokio that stood the Earthquake, coming with his fiancée (or whatever you call the woman you're going to marry when your wife divorces you) to consult Gilbert about something."[46]

Apart from his practice, Roe was much in demand for his opinions on such controversial subjects as capital punishment, prohibition, and, of course, politics generally. In 1927, Roe wrote a long letter to the *New York Times* about the unfairness of the Sacco and Vanzetti trial[47] and made a $2 contribution to the League to Abolish Capital Punishment.[48] The following summer, he responded to an invitation from the *Forum*, a prestigious national magazine, for an opinion piece on capital punishment. His approach was more practical than philosophical. "Society has an undoubted right to protect itself against criminals," he wrote, "and if killing them afforded such protection then it might well be argued that society should kill them. But all experience has shown that the death penalty is no deterrent to crime . . . merely the gratification of the revengeful spirit in primitive man, and is an easy way to escape responsibility for the diseased condition of society, of which crime is merely an expression."[49]

On the issue of prohibition, Roe was ambivalent. In early 1928, he declined an invitation to speak on the subject at the City Club of New York. "I am not in sympathy with many of the methods of the Prohibitionists and I am certainly not in sympathy with the methods of most of the Antis," he wrote club secretary William F. Howe. "If the so-called 'respectable' people would obey the law instead of violating it and conniving at its violation, and spending millions of dollars for bootleg liquor which is the source of all the corruption in the business of which they complain, there would be no Prohibition question." Roe did accept Howe's offer to attend the dinner, promising to "listen with interest to what the partisans on each side of this question have to say."[50]

Later in 1928, Roe declined an invitation to support the candidacy of Franklin D. Roosevelt for governor of New York. In a letter to Oswald Garrison Villard, Roe said he was "so thoroughly out of sympathy with both the Democrat and Republican parties that I do not care to make any declaration in favor of the candidates of either of them. Until such time as we can get a really Progressive party, which I still venture to hope will be within my lifetime, I shall probably vote the Socialist ticket as a protest."[51] True to his word, Roe sent a $25 contribution to the Independent Committee for Norman Thomas, the Socialist Party candidate for president, and allowed the use of his name as a member of the committee. "I am not a Socialist, at least not a regular one, but as a Progressive, I am glad to support Mr. Thomas in this campaign," he wrote Harry W. Laidler. "Indeed, from my point of view there is no other logical

Winding Down

position for Progressives to take."[52] The same day, he wrote Phil La Follette, expressing the hope that Bob Jr., who succeeded his father as senator, would not support Al Smith for president. "[The] effort to corral the La Follette 1924 votes for Smith, and to try and make it appear that Smith is the same kind of a Progressive that your Dad was is disgusting to me at least."[53]

The end of 1928 and the beginning of 1929 were largely taken up with preparations for memorial exercises recognizing Robert La Follette[54] and various court appearances. In February 1929, for example, Roe took on the defense of an attorney, Silas Blake Axtell, who was charged with unprofessional conduct. Hearings in the case began in March and ended in September, with eight hundred pages of testimony taken. In October, all charges except one, self-advertising, were held not established by the evidence.[55]

The *Forum* continued to press Roe for opinion pieces on current issues, such as the need for more liberal justices on the Supreme Court[56] and the debate between atheists and believers. On the latter, Roe wrote, "[To] my mind such a discussion is not only useless but likely to do harm rather than good. The Atheists can no more prove their thesis that there is no God than the religious people can prove theirs that there is a God. Such a discussion never results in making either side more tolerant of the views of the other but generally quite the reverse."[57] Roe spent much of August in Washington, working on the war chapter of La Follette's biography and writing home nearly every day. When he read in the paper that Wisconsin Socialist Party leader Victor Berger had died of his injuries in a Milwaukee streetcar accident, he asked Netha to "send a telegram in our joint names to Mrs. Berger . . . expressing our sympathy and great regret at the death of Mr. Berger, which was not only a great loss to all of his friends but to the country and the world."[58]

Most of his correspondence with Netha was personal, however, regarding daughter Gwyneth's problems passing Latin, son Jack's summer work for his law firm, and—in a handwritten postscript to spare Nellie, the stenographer—the "burning love I am feeling for you this minute."[59] He wrote about the oppressive heat in Washington, suggesting that Netha should come for a visit if it got cooler—"especially if you have any curiosity regarding Nellie's conduct and mine. My personal feeling is that this weather insures perfect chastity on the part of anybody."[60] Jack wrote his father two days later. "Mother has decided not to come down to Washington at all, despite your telegram of last night saying that the weather had become cool. As you may recall, your letter earlier in the week intimated that you were remaining chaste only because of the hot weather. Possibly mother feels that she would be surplussage now that the barometer has changed."⁶¹ Roe promptly sent Jack's letter to Netha. "I am returning a letter recently received from your son. What kind of mother do you think you are that produced so lewd-minded an offspring."⁶²

Roe also remained politically active during 1929, joining the Progressive La Guardia Non-Partisan Committee supporting then U.S. Representative Fiorello La Guardia for mayor of New York City. La Guardia had supported La Follette in 1924, and Roe returned the favor. "I was delighted to receive your letter," La Guardia wrote Roe in August. "I appreciate it so much. Yes indeed, we want to marshal all our forces. I need not tell you the fight that I have been through to get the nomination and the fight I must go to be elected. I am very confident that we can put it over."⁶³ Roe took great offense, however, at the La Guardia campaign's publicly urging socialist Norman Thomas to withdraw from the mayoralty race. "I thought when I joined [the committee] that I was helping to make a fight on Tammany Hall, not on the Socialist party and particularly not upon Mr. Thomas," Roe wrote J. A. H. Hopkins, committee chair. "Both Mr. Thomas and Major La Guardia did heroic service in behalf of the Progressive ticket in the campaign of 1924, and in this campaign both are in my judgment equally entitled to appeal for Progressive votes from their respective points of view."⁶⁴ Roe asked that his name be taken off the committee roster, although he subsequently assured La Guardia of his support. When the *New York World* impugned La Guardia's "progressivism," La Guardia asked Roe to intercede with Robert La Follette Jr., "for [a] proper statement from him,"⁶⁵ Roe wrote back that "any attack by anyone upon your record and character as a Progressive will be resented and denied."⁶⁶

In the fall of 1929, Roe sold the Dutchess County farm at Wappinger's Falls that he and the family had so enjoyed. A corporation called the Dutchess Land Company, with Roe's associate John Scoble as one of the incorporators, would retain some of the land as a farm but also lay out a golf course and tennis courts on the property.⁶⁷ The property would later become known as the Hutchinson Estate, and on it was the house where Franklin Roosevelt's candidacy was planned when the house was owned by his counsel, Judge Samuel Rosenman.⁶⁸ Roe also appeared in his last legal case that fall,⁶⁹ again representing a client who had been victimized by the "unscrupulous methods employed by" Roe's old adversary, Jared Flagg, in financing two properties on West 68th Street. The 1929 case, styled *Kaufman v. Flagg*,⁷⁰ was actually a contest over which among several creditors of Flagg had priority. Roe's client prevailed on a $20,000 mortgage, although other claimants were given priority on another one valued at $40,000.

Winding Down

Gilbert and Netha Roe attended a luncheon in honor of John Dewey's seventieth birthday at the Hotel Astor on October 19.[71] Not long afterward, however, Gilbert fell very ill, probably due to congestive heart failure associated with an oral infection he had suffered for several years.[72] Netha kept family and friends apprised of his progress through letters to "Dear Ones," like the one she sent on Thanksgiving night:

> Daddy and I have had a really peaceful day and a fairly comfortable one for Daddy. He has slept less than an hour all day long. It is the first day I recall that he has not either slept or been "dead for sleep" without being able to accomplish it. It followed one of the best nights he has had, (which means he was awake three or four times after 2:30 but slept again quickly after hot milk or going to the bath room or talking a moment).
>
> The most trying times for Daddy have been the two times when digitalis is discontinued because of threatened nausea. It is rather hard to say at these times whether irritation and weakness due to the nausea makes Daddy question the wisdom of everyone, or whether it is the let-down from withdrawing the digitalis that makes him feel weaker and therefore more discouraged. But as restful sleep has followed both these experiments I have confidence that the direction is right.[73]

Despite that optimistic note, Netha would later annotate the letter in pencil: "This was the last day I dared trust that Gilbert would get well. N." Gilbert Roe died on December 22, 1929, just over a month before his sixty-fifth birthday. Private funeral services were held in the 10th Street apartment, with Netha and the children in attendance.[74]

Epilogue

Gilbert Roe's death in 1929 brought a remarkable outpouring of grief from political and philosophical allies. The most moving obituaries were published in the Wisconsin press closely associated with Roe and La Follette. Madison's *Capital Times* wrote: "The death of Mr. Roe brings an irreparable loss to the Progressive movement and to the cause of good government in this country. He was a man who could have attained to great wealth in the service of corporate interests had he so chosen. But there was the spirit of the rebel and the explorer in his makeup. Never did an attorney more conscientiously follow the oath which every lawyer must take than Gil Roe." In the *Progressive*, successor to *La Follette's Magazine*, Robert La Follette Jr. wrote: "Gilbert E. Roe will be remembered as one of the gallant, courageous figures of his time. . . . Though he never held a public office the contributions he made to the public welfare were so solid and conspicuous as to assure him an enduring place in the history of his country."[75]

The *Truth Seeker*, a magazine of the Freethought movement that Roe had defended in a criminal libel case in 1913, praised Roe in its January 1930 issue. "The New York Bar lost a member it could ill spare when Gilbert E. Roe took his departure, December 22, 1929. For Mr. Roe was something more than a lawyer whose proudest boast was to win cases. He was a defender, often a champion, of the lost cause."[76] Roe's associate, John Scoble, prepared a memorial for the New York City Bar Association's 1930 Yearbook, which quoted La Follette Sr. on his friend Gilbert Roe: "He has always looked upon the profession of law as one that involves to a high degree responsibility to the public, and it would be difficult to find a successful practitioner who combines with his legal skill a keener sense of duty to the public good."[77]

Condolence letters came pouring in from all over the world. One of the first came from Henry R. Linville, president of the Teachers Union, for whom Roe was still working when he died. "We shall miss him more, perhaps, than any friend we have," Linville wrote on December 23.[78] In a longer formal statement issued in February 1930, Linville said that for a "period of eleven years Mr. Roe's work for the Union was characterized by qualities of great skill as a lawyer, of fine courage and intelligence as a man and of devotion as a friend."[79] Ralph Sucher, a Washington journalist who married Mary La Follette, wrote to "Aunt Netha" about the boyhood stories Roe told Ralph's young son Bob when Roe was in Washington during the past summer. When Roe told Bob about an old dog who had died, Bob asked why. "'We all have to die, Bob,'" Roe had told the boy, "'but that isn't important. You want to live and do good things, and be kind and generous to people, and when you are gone they will remember what a good fellow you were, the way we think of your grandfather.'"[80]

"Gil had love to give, and understanding," Lincoln Steffens wrote from Carmel, California. "My grief (there is always a remorse) is that I can't remember having expressed to Gil my love for him; it's as if I had taken his and never thought that he might have liked to know about mine, which wells up warm and big now that it is too late for him."[81] Emma Goldman wrote from St. Tropez, France: "I was terribly shocked to read that so fine a spirit like Gilbert's was no more. And I wanted you to know that I feel profoundly the tragedy that has come to you."[82] Alexander Berkman wrote from Paris: "I have known few men whom I could admire as frankly and unconditionally as I did Gilbert."[83] And Agnes Smedley wrote from Shanghai: "I regard Mr. Roe's death not only as a personal loss, for he was a friend who never failed me in all my troubles since I met him during the world war; but I regard his death as a loss to America. He seemed to be one of those few Americans who, in these days of imperialist plundering, held to and fought for the principles of liberty that existed when he was young."[84]

"The sad news of Gilbert's sudden death was an inexpressible shock to me," wrote socialist lawyer Morris Hillquit. "I loved him dearly as did all those who had the good fortune of coming into close contact with him and observing his quiet courage, unfailing kindness and noble idealism. His passing leaves an awful gap in our midst."[85] Another lawyer, and sometime client, Hobart Bird, wrote, "I was greatly shocked and grieved to read in this morning's press of the death of your very good husband. . . . I counted him as one of my best and most delightful of friends and oh how many many others must have felt the same toward him, because of his humanitarianism both general and specific, always tempering justice with mercy."[86]

Similar sentiments were expressed by his political allies. Former New York governor William Sulzer: "I have just learned, with deep regret, of the death of your good and distinguished husband—who for many years was my personal friend."[87] From Meta Berger, widow of the socialist political leader Victor Berger: "Mr. Berger always admired Mr. Roe so greatly. . . . Here in Wisconsin as in New York, Washington, & elsewhere, Mr. Roe's friends and admirers were legion."[88] And from Marx Lewis, executive secretary of the Socialist Party of America: "[He] had endeared himself to all of us by his fearless and unselfish devotion to the cause of progress and his defense of minority thought and opinion."[89] Roe's publisher, Ben Huebsch, wrote: "Gilbert was so generous in giving of his goodness and kindness and wisdom, to individuals and groups, that he himself must have been unconscious of the far-reaching consequences of his unselfish benefactions."[90]

In early 1930, Netha moved into an apartment at 158 Waverly Place in Greenwich Village recently vacated by Fola La Follette.[91] Later, she moved to Norris, Tennessee, to live with Janet, who directed a nursery school there for the Tennessee Valley Authority. They moved to Washington, D.C., in 1943, and after Janet married Jerome Keller, Netha continued to live with Janet while working on her autobiography.[92] Netha Roe died at age one hundred in 1968.[93] Jack practiced law in Madison, along with Phil La Follette, in the firm of Roberts, Roe & Boardman.[94] He committed suicide in 1956.[95] Gwyneth attended graduate school at the University of Wisconsin and worked as a reporter there and, later, in Michigan and Illinois. She married Edwin M. Murphy of Bethesda, Maryland, and died at age fifty-five in 1971. At the time of her death, she was an information officer of the Prince George's County Public Library in Bladensburg, Maryland.[96]

Conclusion

Gilbert Roe's Legacy

> [We] consider this case against the background of a profound national commitment to the principle that debate on public issues should be uninhibited, robust, and wide-open, and that it may well include vehement, caustic, and sometimes unpleasantly sharp attacks on government and public officials.
>
> New York Times v. Sullivan

> [Government may not] forbid or proscribe advocacy of the use of force or of law violation except where such advocacy is directed to inciting or producing imminent lawless action and is likely to incite or produce such action.
>
> Brandenburg v. Ohio

Gilbert Roe was a loving husband and father, a hard-working and successful lawyer, a fiercely loyal and dedicated friend, a staunch political partisan, and a true pioneer in the evolution of freedom of speech in the United States. With a handful of other notable lawyers, Roe was an acknowledged leader in the fight for free speech from the birth of the progressive movement through the Red Scare of the 1920s. It fell to Roe and the others to translate the constitutional ideal of "freedom of speech" into a practical and sustainable legal doctrine that would actually protect those who tried to exercise that freedom from governmental repression. He failed more often than not in court, but the battles he fought kept the cause alive until, in time, the victory was won.

In the years before the United States entered World War I, the doctrinal tools that Roe used in court were based largely on the theories of Theodore Schroeder, who saw freedom of speech as a right derived from the liberty interest protected by the due process clause of the Fourteenth Amendment. Roe employed arguments based on that theoretical foundation in his representation of anarchists and feminists against the hostility of the government and, indeed, the popular majority. Those arguments fell largely on deaf ears, however, and Roe gradually adopted new arguments based on theoretical foundations advanced by Zecharia Chafee and other civil libertarians who saw freedom of speech not so much as an individual liberty but rather as a practical requirement for the proper functioning of a democratic society.

In his most famous war-related case, *Masses Publishing Co. v. Patten*, Roe's constitutional argument was perfunctory at best, and the case was decided on purely statutory grounds. But by 1919, two years later, Roe would write: "I insist upon freedom of speech and of free press not merely because it is a constitutional right, but because it is a necessity under our form of government."[1] Roe's later argument, grounded in the First Amendment, would eventually gain traction in the courts, most notably in the dissenting opinions of Holmes and Brandeis, but it would still be years before they prevailed.

Perhaps the first inkling that Roe's labors would bear fruit would come two years after his death, in the landmark case of *Near v. Minnesota*,[2] in which Roe's fellow progressive Charles Evans Hughes would declare that the First Amendment prohibited the courts from imposing prior restraints by injunction. Roe had inveighed against the use of injunctions to stifle free speech in connection with his representation of anarchists such as Emma Goldman. In 1915, Roe had told the Commission on Industrial Relations that allowing the courts to enjoin Goldman from speaking because her message might not be welcome was "utterly subversive of free assemblage and free speech."[3] In 1931, the U.S. Supreme Court fully ratified that view.

Eighteen years later, the U.S. Supreme Court took up another abridgement of freedom of speech that Roe had fought against—and lost—years earlier defending the socialist author Upton Sinclair. Sinclair's 1914 conviction for demonstrating in front of John D. Rockefeller's New York City offices had been largely predicated on the likelihood that his protest would result in a breach of the peace. In 1949, in *Terminiello v. Chicago*, the court ruled in favor of a Catholic priest who made inflammatory remarks during a speech in Chicago and was fined for violating the city's "breach of peace" ordinance. The court declared that no speaker could be convicted on the ground that his speech "stirred people to anger, invited public dispute, or brought about a condition of unrest."[4]

Roe's struggles against the seditious libel provisions of the Espionage Act had come to naught, but half a century later, the U.S. Supreme Court invoked the now-presumed unconstitutionality of that repressive legislation to prohibit the use of Alabama libel law to punish those who would criticize government. In the 1964 case of *New York Times v. Sullivan*, the court effectively abolished the kind of seditious libel laws that Roe had consistently fought against.[5] L. B. Sullivan was the police commissioner of Montgomery, Alabama, at the height of the civil rights movement. Using a time-honored practice of southern segregationist officials, he sued the *Times* for libel based on an ad placed in the paper supporting Dr. Martin Luther King. The Supreme Court saw the lawsuit for what it really was—an attempt to punish criticism of government—and it raised the bar dramatically for libel suits filed by public officials. "[S]editious libel, like heresy, is now firmly outside the American tradition," wrote scholar Harry Kalven Jr. "The central meaning of the First Amendment is that seditious libel cannot be made the subject of government sanction."[6]

Not only did *New York Times v. Sullivan* drive the final nail in the coffin of seditious libel, but it also constitutionalized libel law itself. Predicting the outcome of any lawsuit is always a risky business, but it is likely that Roe's first important case—the libel suit against *McClure's Magazine*—would have had a very different outcome after 1964. The heavy presumption of liability on the part of the defendant would no longer exist. Instead, the burden would be on the plaintiff to prove that the defendant was not only wrong but also negligent or malicious. Today, Roy Stannard Baker's reliance on the errors in the government report might well have resulted in complete vindication for the pioneering muckraker. But that case arose before the First Amendment was a common or useful defense, not only for libel cases but for all manner of freedom of speech cases. The First Amendment was not mentioned anywhere in the record, by Roe or any judge who heard the case, and any argument based on the First Amendment would probably have been summarily dismissed. But Roe's work for freedom of speech during these "forgotten years"[7] helped to lay a foundation for modern First Amendment jurisprudence.

Finally, the case that most closely embodies the principles established in the brilliant *Masses* opinion of Learned Hand, albeit couched now in constitutional rather than statutory terms, was *Brandenburg v. Ohio*, decided in 1969. Brandenberg involved a Ku Klux Klan leader who violated Ohio's Criminal Syndicalism Statute by "advocating . . . the duty, necessity, or propriety of . . . violence . . . as a means of accomplishing . . . political reform." Without reference to *Masses*—which had been quickly and decisively reversed back in 1917—the U.S. Supreme Court adopted Hand's central distinction between advocacy and incitement to hold that government may not "forbid or proscribe advocacy of the use of force or of law violation except where such advocacy is directed to inciting or producing imminent lawless action and is likely to incite or produce such action."[8]

If Roe's legacy had been merely helping to establish the foundations for *Near*, *Terminiello*, *Sullivan*, and *Brandenburg*, that would be more than enough to guarantee him an honored place in the history of free speech law. But his career should also inspire civil libertarians, and especially civil libertarian lawyers, to continue giving voice to the unpopular, radical, even subversive views that comprise the American experience.

Notes

Introduction

1. Testimony of Charles Bamberger on Cross-Examination, Papers on Appeal from Order at 38, New York v. Sanger, 33 N.Y. Crim. R. 415 (1915).
2. MARGARET SANGER, MY FIGHT FOR BIRTH CONTROL 120 (1931).
3. Testimony of Charles Bamberger on Cross-Examination, *supra* note 1.
4. Testimony of Charles Bamberger on Direct Examination, Papers on Appeal from Order at 37, New York v. Sanger, 33 N.Y. Crim. R. 415 (1915).
5. William Sanger, *Birth Control*, in JAILED FOR BIRTH CONTROL: THE TRIAL OF WILLIAM SANGER, SEPTEMBER 10, 1915, at 6 (James Waldo Fawcett ed., 1917). In her autobiography, Margaret wrote that William explained to Heller that "we had agreed that I was to carry on my work independently of him, and he did not even think he had any of the pamphlets. However, the man's story was so pathetic that he rummaged around and by chance found one in the library drawer." MARGARET SANGER, MARGARET SANGER: AN AUTOBIOGRAPHY 176 (1938) [hereinafter MARGARET SANGER].
6. MARGARET SANGER, *supra* note 5, at 176.
7. MARK A. GRABER, TRANSFORMING FREE SPEECH 54 (1991).
8. JOHN D. BUENKER, 4 THE HISTORY OF WISCONSIN: THE PROGRESSIVE ERA, 1893–1914, at 6–11 (Nook ed., 2013).
9. ALFRED H. KELLY, WINFRED A. HARBISON & HERMAN BELZ, 2 THE AMERICAN CONSTITUTION, ITS ORIGINS AND DEVELOPMENT 386 (1991).
10. U.S. CONST., amend. XIV, §1. The plain language of the amendment says that no state shall "deprive any person of life, liberty, or property, without due process of law."
11. 165 U.S. 578 (1897).
12. KELLY, HARBISON & BELZ, *supra* note 9, at 403.
13. GRABER, *supra* note 7, at 18 (quoting William Graham Sumner).
14. *Id.* at 34–35.
15. Lochner v. New York, 198 U.S. 45 (1905).

16. GRABER, *supra* note 7, at 56–62.
17. INDUSTRIAL RELATIONS, FINAL REPORT AND TESTIMONY, S. DOC. NO. 415, at 10469–72 (1916).
18. GRABER, *supra* note 7, at 4.
19. Masses Publ. Co. v. Patten, 244 F. 535, 540 (S.D.N.Y. 1917).
20. Schenck v. United States, 249 U.S. 47 (1919).
21. GRABER, *supra* note 7, at 118–26.
22. *Espionage and Interference with Neutrality: Hearings on H.R. 291 Before the H. Comm. on the Judiciary*, 65th Cong. (1917), at 40–41.
23. Gilbert E. Roe, *The Espionage Law*, PEARSON'S MAG., March 1919, at 197.

CHAPTER 1. GETTING STARTED

1. Notes, in Gwyneth King Roe Papers, 1880–1968, Wisconsin Historical Society, Mss 151 [hereinafter GKR Papers], Box 8, Folder 6.
2. Diploma, in GKR Papers, Box 7, Folder 6.
3. Letter from Gilbert E. Roe to Mrs. Fred A. Baker (June 10, 1915), in GKR Papers, Box 1, Folder 16.
4. Gilbert E. Roe, *Stability of the American Government* (unpublished high school graduation oration), in GKR Papers, Box 7, Folder 6.
5. Diploma, in GKR Papers, Box 7, Folder 6.
6. *The Aegis*, U. Wis., Vol. 1 (November 22 & 23 & March 4, 1887), in GKR Papers, Box 7, Folder 7.
7. Certificate, in GKR Papers, Box 7, Folder 6.
8. Certificates, in GKR Papers, Box 7, Folder 6.
9. MADISON CITY DIRECTORY, 1890–91, at 24, http://ancestry.com.
10. BELLE CASE & FOLA LA FOLLETTE, ROBERT M. LA FOLLETTE 41, 21 (1953) [hereinafter LA FOLLETTE].
11. La Follette Family Papers, Library of Congress, Box 230, Folder 4 — Cases of La Follette, Harper, Roe & Zimmerman.
12. U.S. Fed. Census, Milford, Jefferson, Wis., Roll: 1430, Family History Film: 1255430, Page: 200A, Enumeration District: 173.
13. Gwyneth King Roe, *Two Views of the La Follettes: 1. Madison, the '90s*, WISCONSIN MAGAZINE OF HISTORY, Winter 1958–59, at 104. This is a published version of a draft chapter entitled *Madison, Wisconsin*, in Gwyneth Roe's unpublished autobiography, available in GKR Papers, Box 4, Folder 3, at 4–5.
14. *Two Views of the La Follettes*, *supra* note 13, at 104.
15. *Madison, Wisconsin*, *supra* note 13, at 14.
16. LA FOLLETTE, *supra* note 10, at 109.
17. Gwyneth King Roe, draft introduction to her unpublished autobiography, entitled *Prelude*, in GKR Papers, Box 4, Folder 4.

18. Gwyneth King Roe, draft chapter 1 to her unpublished autobiography, entitled *New Providence, Eldora and Hampton, Iowa*, in GKR Papers, Box 4, Folder 4.

19. Gwyneth King Roe, draft chapter 2 to her unpublished autobiography, entitled *Founding a Town on the Bank of a River*, in GKR Papers, Box 4, Folder 4.

20. Gwyneth Roe Murphy, untitled draft obituary of her mother, Gwyneth King Roe, undated, in GKR Papers, Box 9, Folder 3.

21. *Two Views of the La Follettes*, supra note 13, at 104.

22. LA FOLLETTE, supra note 10, at 112.

23. *Madison, Wisconsin*, supra note 13, at 7–8.

24. *Two Views of the La Follettes*, supra note 13, at 107.

25. Letter from Gilbert Roe to Gwyneth King (undated), in GKR, Box 2, Folder 13.

26. Gwyneth King Roe, draft chronology, in GKR Papers, Box 4, Folder 1.

27. *See* GKR Papers, Box 2, Folder 9, for detailed materials regarding this trip.

28. *See, e.g.*, *La Follette Lieutenant Marries Miss Gwyneth King of Chicago*, WISCONSIN WEEKLY ADVOCATE, November 16, 1899, page number unknown.

29. Letter from Fola La Follette to Gilbert Roe (August 3, 1899), in GKR Papers, Box 1, Folder 9.

30. Petition for Admission, in GKR Papers, Box 7, Folder 6.

31. Letter from Gilbert Roe to Alfred Rogers, La Follette political aide and law partner (December 10, 1900), showing addresses on letterhead, in Gilbert E. Roe Papers, 1887–1961, in La Follette Family Papers, 1781–1988, Manuscript Division, Library of Congress, Washington, D.C. [hereinafter Roe Papers], Box H4, Folder 1910.

32. U.S. Fed.Census.

33. U.S. Fed.Census.

34. Petition and Order (January 19, 1900), in GKR Papers, Box 7, Folder 6. Roe was admitted to practice in the federal courts in New York in 1903. Certificate of Admission (April 24, 1903), in GKR Papers, Box 7, Folder 6.

35. Fragment of Draft Autobiography, in GKR Papers, Box 5, Folder 7.

36. Van Tine v. Hilands, 131 F. 124, 125 (S.D.N.Y. 1904).

37. Erie City Iron Works v. Thomas, 139 F. 995 (S.D.N.Y. 1905).

38. Milliken Bros. v. City of N.Y., 135 A.D. 598 (1909).

39. Haenschen v. Roebling Const. Co., 194 N.Y. 533 (1909); Bier v. Roebling Const. Co., 134 A.D. 356 (N.Y. App. 1909).

40. Clark v. Johnston, 141 A.D. 926 (N.Y. App. 1910).

41. Fragment of Draft Autobiography, in GKR Papers, Box 5, Folder 7.

42. Letter from Gilbert Roe to John D. Leedy (May 14, 1901), in Roe Papers, Box H4, Folder 1901.

43. Fragment of Draft Autobiography, in GKR Papers, Box 5, Folder 7.

44. Letter from Gilbert Roe to Alfred Rogers (July 6, 1906), in Roe Papers, Box H4, Folder 1906.

45. Letter from Gilbert Roe to Alfred Rogers (July 17, 1906), in Roe Papers, Box H4, Folder 1906.

46. Letter from Gilbert Roe to Alfred Rogers (December 15, 1906), in Roe Papers, Box H4, Folder 1906.
47. Strauss v. Union Cent. Life Ins. Co., 67 N.Y.S. 509, 509 (N.Y. Sup. Ct. 1900).
48. Strauss v. Union Cent. Life Ins. Co., 63 N.E. 347, 350 (N.Y. 1902), *aff'g* 70 N.Y.S. 1149 (N.Y. App. 1901).
49. McCoy v. Mutual Reserve Life Ins. Co., 82 N.Y.S. 638 (N.Y. App. Div. 1903).
50. *See, e.g.*, Lambert v. Mutual Reserve Life Ins. Co., 90 N.Y.S. 1103 (N.Y. App. Div. 1904) (memorandum opinion deciding eight actions); Johnston v. Mutual Reserve Life Ins. Co., 93 N.Y.S. 1062 (N.Y. App. Div. 1905) (deciding 13 actions).
51. Mutual Reserve Life Ins. Co. v. Birch, 200 U.S. 612 (1905).
52. Birch v. Mutual Reserve Life Ins. Co., 86 N.Y.S. 872, 873 (N.Y. App. Div. 1904).
53. Letter from Theodore Schroeder to U.S. Sen. John C. Spooner, February 11, 1903, in Theodore Schroeder Papers, 1842–1957, Special Collections Research Center, Southern Illinois University Carbondale, Box 6, Folder 2 [hereinafter Schroeder Papers].
54. *Birch*, 86 N.Y.S. at 874.
55. *Birch*, 200 U.S. at 612.
56. Robinson v. Mutual Reserve Life Ins. Co., 182 F. 850, 863–64 (S.D.N.Y. 1910).
57. Joseph Ishill, *Theodore Schroeder, in* A NEW CONCEPT OF LIBERTY: FROM AN EVOLUTIONARY PSYCHOLOGIST: THEODORE SCHROEDER x–xxxvii (Joseph Ishill ed., 1940).
58. Letter from Theodore Schroeder to John C. Spooner (February 11, 1903), in Schroeder Papers, Box 6, Folder 2.
59. JOHN D. BUENKER, 4 THE HISTORY OF WISCONSIN: THE PROGRESSIVE ERA, 1893–1914, at 560 (Nook ed., 2013).
60. Ishill, *supra* note 57, at xxxviii.
61. Partnership Announcement, in GKR Papers, Box 7, Folder 6.
62. LA FOLLETTE, *supra* note 10, at 444.
63. Annotated photograph, in GKR Papers, Box 8, Folder 3.
64. Handwritten notes from Belle La Follette to Gilbert Roe, May 14 and September 16, 1906, in Roe Papers, Box H1, Folder 1906.
65. Samuel G. Blythe, *The Lonely Man of the Senate*, SATURDAY EVENING POST, June 10, 1911, at 4, 49; U.S. Senate, Senate History, 1878–1920, http://www.senate.gov/artandhistory/history/minute/Maiden_Speeches.htm).
66. Letter from Gilbert Roe to Belle La Follette (April 26, 1906), in Roe Papers, Box H4, Folder 1906.
67. Handwritten note from Belle La Follette to "Netha" (May 14, 1906), in Roe Papers, Box H1, Folder 1906.
68. Handwritten note from Belle La Follette to Gwyneth Roe (September 16, 1906), in Roe Papers, Box H1, Folder 1906. Underlining in the original.
69. Letter from Alfred Rogers to Gilbert Roe (January 16, 1906), in Roe Papers, Box H6, Folder 1906.
70. Letter from Gilbert Roe to Alfred Rogers (January 19, 1906), in Roe Papers, Box H4, Folder 1906.

71. Letter from Alfred Rogers to Gilbert Roe (December 27, 1906), in Roe Papers, Box H6, Folder 1906.

72. Letter from Belle La Follette to Gilbert Roe (May 31, 1907), in Roe Papers, Box H6, Folder 1906.

73. SELECTED OPINIONS OF LUTHER DIXON AND EDGAR RYAN, LATE CHIEF JUSTICES OF THE SUPREME COURT OF WISCONSIN iii (Gilbert E. Roe ed., 1907).

74. Letter from Gilbert Roe to Alfred Rogers (July 9, 1906), in Roe Papers, Box H4, Folder 1907.

75. *See, e.g.*, letter from Gilbert Roe to H. B. Maurer, Brooklyn (February 14, 1907), in Roe Papers, Box H4, Folder 1907 (suggesting how to boost attendance at a La Follette speech Maurer was hosting and ordering ten tickets himself).

76. *See, e.g.*, letter from Gilbert Roe to Walter Drew, Madison (July 23, 1907), in Roe Papers, Box H4, Folder 1907 (offering to compile a book on the history of primary election law in La Follette's own words).

77. Letter from Gilbert Roe to Alfred Rogers (September 9, 1910), in Roe Papers, Box H4, Folder 1910.

78. Handwritten note from Belle La Follette to the Roes (October 15, 1910), in Roe Papers, Box H1, Folder 1910.

79. Letter from Gilbert Roe to William McCombs (September 27, 1911), in Roe Papers, Box H4, Folder 1911.

80. Letter from Belle La Follette to Gwyneth King Roe (September 8, 1911), in Roe Papers, Box H1, Folder 1911.

81. DORIS KEARNS GOODWIN, THE BULLY PULPIT: THEODORE ROOSEVELT, WILLIAM HOWARD TAFT AND THE GOLDEN AGE OF JOURNALISM 843–44 (Nook ed., 2013).

82. Letter from Gilbert Roe to Francis McGovern (October 10, 1910), in Roe Papers, Box H4, Folder 1910.

83. GOODWIN, *supra* note 81, at 822–30.

84. Letter from Gilbert Roe to Alfred Baker (November 2, 1911), in Roe Papers, Box H4, Folder 1911.

85. Mark Sullivan, *The Situation to Date*, COLLIER'S THE NAT'L WKLY., December 23, 1911, at 18.

86. Letter from Gilbert Roe to COLLIER'S (December 30, 1911), in Roe Papers, Box H4, Folder 1911.

87. GOODWIN, *supra* note 81, at 830–31.

88. LA FOLLETTE, *supra* note 10, at 375.

89. GOODWIN, *supra* note 81, at 833–34.

90. LA FOLLETTE, *supra* note 10, at 387–90.

91. GOODWIN, *supra* note 81, at 834.

92. Letter from Belle La Follette to Gilbert Roe (February 6, 1912), in LA FOLLETTE, *supra* note 10, at 411.

93. GOODWIN, *supra* note 81, at 837.

94. Letter from Robert La Follette to Gilbert Roe (February 6, 1912), in LA FOLLETTE, *supra* note 10, at 413–14.

95. Letter from Gilbert Roe to Rudolph Spreckels (April 13, 1912), in LA FOLLETTE, *supra* note 10, at 418.
96. Letter from Gilbert Roe to Robert La Follette (February 8, 1912), in Roe Papers, Box H4, Folder 1912.
97. GOODWIN, *supra* note 81, at 844.
98. Letter from Gilbert Roe to P. S. Scales, Esq., c/o Rudolph Spreckels (May 23, 1912), in Roe Papers, Box H4, Folder 1912.
99. GOODWIN, *supra* note 81, at 850–67.
100. LA FOLLETTE, *supra* note 10, at 435.
101. Letter from Gilbert Roe to Robert La Follette (June 8, 1912), in Roe Papers, Box H4, Folder 1912.
102. LA FOLLETTE, *supra* note 10, at 435–37.
103. GOODWIN, *supra* note 81, at 867, 884.
104. Letter from Gilbert Roe to W. S. Elder, Esq., Deadwood, S.D. (June 26, 1912), in Roe Papers, Box H4, Folder 1912.
105. Letter from Gilbert Roe to I. A. Webb, Deadwood, S.D. (August 5, 1912), in Roe Papers, Box H4, Folder 1912.
106. Letter from Gilbert Roe to Grant Thomas, Esq., Portland, Ore. (August 20, 1912), in Roe Papers, Box H4, Folder 1912.
107. Letter from Gilbert Roe to Robert La Follette (October 9, 1912), in Roe Papers, Box H4, Folder 1912.
108. Named for Lochner v. New York, 198 U.S. 45 (1905) (striking down state legislation limiting the working hours of bakers).
109. GILBERT E. ROE, OUR JUDICIAL OLIGARCHY 23, 198–99 (1912).
110. GOODWIN, *supra* note 81, at 844.
111. Letter from Gilbert Roe to Robert M. La Follette (February 8, 1912), in Roe Papers, Box H4, Folder 1912.
112. Letter from Gilbert Roe to Dick Jones, *State Journal* (November 18, 1912), in Roe Papers, Box H4, Folder 1912.
113. *See* ANDREW L. KAUFMAN, CARDOZO 117 (2000).
114. *Urge G. E. Roe for Bench*, N.Y. TIMES, July 23, 1913, at 2.
115. Letter from Gilbert Roe to Robert La Follette (July 30, 1913), in Roe Papers, Box H4, Folder 1913.
116. Letter from Gilbert Roe to Robert La Follette (August 11, 1913), in Roe Papers, Box H4, Folder 1913.
117. Letter from Gilbert Roe to Robert La Follette (August 15, 1913), in Roe Papers, Box H4, Folder 1913.
118. KAUFMAN, *supra* note 113, at 125.
119. Letter from Gilbert Roe to William Sulzer (May 9, 1913), in Roe Papers, Box H4, Folder 1913.
120. KAUFMAN, *supra* note 113, at 120.
121. *Will Seek Writ to Free Garrison*, N.Y. TIMES, September 20, 1913, at 1.

122. *Assembly Jails Sulzer's Friend*, ROME (N.Y.) DAILY SENTINEL, September 19, 1913, at 1.

123. *Will Seek Writ, supra* note 121.

124. *Garrison Is Freed by Court*, DUNKIRK (N.Y.) EVENING OBSERVER, October 30, 1913, at 1.

125. *Court Sets Garrison Free*, N.Y. TIMES, October 31, 1913, at 3.

126. *Sulzer Elected to Assembly Two to One in Sixth*, N.Y. TIMES, November 5, 1913, at 1.

127. GERALD GUNTHER, LEARNED HAND: THE MAN AND THE JUDGE 235–36 (1994).

128. Letter from Gilbert Roe to Learned Hand (November 6, 1913), in Roe Papers, Box H4, Folder 1913.

129. Letter from Learned Hand to Gilbert Roe (November 7, 1913), in Roe Papers, Box H6, Special Correspondence.

130. F. 910 (2d Cir. 1909). *See infra* Chapter 2.

131. Letter from Gilbert Roe to Rudolph Spreckles (August 6, 1914), in Roe Papers, Box H4, Folder 1914.

132. LA FOLLETTE, *supra* note 10, at 516.

133. Loewe v. Lawlor, 208 U.S. 274 (1908).

134. Letter from Gilbert Roe to Robert M. La Follette (May 6, 1915), in Roe Papers, Box H4, Folder 1915.

135. Telegram from Gilbert Roe to Robert M. La Follette (May 9, 1915), in Roe Papers, Box H4, Folder 1915.

136. Gilbert E. Roe, *Argument of Gilbert E. Roe before the Judiciary Committee of the Constitutional Convention, June 24, 1915* (reprint), in Roe Papers, Box H14.

137. Cook v. Flagg, 255 F. 195, 199 (S.D.N.Y. 1915); Cook v. Flagg, 233 F. 426, 428 (2d Cir. 1916); Cook v. Flagg, 251 F. 5, 12 (2d Cir. 1918).

138. Flagg v. Cook, 247 U.S. 508 (1918).

139. Letter from Belle Case La Follette to Gwyneth King Roe (January 25, 1918), in GKR Papers, Box 1, Folder 8.

140. Letter from Gilbert Roe to Robert La Follette (August 5, 1916), in Roe Papers, Box H5, Folder 1916.

141. Letter from Gilbert Roe to William Chilton (February 2, 1916), in Roe Papers, Box H5, Folder 1916.

142. LA FOLLETTE, *supra* note 10, at 584.

143. Letter from Gilbert Roe to Robert La Follette (November 8, 1916), in Roe Papers, Box H5, Folder 1916.

144. Letter from Gilbert Roe to Robert La Follette (May 24, 1916), in Roe Papers, Box H5, Folder 1916.

145. Telegram from Gilbert Roe to Belle Case La Follette (May 25, 1916), in Roe Papers, Box H5, Folder 1916.

146. Letter from Gilbert Roe to John Hannan (May 27, 1916), in Roe Papers, Box H5, Folder 1916.

147. Letter from Gilbert Roe to Belle Case La Follette (May 31, 1916), in Roe Papers, Box H5, Folder 1916.
148. Letter from Gilbert Roe to Robert La Follette (June 6, 1916), in Roe Papers, Box H5, Folder 1916.
149. Letter from Gilbert Roe to Robert La Follette Jr. (Bobbie) (June 2, 1916), in Roe Papers, Box H5, Folder 1916.
150. LA FOLLETTE, *supra* note 10, at 656.
151. DAVID M. KENNEDY, OVER HERE 30–34 (2004).
152. Letter from Gwyneth King Roe to Carrie Chapman Catt (February 25, 1917), in GKR Papers, Box 1, Folder 3.
153. Letter from Mrs. Norman de R. Whitehouse to Gwyneth King Roe (February 28, 1917), in GKR Papers, Box 2, Folder 4.
154. Letter from Gwyneth King Roe to Carrie Chapman Catt, *supra* note 152.
155. Letter from Gilbert Roe to Robert La Follette (February 27, 1917), in Roe Papers, Box H5, Folder 1917.
156. KENNEDY, *supra* note 151, at 11.
157. LA FOLLETTE, *supra* note 10, at 666–67.

CHAPTER 2. THE MUCKRAKERS

1. Letter from Robert M. La Follette to Gilbert Roe (July 27, 1904), in Roe Papers, Box H6, Folder 1904.
2. JOHN D. BUENKER, 4 THE HISTORY OF WISCONSIN: THE PROGRESSIVE ERA, 1893–1914, at 540–79 (Nook ed., 2013).
3. JUSTIN KAPLAN, LINCOLN STEFFENS: A BIOGRAPHY 95–96, 130–39 (1974).
4. DORIS KEARNS GOODWIN, THE BULLY PULPIT 206–62 (Nook ed., 2013).
5. ARTHUR & LILI WEINBERG, THE MUCKRAKERS 1902–1912, at xvi–xvii (1961).
6. KAPLAN, *supra* note 3, at 113.
7. ARTHUR & LILI WEINBERG, *supra* note 5, at xvii.
8. KAPLAN, *supra* note 3, at 126.
9. Letter from Robert M. La Follette to Gilbert Roe (July 27, 1904), in Roe Papers, Box H6, Folder 1904.
10. Letter from Gilbert Roe to Hon. A. R. Hall (September 27, 1904), Box H4, Folder 1901–03 ("I have come to know Steffens very well, and he certainly is a great fellow"). Hall was a pro–La Follette, anti-railroad legislator in the Wisconsin assembly.
11. Letter from Lincoln Steffens to Gwyneth Roe (December 24, 1929), in GKR Papers, Box 2, Folder 2.
12. MCCLURE'S 563 (October 1904).
13. BELLE CASE & FOLA LA FOLLETTE, ROBERT M. LA FOLLETTE 185 (1953) [hereinafter LA FOLLETTE].

14. KAPLAN, *supra* note 3, at 139.
15. BUENKER, *supra* note 2, at 540.
16. S. S. McClure Co. v. Philipp, 170 F. 910, 911 (2d Cir. 1909).
17. Record Extract at 36–41, 153, S. S. McClure Co. v. Philipp, 170 F. 910 (2d Cir. 1909) (No. 219).
18. Ray Stannard Baker, *Editorial: Some of the Difficulties Encountered in Investigating the Railroad Problem*, 26 MCCLURE'S MAGAZINE 672 (April 1906).
19. Ray Stannard Baker, *The Railroad Rate*, 26 MCCLURE'S MAGAZINE 47 (November 1905); *Railroad Rebates*, 26 MCCLURE'S MAGAZINE 179 (December 1905); and *Railroads on Trial*, 26 MCCLURE'S MAGAZINE 318–26 (January 1906), 398 (February 1906), and 535 (March 1906). Complete set of MCCLURE'S MAGAZINE is available at http://www.unz.org/Pub/McClures-1904oct-00563?View=PDFPages.
20. Complaint, dated January 12, 1906; filed January 15, 1906, Record Extract at 8, S. S. McClure Co. v. Philipp, 170 F. 910 (2d Cir. 1909) (No. 219). *See also* Complaint in Union Refrigerator Transit Co. v. S. S. McClure, undated, in Roe Papers, Box H9, Folder 1906.
21. Complaint, dated January 12, 1906; filed January 15, 1906, Record Extract at 8–9, S. S. McClure Co. v. Philipp, 170 F. 910 (2d Cir. 1909) (No. 219).
22. Rodney Smolla, 1 LAW OF DEFAMATION §1.15 (2d ed.) (2015).
23. Complaint, dated January 12, 1906; filed January 15, 1906, Record Extract at 9–29, S. S. McClure Co. v. Philipp, 170 F. 910 (2d Cir. 1909) (No. 219).
24. KAPLAN, *supra* note 3, at 124.
25. Letter from Gilbert Roe to Albert Boyden (September 27, 1904), in Roe Papers, Box H4, Folder 1906 (misfiled).
26. BUENKER, *supra* note 2, at 568.
27. Letter from Gilbert Roe to Alfred Rogers (February 10, 1906), in Roe Papers, Box H4, Folder 1906.
28. Answer, Record Extract at 42, S. S. McClure Co. v. Philipp, 170 F. 910 (2d Cir. 1909) (No. 219).
29. Letter from Gilbert Roe to Alfred Rogers (February 10, 1906), in Roe Papers, Box H4, Folder 1906.
30. Letter from Gilbert Roe to Robert La Follette (October 16, 1914), in Roe Papers, Box H7, Folder 1914.
31. Union Refrigerator Transit Co. v. S. S. McClure Co., 146 F. 623 (S.D.N.Y. 1906).
32. Letter from S. S. McClure to Gilbert Roe (April 10, 1908), in Roe Papers, Box H3, Folder Mc.
33. Answer, Record Extract at 32–43, S. S. McClure Co. v. Philipp, 170 F. 910 (2d Cir. 1909) (No. 219).
34. Letter from Gilbert Roe to Robert La Follette (February 27, 1906), in Roe Papers, Box H6, Folder 1906.
35. Letter from H. P. Myrick, Editor, *Milwaukee Free Press*, to Gilbert Roe (April 24, 1908), in Roe Papers, Box H3, Folder M.

36. Letter from Gilbert Roe to Robert La Follette (February 27, 1906), in Roe Papers, Box H6, Folder 1906.

37. Letter from Gilbert Roe to Alfred Rogers (March 2, 1906), in Roe Papers, Box H4, Folder 1906.

38. Letter from Gilbert Roe to Robert La Follette (March 6, 1906), in Roe Papers, Box H4, Folder 1906.

39. Baker, *supra* note 19, at 672–74.

40. GOODWIN, *supra* note 4, at 608.

41. KAPLAN, *supra* note 3, at 154.

42. GOODWIN, *supra* note 4, at 608–11.

43. Letter from Gilbert Roe to Phillips Publishing Co. (June 29, 1906), in Roe Papers, Box H4, Folder 1906.

44. Fragment of Draft Autobiography, in GKR Papers, Box 5, Folder 7.

45. Letter from Edith Lewis to Gilbert Roe (December 24, 1912), in Roe Papers, Box H3, Folder L.

46. Record Extract at 60, S. S. McClure Co. v. Philipp, 170 F. 910 (2d Cir. 1909) (No. 219).

47. 245 F. 102, 106–7 (2d Cir. 1917); *see infra* Chapter 6.

48. Reply Brief for Plaintiff in Error (*McClure's*), filed April 8, 1909, Record Extract at 10, S. S. McClure Co. v. Philipp, 170 F. 910 (2d Cir. 1909) (No. 219).

49. Record Extract at 245, S. S. McClure Co. v. Philipp, 170 F. 910 (2d Cir. 1909) (No. 219).

50. Brief for Defendant in Error (Philipp), filed March 26, 1909, Record Extract at 17, S. S. McClure Co. v. Philipp, 170 F. 910 (2d Cir. 1909) (No. 219).

51. Answer, Record Extract at 46, S. S. McClure Co. v. Philipp, 170 F. 910 (2d Cir. 1909) (No. 219).

52. Record Extract at 244–5, S. S. McClure Co. v. Philipp, 170 F. 910 (2d Cir. 1909) (No. 219).

53. Trial Transcript, Record Extract at 70–236, S. S. McClure Co. v. Philipp, 170 F. 910 (2d Cir. 1909) (No. 219).

54. Letter from Gilbert Roe to Robert La Follette (April 13, 1908), in Roe Papers, Box H4, Folder 1908.

55. Trial Transcript, Record Extract at 235–289, S. S. McClure Co. v. Philipp, 170 F. 910 (2d Cir. 1909) (No. 219).

56. Order Staying Execution of the Judgment, April 16, 1908, Record Extract at 58, S. S. McClure Co. v. Philipp, 170 F. 910 (2d Cir. 1909) (No. 219).

57. Letter from S. S. McClure to Gilbert Roe (April 10, 1908), in Roe Papers, Box H3, Folder Mc.

58. Letter from Gilbert Roe to S. S. McClure (April 11, 1908), in Roe Papers, Box H4, Folder 1908.

59. Order Denying Motion for a New Trial, April 16, 1908, Record Extract at 56, S. S. McClure Co. v. Philipp, 170 F. 910 (2d Cir. 1909) (No. 219).

60. Order Staying Execution of the Judgment, April 16, 1908, Record Extract at 58, S. S. McClure Co. v. Philipp, 170 F. 910 (2d Cir. 1909) (No. 219).

61. Judgment, Record Extract at 60, S. S. McClure Co. v. Philipp, 170 F. 910 (2d Cir. 1909) (No. 219).

62. Letter from H. P. Myrick to Gilbert Roe (April 18, 1908), in Roe Papers, Box H3, Folder M.

63. Assignment of Errors, Record Extract at 308–76, S. S. McClure Co. v. Philipp, 170 F. 910 (2d Cir. 1909) (No. 219).

64. Petition, Record Extract at 1, S. S. McClure Co. v. Philipp, 170 F. 910 (2d Cir. 1909) (No. 219).

65. Order, Record Extract at 384, S. S. McClure Co. v. Philipp, 170 F. 910 (2d Cir. 1909) (No. 219).

66. Order from Circuit Judge E. Henry Lacombe, dated September 23, 1908, giving Roe until October 22, 1908, to file the transcript of record on appeal, and receipts for copies of the record from both law firms, December 10, 1908, S. S. McClure Co. v. Philipp, 170 F. 910 (2d Cir. 1909) (No. 219).

67. Brief for Defendant in Error at 1, March 26, 1909, S. S. McClure Co. v. Philipp, 170 F. 910 (2d Cir. 1909) (No. 219) (Roe's initial brief was not preserved).

68. *S. S. McClure*, 170 F. at 915.

69. Brief for Defendant in Error at 2, 13 *et seq.*, March 26, 1909, S. S. McClure Co. v. Philipp, 170 F. 910 (2d Cir. 1909) (No. 219).

70. Reply Brief of Plaintiff in Error at 1, 10–11, April 8, 1909, S. S. McClure Co. v. Philipp, 170 F. 910 (2d Cir. 1909) (No. 219).

71. *S. S. McClure*, 170 F. at 912–15.

72. Letter from Robert La Follette to Gilbert Roe (undated), in Roe Papers, Box H4, Folder 1914.

73. Letter from Gilbert Roe to Robert La Follette (October 16, 1914), in Roe Papers, Box II4, Folder 1914.

74. Stanley P. Caine and Roger E. Wyman, *Introduction*, in EMANUEL L. PHILIPP, POLITICAL REFORM IN WISCONSIN xxi (1973) (1910).

CHAPTER 3. THE ANARCHISTS

1. EMMA GOLDMAN, LIVING MY LIFE 484 (1931) [hereinafter LIVING MY LIFE].

2. *See* MICHAEL KAZIN, AMERICAN DREAMERS 162 (Nook ed. 2011).

3. Joseph Ishill, *Theodore Schroeder, in* A NEW CONCEPT OF LIBERTY: FROM AN EVOLUTIONARY PSYCHOLOGIST: THEODORE SCHROEDER xxxv (Joseph Ishill ed., 1940) (quoting *Truth* (May 6, 1905)).

4. JANICE RUTH WOOD, THE STRUGGLE FOR FREE SPEECH IN THE UNITED STATES, 1872–1915: EDWARD BLISS FOOTE, EDWARD BOND FOOTE, AND ANTI-COMSTOCK OPERATIONS 27 (2008).

5. An Act for the Suppression of Trade in, and Circulation of, Obscene Literature and Articles of Immoral Use, ch. 258, 17 Stat. 598 (1873) [hereinafter Comstock Act].

6. *See, e.g.,* CHARLES REMBAR, THE END OF OBSCENITY 21 (1968); 2 EMMA GOLDMAN, MAKING SPEECH FREE, 1902–1909 [hereinafter MAKING SPEECH FREE], at 516, 557 (Candace Falk ed., 2005).

7. Comstock Act, *supra* note 5, at §148.

8. DAVID M. RABBAN, FREE SPEECH IN ITS FORGOTTEN YEARS, 1870–1920, at 44 (1999).

9. MAKING SPEECH FREE, *supra* note 6, at 557.

10. *A Call for Concerted Action,* LUCIFER: THE LIGHT-BEARER, May 1, 1902, at 122.

11. An Act to Regulate the Immigration of Aliens into the United States, ch. 1012, 32 Stat. 1222 (1903).

12. RABBAN, *supra* note 8, at 46.

13. MAKING SPEECH FREE, *supra* note 6, at 557.

14. RABBAN, *supra* note 8, at 47.

15. *Ruminations,* LUCIFER: THE LIGHT-BEARER, June 5, 1902, at 161.

16. EDWIN C. WALKER, FREE SPEECH LEAGUE, DECLARATION OF CONCEPTS AND PRINCIPLES (1903). *See* WOOD, *supra* note 4, at 77.

17. Ida Craddock, *The Danse du Ventre as Performed in the Cairo Street Theatre, Midway Plaisance, Chicago: Its Value as an Educator in Marital Duties,* NEW YORK WORLD, August 13, 1893; VERE CHAPPELL, SEXUAL OUTLAW, EROTIC MYSTIC: THE ESSENTIAL IDA CRADDOCK 5 (2010).

18. MAKING SPEECH FREE, *supra* note 6, at 557.

19. LIVING MY LIFE, *supra* note 1, at 553.

20. RABBAN, *supra* note 8, at 64–65.

21. ALICE WEXLER, EMMA GOLDMAN, AN INTIMATE LIFE 118–19 (1984).

22. U.S. ex rel. Turner v. Williams, 194 U.S. 279, 289–94 (1904).

23. WEXLER, *supra* note 21, at 119.

24. LIVING MY LIFE, *supra* note 1, at 348–50 (1931).

25. WEXLER, *supra* note 21, at 118.

26. LIVING MY LIFE, *supra* note 1, at 362.

27. *Id.* at 558.

28. Letter from Gilbert E. Roe to Edwin Foote Jr. (November 9, 1909), in Schroeder Papers, Box 9, Folder 1.

29. RABBAN, *supra* note 8, at 50.

30. *Id.* Foote scholar Janice Ruth Wood suggests Foote's bequest to Schroeder may have preceded Roe's advice: "By February 27, 1908, Foote Jr. had become concerned for the League's welfare upon his death and set up a fund that Schroeder would administer. He specified three priorities for the fund. Its primary use was to be for the Free Speech League and its propaganda, for defense of victims, for encouragement of papers that favor it and postal progress reforms, and lastly, for comfort and relief of its friends when

'down and out.' Secondly, the fund could be applied to publishing Schroeder's research on what Foote Jr. described as the 'sex origin of religious motives,' Schroeder's own form of sexually based psychology related to spiritual beliefs. Lastly, Foote Jr. requested that additional arrangements be made for someone to take charge of the fund in the event of Schroeder's death.

"Schroeder did name Foote Jr. as his own benefactor in a February 1910 letter to League attorney Gilbert Roe, to whom he explained that he had paid printers from the income of a fund provided by Foote Jr. for the furtherance of his free-speech work." WOOD, *supra* note 4, at 79.

31. RABBAN, *supra* note 8, at 53–55.
32. Letter from Theodore Schroeder to Gilbert Roe (February 21, 1910), in Schroeder Papers, Box 9, Folder 2, quoted in RABBAN, *supra* note 8, at 53–54.
33. This account of the incorporation of the Free Speech League was reprinted in league publications such as THE FREE SPEECH CASE OF JAY FOX, presumably written by Schroeder and released by the league in September 1912 to raise money for the Fox appeals. *See infra*, text accompanying note 51.
34. MAKING SPEECH FREE, *supra* note 6, at 558.
35. RABBAN, *supra* note 8, at 72.
36. CHARLES PIERCE LEWARNE, UTOPIAS ON PUGET SOUND, 1885–1915, 171–73, 221 (1975).
37. Mary M. Carr, *Jay Fox: Anarchist of Home*, COLUM. MAG., Spring 1990, at 3–7.
38. ERNESTO A. LONGA, ANARCHIST PERIODICALS IN ENGLISH PUBLISHED IN THE UNITED STATES (1833–1955) 43–48, 199 (2010).
39. Carr, *supra* note 37, at 6.
40. LEWARNE, *supra* note 36, at 215–16.
41. Carr, *supra* note 37, at 5–6.
42. LEWARNE, *supra* note 36, at 216.
43. Transcript of Record at 1, Fox v. Washington, 236 U.S. 273 (1915) (No. 134).
44. *Id.* Although not specifically mentioned in the information, the charge implicated a Washington statute that stated: "Every person who shall willfully print, publish, edit, issue or knowingly circulate, sell, distribute or display any book, paper, document or written or printed matter in any form, advocating, encouraging or inciting, or having a tendency to encourage or incite the commission of any crime, breach of the peace or act of violence, *or which shall tend to encourage or advocate disrespect for law or for any court or courts of justice*, shall be guilty of a gross misdemeanor." Rem. & Bal. §2564 (emphasis in THE FREE SPEECH CASE OF JAY FOX, *supra* note 33, at 3).
45. Transcript of Record at 1–4, Fox v. Washington, 236 U.S. 273 (1915) (No. 134).
46. LEWARNE, *supra* note 36, at 216–18.
47. *Id.* at 217 (quoting the TACOMA DAILY LEDGER, January 12, 1912).
48. Transcript of Record at 25–29, Fox v. Washington, 236 U.S. 273 (1915) (No. 134).
49. LEWARNE, *supra* note 36, at 4–6, 217–18.

50. Transcript of Record at 7–9, Fox v. Washington, 236 U.S. 273 (1915) (No. 134).

51. THE FREE SPEECH CASE OF JAY FOX, *supra* note 33, at 3–9.

52. Appellant's Brief at 9–26, Washington v. Fox, 71 Wash. 185, 127 P. 1111 (1912).

53. *Id.* at 31–44. Anderson refers in particular to one of the freight rate cases in which the judge cited an alleged provision of the Chinese penal code: "Whoever is guilty of improper conduct and of such as is contrary to the spirit of the laws, though not a breach of any specific part of it, shall be punished at least forty blows, and when the impropriety is of a serious nature, with eighty blows." That judge found little difference between that statute and one punishing unreasonably high railroad rates, without specifying what rates were reasonable. Anderson thought the analogy applied equally to criminalizing language "which shall tend to encourage or advocate disrespect for the law." *Id.* at 40 (citing Chi. & N.W. Ry. Co. v. Dey, 35 F. 866 (C.C. S.D. Iowa 1888)).

54. Appellant's Brief at 26–31, Washington v. Fox, 71 Wash. 185, 127 P. 1111 (1912).

55. Respondent's Brief at 17, Washington v. Fox, 71 Wash. 185, 127 P. 1111 (1912) (quoting Wash. Const. art. I §5).

56. Respondent's Brief at 18, Washington v. Fox, 71 Wash. 185, 127 P. 1111 (1912) (quoting New York v. Most, 171 N.Y. 423, 431, 64 N.E. 175, 178 (1902)).

57. Respondent's Brief at 4, Washington v. Fox, 71 Wash. 185, 127 P. 1111 (1912).

58. Appellant's Reply Brief at 4, 25–37, Washington v. Fox, 71 Wash. 185, 127 P. 1111 (1912).

59. RABBAN, *supra* note 8, at 73.

60. Appellant's Reply Brief at 38, Washington v. Fox, 71 Wash. 185, 127 P. 1111 (1912) (citing Patterson v. Colorado, 205 U.S. 454, 464–65 (1907) (Harlan, J., dissenting)).

61. Washington v. Fox, 71 Wash. at 186–89, 127 P. at 1112–13 (1912).

62. Transcript of Record at 12, Fox v. Washington, 236 U.S. 273 (1915) (No. 134).

63. Letter from Gilbert Roe to Theodore Schroeder (December 31, 1912), in Schroeder Papers, Box 10, Folder 3.

64. Letter from Theodore Schroeder to Gilbert Roe (January 6, 1913), in Schroeder Papers, Box 10, Folder 4.

65. Letter from Gilbert Roe to Theodore Schroeder (January 10, 1913), in Schroeder Papers, Box 10, Folder 4.

66. Letter from Gilbert Roe to Theodore Schroeder (January 13, 1913), in Schroeder Papers, Box 10, Folder 4.

67. *Id.* The exception to the mootness rule for causes that are "capable of repetition yet evading review" was still quite new in 1913. Weinstein v. Bradford, 423 U.S. 147, 148 (1975) (noting that Southern Pacific Terminal Co. v. ICC, 219 U.S. 498 (1911), was the first case to enunciate the "capable of repetition, yet evading review" doctrine).

68. Letter from Gilbert Roe to Theodore Schroeder (January 16, 1913), in Schroeder Papers, Box 10, Folder 4.

69. Transcript of Record at 15–23, Fox v. Washington, 236 U.S. 273 (1915) (No. 134).

70. Letter from Gilbert Roe to Theodore Schroeder (March 21, 1913), in Schroeder Papers, Box 10, Folder 4.

71. Letter from Gilbert Roe to Theodore Schroeder (March 27, 1913), in Schroeder Papers, Box 10, Folder 4.

72. Transcript of Record at 24, Fox v. Washington, 236 U.S. 273 (1915) (No. 134).

73. Brief for Plaintiff-in-Error [Jay Fox] at 7, 17, Fox v. Washington, 236 U.S. 273 (1915) (No. 134).

74. MARK A. GRABER, TRANSFORMING FREE SPEECH 62 (1991).

75. Brief for Plaintiff-in-Error [Jay Fox] at 7–13, Fox v. Washington, 236 U.S. 273 (1915) (No. 134).

76. 212 U.S. 86 (1909).

77. Brief for Plaintiff-in-Error [Jay Fox] at 13, 16, Fox v. Washington, 236 U.S. 273 (1915) (No. 134).

78. Brief for Defendant-in-Error [Washington] at 4–10, Fox v. Washington, 236 U.S. 273 (1915) (No. 134). The brief refers no New York v. Most, 64 N.E. 175 (N.Y. 1902).

79. Fox v. Washington, 236 U.S. 273, 277 (1915).

80. Letter from Gilbert Roe to Richard W. Jamieson, Tacoma, Wash. (June 5, 1916), in Roe Papers, Box H5, Folder 1916.

81. LEWARNE, *supra* note 36 at 219–20.

82. Carr, *supra* note 37, at 9–10.

83. ELIZABETH GURLEY FLYNN, THE REBEL GIRL 154–162 (1955).

84. Brief of Michael Dunn, Prosecutor of the Pleas for the County of Passaic, on behalf of the State, Defendant in Error, at 3–4, New Jersey v. Boyd, 93 A. 599, 94 A. 807 (N.J. 1915) (Nos. 61 & 62).

85. Ch. 278, P.L. 1908.

86. Brief of Michael Dunn, *supra* note 84, at 3–4.

87. Letter from Gilbert Roe to Robert La Follette (June 12, 1913), in Roe Papers, Box H4, Folder 1913.

88. Motions on Indictment, Case Record at 18–20, New Jersey v. Boyd, 93 A. 599, 94 A. 807 (N.J. 1915) (Nos. 61 & 62).

89. Trial Transcript, Case Record at 21–45, New Jersey v. Boyd, 93 A. 599, 94 A. 807 (N.J. 1915) (Nos. 61 & 62).

90. Proceedings on Indictment, Case Record at 7, New Jersey v. Boyd, 93 A. 599, 94 A. 807 (N.J. 1915) (Nos. 61 & 62).

91. Specification of Causes for Reversal, Case Record at 46–47, New Jersey v. Boyd, 93 A. 599, 94 A. 807 (N.J. 1915) (Nos. 61 & 62).

92. New Jersey v. Boyd, 91 A. 586–88 (N.J.S.Ct. 1914).

93. New Jersey v. Quinlan, 91 A. 111 (N.J.S.Ct. 1913).

94. New York v. Most, 64 N.E. 175 (N.Y. 1902).

95. *Boyd*, 91 A. at 588.

96. Letter from Gilbert Roe to Ann Sumner Boyd (August 14, 1914), in Roe Papers, Box H4, Folder 1914.

97. Assignments of Error, Case Record at 55–58, New Jersey v. Boyd, 93 A. 599, 94 A. 807 (N.J. 1915) (Nos. 61 & 62). *See also* Brief for Plaintiff-in-Error, New Jersey v. Boyd, 93 A. 599, 94 A. 807 (N.J. 1915) (Nos. 61 & 62).

98. *Boyd*, 93 A. at 599.

99. *Boyd*, 94 A. at 808.

100. *The Recantation of Frederick Sumner Boyd*, N.Y. Call, March 25, 1915, reprinted in MOTHER EARTH BULLETIN, April 1915, at 78–80.

101. *Observations and Comments*, MOTHER EARTH BULLETIN, April 1915, at 68–69.

102. *Lincoln Steffens on Violence*, 18 PUBLIC 355 (April 9, 1915).

103. I.W.W. History Project, U. Washington, http://depts.washington.edu/iww/persecution.shtml.

104. MAKING SPEECH FREE, *supra* note 6, at 558.

105. National Free Speech Committee, *Free Speech Manifesto*, reprinted in ALDEN FREEMAN, THE FIGHT FOR FREE SPEECH 30 (1909). Available in Jewish Women's Archive, http://jwa.org/media/fight-for-free-speech-pamphlet-published-by-alden-freeman.

106. During a trip to Chicago in October–November 1914, Goldman renewed a relationship with the lesbian couple Margaret Anderson, editor of the *Little Review*, and Harriett Dean (known as Deansie). In her autobiography, Goldman reminisces: "Since the unforgettable days I had spent with Margaret in the spring when we had both enjoyed the hospitality of Mr. and Mrs. Roe at their home in Pelham Manor, something new and precious had grown up between us." LIVING MY LIFE, *supra* note 1, at 548. Wexler intimates that Goldman and Anderson may have had an affair at the time. *See* WEXLER, *supra* note 21, at 198–99.

107. Letter from Gilbert Roe to Theodore Schroeder (September 9, 1910), in Schroeder Papers, Box 9, Folder 2.

108. LIVING MY LIFE, *supra* note 1, at 483–85.

109. *Id.* at 540–41.

110. Gilbert E. Roe, *A Tribute*, 10 MOTHER EARTH 430 (March 1915).

111. Gilbert E. Roe, *Reasonable Restrictions upon Freedom of Assemblage*, reprinted from 9 PUBLICATIONS OF THE AM. SOCIOLOGICAL SOC. 1914, at 4–7.

112. LIVING MY LIFE, *supra* note 1, at 562–63.

113. *See, e.g.*, The Clarence Darrow Digital Collection, Univ. of Minn. L. Lib., http://darrow.law.umn.edu/trials.php?tid=2.

114. Letter from Alexander Berkman to Gilbert Roe (February 17, 1915), in Roe Papers, Box H2, Folder B.

115. LIVING MY LIFE, *supra* note 1, at 563.

116. Letter from Alexander Berkman to Gwyneth King Roe (March 25, 1930), in GKR Papers, Box 3, Folder 5–9. *See also* Letter from Berkman to Leonard Abbott (February 2, 1930), a copy of which was attached to the GKR letter.

117. Letter from Alexander Berkman to Gilbert Roe (February 17, 1915), in Roe Papers, Box H2, Folder B.
118. Letter from Gilbert Roe to Alexander Berkman (September 1, 1916), in Roe Papers, Box H5, Folder 1916.
119. Letter from Alexander Berkman to Gwyneth King Roe (March 25, 1930), in GKR Papers, Box 3, Folder 5–9.

Chapter 4. The Feminists

1. Robert M. La Follette, Autobiography 315 (1913).
2. Letter from Francis Maule Bjorkman to Gilbert Roe (April 10, 1912), in Roe Papers, Box H2, Folder B.
3. Autobiography, *supra* note 1, at 317–18.
4. Belle Case and Fola La Follette, Robert M. La Follette 693, 891 (1953) [hereinafter La Follette].
5. Postcard from Emily M. Bishop to Gwyneth King Roe (March 17, 1909), in Roe Papers, Box H4, Folder 1909.
6. Letter from Gwyneth King Roe to Theodore Schroeder (ca. April 16, 1912), in Schroeder Papers, Box 10, Folder 1.
7. Letter from Theodore Schroeder to Gwyneth King Roe (April 16, 1912), in Schroeder Papers, Box 10, Folder 1.
8. Letter from Caroline [unreadable surname] to Gilbert Roe (June 29, 1910), in Roe Papers, Box H2, Folder L.
9. La Follette, *supra* note 4, at 377; *Women Parade and Rejoice in the End*, N.Y. Times, May 7, 1911, at 1.
10. La Follette, *supra* note 4, at 377.
11. Gilbert E. Roe, Discriminations against Women in the Laws of New York 2, 18–19 (1914).
12. Letter from Gilbert Roe to Harriet Stanton Blatch (December 12, 1914), in Roe Papers, Box H4, Folder 1914.
13. *See, e.g.*, letter from Roe to Mrs. James L. Laidlaw, President, Woman Suffrage Party (October 1, 1915), promising to speak at an October 6, 1915, meeting at the Republican Club; letters from Gilbert Roe to lawyer Samuel Untermyer soliciting and acknowledging a donation to the suffrage campaign (September 29 & October 4, 1915), in Roe Papers, Box H5, Folder 1915.
14. Letter from Gilbert Roe to Fola La Follette (October 11, 1915), in Roe Papers, Box H5, Folder 1915.
15. Letter from Gilbert Roe to Frederick C. Howe (October 29, 1915), in Roe Papers, Box H5, Folder 1915.
16. Letter from Gilbert Roe to Robert La Follette (November 6, 1915), in Roe Papers, Box H5, Folder 1915.

17. *See, e.g.*, LINDA GORDON, THE MORAL PROPERTY OF WOMEN (2002).

18. MARGARET SANGER, MY FIGHT FOR BIRTH CONTROL 57 (1931) [hereinafter MY FIGHT].

19. Margaret Sanger, *Amusement*, 1 WOMAN REBEL 11 (April 1914).

20. Letter from Gilbert Roe to Leonard Abbott (April 24, 1916), in Roe Papers, Box H5, Folder 1916.

21. MARGARET SANGER, MARGARET SANGER: AN AUTOBIOGRAPHY 70–77 (1938) [hereinafter MARGARET SANGER].

22. EMMA GOLDMAN: MADE FOR AMERICA, 1890–1901 at 55 (Candace Falk ed., 2003).

23. EMMA GOLDMAN, LIVING MY LIFE 552–53 (1931).

24. MY FIGHT, *supra* note 18, at 62.

25. MARGARET SANGER, *supra* note 21, at 104–12.

26. MY FIGHT, *supra* note 18, at 86.

27. NolleProsequi, United States v. Sanger (S.D.N.Y. February 18, 1916).

28. MARGARET SANGER, *supra* note 21, at 115–20.

29. MY FIGHT, *supra* note 18, at 120–21.

30. Affidavit of William Sanger, Papers on Appeal from Order at 6–10, New York v. Sanger, 33 N.Y. Crim. R. 415 (1915).

31. MARGARET SANGER, *supra* note 21, at 177.

32. Letter from Gilbert Roe to City Magistrate (January 19, 1915), in Roe Papers, Box H4, Folder 1915.

33. Letter from Gilbert Roe to the Armstrong Agency (January 23, 1915), in Roe Papers, Box H4, Folder 1915.

34. Complaint, Papers on Appeal from Order at 30, New York v. Sanger, 33 N.Y. Crim. R. 415 (1915).

35. MARGARET SANGER, FAMILY LIMITATION 2–5 (1914).

36. MARGARET SANGER, *supra* note 21, at 177.

37. Complaint, Papers on Appeal from Order at 32–33, New York v. Sanger, 33 N.Y. Crim. R. 415 (1915).

38. Letter from Emma Goldman to Gilbert Roe (February 1, 1915), in Roe Papers, Box H7, Folder Goldman.

39. Testimony of Charles Bamberger on Direct Examination, Papers on Appeal from Order at 37, New York v. Sanger, 33 N.Y. Crim. R. 415 (1915).

40. Testimony of Anthony Comstock on Direct Examination, Papers on Appeal from Order at 40–41, New York v. Sanger, 33 N.Y. Crim. R. 415 (1915).

41. Testimony of Anthony Comstock on Cross-Examination, Papers on Appeal from Order at 42, New York v. Sanger, 33 N.Y. Crim. R. 415 (1915).

42. Rulings of Hon. Matthew P. Breen, City Magistrate, Papers on Appeal from Order at 43, New York v. Sanger, 33 N.Y. Crim. R. 415 (1915).

43. Letter from Gilbert Roe to Leonard Abbott (February 4, 1915), in Roe Papers, Box H4, Folder 1915.

44. Letter from Leonard Abbott to Gilbert Roe (February 5, 1915), in Roe Papers, Box H7, Folder Abbott.

45. Letter from Gilbert Roe to Leonard Abbott (February 6, 1915), in Roe Papers, Box H4, Folder 1915.

46. Letter from Leonard Abbott to Gilbert Roe (undated), in Roe Papers, Box H7, Folder Abbott.

47. Max Eastman, *Is the Truth Obscene?*, MASSES, March 1915, at 5, 6.

48. Letter from Free Speech League (unaddressed, undated), in Roe Papers, Box H4, Folder 1915.

49. Affidavit of William Sanger, Papers on Appeal from Order at 7, New York v. Sanger, 33 N.Y. Crim. R. 415 (1915).

50. Letter from Gilbert Roe to Leonard Abbott (February 16, 1915), in Roe Papers, Box H4, Folder 1915.

51. Letter from Leonard Abbott to Gilbert Roe (February 17, 1915), in Roe Papers, Box H7, Folder Abbott.

52. Letter from Alexander Berkman to Gilbert Roe (February 17, 1915), in Roe Papers, Box H2, Folder B.

53. Letter from Gilbert Roe to Leonard Abbott (February 19, 1915), in Roe Papers, Box H4, Folder 1915.

54. Letter from Gilbert Roe to Max Eastman (August 4, 1915), in Roe Papers, Box H5, Folder 1915.

55. Letter from Gilbert Roe to Mr. Wheeler, *Harper's Magazine* (May 3, 1915), in Roe Papers, Box H4, Folder 1915.

56. Letter from Gilbert Roe to Leonard Abbott (February 19, 1915), in Roe Papers, Box H4, Folder 1915.

57. Fox v. Washington, 236 U.S. 275, 278 (1915).

58. Motion to Prosecute by Indictment, Papers on Appeal from Order at 4–5, New York v. Sanger, 33 N.Y. Crim. R. 415 (1915).

59. Affidavit of William Sanger, Papers on Appeal from Order at 5, 10–11, New York v. Sanger, 33 N.Y. Crim. R. 415 (1915).

60. Letter from Leonard Abbott to Gilbert Roe (March 3, 1915), in Roe Papers, Box H7, Folder Abbott.

61. Letter from Leonard Abbott to Gilbert Roe (March 23, 1915), in Roe Papers, Box H7, Folder Abbott.

62. Letter from Leonard Abbott to Gilbert Roe (March 26, 1915), in Roe Papers, Box H7, Folder Abbott.

63. Letter from Gilbert Roe to Mr. Lockhart, Ass't Dist. Atty. (March 15, 1915), in Roe Papers, Box H4, Folder 1915.

64. Letter from Gilbert Roe to Leonard Abbott (March 26, 1915), in Roe Papers, Box H4, Folder 1915.

65. Letter from Leonard Abbott to Gilbert Roe (March 27, 1915), in Roe Papers, Box H7, Folder Abbott.

66. Letter from Gilbert Roe to Leonard Abbott (March 30, 1915), in Roe Papers, Box H4, Folder 1915.

67. Letter from Gilbert Roe to Leonard Abbott (March 31, 1915), in Roe Papers, Box H4, Folder 1915.

68. Letter from Leonard Abbott to Gilbert Roe (April 1, 1915), in Roe Papers, Box H7, Folder Abbott.

69. Letter from Leonard Abbott to Gilbert Roe (March 27, 1915), in Roe Papers, Box H7, Folder Abbott.

70. Letter from Leonard Abbott to Gilbert Roe (undated), in Roe Papers, Box H7, Folder Abbott.

71. Letter from Gilbert Roe to Leonard Abbott (March 30, 1915), in Roe Papers, Box H4, Folder 1915.

72. Letter from Leonard Abbott to Gilbert Roe (April 2, 1915), in Roe Papers, Box H7, Folder Abbott.

73. Letter from Gilbert Roe to Leonard Abbott (April 2, 1915), in Roe Papers, Box H4, Folder 1915.

74. Letter from Gilbert Roe to Leonard Abbott (April 5, 1915), in Roe Papers, Box H4, Folder 1915.

75. Letter from Leonard Abbott to Gilbert Roe (March 27, 1915), in Roe Papers, Box H7, Folder Abbott.

76. Letter from Leonard Abbott to Gilbert Roe (undated), in Roe Papers, Box H7, Folder Abbott.

77. Letter from Gilbert Roe to Leonard Abbott (April 5, 1915), in Roe Papers, Box H4, Folder 1915.

78. Order Appealed From, Papers on Appeal from Order at 2–3, New York v. Sanger, 33 N.Y. Crim. R. 415 (1915).

79. Notice of Appeal, Papers on Appeal from Order at 2, New York v. Sanger, 33 N.Y. Crim. R. 415 (1915).

80. *William Sanger Trial Postponed to June 18*, N.Y. CALL, May 12, 1915.

81. Appellant's Brief, New York v. Sanger, 33 N.Y. Crim. R. 415 (1915).

82. Letter from Leonard Abbott to Gilbert Roe (April 27, 1915), in Roe Papers, Box H7, Folder Abbott.

83. Letter from Gilbert Roe to Leonard Abbott (April 29, 1915), in Roe Papers, Box H4, Folder 1915.

84. Letter from Leonard Abbott to Margaret Sanger (May 1, 1915), in The Margaret Sanger Papers, http://wyatt.electricbeanstalk.com/mep/MS/xml/s104419.html.

85. *William Sanger Trial Postponed to June 18*, N.Y. CALL, May 12, 1915.

86. Letter from Leonard Abbott to Gilbert Roe (June 8, 1915), in Roe Papers, Box H7, Folder Abbott.

87. Letter from Gilbert Roe to Leonard Abbott (June 16, 1915), in Roe Papers, Box H5, Folder 1915.

88. Letter from Gilbert Roe to Leonard Abbott (June 18, 1915), in Roe Papers, Box H5, Folder 1915.

89. Letter from William Sanger to Gilbert Roe (June 21, 1915), in Roe Papers, Box H7, Folder Sanger.

90. Letter from Gilbert Roe to William Sanger (June 23, 1915), in Roe Papers, Box H5, Folder 1915.

91. Letter from Gilbert Roe to Leonard Abbott (June 23, 1915), in Roe Papers, Box H5, Folder 1915.

92. Letter from Leonard Abbott to Gilbert Roe (June 23, 1915), in Roe Papers, Box H7, Folder Abbott.

93. Letter from Gilbert Roe to Leonard Abbott (June 28, 1915), in Roe Papers, Box H5, Folder 1915.

94. Letter from Leonard Abbott to Gilbert Roe (June 29, 1915), in Roe Papers, Box H7, Folder Abbott.

95. Letter from Gilbert Roe to Belle Case La Follette (July 2, 1915), in Roe Papers, Box H5, Folder 1915.

96. Letter from Gilbert Roe to Floyd Wilmot (July 6, 1915), in Roe Papers, Box H5, Folder 1915.

97. Letter from Gilbert Roe to Leonard Abbott (July 9, 1915), in Roe Papers, Box H5, Folder 1915.

98. Letter from Gilbert Roe to Leonard Abbott (July 12, 1915), in Roe Papers, Box H5, Folder 1915.

99. New York v. Sanger, 33 N.Y. Crim. R. 415 (1915).

100. Letter from Gilbert Roe to Leonard Abbott (July 12, 1915), in Roe Papers, Box H5, Folder 1915.

101. *Clash over Comstock*, N.Y. TIMES, July 19, 1915, at 16.

102. Letter from Leonard Abbott to Gilbert Roe (July 19, 1915), in Roe Papers, Box H7, Folder Abbott.

103. Letter from Gilbert Roe to Mr. Lockhart, Ass't Dist. Atty. (August 2, 1915), in Roe Papers, Box H5, Folder 1915.

104. Letter from Gilbert Roe to Leonard Abbott (August 23, 1915), in Roe Papers, Box H5, Folder 1915.

105. Letter from Leonard Abbott to Gilbert Roe (August 30, 1915), in Roe Papers, Box H7, Folder Abbott.

106. Letter from Gilbert Roe to Floyd Wilmot (September 7, 1915), in Roe Papers, Box H5, Folder 1915.

107. William Sanger, *Birth Control*, in JAILED FOR BIRTH CONTROL: THE TRIAL OF WILLIAM SANGER, September 10, 1915, at 4 (James Waldo Fawcett ed., 1917).

108. *Disorder in Court as Sanger Is Fined*, N.Y. TIMES, September 11, 1915, at 7.

109. MY FIGHT, *supra* note 18, at 122.

110. Letter from Leonard Abbott to Gilbert Roe (October 5, 1915), in Roe Papers, Box H7, Folder Abbott.

111. MY FIGHT, *supra* note 18, at 123.

112. Letter from Gilbert Roe to Leonard Abbott (October 6, 1915), in Roe Papers, Box H5, Folder 1915.

113. Letter from Leonard Abbott to Gilbert Roe (October 5, 1915), in Roe Papers, Box H7, Folder Abbott.

114. Letter from Leonard Abbott to Gilbert Roe (December 14, 1915), in Roe Papers, Box H7, Folder Abbott.

115. MY FIGHT, *supra* note 18, at 131.

116. MARGARET SANGER, *supra* note 21, at 187, 237. *See also* JEAN H. BAKER, MARGARET SANGER: A LIFE OF PASSION 119 (2011).

117. Letter from Gilbert Roe to Hon. Arthur M. Woods, Police Comm'r (October 21, 1916), in Roe Papers, Box H5, Folder 1916.

118. *See, generally,* Patricia A. Carter, *Henrietta Rodman and the Fight to Further Women's Economic Autonomy*, in WOMEN EDUCATORS, LEADERS AND ACTIVISTS 152, 156 (Tanya Fitzgerald & Elizabeth M. Smyth eds., 2014).

119. Handwritten note from Henrietta Rodman to Gilbert Roe (undated), in Roe Papers, Box H6, Folder Rodman.

120. *Weds Secretly to Fool School Board*, N.Y. TRIB., March 19, 1913, at 1; *Henrietta Rodman Defies the Board*, BROOKLYN DAILY EAGLE, March 19, 1913, at 28.

121. Carter, *supra* note 118, at 157.

122. Masten v. Maxwell, 83 N.Y.S. 1098, 1098–99 (N.Y. App. Div. 1903).

123. *Id.* at 1101 (Hirschberg, J., concurring).

124. Murphy v. Maxwell, 69 N.E. 1092, 1093–94 (N.Y. 1904).

125. Grendon v. Bd. of Educ., 100 N.Y.S. 253, 253 (N.Y. App. Div. 1906).

126. Carter, *supra* note 118, at 157–59.

127. *See, e.g., Weds Secretly to Fool School Board, supra* note 120; *Henrietta Rodman Defies the Board, supra* note 120.

128. *School Teachers Secretly Married*, DUNKIRK (N.Y.) EVE. OBSERVER, March 19, 1913, at 1.

129. *Henrietta Rodman Defies the Board, supra* note 120.

130. Affidavit of Henrietta Rodman (undated), in Roe Papers, Box H6, Folder Rodman.

131. Letter from Henrietta Rodman to Gilbert Roe (undated), in Roe Papers, Box H6, Folder Rodman.

132. Letter from Gilbert Roe to Henrietta Rodman (undated), in Roe Papers, Box H4, Folder 1913.

133. Letter from Henrietta Rodman to Gilbert Roe (undated), in Roe Papers, Box H6, Folder Rodman.

134. *See* Peixotto v. Bd. of Educ., 144 N.Y.S. 87 (N.Y. Sup. Ct. 1913), *rev'd*, 145 N.Y.S. 853 (N.Y. App. Div. 1914), *aff'd*, 146 N.Y.S. 1108 (N.Y. 1914).

135. *Mother-Teachers Fight*, BROOKLYN DAILY EAGLE, October 1, 1914, at 16.

136. *Sporting Note*, "The Conning Tower," N.Y. TRIB., November 10, 1914, at 8.

137. *Maxwell Orders Charges*, BROOKLYN DAILY EAGLE, November 12, 1914, at 3.

138. *Teacher under Ban in "Mother Baiting" Censure*, N.Y. TRIB., November 12, 1914, at 1.

139. *The Board of Education Meets* (editorial), N.Y. TRIB., November 12, 1914, at 8.
140. *Teachers to Get Maternity Leave*, N.Y. TIMES, November 13, 1914, at 8.
141. *Teachers Hiss Grace Strachan*, N.Y. TRIB., November 14, 1914, at 7.
142. *Mother-Teacher to Fight*, N.Y. TIMES, November 15, 1914, at 13.
143. *Ask Mayor's Aid for Teacher-Mothers*, BROOKLYN DAILY EAGLE, November 16, 1914, at 3.
144. *She Hears the Charges*, BROOKLYN DAILY EAGLE, November 18, 1914, at 24; *Miss Rodman Arraigned*, N.Y. TIMES, November 18, 1914, at 7.
145. *Teacher-Mother Tells of Baby Boy*, N.Y. TRIB., December 1, 1914, at 4.
146. *Henrietta Rodman Loses Her Counsel*, BROOKLYN DAILY EAGLE, December 17, 1914, at 24.
147. *Henrietta Rodman Unready for Trial*, BROOKLYN DAILY EAGLE, December 16, 1914, at 15.
148. *School Board "Despotic,"* BROOKLYN DAILY EAGLE, December 24, 1914, at 2.
149. Carter, *supra* note 118, at 169.
150. *She Had Only One Friend*, BROOKLYN DAILY EAGLE, December 24, 1914, at 18.
151. *Miss Rodman Will Appeal Fine of $1,800*, N.Y. TRIB., December 24, 1914, at 1.
152. Marguerite Mooers Marshall, *Decision in Peixotto Case Makes This Possible*, N.Y. EVENING WORLD, January 13, 1915, at 3.
153. Letter from Frank B. Gilbert, Chief, Law Division, State Board of Education to Gilbert Roe (February 10, 1915), in Roe Papers, Box H2, Folder G.
154. *Henrietta Rodman Loses Her Appeal*, BROOKLYN DAILY EAGLE, June 9, 1915, at 24; *Henrietta Rodman Loses on Appeal*, N.Y. TIMES, June 9, 1915, at 9; *Miss Rodman Loses Suspension Fight*, N.Y. SUN, June 9, 1914.
155. *For Opportunity Classes*, N.Y. TIMES, June 24, 1915, at 11.
156. Carter, *supra* note 118, at 164, 172–73.
157. Letter from Gilbert Roe to Ira S. Wile (June 15, 1915), in Roe Papers, Box H5, Folder 1915.
158. Letter from Henrietta Rodman to Gilbert Roe (March 15, 1916), in Roe Papers, Box H7, Folder Rodman.
159. Letter from Gilbert Roe to Henrietta Rodman (March 20, 1916), in Roe Papers, Box H5, Folder 1916.
160. Letter from Henry R. Linville to Gwyneth King Roe (December 23, 1929), in GKR Papers, Box 3, Folder 5–9.

CHAPTER 5. THE SOCIALISTS

1. Floyd Dell, *Proem: The Rise of Greenwich Village*, in FLOYD DELL, LOVE IN GREENWICH VILLAGE (1926), http://www.bohemianlit.com/full_text/dell/proem.htm.
2. WILLIAM L. O'NEILL, THE LAST ROMANTIC: A LIFE OF MAX EASTMAN 30 (1991).

3. *Id.* at 29; REBECCA ZURIER, ART FOR THE MASSES 32 (1988).
4. ZURIER, *supra* note 3, at 35.
5. *Editorial Notice*, MASSES, December 1912, at 3.
6. O'NEILL, *supra* note 2, at 40.
7. MASSES, February 1913, at 2.
8. *Poisoned at the Source* (cartoon) and *The Worst Monopoly* (editorial), MASSES, July 1913, at 6.
9. BELLE CASE & FOLA LA FOLLETTE, ROBERT M. LA FOLLETTE 297 (1953) [hereinafter LA FOLLETTE].
10. DOUGLAS W. RAE, CITY: URBANISM AND ITS END 107 (2003).
11. Letter from Gilbert Roe to Robert La Follette (May 19, 1910), in Roe Papers, Box H4, Folder 1910.
12. LA FOLLETTE, *supra* note 9, at 297.
13. Letter from Gilbert Roe to Robert La Follette (May 19, 1910), in Roe Papers, Box H4, Folder 1910.
14. West Virginia State Archives, *West Virginia's Mine Wars*, http://www.wvculture.org/history/minewars.html.
15. *Id.* Other demands were an end to blacklisting of organizers, alternatives to company stores, an end to use of mine guards, prohibition on cribbing (a system of cheating the miners in weighing the coal they produced), installation of accurate scales, and union-hired check weighmen.
16. Roger Fagge, *Eugene Debs in West Virginia, 1913: A Reappraisal*, 52 W. VA. HISTORY 1 (1993) (Fagge points out that these commissions were unconstitutional, since the civilian courts were still operating, and that miners were deprived of their right to counsel).
17. UPTON SINCLAIR, THE BRASS CHECK 335–38 (Nook ed., 1916) (quoting an affidavit from Lee Calvin, a mine guard from the Baldwin-Felts Detective Agency).
18. *Id.* at 328–29.
19. Undated statement of Max Eastman, in Roe Papers, Box H9, Folder 1914.
20. *Poisoned at the Source* (cartoon) and *The Worst Monopoly* (editorial), *supra* note 8.
21. Floyd Dell, *Indicted for Criminal Libel*, MASSES, January 1914, at 3.
22. Indictment, New York v. Eastman, N.Y. Cnty. Ct. Gen. Sess., No. 97005, June 26, 1913.
23. *Id.* (annotations ascribed to Theodore Schroeder by Gwyneth King Roe).
24. SINCLAIR, *supra* note 17, at 128 (quoting N. Y. EVENING POST, date unknown).
25. *Id.* at 248 (quoting Senate Document 56, 62nd Cong., 1st Sess., Vol. 2).
26. *Train Succeeds Nott*, N.Y. TIMES, November 7, 1913, at 8.
27. Amos Pinchot, *To the Editor of the Sun*, N.Y. SUN, March 10, 1914, at 18.
28. Memorandum of Points to Look Up under the Noyes Indictment (undated), in Roe Papers, Box H9, Folder 1914.
29. Dell, *supra* note 21.
30. Letter to Arthur Brisbane, author unknown (December 30, 1913), in Roe Papers,

Box H9, Folder 1914 (a penciled notation on the letter, possibly by Netha Roe, suggests the letter may have been sent by Mrs. Eastman).

31. New York v. Eastman, 152 N.Y.S. 314, 317–20 (N.Y. Cnty. Ct. Gen. Sess. 1915) (overruling Noyes demurrer).

32. Letter from Gilbert Roe to Robert La Follette (January 30, 1914), in Roe Papers, Box H4, Folder 1914.

33. Letter from Gilbert Roe to Max Eastman (June 10, 1914), in Roe Papers, Box H4, Folder 1914.

34. Letter from William Rand to Gilbert Roe (January 28, 1914), in Roe Papers, Box H3, Folder R.

35. Statement by Thomas Carnes (January 1, 1914), in Roe Papers, Box H9, Folder 1914.

36. Statement by W. Bruce Reid (January 2, 1914), in Roe Papers, Box H9, Folder 1914.

37. *Plan Meeting of Protest*, N.Y. TIMES, March 2, 1914, at 7.

38. ZURIER, *supra* note 3, at 45.

39. *Hard Words for the Newspapers*, N.Y. TIMES, March 6, 1914, at 20; *Speakers Condemn A.P. as Monopoly*, N.Y. SUN, March 6, 1914, at 2.

40. *Hard Words for the Newspapers*, *supra* note 39, at 20.

41. *Speakers Condemn A.P. as Monopoly*, *supra* note 39.

42. *Hard Words for the Newspapers*, *supra* note 39, at 20.

43. *Investigating the Associated Press*, N.Y. TIMES, March 7, 1914, at 10.

44. Amos Pinchot, *To the Editor of the Sun*, *supra* note 27, at 18.

45. *Eastman Defends "Rights,"* BROOKLYN DAILY EAGLE, March 25, 1914, at 20.

46. Letter from Gilbert Roe to La Follette (March 11, 1914), in Roe Papers, Box H4, Folder 1914.

47. Letter from Gilbert Roe to John O'Hara Cosgrave (April 17, 1914), in Roe Papers, Box H4, Folder 1914.

48. Letter from Arthur C. Train to Gilbert Roe (February 11, 1914), in Roe Papers, Box H3, Folder T.

49. Letter from Gilbert Roe to John O'Hara Cosgrave (April 17, 1914), in Roe Papers, Box H4, Folder 1914.

50. Letter from Gilbert Roe to Max Eastman (June 10, 1914), in Roe Papers, Box H4, Folder 1914.

51. Letter from Max Eastman to Gilbert Roe (June 13, 1914), in Roe Papers, Box H7, Folder Eastman.

52. Letter from Gilbert Roe to Max Eastman (June 24, 1914), in Roe Papers, Box H4, Folder 1914.

53. Letter from Gilbert Roe to James M. Pierce (March 14, 1914), in Roe Papers, Box H4, Folder 1914.

54. Various documents, in Roe Papers, Box H9, Folder Montessori Case.

55. Letter from Gilbert Roe to Harry W. Laidler (March 5, 1914), in Roe Papers, Box H4, Folder 1914.
56. Letter from Gilbert Roe to Caro Lloyd (May 12, 1914), in Roe Papers, Box H4, Folder 1914.
57. Untitled clipping, N.Y. CALL (May 17, 1914), in Roe Papers, Box H7, Folder 1914.
58. Letter from Gilbert Roe to Mabel Dodge (April 4, 1914), in Roe Papers, Box H4, Folder 1914.
59. Letter from Gilbert Roe to Max Eastman (June 24, 1914), in Roe Papers, Box H4, Folder 1914.
60. SINCLAIR, *supra* note 17, at 332.
61. Letter from Gilbert Roe to John O'Hara Cosgrave (July 28, 1914), in Roe Papers, Box H4, Folder 1914.
62. Letter from Max Eastman to Gilbert Roe (July 23, 1914), in Roe Papers, Box H7, Folder Eastman.
63. Letter from Gilbert Roe to Max Eastman (July 28, 1914), in Roe Papers, Box H4, Folder 1914.
64. Letter from Gilbert Roe to John O'Hara Cosgrave (July 28, 1914), in Roe Papers, Box H4, Folder 1914.
65. Letter from Gilbert Roe to John O'Hara Cosgrave (August 3, 1914), in Roe Papers, Box H4, Folder 1914.
66. Letter from Gilbert Roe to Max Eastman (August 4, 1914), in Roe Papers, Box H4, Folder 1914.
67. Letter from Max Eastman to Gilbert Roe (August 5, 1914), in Roe Papers, Box H7, Folder Eastman.
68. Letter from Amos Pinchot to Gilbert Roe (August 31, 1914), in Roe Papers, Box H7, Folder Pinchot.
69. Letter from Max Eastman to Gilbert Roe (September 3, 1914), in Roe Papers, Box H7, Folder Eastman.
70. Letter from Gilbert Roe to Robert La Follette (August 4, 1914), in Roe Papers, Box H4, Folder 1914.
71. New York v. Eastman, 152 N.Y.S. 314, 318–320 (1915).
72. Letter from Gilbert Roe to Amos Pinchot (June 4, 1915), in Roe Papers, Box H5, Folder 1915.
73. Letter from Amos Pinchot to Gilbert Roe (June 2, 1915) in Roe Papers, Box H7, Folder Pinchot.
74. Letter from Gilbert Roe to Amos Pinchot (June 4, 1915), in Roe Papers, Box H5, Folder 1915.
75. Letter from Marlen E. Pew to Gilbert Roe (May 22, 1915), in Roe Papers, Box H3, Folder P.
76. Letter from Max Eastman to Gilbert Roe (July 29, 1915), in Roe Papers, Box H7, Folder Eastman.

77. Letter from Gilbert Roe to Max Eastman (August 4, 1915), in Roe Papers, Box H5, Folder 1915.

78. Letter from Max Eastman to Gilbert Roe (September 7, 1915), in Roe Papers, Box H7, Folder Eastman.

79. Letters from Gilbert Roe to Max Eastman (September 10 & 11, 1915), in Roe Papers, Box H5, Folder 1915.

80. Letter from Gilbert Roe to Amos Pinchot (September 19, 1916), in Roe Papers, Box H5, Folder 1916.

81. Letter from Amos Pinchot to Gilbert Roe (October 19, 1916), in Roe Papers, Box H3, Folder P.

82. Letter from Gilbert Roe to Art Young (November 24, 1915), in Roe Papers, Box H5, Folder 1915.

83. Letter from Gilbert Roe to John O'Hara Cosgrave (August 24, 1916), in Roe Papers, Box H5, Folder 1916.

84. Letter from Gilbert Roe to Art Young (December 1, 1915), in Roe Papers, Box H5, Folder 1915. Eastman would receive a letter from Roe's secretary, Ida C. Smith, apprising him of the dismissal. Letter from Smith to Max Eastman (December 18, 1915), in Roe Papers, Box H5, Folder 1915.

85. SINCLAIR, *supra* note 17, at 250.

86. Letter from Gilbert Roe to John O'Hara Cosgrave (August 24, 1916), in Roe Papers, Box H5, Folder 1916.

87. *April Fool* (cartoon), MASSES, April 1916, at 16–17.

88. ANTHONY ARTHUR, RADICAL INNOCENT: UPTON SINCLAIR 31–180 (2006).

89. *Id.* at 180. In *The Brass Check*, Sinclair writes that the morning after the Ludlow Massacre, "I opened the newspapers, and found an account in *The New York Call*, a Socialist paper, and two inches in the *New York World*—and not a line in any other paper!" SINCLAIR, *supra* note 17, at 120. Sinclair was wrong. *See, e.g., Thirteen Die in Miners' Battle*, N.Y. SUN, April 21, 1914, at 1; *Thirteen Killed in Strike Battle*, N.Y. TRIB., April 21, 1914, at 6; *Trinidad Dead, Thirteen*, BROOKLYN DAILY EAGLE, April 21, 1914, at 1; *45 Dead, 20 Hurt, Score Missing in Strike War*, N.Y. TIMES, April 22, 1914, at 7.

90. ARTHUR, *supra* note 88, at 181.

91. *Crape Wearers to March by Rockefeller To-Day*, N.Y. SUN, April 29, 1914, at 2.

92. *Women Form Picket Line before Rockefeller Office*, N.Y. TRIB., April 29, 1914, at 6.

93. *See, e.g., Woman Anarchist Threatens to Kill J. D. Rockefeller Jr.*, N.Y. EVENING WORLD, April 30, 1914, at 1.

94. ARTHUR, *supra* note 88, at 182.

95. *Sinclair Arrested with Four Pickets in Strike Protest*, BROOKLYN DAILY EAGLE, April 29, 1914, at 1.

96. *Sinclair Organizes "Free Silence" Band*, N.Y. TRIB., April 30, 1914, at 6.

97. *Sinclair Arrested with Four Pickets in Strike Protest*, *supra* note 95.

98. *Sinclair Organizes "Free Silence" Band*, *supra* note 96.

99. *Night Picketing at Rockefeller's*, N.Y. TIMES, May 1, 1914, at 4.

100. ARTHUR, *supra* note 88, at 182.

101. *Night Picketing at Rockefeller's*, *supra* note 99.

102. *Upton Sinclair Goes to Jail*, KINGSTON (N.Y.) DAILY FREEMAN, April 30, 1914, at 1.

103. ARTHUR, *supra* note 88, at 183.

104. Sinclair did express sympathy for Arthur Caron, an anarchist who died building a bomb intended for Rockefeller, although he refused to sanction the violence. *Id.* at 185.

105. ARTHUR, *supra* note 88, at 184.

106. Upton Sinclair, *John D.'s Governor of Colorado Lied to President Wilson and Associated Press Suppressed the Facts, Says Sinclair*, APPEAL TO REASON, May 30, 1914, at 1.

107. Letter from Gilbert Roe to Max Eastman (June 10, 1914), in Roe Papers, Box H4, Folder 1914.

108. Letter from Gilbert Roe to Andrew O'Rourke (June 5, 1914), in Roe Papers, Box H4, Folder 1914.

109. Letter from Gilbert Roe to Andrew O'Rourke (June 9, 1914), in Roe Papers, Box H4, Folder 1914.

110. SINCLAIR, *supra* note 17, at 122.

111. Letter from Gilbert Roe to Mary Craig Sinclair (May 25, 1914), in Roe Papers, Box H4, Folder 1914.

112. Letter from Gilbert Roe to Upton Sinclair (May 26, 1914), in Roe Papers, Box H4, Folder 1914.

113. Letter from Gilbert Roe to Mary Craig Sinclair (June 20, 1914), in Roe Papers, Box H4, Folder 1914.

114. Letter from John Scoble to Mary Craig Sinclair (July 7, 1914), in Roe Papers, Box H4, Folder 1914.

115. New York v. Sinclair, 149 N.Y.S. 54, 60–63 (Ct. Gen. Sess. 1914).

116. *Id.* at 56 (citing Laws of 1882, ch. 410, §1458).

117. *Id.* Rockefeller was not identified in the record below, and Roe argued, unsuccessfully, that this was fatal to the prosecution's assertion that Sinclair's actions were intended as a rebuke to Rockefeller.

118. Letter from Upton Sinclair to Gilbert Roe (July 15, 1914), in Roe Papers, Box H3, Folder S.

119. Letter from John Scoble to Upton Sinclair (July 17, 1914), in Roe Papers, Box H4, Folder 1914.

120. Letter from Upton Sinclair to Gilbert Roe (July 22, 1914), in Roe Papers, Box H3, Folder S.

121. Letter from Upton Sinclair to Gilbert Roe (September 24, 1914), in Roe Papers, Box H3, Folder S.

122. New York v. Sinclair, 151 N.Y.S. 1136 (N.Y. App. Div. 1915).

123. Letter from Gilbert Roe to Upton Sinclair (February 6, 1915), in Roe Papers, Box H4, Folder 1915.

124. Letter from Upton Sinclair to Gilbert Roe (April 22, 1915), in Roe Papers, Box H3, Folder S.

125. Letter from Gilbert Roe to Upton Sinclair (April 26, 1915), in Roe Papers, Box H4, Folder 1915.

126. Undated, unaddressed letter from Gwyneth King Roe, in GKR Papers, Box 1, Folder 16.

127. JAMES H. MAURER, IT CAN BE DONE 150–55, 191–92 (1938).

128. Letter from Gilbert Roe to William S. Furst (August 30, 1916), in Roe Papers, Box H5, Folder 1916.

129. MAURER, *supra* note 127, at 192–93.

130. Letter from Gilbert Roe to the Editor, N.Y. TRIB. (December 13, 1916), in Roe Papers, Box H5, Folder 1916.

131. *Justice for James Maurer*, N.Y. TRIB., December 19, 1916, at 5.

132. Letter from Gilbert Roe to Carl Beck (December 20, 1916), in Roe Papers, Box H5, Folder 1916.

133. Letter from James Maurer to Gilbert Roe (April 3, 1919), in Roe Papers, Box H3, Folder M.

CHAPTER 6. THE PACIFISTS I

1. Geoffrey R. Stone, *Judge Learned Hand and the Espionage Act of 1917: A Mystery Unraveled*, 70 U. CHI. L. REV. 335, 345–46 (2003).

2. Letter from Gilbert Roe to Robert La Follette (April 7, 1917), in Roe Papers, Box H5, Folder 1917.

3. *Espionage and Interference with Neutrality: Hearings on H.R. 291 Before the H. Comm. on the Judiciary*, 65th Cong. (1917).

4. Letter from Gilbert Roe to Robert La Follette (April 30, 1917), in Roe Papers, Box H5, Folder 1917.

5. *Espionage and Interference with Neutrality*, *supra* note 3, at 36–62.

6. STAT. 217, 219 (1917).

7. Letter from Gilbert Roe to Robert La Follette (April 19, 1917), in Roe Papers, Box H5, Folder 1917.

8. Resolutions of the American Newspaper Publishers Association, 65th Cong. (1st Sess. 1917), *in* 55 Cong. Rec. S1861 (May 5, 1917).

9. *See* Stone, *supra* note 1, at 346.

10. DAVID M. KENNEDY, OVER HERE 25–28 (2004).

11. Stone, *supra* note 1, at 346.

12. Letter from Gilbert Roe to Robert La Follette (April 19, 1917), in Roe Papers, Box H5, Folder 1917.

13. Letter from Gilbert Roe to Robert La Follette (May 8, 1917), in Roe Papers, Box H5, Folder 1917.

14. Ch. 30, 40 STAT. 217, 230–31 (1917).

15. Letter from Gilbert Roe to Roger Baldwin (June 30, 1917) (cited in Donald

Johnson, *Wilson, Burleson, and Censorship in the First World War*, 28 J. SOUTHERN HISTORY 46, 47 (1962)).

16. KENNEDY, *supra* note 10, at 27. *See also Socialist Paper Held Up*, N.Y. TIMES, July 1, 1917, at 12 (*American Socialist* held up prior to enactment).

17. Johnson, *supra* note 15, at 48.

18. Affidavit of Merrill Rogers, Transcript of Record at 17, Masses Pub. Co. v. Patten, 246 F. 24 (2d Cir. 1917) (No. 123).

19. Brief for Complainant-Appellee at 2, Masses Pub. Co. v. Patten, 246 F. 24 (2d Cir. 1917) (No. 123).

20. Deposition of William H. Lamar, Transcript of Record at 26, Masses Pub. Co. v. Patten, 246 F. 24 (2d Cir. 1917) (No. 123).

21. Affidavit of Merrill Rogers, Transcript of Record at 17, Masses Pub. Co. v. Patten, 246 F. 24 (2d Cir. 1917) (No. 123).

22. Bill of Complaint, Transcript of Record at 7, Masses Pub. Co. v. Patten, 246 F. 24 (2d Cir. 1917) (No. 123).

23. Affidavit of Merrill Rogers, Transcript of Record at 17-18, Masses Pub. Co. v. Patten, 246 F. 24 (2d Cir. 1917) (No. 123).

24. Affidavit of A. S. Burleson, Transcript of Record at 20, Masses Pub. Co. v. Patten, 246 F. 24 (2d Cir. 1917) (No. 123).

25. *Emma Goldman and Berkman Get Two Years*, N.Y. SUN, July 10, 1917, at 1.

26. Affidavit of A. S. Burleson, Transcript of Record at 20, 23, Masses Pub. Co. v. Patten, 246 F. 24 (2d Cir. 1917) (No. 123).

27. *Emma Goldman and Berkman Get Two Years*, *supra* note 25.

28. Bill of Complaint, Transcript of Record at 5-9, Masses Pub. Co. v. Patten, 246 F. 24 (2d Cir. 1917) (No. 123).

29. United States v. Kennerly, 209 Fed. 119 (S.D.N.Y. 1913). *See also* GERALD GUNTHER, LEARNED HAND 148-51 (1994).

30. *See, e.g.*, Massachusetts v. Friede, 171 N.E. 472, 473 (Mass. 1930).

31. Butler v. Michigan 352 U.S. 380 (1957). *See also* Roth v. United States, 354 U.S. 476 (1957).

32. Order to Show Cause, Transcript of Record at 12-13, Masses Pub. Co. v. Patten, 246 F. 24 (2d Cir. 1917) (No. 123).

33. *"The Masses" Must Wait*, N.Y. TIMES, July 17, 1917, at 7.

34. Letter from Gilbert Roe to Robert La Follette (July 18, 1917), in Roe Papers, Box H5, Folder 1917.

35. *Hillquit Reports on Mail Protest*, N.Y. TIMES, July 18, 1917, at 4. According to Donald Johnson, the group consisted of Hillquit, Darrow, Walsh, and lawyer Seymour Stedman. Johnson, *supra* note 15, at 49. Baldwin's name appears in BELLE CASE & FOLA LA FOLLETTE, ROBERT M. LA FOLLETTE 739 (1953) [hereinafter LA FOLLETTE].

36. *Hillquit Reports on Mail Protest*, *supra* note 35, at 4.

37. LA FOLLETTE, *supra* note 35, at 739.

38. Johnson, *supra* note 15, at 49–51.
39. Deposition of John M. Scoble at 2 (August 15, 1917), Masses Pub. Co. v. Patten, 246 F. 24 (2d Cir. 1917) (No. 123).
40. *Judge Makes Point in "Masses" Favor*, N.Y. Times, July 22, 1917, at 1.
41. *Id. See also* Affidavits of A. S. Burleson & William H. Lamar, Transcript of Record at 19–27, Masses Pub. Co. v. Patten, 246 F. 24 (2d Cir. 1917) (No. 123).
42. Affidavit of A. S. Burleson, Transcript of Record at 20–25, Masses Pub. Co. v. Patten, 246 F. 24 (2d Cir. 1917) (No. 123).
43. Masses, August 1917, at 9–29.
44. *Id.* at 36. Excerpts from all four text items appear in an appendix to the Hand decision, Masses Pub. Co. v. Patten, 244 F. 535, 543–46 (S.D.N.Y. 1917).
45. *Judge Makes Point in "Masses" Favor*, *supra* note 40.
46. *"Masses" in Court Called Foe of U.S.*, N.Y. Sun, July 22, 1917, at 9.
47. *Cartoon Cause Suppression of "The Masses,"* N.Y. Trib., July 22, 1917, at 16.
48. *Judge Makes Point in "Masses" Favor*, *supra* note 40.
49. Affidavit of Max Eastman, Transcript of Record at 28, Masses Pub. Co. v. Patten, 246 F. 24 (2d Cir. 1917) (No. 123).
50. Amendment to Complaint, Transcript of Record at 29, Masses Pub. Co. v. Patten, 246 F. 24 (2d Cir. 1917) (No. 123).
51. Masses Pub. Co. v. Patten, 244 F. 535, 540 (S.D.N.Y. 1917).
52. Order Granting Temporary Injunction, Transcript of Record at 50, Masses Pub. Co. v. Patten, 246 F. 24 (2d Cir. 1917) (No. 123).
53. *Masses Pub. Co.*, 244 F. at 538–43.
54. Order Granting Temporary Injunction, Transcript of Record at 50, Masses Pub. Co. v. Patten, 246 F. 24 (2d Cir. 1917) (No. 123).
55. Masses Pub. Co. v. Patten, 245 F. 102, 104 (2d Cir. 1917).
56. Assignment of Error, Transcript of Record at 53, Masses Pub. Co. v. Patten, 246 F. 24 (2d Cir. 1917) (No. 123).
57. Citation on Appeal, Transcript of Record at 55, Masses Pub. Co. v. Patten, 246 F. 24 (2d Cir. 1917) (No. 123).
58. Letter from Gilbert Roe to Robert La Follette (July 26, 1917), in Roe Papers, Box H5, Folder 1917.
59. La Follette, *supra* note 35, at 741–42.
60. Letter from Gilbert Roe to Robert La Follette (August 3, 1917), in Roe Papers, Box H5, Folder 1917.
61. Deposition of Frederick G. Mulker at 1 (August 22, 1917), Masses Pub. Co. v. Patten, 246 F. 24 (2d Cir. 1917) (No. 123).
62. *"The Masses" Now Using Mails to Increase Sales Cut Down by Postal Ban*, N.Y. Trib., August 23, 1917, at 4.
63. Masses Pub. Co. v. Patten, 245 F. 102, 104–106 (2d Cir. 1917).
64. Deposition of John M. Scoble at 3 (August 15, 1917), Masses Pub. Co. v. Patten, 246 F. 24 (2d Cir. 1917) (No. 123).

65. Deposition of Frederick G. Mulker at 2–3 (August 22, 1917), Masses Pub. Co. v. Patten, 246 F. 24 (2d Cir. 1917) (No. 123).

66. *Ban on "Masses" Is Denounced*, N.Y. TRIB., August 15, 1917, at 3.

67. Deposition of Frederick G. Mulker at 2–4 (August 22, 1917), Masses Pub. Co. v. Patten, 246 F. 24 (2d Cir. 1917) (No. 123).

68. John Sayer, *Art and Politics, Dissent and Repression: The Masses Magazine versus the Government*, 32 AM. J. L. HIST. 42, 50 (1988) (quoting ARTHUR YOUNG, ART YOUNG: HIS LIFE AND TIMES 318 (1939)).

69. *Paper Barred, Opens Suit*, BROOKLYN DAILY EAGLE, August 18, 1917, at 2.

70. Deposition of John M. Scoble at 4–5 (August 15, 1917), Masses Pub. Co. v. Patten, 246 F. 24 (2d Cir. 1917) (No. 123) (quoting *Masses Pub. Co.*, 245 F. at 106).

71. Deposition of Frederick G. Mulker at 4 (August 22, 1917), Masses Pub. Co. v. Patten, 246 F. 24 (2d Cir. 1917) (No. 123).

72. *Id.* at 6 (quoting N.Y. TRIB., August 18, 1917).

73. Letter from Gilbert Roe to Robert La Follette (August 24, 1917), in Roe Papers, Box H5, Folder 1917.

74. *"Masses" Mail Ban Upheld by Court*, N.Y. SUN, September 15, 1917, at 4 (quoting Masses Pub. Co. v. Patten (S.D.N.Y. September 12, 1917) (unpublished) (printed in U.S. Dept. of Justice, *Interpretation of War Statutes Bulletin No. 6*)).

75. Sayer, *supra* note 68, at 51 (quoting Masses Pub. Co. v. Patten (S.D.N.Y. September 12, 1917) (unpublished) (printed in U.S. Dept. of Justice, *Interpretation of War Statutes Bulletin No. 6*)).

76. *Burleson Calls "The Masses" and Watson Seditious*, N.Y. TRIB., August 23, 1917, at 4.

77. Sayer, *supra* note 68, at 50 (quoting Masses Pub. Co. v. Patten (S.D.N.Y. September 12, 1917) (unpublished) (printed in U.S. Dept. of Justice, *Interpretation of War Statutes Bulletin No. 6*)).

78. *May Bar "The Masses" from City Libraries*, N.Y. TRIB., September 12, 1917, at 5.

79. Sayer, *supra* note 68, at 51.

80. *Mr. Wilson Writes to Max Eastman*, N.Y. TRIB., September 28, 1917, at 1.

81. *Hard to Draw Line, Wilson Tells Eastman; Things Innocent in Peace Perilous in War*, N.Y. TIMES, September 28, 1917, at 1.

82. Letter from Gilbert Roe to John Hannan (September 20, 1917), in Roe Papers, Box H5, Folder 1917.

83. Ch. 106, §19, 40 STAT. 411, 426 (October 6, 1917).

84. Sayer, *supra* note 68, at 51 (citing 55 LITERARY DIGEST 12 (October 6, 1917)).

85. *Id.* (citing letter from Lamar to Oswald Garrison Villard, in OSWALD GARRISON VILLARD, FIGHTING YEARS: MEMOIRS OF A LIBERAL EDITOR 357 (1939)).

86. *Masses Seeks Mail Rights*, N.Y. TIMES, October 25, 1917, at 15.

87. Brief of Defendant-Respondent at 4–32 (September 16, 1917), Masses Pub. Co. v. Patten, 246 F. 24 (2d Cir. 1917) (No. 123). The case Caffey cites is Jeffersonian Pub. Co. v. West, 245 F. 585, 589 (S.D. Ga, 1917).

88. Brief of Complainant-Appellee at 20–43 (October 1, 1917), Masses Pub. Co. v. Patten, 246 F. 24 (2d Cir. 1917) (No. 123).
89. 247 F. 124 (D.C. Md. 1917).
90. Brief of Complainant-Appellee at 52–58 (October 1, 1917), Masses Pub. Co. v. Patten, 246 F. 24 (2d Cir. 1917) (No. 123).
91. Telephone Logs, in GKR Papers, Box 7, Folder 7.
92. Masses Pub. Co. v. Patten, 246 F. 24, 27 (1917).
93. *Id.* (quoting 4 WILLIAM BLACKSTONE, COMMENTARIES *151).
94. *Masses Pub. Co.*, 246 F. at 27–39.
95. *Seditious Publications Face Grand Jury Act*, N.Y. EVENING WORLD, November 3, 1917, at 3.
96. *Indict Seven Members of "The Masses"—Bench Warrants Are Issued*, BROOKLYN DAILY EAGLE, November 19, 1917, at 1.
97. *Masses Pleads Not Guilty*, BROOKLYN DAILY EAGLE, November 21, 1917, at 2. Roe had supported Hillquit's unsuccessful run for mayor of New York City earlier that month on the Socialist ticket. MICHAEL KAZIN, WAR AGAINST WAR 235 (2017).
98. *Her First Poem Gets Her Indicted*, N.Y. TRIB., November 21, 1917, at 6.
99. *Max Eastman Held Under $5,000 Bond*, N.Y. TRIB., November 22, 1917, at 7.
100. *Cut Off Radical Press*, N.Y. TIMES, November 6, 1917, at 8.
101. *"The Masses" Sings Swan Song at Ball*, N.Y. TRIB., December 8, 1917.
102. GUNTHER, *supra* note 29, at 152–55.
103. Sayer, *supra* note 68, at 60–74.
104. Letter from Gilbert Roe to Belle La Follette (December 5, 1917), in Roe Papers, Box H5, Folder 1917.

CHAPTER 7. THE PACIFISTS II

1. Letter from Belle Case La Follette to Gwyneth Roe, September 26, 1917, in Roe Papers, Box H7, Folder 1917 Belle Case La Follette.
2. BELLE CASE & FOLA LA FOLLETTE, ROBERT M. LA FOLLETTE 656, 797 (1953) [hereinafter LA FOLLETTE].
3. *Id.* at 629.
4. Letter from Gilbert Roe to Robert La Follette (March 7, 1917), in Roe Papers, Box H5, Folder 1917.
5. LA FOLLETTE, *supra* note 2, at 666–67.
6. *Id.* at 746–76.
7. S. COMM. ON PRIVILEGES & ELECTIONS, SPEECH OF SENATOR ROBERT M. LA FOLLETTE, HEARINGS 4 (Comm. Prints 1917 & 1918) [hereinafter HEARINGS]. The hearings were printed in two volumes, consecutively paginated, but the first volume is identified as a subcommittee hearing, the second as a full committee hearing.

8. La Follette, *supra* note 2, at 776–80.
9. Hearings, *supra* note 7, at 2.
10. La Follette, *supra* note 2, at 797–802.
11. Hearings, *supra* note 7, at 12–27.
12. Brief in Behalf of Senator Robert M. La Follette, In the Matter of the Investigation by the Senate of the United States of the Charge Made by the Minnesota Commission on Public Safety that on the 20th Day of September, 1917, Senator Robert M. La Follette Made an Address of "A Disloyal and Seditious Nature" at a Public Meeting before a Large Audience at St. Paul, Minnesota 8–10 (undated).
13. La Follette, *supra* note 2, at 804–10.
14. Hearings, *supra* note 7, at 29.
15. La Follette, *supra* note 2, at 815, 874–75.
16. Letter from Gilbert Roe to Morris Hillquit, referenced in Telephone Logs, GKR Papers, Box 7, Folder 7.
17. Letter from Gilbert Roe to Atlee Pomerene (April 24, 1918), in Roe Papers, Box H5, Folder 1918.
18. Letter from Gilbert Roe to Atlee Pomerene (May 9, 1918), in Roe Papers, Box H5, Folder 1918.
19. Letter from Gilbert Roe to Atlee Pomerene (May 13, 1918), in Roe Papers, Box H5, Folder 1918.
20. La Follette, *supra* note 2, at 876.
21. Hearings, *supra* note 7, at 53–98.
22. *Id.* at 99 (the document under discussion was S. Comm. on Privileges & Elections, Speech of Senator Robert M. La Follette, Memorandum of Information (Comm. Print 1918)).
23. *Id.* at 100–159.
24. La Follette, *supra* note 2, at 883–921.
25. Debs v. United States, 249 U.S. 211 (1919).
26. Schenck v. United States, 249 U.S. 47 (1919).
27. Sugarman v. United States, 249 U.S. 182 (1919).
28. Frohwerk v. United States, 249 U.S. 204 (1919).
29. David Ray Papke, The Pullman Case 8–10 (1999).
30. *Id.* at 86. *See also* In re Debs, 158 U.S. 564 (1895).
31. Papke, *supra* note 29, at 87.
32. Max Eastman, The Trial of Eugene Debs 3 (1918).
33. Peter Carlson, Roughneck: The Life and Times of Big Bill Haywood 156–59 (1983).
34. Scott Nearing, The Debs Decision 6 (1919).
35. *Id. See also* Ruthenberg v. United States, 245 U.S. 480 (1918).
36. Nearing, *supra* note 34, at 8–9. *See also Debs*, 249 U.S. at 213.
37. Nearing, *supra* note 34, at 11. *See also* Stokes v. United States, 274 F. 18 (1920) (reversing Stokes's conviction).
38. Nearing, *supra* note 34, at 11–35.

39. David L. Sterling, *In Defense of Debs: The Lawyers and the Espionage Act Case*, 83 IND. MAG. OF HIST. 17, 22–23 (1987).

40. Brief of Plaintiff in Error at 62–87, Debs v. United States, 249 U.S. 211 (1919) (No. 714).

41. Brief of Gilbert E. Roe as Amicus Curiae at 2–46, Debs v. United States, 249 U.S. 211 (1919) (No. 714).

42. Brief for the United States at I-II, Debs v. United States, 249 U.S. 211 (1919) (No. 714).

43. Brief for the United States in Reply to Brief of Gilbert E. Roe, as Amicus Curiae at 2–3, 16, Debs v. United States, 249 U.S. 211 (1919) (No. 714).

44. *Id.* at 17. For a more detailed summary of the arguments in the case, see David M. Rabban, *The Emergence of Modern First Amendment Doctrine*, 50 U. CHI. L. REV. 1205, 1247–57 (1983).

45. LA FOLLETTE, *supra* note 2, at 937.

46. *Debs*, 249 U.S. at 215.

47. *Schenck*, 249 U.S. at 48–52.

48. *Sugarman*, 249 U.S. at 183.

49. *Frohwerk*, 249 U.S. at 205–7.

50. Abrams v. United States, 250 U.S. 616, 627–31 (1919) (Holmes, J., dissenting).

51. THOMAS HEALY, THE GREAT DISSENT 108 (2013).

52. Gilbert E. Roe, *The Espionage Law*, PEARSON'S MAG., March 1919, at 196.

53. *See* the Village of Arden, http://arden.delaware.gov/, for information on Arden today.

54. Indictment, United States v. Stephens, No. 13 (D. Del. May 1, 1918).

55. ANTHONY ARTHUR, RADICAL INNOCENT: UPTON SINCLAIR 152 (2006).

56. Demurrer, United States v. Stephens, No. 13 (D. Del. May 16, 1918).

57. *Stephens Acquitted of Any Violation of Espionage Act*, WILMINGTON SUNDAY MORNING STAR, June 23, 1918, at 1, 9.

58. Letter from Frank Stephens to Gwyneth King Roe, July 1, 1918, in GKR Papers, Box 2, Folder 1.

59. Pencil note on the back of a Camp Dix Reservation Pass, dated September 4, 1918, probably written by Gwyneth King Roe ("only occasion where Gilbert appeared in a court martial case"), in GKR Papers, Box 7, Folder 7.

60. *See, e.g.*, letters from F. P. Keppel, Third Assistant Secretary of War (January 23, 1919, and February 6, 1919), in Roe Papers, Box H8, Folder 1919. *See also* letter from J. W. Riley, Adjutant General, declining to intercede to reduce Alexander's sentence (February 14, 1919), in Roe Papers, Box H8, Folder 1919.

61. Testimony of Louis B. Nagler, Transcript of Record at 54–57, Nagler v. United States, 254 U.S. 661 (1920) (No. 64).

62. Indictment, Transcript of Record at 6, Nagler v. United States, 254 U.S. 661 (1920) (No. 64).

63. Testimony of Louis B. Nagler, Transcript of Record at 54–57, Nagler v. United States, 254 U.S. 661 (1920) (No. 64).

64. Indictment, Transcript of Record at 7, Nagler v. United States, 254 U.S. 661 (1920) (No. 64).

65. United States v. Nagler, 252 F. 217, 219 (W.D. Wis. 1918).

66. *See, e.g.*, Proclamation of President Taft, December 27, 1911; Order of Secretary of War, July 5, 1917; and Executive Order as to Y.M.C.A., November 1, 1917, Transcript of Record at 13–16, Nagler v. United States, 254 U.S. 661 (1920) (No. 64).

67. *Nagler*, 252 F. at 221–23.

68. *Thirty Months in Prison for Slander of Red Cross*, NEWS LETTER, American Red Cross, Atlantic Division, September 23, 1918, at 6.

69. Assignment of Errors and Petition for Writ of Error, Transcript of Record at 99–116, Nagler v. United States, 254 U.S. 661 (1920) (No. 64).

70. Nagler v. United States, 254 U.S. 661 (1920).

71. *Surrender of Draft Defendants Is Offered*, OAKLAND TRIB., August 9, 1917, at 1.

72. Indictment, Transcript of Record at 2–4, O'Connell v. United States, 253 U.S. 142 (1920) (No. 221).

73. Demurrer to Indictment, Transcript of Record at 6–15, O'Connell v. United States, 253 U.S. 142 (1920) (No. 221).

74. Arraignment and Orders, Transcript of Record at 16, O'Connell v. United States, 253 U.S. 142 (1920) (No. 221).

75. *O'Connell Bail Is $25,000 as Appeal Pends*, OAKLAND TRIB., September 26, 1917, at 1–2.

76. *"Free Speech" Has Limits, O'Connell Jury Is Informed*, OAKLAND TRIB., September 26, 1917, at 2.

77. Verdict, Transcript of Record at 172, O'Connell v. United States, 253 U.S. 142 (1920) (No. 221).

78. Sentence, Transcript of Record at 192, O'Connell v. United States, 253 U.S. 142 (1920) (No. 221).

79. Brief of Daniel O'Connell and Carl J. F. Wacker, O'Connell v. United States, 253 U.S. 142 (1920) (No. 221) (O'Connell Brief).

80. Brief for Plaintiffs-in-Error, Daniel O'Connell and Carl J. F. Wacker, O'Connell v. United States, 253 U.S. 142 (1920) (No. 221) (Roe Brief).

81. Supplemental or Reply Brief for Plaintiffs-in-Error, Daniel O'Connell and Carl J. F. Wacker, O'Connell v. United States, 253 U.S. 142 (1920) (No. 221).

82. O'Connell v. United States, 253 U.S. 142, 147–48 (1920).

83. In the Matter of Daniel O'Connell, 194 P. 1010, 1010 (Cal. 1920).

84. Letter from Roger Baldwin to Gwyneth King Roe (January 9, 1930), in GKR Papers, Box 3, Folder 8.

85. DAVID M. RABBAN, FREE SPEECH IN ITS FORGOTTEN YEARS 308 (1997).

CHAPTER 8. THE COMMUNISTS

1. JUSTIN KAPLAN, LINCOLN STEFFENS 233 (1974) (quoting THEODORE DRAPER, THE ROOTS OF AMERICAN COMMUNISM 101 (1957)).

2. ANTHONY ARTHUR, RADICAL INNOCENT: UPTON SINCLAIR 201–204 (2006).
3. DAVID M. KENNEDY, OVER HERE 26–28 (2004).
4. BELLE CASE & FOLA LA FOLLETTE, ROBERT M. LA FOLLETTE 521–36 (1953) [hereinafter LA FOLLETTE].
5. KENNEDY, *supra* note 3, at 28–29.
6. Postcard from Lincoln Steffens to Gwyneth King Roe, May 29, 1917, in GKR Papers, Box 2, Folder 2.
7. KAPLAN, *supra* note 1, at 233 (quoting Steffens's recollections in 1926 from THE LETTERS OF LINCOLN STEFFENS 724 (Ella Winter & Granville Hicks eds., 1938)).
8. Letter from Lincoln Steffens to Gwyneth King Roe (April 30, 1933), in GKR Papers, Box 2, Folder 2.
9. KAPLAN, *supra* note 1, at 237.
10. ERIC HOMBERGER, JOHN REED 48–49 (1990).
11. Letter from Gilbert Roe to Edward Eyre Hunt (January 20, 1914), in Roe Papers, Box H4, Folder 1914.
12. HOMBERGER, *supra* note 10, at 55.
13. Letter from John Reed to Gilbert Roe (December 31, 1913), in Roe Papers, Box H3, Folder R.
14. Undated letter from Mabel Dodge to Gilbert Roe asking Roe to take her divorce case because she could not get a Paris divorce because of the war. In Roe Papers, Box H7, Folder 1914. *See also* undated letter from Edwin S. Dodge ("My wife, Mrs. Mabel Dodge of 23 Fifth Avenue writes me that she has retained you as her lawyer"), in Roe Papers, Box H2, Folder D.
15. Letter from Gilbert Roe to Mabel Dodge (April 4, 1914), in Roe Papers, Box H4, Folder 1914.
16. HOMBERGER, *supra* note 10, at 74.
17. Letter from John Reed to Gwyneth King Roe (March 24, 1915), in GKR Papers, Box 1, Folder 15. It is not certain which poem Reed edited, but it may have been Netha's powerful antiwar poem "Go Tell the Emperor." That poem was published in *Harper's Weekly* on June 5, 1915, which bore the cover headline, "When Will the War End?" The final, heavily edited poem, originally entitled "A Message for the Emperor," begins:

> Sick with reading unauthentic news,
> Knowing that, false or true, there could be nothing worse,
> With futile rage and horror chasing like phantoms thro' my brain,
> I must have fallen asleep,
> For though I feel what followed happened clear,
> It must have been a dream.
>
> I was a messenger, and on the battle-field,
> Blood everywhere. The sight of it! The smell of it!
> And they who lay there felt blood, tasted blood,
> And when the last gun ceased, we heard blood drip.

> Through the hostile field I crept till all my senses reeled
> At the sight of it, the smell of it, the feel of it.
> And then I came to the victor's field—
> More blood—more dead—and still more blood.

18. Letter from John Reed to Gwyneth King Roe (March 24, 1915), in GKR Papers, Box 1, Folder 15.

19. HOMBERGER, *supra* note 10, at 103–132.

20. Draft obituary of Gwyneth King Roe (March 30, 1968), in GKR Papers, Box 9, Folder 3.

21. JANICE R. AND STEPHEN R. MACKINNON, AGNES SMEDLEY: THE LIFE AND TIMES OF AN AMERICAN RADICAL 142 (1988).

22. RUTH PRICE, THE LIVES OF AGNES SMEDLEY 8 (2005).

23. *Id.* at 82. Proving or disproving Smedley's Soviet connection is far beyond the scope of this book, but Price's biography is based on sources that the MacKinnons could not have seen. Price's self-identification as a "leftist" and her continuing appreciation for Smedley lend further credence to her account. This sketch assumes, without proving, that the Price narrative is the more accurate one.

24. *Id.* at 14–69.

25. MACKINNON, *supra* note 21, at 46.

26. PRICE, *supra* note 22, at 69–71.

27. Indictment, United States v. Salindranath Ghose et al. (S.D.N.Y. April 1, 1918) (Nat'l Archives, S.D.N.Y. Record C-11-360). Many of the legal documents in related cases spell Ghose's name "Sailendra Nath," which is the spelling used by the defendants' supporters, but the records flowing from this indictment use "Salindranath." Both spellings are correct, reflecting different regional pronunciations of the original Bengali. These notes use the spelling on the referenced documents.

28. MACKINNON, *supra* note 21, at 46. Price says the bail money was raised by Dr. Percy Stickney Grant, a socialist clergyman. Price, *supra* note 22, at 72.

29. PRICE, *supra* note 22, at 73.

30. Indictment (pencil notation), United States v. Salindranath Ghose et al. (S.D.N.Y. April 1, 1918) (Nat'l Archives, S.D.N.Y. Record C-11-360).

31. Demurrer, Salindranath Ghose et al. (S.D.N.Y. April 9, 1918) (Nat'l Archives, S.D.N.Y. Record C-11-360).

32. Indictment (pencil notation), United States v. Salindranath Ghose et al. (S.D.N.Y. April 1, 1918) (Nat'l Archives, S.D.N.Y. Record C-11-360).

33. PRICE, *supra* note 22, at 72.

34. MACKINNON, *supra* note 21, at 46; *see also* MARGARET SANGER, MARGARET SANGER: AN AUTOBIOGRAPHY 351 (1938).

35. PRICE, *supra* note 22, at 71.

36. Indictment, Exhibit 1A, Transcript of Record at 10, Smedley v. McCarthy, 251 U.S. 564 (1919) (No. 245).

Notes to Pages 173–176

37. Certification, Transcript of Record at 16, Smedley v. McCarthy, 251 U.S. 564 (1919) (No. 245).

38. Complaint, Transcript of Record at 8, Smedley v. McCarthy, 251 U.S. 564 (1919) (No. 245).

39. Petition, United States v. Salindranath Ghose et al. (S.D.N.Y. August 23, 1918) (Nat'l Archives, S.D.N.Y. Record C-11-360).

40. Show Cause Order, United States v. Salindranath Ghose et al. (S.D.N.Y. August 29, 1918) (Nat'l Archives, S.D.N.Y. Record C-11-360).

41. Record Notation, United States v. Salindranath Ghose et al. (S.D.N.Y. August 29, 1918) (Nat'l Archives, S.D.N.Y. Record C-11-360).

42. MacKinnon, *supra* note 21, at 60–61.

43. Petition for Writ of Habeas Corpus, Transcript of Record at 3–7, Smedley v. McCarthy, 251 U.S. 564 (1919) (No. 245).

44. Orders, Transcript of Record at 16–18, Smedley v. McCarthy, 251 U.S. 564 (1919) (No. 245).

45. Opinion of Judge A. N. Hand, Transcript of Record at 19–22, Smedley v. McCarthy, 251 U.S. 564 (1919) (No. 245).

46. Petition and Order, Transcript of Record at 22–23, Smedley v. McCarthy, 251 U.S. 564 (1919) (No. 245).

47. Bond for Costs, Transcript of Record at 24–26, Smedley v. McCarthy, 251 U.S. 564 (1919) (No. 245).

48. Petition and Order, United States v. Salindranath Ghose et al. (S.D.N.Y. December 10, 1918) (Nat'l Archives, S.D.N.Y. Record C-11-360) (quoting letter from Roe to Caffey and Stephenson, November 18, 1918).

49. Order, United States v. Salindranath Ghose et al. (S.D.N.Y. December 16, 1918) (Nat'l Archives, S.D.N.Y. Record C-11-360).

50. Nolle Prosequi as to Pulin B. Bose, Taraknath Das, Jadu Gopal Mukerjee and Bhai Bhagwan Singh, United States v. Salindranath Ghose et al. (S.D.N.Y. June 5, 1923) (Nat'l Archives, S.D.N.Y. Record C-11-360).

51. Price, *supra* note 22, at 76–78.

52. *Id.* at 81 (citing letter from Gilbert Roe to John Lord O'Brian (January 13, 1919), in DOJ records).

53. *Id.* at 78–79. Price abbreviates Friends of Freedom for India as FFFI.

54. *Id.* at 77; MacKinnon, *supra* note 21, at 56.

55. Price, *supra* note 22, at 80.

56. Motion on Behalf of Appellee to Dismiss or Affirm and Brief in Support at 1–11, Smedley v. McCarthy, 251 U.S. 564 (1919) (No. 245).

57. Brief on Behalf of Appellants in Opposition to Motion to Dismiss the Appeal or Affirm the Judgment of the District Court at 3–60, Smedley v. McCarthy, 251 U.S. 564 (1919) (No. 245).

58. Price, *supra* note 22, at 82.

59. Smedley v. McCarthy, 251 U.S. 564 (1919).

60. Friends of Freedom for India, India's Freedom in American Courts 10, April 1919, https://www.saadigitalarchive.org.

61. MACKINNON, *supra* note 21, at 63–64.

62. Letter from Robert Morss Lovett to Gilbert Roe (February 6, 1920), in Roe Papers, Box H3, Folder L.

63. Letter from Robert Morss Lovett & Agnes Smedley to "Dear Friends" (November 2, 1920), https://www.saadigitalarchive.org/item/20130513-2757.

64. MACKINNON, *supra* note 21, at 68.

65. PRICE, *supra* note 22, at 143; MacKinnon, *supra* note 21, at 110.

66. MACKINNON, *supra* note 21, at 131.

67. Letters from Agnes Smedley to Gilbert Roe (April 12, 1929, and June 5, 1929), in Roe Papers, Box H8, Folder 1929.

68. CELIA LEWIS ZITRON, THE NEW YORK CITY TEACHERS UNION 1916–1964 at 164–65 (1968).

69. THOMAS MUFSON, THE TRIAL OF THE THREE SUSPENDED TEACHERS OF THE DE WITT CLINTON HIGH SCHOOL 7 (1918) (purporting to be a transcript of the hearings).

70. ZITRON, *supra* note 68, at 166.

71. MUFSON, *supra* note 69, at 12, 18.

72. Zitron suggests that Paul learned of the assignment through a network of student spies directed by a teacher, Aaron I. Dotey. ZITRON, *supra* note 68, at 165.

73. MUFSON, *supra* note 69, at 21–108.

74. *Arraigns Methods in Trying Teachers*, N.Y. TIMES, December 16, 1917, at 5.

75. *Dismiss Teachers after Hot Debate*, N.Y. TIMES, December 20, 1917, at 1.

76. *Will Fight Dismissals*, N.Y. TIMES, December 21, 1917, at 20.

77. TEACHERS UNION OF THE CITY OF NEW YORK, TOWARD A NEW EDUCATION: THE CASE AGAINST AUTOCRACY IN OUR PUBLIC SCHOOLS 134–143 (1918) (Roe's brief on behalf of Schmalhausen, Schneer, and Mufson appears in an appendix to this pamphlet, prepared by the Teachers Union in response to a report by the American Defense Society that strongly condemned the three teachers.).

78. *Dismissed Teachers Appeal to Finley*, BROOKLYN DAILY EAGLE, January 19, 1918, at 18.

79. *Teachers Disloyal, Dr. Finegan Holds*, BROOKLYN DAILY EAGLE, November 6, 1918, at 8.

80. STEPHEN F. BRUMBERG, NEW YORK CITY SCHOOLS MARCH OFF TO WAR (presented at the Annual Meeting of the American Educational Research Association, New Orleans, La., April 6, 1988) (available from Educational Resources Information Center).

81. *Socialists Hear Expelled Teachers and Denounce the Board of Education*, N.Y. TRIB., January 21, 1918, at 5; *Socialists Attack New School Board*, N.Y. SUN, January 21, 1918, at 2.

82. Notice of Suspension, in The Teachers' Union, Brief and Argument of Gilbert E. Roe in Behalf of Benjamin Glassberg, Teacher 3 (1919) [hereinafter Brief and Argument].

83. *Union to Defend Teacher Ousted on Disloyalty Charge*, N.Y. TRIB., January 21, 1919, at 5.

84. *Quiz Teacher on Trotzky*, N.Y. TIMES, January 19, 1918.
85. Brief and Argument, *supra* note 82, at 6.
86. Charge and Specifications, in Brief and Argument, *supra* note 82, at 6–7 (1919).
87. *C.H.S. Boys Testify at Teacher's Trial*, BROOKLYN DAILY EAGLE, March 29, 1919, at 12.
88. *Accused Teacher Aided by Students*, BROOKLYN DAILY EAGLE, May 3, 1919, at 5.
89. Brief and Argument, *supra* note 82, at 9.
90. *Raymond Robins Testifies in Behalf of Deposed Teacher*, N.Y. TRIB., April 4, 1919, at 10.
91. Stipulation, in Brief and Argument, *supra* note 82, at 9–10.
92. Statement of Benjamin Glassberg, attached to Brief and Argument, *supra* note 82, at 28.
93. *Hot Disputes Mark Trial of Glassberg*, N.Y. TRIB., May 10, 1919, at 3.
94. *Id. See also Radicals Close Schools; Too Much Publicity*, N.Y. TRIB., May 12, 1919, at 11.
95. *Accused Teacher Aided*, *supra* note 88.
96. Brief and Argument, *supra* note 82, at 8–26.
97. *Teacher Is Found Guilty*, N.Y. TIMES, May 27, 1919, at 15.
98. *Id.; Benjamin Glassberg, Socialist Teacher, Is Found Guilty*, N.Y. TRIB., May 28, 1919, at 10.
99. *Teacher Will Appeal Bolshevism Verdict*, N.Y. TRIB., May 30, 1919, at 4.
100. *Dismissed Teacher Attacks Instruction Methods at Protest Meeting*, N.Y. TRIB., June 12, 1919, at 8.
101. *Quakeress Loses Appeal*, BROOKLYN DAILY EAGLE, November 22, 1919, at 9.
102. *Glassberg Appeal Heard*, BROOKLYN DAILY EAGLE, November 29, 1919, at 20.
103. The Glass Berg Case, undated memorandum, in Roe Papers, Box H12, Folder Glassberg.
104. In the Matter of the Dismissal of Benjamin Glassberg, 33 STATE EDUC. DEPT. REPT. 261, 265–67 (1925).
105. David A. Lincove, *Radical Publishing to "Reach the Million Masses,"* 10 LEFT HIST. 85, 92 (2014).
106. *Glassberg Seeks Reinstatement as School Teacher*, BROOKLYN DAILY EAGLE, August 11, 1923, at 7.
107. Letter from Benjamin Glassberg to Gilbert Roe (January 3, 1927), in GKR Papers, Box 1, Folder 5.
108. Letter from Gilbert Roe to Benjamin Glassberg (January 10, 1927), in GKR Papers, Box 1, Folder 5.
109. ZITRON, *supra* note 68, at 175–76.
110. Letter from Benjamin Glassberg to Gwyneth King Roe (December 27, 1929), in GKR Papers, Box 1, Folder 5.
111. Letter from William L. Ettinger to the Board of Education (March 16, 1921), in Roe Papers, Box H12, Folder Hyams Case.

112. Letter from Board of Education to Gilbert Roe (February 16, 1922), in Roe Papers, Box H12, Folder Hyams Case.

113. ZITRON, *supra* note 68, at 172–73.

114. *Id.* at 173–74 (quoting Howard K. Beale, *Are American Teachers Free? Part XII*, REPORT OF AMERICAN COMMISSION ON SOCIAL STUDIES at 61–62 (1936)).

115. ZITRON, *supra* note 68, at 175.

116. Draft of Teachers Union protest against the Lusk Laws, in Roe Papers, Box H12, Folder 1922.

117. Statement of the Teachers Union on the Services of Mr. Gilbert E. Roe, Counsel of the Union for Eleven Years (February 18, 1930), in GKR Papers, Box 1, Folder 5.

118. ZITRON, *supra* note 68, at 175.

119. KENNEDY, *supra* note 3, at 289–90.

120. *Ousted Socialists Will Get Hearing Next Week; Leaders in Assembly Sure of Stand*, BROOKLYN DAILY EAGLE, January 8, 1920, at 1.

121. *Ousted Socialists Begin Fight for Assembly Seats*, BROOKLYN DAILY EAGLE, January 8, 1920, at 1.

122. *Socialists Plan New Lusk Attack*, N.Y. TIMES, January 12, 1920, at 1.

123. *Sweet Blocks Move to Seat Socialists*, N.Y. TIMES, January 20, 1920, at 3.

124. Answer, In the Matter of the Investigation by the Assembly of the State of New York, February 1920, at 1–3, in Roe Papers, Box H12, Folder Assemblymen Case.

125. Gilbert E. Roe, *The Socialist Trial at Albany*, LA FOLLETTE'S MAG., April 1920, at 64.

126. *Socialists Close Defence Abruptly*, SUN & N.Y. HERALD, February 28, 1920, at 4.

127. *Ousted Socialists Called Traitors*, SUN & N.Y. Herald, March 5, 1920, at 5.

128. *Hillquit Attacks Committee Power in Socialist Trial*, N.Y. EVENING WORLD, March 3, 1920, at 3; *Stedman Likens Assembly to Czar in Socialist Trial*, N.Y. EVENING WORLD, March 5, 1920, at 8.

129. *Expel the Five Socialist Assemblymen, Urges Majority Report, Charging Treason; Roosevelt to Oppose Ouster Motion*, N.Y. TIMES, March 31, 1920, at 1.

130. *Democratic Filibusters Delay Vote on Expulsion of Socialists in Stormy Debate in Assembly*, N.Y. TIMES, April 1, 1920, at 1.

131. *Assembly Expels All Five Socialists by Big Vote after a Thrilling Session*, BROOKLYN DAILY EAGLE, April 1, 1920, at 1.

132. Gilbert E. Roe, *The Socialist Trial at Albany*, LA FOLLETTE'S MAG., April 1920, at 64.

133. *Special Elections Refused Socialists*, SUN & N.Y. HERALD, April 13, 1920, at 1.

134. *Fusion Completed against Socialism*, N.Y. TIMES, August 13, 1920, at 3.

135. *Five Socialists Assemblymen Are Reelected*, SUN & N.Y. HERALD, September 17, 1920, at 22.

136. *Assembly Again Expels Three Socialists*, N.Y. TIMES, September 22, 1920, at 1.

137. Undated note from Morris Hillquit to Gilbert Roe, in Roe Papers, Box H8, File 1920.

Chapter 9. Winding Down

1. Notation by Gwyneth Roe Murphy on pamphlet about Pelham Manor (January 1970), in GKR papers, Box 8, Folder 3.
2. Jack Roe, *Airplane Exposition at the Seventy-First's Armory*, ROE FAMILY NEWS, March 12, 1920, at 1, in GKR Papers, Box 8, Folder 4.
3. Jack Roe, *Atlantic City Trip, Extra Extra*, ROE FAMILY NEWS, March 20, 1920, at 2, in GKR Papers, Box 8, Folder 4.
4. Jack Roe, *Mrs. Baker Reads to Group of Distinguished Friends*, ROE FAMILY NEWS, February 25, 1921, at 1, in GKR Papers, Box 8, Folder 4.
5. Fragmentary page from unpublished GKR autobiography, in GKR Papers, Box 5 Folder 9.
6. Jack Roe, *Family to Go to Farm!!!*, ROE FAMILY NEWS, March 23, 1920, at 1, in GKR Papers, Box 8, Folder 4.
7. Jack Roe, *Girls Weed Garden, Jack Works in Hayfield*, ROE FAMILY NEWS, June 5, 1920, at 1, in GKR Papers, Box 8, Folder 4.
8. Undated, handwritten essay, in GKR Papers, Box 8, Folder 3.
9. Jack Roe, *Family Visits Washington and Sees Harding's Inauguration*, ROE FAMILY NEWS, March 23, 1920, at 1, in GKR Papers, Box 8, Folder 4.
10. Jack Roe, *Mr. and Mrs. Roe to Visit Washington Soon*, ROE FAMILY NEWS, April 22, 1920, at 1, in GKR Papers, Box 8, Folder 4.
11. Nagler v. United States, 254 U.S. 661 (1920).
12. Donnelly v. Anderson Brown & Co., 275 F. 438 (S.D.N.Y. 1921); Rolle v. Rolle, 194 N.Y.S. 661 (N.Y. App. 1922); and May v. Hetrick Bros. Co., 235 N.Y. 601 (1923).
13. S. Res. 295, 62 Cong. Rec. 8140, 67th Cong., 2d Sess., June 5, 1922.
14. S. Res. 292, 62 Cong. Rec. 6867, 67th Cong., 2d Sess., May 13, 1922.
15. J. Leonard Bates, *The Teapot Dome Scandal and the Election of 1924*, 60 AM. HIST. REV. 303, 303–5 (1955).
16. BELLE CASE & FOLA LA FOLLETTE, ROBERT M. LA FOLLETTE 1124 (1953) [hereinafter LA FOLLETTE].
17. NANCY C. UNGER, FIGHTING BOB LA FOLLETTE: THE RIGHTEOUS REFORMER 305 (Nook ed., 2000). *See also* JOHN D. HICKS, REPUBLICAN ASCENDANCY 1921–1933, at 88–92 (1960).
18. Bates, *supra* note 15, at 319.
19. James C. Prude, *William Gibbs McAdoo and the Democratic National Convention of 1924*, 38 J. S. HIST. 621, 621 (1972).
20. LA FOLLETTE, *supra* note 16, at 1110.

21. *Id.* at 1114–15 (quoting letter from Gilbert Roe to Robert La Follette (June 17, 1924), in Roe Papers, Box H5, Folder 1924).

22. UNGER, *supra* note 17, at 308; *see also* LA FOLLETTE, *supra* note 16, at 1114–17.

23. Fred E. Haynes, *The Significance of the Latest Third Party Movement*, 12 MISS. VALLEY HIST. REV. 177, 179 (1925).

24. See letter from Gilbert Roe to Robert La Follette (September 2, 1924), in Roe Papers, Box H12, Folder 1924 (listing Roe's responsibilities as New York, New Jersey, Pennsylvania, Delaware, Connecticut, Rhode Island, New Hampshire, Vermont, Maine, and Massachusetts).

25. Memorandum (September 2, 1924), in Roe Papers, Box H5, Folder 1924.

26. See letter from Gilbert Roe to Robert La Follette Jr. (January 7, 1924), in Roe Papers, Box H5, Folder 1924 (critiquing a draft constitutional amendment allowing Congress to override Supreme Court holdings of unconstitutionality).

27. LA FOLLETTE-WHEELER JOINT NATIONAL COMMITTEE PUBLICITY DEPT., LA FOLLETTE AND THE PROGRESSIVES ON THE COURTS, Leaflet No. 4, at 1–5 (1924).

28. Letter from Belle Case La Follette to Gwyneth King Roe (August 25, 1924), in GKR Papers, Box 1, Folder 8.

29. James H. Shideler, *The La Follette Progressive Party Campaign of 1924*, 33 WIS. MAG. OF HIST. 444, 454–55 (1950).

30. Telegram from Robert La Follette to Gilbert Roe (October 17, 1924), in Roe Papers, Box H5, Folder 1924.

31. David Leip, 1924 Presidential General Election Results, https://web.archive.org/web/20120307165705/, http://uselectionatlas.org/RESULTS/national.php?year=1924 (2012).

32. LA FOLLETTE, *supra* note 16, at 1148, 1164.

33. Letter from Robert La Follette Jr. to Gilbert Roe (June 16, 1925), in Roe Papers, Box H8, Folder 1925.

34. LA FOLLETTE, *supra* note 16, at 1169–70.

35. Letter from Belle Case La Follette to Gilbert Roe (December 17, 1925), in GKR Papers, Box 1, Folder 8.

36. Letter from Belle Case La Follette to Gilbert Roe (June 6, 1926), in GKR Papers, Box 1, Folder 8.

37. Gilbert E. Roe, *Senator La Follette and the World War*, draft manuscript annotated by GKR, in Roe Papers, Box H13, Folder 1929.

38. Gilbert E. Roe, *In Memoriam, Robert Marion La Follette* (March 30, 1929), presented at Dane County Bar Association, in Roe Papers, Box H14, Folder 1926–29 La Follette.

39. LA FOLLETTE, *supra* note 16, at 1178.

40. Letter from Gilbert Roe to Percey Stickney Grant (January 6, 1927), in Roe Papers, Box H5, Folder 1927.

41. Lease, signed July 30, 1926, in GKR Papers, Box 8, Folder 1.

42. Fragmentary pages from unpublished GKR autobiography, in GKR Papers, Box 5 Folder 10.

43. *Return of Alien Property—No. 4, Hearings before the Committee on Ways and Means, House of Representatives*, 69th Cong., Interim 1st & 2d Sess., November 22, 1926, at 410–18.

44. Office Accounts, 1927–1929, in GKR Papers, Box 5, Folder 3.

45. Memorandum (June 15, 1928), in GKR Papers, Box 2, Folder 1.

46. Letter from Gwyneth King Roe to Lorena "Loey" King (April 5, 1927), in Roe Papers, Box H5, Folder 1927.

47. Letter from Gilbert Roe to Editor, N.Y. TIMES (August 18, 1927), in Roe Papers, Box H5, Folder 1927.

48. Letter from Gilbert Roe to League to Abolish Capital Punishment (September 8, 1927), in Roe Papers, Box H5, Folder 1927.

49. Letter from Gilbert Roe to Editor, FORUM (July 7, 1928), in Roe Papers, Box H5, Folder 1928.

50. Letter from Gilbert Roe to William F. Howe (February 25, 1928), in Roe Papers, Box H5, Folder 1928.

51. Letter from Gilbert Roe to Oswald Garrison Villard (October 18, 1928), in Roe Papers, Box H5, Folder 1928.

52. Letter from Gilbert Roe to Harry W. Laidler (October 20, 1928), in Roe Papers, Box H5, Folder 1928.

53. Letter from Gilbert Roe to Phil La Follette (October 20, 1928), in Roe Papers, Box H5, Folder 1928.

54. Letter from Gilbert Roe to Phil La Follette (May 16, 1929), in Roe Papers, Box H5, Folder 1929.

55. Memorandum (undated), in GKR Papers, Box 7, Folder 7.

56. Letter from Henry Goddard Leach to Gilbert Roe (June 18, 1929), in Roe Papers, Box H3, Folder L.

57. Letter from Gilbert Roe to Henry Goddard Leach (July 12, 1929), in Roe Papers, Box H5, Folder 1929.

58. Letter from Gilbert Roe to Gwyneth King Roe (August 8, 1929), in Roe Papers, Box H1, Folder 1929.

59. Letter from Gilbert Roe to Gwyneth King Roe (August 12, 1929), in Roe Papers, Box H1, Folder 1929.

60. Letter from Gilbert Roe to Gwyneth King Roe (August 13, 1929), in Roe Papers, Box H1, Folder 1929.

61. Letter from Jack Roe to Gilbert Roe (August 15, 1929), in Roe Papers, Box H1, Folder 1929.

62. Letter from Gilbert Roe to Gwyneth King Roe (August 16, 1929), in Roe Papers, Box H1, Folder 1929.

63. Letter from Fiorello La Guardia to Gilbert Roe (August 6, 1929), in Roe Papers, Box H3, Folder L.

64. Letter from Gilbert Roe to J. A. H. Hopkins (October 23, 1929), in Roe Papers, Box H5, Folder 1929.

65. Telegram from Fiorello H. La Guardia to Gilbert Roe c/o Belle Case La Follette (October 26, 1929), in Roe Papers, Box H3, Folder L.

66. Letter from Gilbert Roe to Fiorello H. La Guardia (October 28, 1929), in Roe Papers, Box H5, Folder 1929.

67. *Golf Course near Falls; Dutchess Land Company Formed to Take Over Gilbert Roe Farm*, unknown newspaper clipping, undated, in GKR Papers, Box 8, Folder 3.

68. *Sell House Where Mr. Roosevelt's Candidacy Was Planned in Dutchess*, unknown newspaper clipping, undated, in GKR Papers, Box 8, Folder 3.

69. "I think this was the last case in which Gilbert appeared," pencil annotation by Gwyneth King Roe, in GKR Papers, Box 5, Folder 7.

70. 237 N.Y.S. 26, 30–31 (N.Y. Sup. Ct. App. Div. 1929).

71. Luncheon program, October 19, 1929, in GKR Papers, Box 9, Folder 1.

72. *See* letter from Belle Case La Follette to Gwyneth King Roe (January 24, 1926), in GKR Papers, Box 1, Folder 8.

73. Letter from Gwyneth King Roe to "Dear Ones" (Thanksgiving night, 1929), in GKR Papers, Box 2, Folder 10.

74. *Gilbert Roe Dies in N.Y. at 65 after Long Illness*, CAPITAL TIMES, December 23, 1929.

75. Robert M. La Follette Jr., *Gilbert E. Roe*, PROGRESSIVE, December 28, 1929, at 1.

76. *Gilbert Roe*, TRUTH SEEKER, January 1930, at 22.

77. John M. Scoble, *Memorial of Gilbert E. Roe*, in 1930 YEARBOOK OF THE ASSOCIATION OF THE BAR OF THE CITY OF NEW YORK.

78. Letter from Henry R. Linville to Gwyneth King Roe (December 23, 1929), in GKR Papers, Box 2, Folder 5.

79. Henry R. Linville, Statement of the Teachers Union on the Service of Mr. Gilbert E. Roe, Counsel of the Union for Eleven Years (February 16, 1930), in GKR Papers, Box 2, Folder 5.

80. Letter from Ralph Sucher to Gwyneth King Roe (December 25, 1929), in GKR Papers, Box 2, Folder 3.

81. Letter from Lincoln Steffens to Gwyneth King Roe (December 24, 1929), in GKR Papers, Box 2, Folder 2.

82. Letter from Emma Goldman to Gwyneth King Roe (January 13, 1930), in GKR Papers, Box 1, Folder 5.

83. Letter from Alexander Berkman to Gwyneth King Roe (March 25, 1930), in GKR Papers, Box 1, Folder 1.

84. Letter from Agnes Smedley to Gwyneth King Roe (February 22, 1930), in GKR Papers, Box 2, Folder 1.

85. Letter from Morris Hillquit to Gwyneth King Roe (December 23, 1929), in GKR Papers, Box 3, Folder 5.

86. Letter from Hobart Bird to Gwyneth King Roe (December 23, 1929), in GKR Papers, Box 3, Folder 5.

87. Letter from William Sulzer to Gwyneth King Roe (December 23, 1929), in GKR Papers, Box 3, Folder 6.

88. Letter from Meta Berger to Gwyneth King Roe (December 25, 1929), in GKR Papers, Box 3, Folder 6.

89. Letter from Marx Lewis to Gwyneth King Roe (December 24, 1929), in GKR Papers, Box 3, Folder 6.

90. Letter from Ben Heubsch to Gwyneth King Roe (December 23, 1929), in GKR Papers, Box 3, Folder 6.

91. Letter from Belle Case La Follette to Gwyneth King Roe (February 17, 1930), in GKR Papers, Box 1, Folder 8.

92. Gwyneth Roe Murphy, draft press release on her mother's one hundredth birthday party, in GKR Papers, Box 9, Folder 3.

93. Social Security Death Index. Gwyneth Roe Murphy, untitled draft obituary of her mother, Gwyneth King Roe, undated, at 2, in GKR Papers, Box 9, Folder 3.

94. Untitled clipping from the GRAND RAPIDS (MICH.) HERALD, May 8, 1949, in GKR Papers, Box 9, Folder 2.

95. Letter from William Beard to Gwyneth King Roe (March 6, 1958), in GKR Papers, Box 1, Folder 2, and Gwyneth Roe Murphy, draft press release on her mother's one hundredth birthday party, in GKR Papers, Box 9, Folder 3.

96. *Daughter of Gilbert Roe Is Dead at Age 55*, CAPITAL TIMES (Madison), June 11, 1971.

CONCLUSION

1. *See supra* Introduction.
2. 283 U.S. 697 (1931).
3. *See supra* Introduction.
4. 337 U.S. 1, 5 (1949).
5. 376 U.S. 254 (1964).
6. HARRY KALVEN JR., A WORTHY TRADITION: FREEDOM OF SPEECH IN AMERICA 66–67 (1988).
7. *See generally* DAVID RABBAN, FREE SPEECH IN ITS FORGOTTEN YEARS (1997).
8. 395 U.S. 444, 448 (1969) (per curiam). Indeed, Harvard law professor Martha A. Field, who clerked for Justice Abe Fortas when he wrote the *Brandenburg* decision, has denied that Fortas had *Masses* in mind at the time. Martha A. Field, Brandenburg v. Ohio *and Its Relationship to* Masses Publishing Co. v. Patten, 50 ARIZ. ST. L.J. 791, 792 (2018).

Table of Cases

Abrams v. United States, 250 U.S. 616 (1919), 160, 239n50

Allgeyer v. Louisiana, 165 U.S. 578 (1897), 7, 205n11

Bier v. Roebling Const. Co., 134 A.D. 356 (N.Y. App. 1909), 15, 207n39

Birch v. Mutual Reserve Life Ins. Co., 86 N.Y.S. 872 (App. Div. 1904), aff'd, Mutual Reserve Life Ins. Co. v. Birch, 200 U.S. 612 (1905), 16, 17, 20, 208nn51–52, 54–55

Brandenburg v. Ohio, 395 U.S. 444 (1969), 203, 251n8

Butler v. Michigan, 352 U.S. 380 (1957), 132, 234n31

Chi. & N.W. Ry. Co. v. Dey, 35 F. 866 (C.C.S.D. Iowa 1888), 38, 218n53

Clark v. Johnston, 141 A.D. 926 (N.Y. App. 1910), 15, 207n40

Cook v. Flagg, 251 F. 195 (S.D.N.Y. 1918), cert. denied, Flagg v. Cook, 247 U.S. 508 (1918); see also, Cook v. Flagg, 233 F. 426 (2d Cir. 1916), Cook v. Flagg, 255 F. 195 (S.D.N.Y 1915), 26, 211nn137–38

Debs v. United States, 249 U.S. 211 (1919), 155–61, 164, 238nn25, 36, 239nn40–44, 46

Donnelly v. Anderson Brown & Co., 275 F. 438 (S.D.N.Y. 1921), 190, 247n12

Erie City Iron Works v. Thomas, 139 F. 995 (S.D.N.Y. 1905), 15, 207n37

Fox v. Washington, 236 U.S. 273 (1915), aff'g Washington v. Fox, 71 Wash. 185 (1912), 52, 54–63, 67, 217nn43–45, 48, 218nn50, 52–58, 60–62, 219nn69, 72–73, 75, 77–79, 223n57

Frohwerk v. United States, 249 U.S. 204 (1919), 156, 238n28, 239n49

Grendon v. Bd. of Educ., 100 N.Y.S. 253 (N.Y. 1904), 89–90, 226n125

Haenschen v. Roebling Const. Co., 194 N.Y. 533 (1909), 15, 207n39

In re Daniel O'Connell, 194 P. 1010 (Cal. 1920), 166, 240n83

Jeffersonian Pub. Co. v. West, 245 F. 585 (S.D. Ga. 1917), 143, 236n87

Johnston v. Mutual Reserve Life Ins. Co., 93 N.Y.S. 1062 (N.Y. App. Div. 1905), 16, 17, 20, 208n50

Kaufman v. Flagg, 237 N.Y.S. 26 (1929), 196, 250n70

Lambert v. Mutual Reserve Life Ins. Co., 90 N.Y.S. 1103 (N.Y. App. Div. 1904), 16, 17, 20, 208n50

Lochner v. New York, 198 U.S. 45 (1903), 7, 23, 205n15, 210n108

Loewe v. Lawlor, 208 U.S. 274 (1908), 26, 211n133

Massachusetts v. Friede, 171 N.E. 472 (Mass. 1930), 132, 234n30

Masses Publishing Co. v. Patten, 244 F. 535 (S.D.N.Y. 1917), stayed, 245 F. 102 (2d Cir. 1917), rev'd, 246 F. 24 (2d Cir. 1917), 4–5, 9, 10, 37, 131–48, 157–58, 166, 202, 203,

Masses Publishing Co. v. Patten (*continued*) 206n19, 234nn18–24, 26, 28, 32, 235nn41–42, 44, 49–57, 61, 63–64, 236nn65, 67, 70–71, 87, 237nn88, 92, 94

Masten v. Maxwell, 83 N.Y.S. 1098 (N.Y. App. Div. 1903), 89, 226nn122–23

May v. Hetrick Bros. Co., 235 N.Y. 601 (1923), 190, 247n12

McCoy v. Mutual Reserve Life Ins. Co., 82 N.Y.S. 638 (N.Y. App. Div. 1903), 17, 20, 208n49

Milliken Bros. v. City of N.Y., 135 A.D. 598 (1909), 15, 207n38

Murphy v. Maxwell, 69 N.E. 1092 (N.Y. 1904), 89, 226n124

Mutual Reserve Life Ins. Co. v. Birch, 200 U.S. 612 (1905), *aff'g* Birch v. Mutual Reserve Life Ins. Co., 86 N.Y.S. 872 (App. Div. 1904), 16, 17, 20, 208n51

Nagler v. United States, 254 U.S. 661 (1920), *rev'g* United States v. Nagler, 252 F. 217 (W.D. Wis. 1918), 162–64, 239nn61–63, 240nn64–67, 69–70, 247n11

Near v. Minnesota, 283 US 697 (1931), 202, 251n2

New Jersey v. Boyd, 91 A. 586 (N.J. S.Ct. 1914), *aff'd in part*, 93 A. 599 (N.J. Err. & App. 1915), *rev'd in part*, 94 A. 807 (N.J. Err. & App. 1915), 63–66, 219nn84, 86, 88–92, 220nn95, 97–99

New Jersey v. Quinlan, 91 A. 111 (N.J. S.Ct. 1913), 63, 65, 219n93

New York v. Eastman, 152 N.Y.S. 314 (N.Y. Cnty. Ct. Gen. Sess. 1915), 105–17, 228nn22–23, 229n31, 230n71

New York v. Most, 64 N.E. 175 (N.Y. 1902), 62, 218n56, 219n94

New York v. Sanger (William), 33 N.Y. Crim. R. 415 (N.Y. App. Div. 1915), 3–4, 73–88, 205nn1, 3–4, 222nn30, 34, 37, 39–42, 223nn49, 58–59, 224nn78–79, 81, 225n99

New York v. Sinclair, 149 N.Y. 54 (N.Y. Ct. Gen. Sess. 1914), *aff'd*, 151 N.Y. 1136 (N.Y. App. Div. 1915), 120–23, 232nn115–17, 122

New York Times v. Sullivan, 376 U.S. 254 (1964), 203, 251n5

O'Connell v. United States, 253 U.S. 142 (1920), 164–66, 240nn72–74, 77–83

Patterson v. Colorado, 205 U.S. 454 (1907), 58, 61, 62, 218n60

Peixotto v. Bd. of Educ., 144 N.Y.S. 87 (N.Y. Sup. Ct. 1913), *rev'd*, 145 N.Y.S. 853 (N.Y. App. Div. 1914), *aff'd*, 146 N.Y.S. 1108 (N.Y. 1914), 91, 226n134

Philipp v. S. S. McClure Co., *aff'd*, S.S. McClure Co. v. Philipp, 170 F. 910 (2d Cir. 1909), 25, 35, 37, 137, 213nn16–17, 20–21, 23, 28, 33, 214nn46, 48–53, 55–56, 59, 251nn60–61, 63–71

Robinson v. Mutual Reserve Life Ins. Co., 182 F. 850 (S.D.N.Y. 1910), 17, 20, 208n56

Rolle v. Rolle, 194 N.Y.S. 661 (N.Y. App. Div. 1922), 190, 247n12

Roth v. United States, 354 U.S. 476 (1957), 132, 234n31

Ruthenberg v. United States, 245 U.S. 480 (1918), 157, 238n35

Schenck v. United States, 249 U.S. 47 (1919), 10, 156, 159, 160, 206n20, 238n26, 239n47

Smedley v. McCarthy, 251 U.S. 564 (1919), 173–76, 242n36, 243nn37–38, 43–47, 56–57, 59

Southern Pacific Terminal Co. v. ICC, 219 U.S. 498 (1911), 218n67

S. S. McClure Co. v. Philipp, 170 F. 910 (2d Cir. 1909), *aff'g* Philipp v. S.S. McClure Co., 25, 35, 37, 137, 213nn16–17, 20–21, 23, 28, 33, 214nn46, 48–53, 55–56, 59, 251nn60–61, 63–71

Stokes v. United States, 274 F. 18 (1920), 157, 238n37

Strauss v. Union Cent. Life Ins. Co., 63 N.E. 347 (N.Y. 1902), *aff'g* 70 N.Y.S. 1149 (N.Y. App. Div. 1901), *aff'g* 67 N.Y.S. 509 (N.Y. Sup. Ct. 1900), 16, 208nn47–48

Sugarman v. United States, 249 U.S. 182 (1919), 156, 160, 238n27, 239n48

Terminiello v. Chicago, 337 U.S. 1 (1949), 202, 251n4

Table of Cases

Turner v. Williams, 194 U.S. 279 (1904), 49–50, 216n22

Union Refrigerator Transit Co. v. S. S. McClure, 146 F. 623 (S.D.N.Y. 1906), 33–35, 213nn20, 31

United States v. Baker, 247 F. 124 (D. Md. 1917), 145, 237n89

United States v. Kennerly, 209 F. 119 (S.D.N.Y. 1913), 132, 234n29

United States v. Nagler, 252 F. 217 (W.D. Wis. 1918), rev'd, Nagler v. United States, 254 U.S. 661 (1920), 162–64, 239nn61–63, 240nn64–67, 69–70, 247n11

United States v. Salindranath Ghose et al. (S.D.N.Y. April 1, 1918), 172–75, 242nn27, 30–32, 243nn39–41, 48–50

United States v. Sanger (Margaret) (S.D.N.Y. 1916) (nolle prosequi), 75, 87–88, 222n27

United States v. Stephens, No. 13 (D. Del. May 16, 1918), 160–62, 164, 239nn54, 56

Van Tine v. Hilands, 131 F. 124 (S.D.N.Y. 1904), 15, 207n36

Washington v. Fox, 71 Wash. 185 (1912), aff'd, Fox v. Washington, 236 U.S. 273 (1915), 52, 54–63, 67, 217nn43–45, 48, 218nn50, 52–58, 60–62, 219nn69, 72–73, 75, 77–79, 223n57

Waters-Pierce Oil Co. v. Texas, 212 U.S. 86 (1909), 62, 219n76

Weinstein v. Bradford, 423 U.S. 147 (1975), 218n67

Index

In subentries, "La Follette" refers to Robert M. La Follette Sr., "Netha" refers to Gwyneth King Roe, and "Roe" refers to Gilbert E. Roe.

Abbot, Francis, 47
Abbott, Leonard: and Free Silence League, 120; and Free Speech League, 4, 51; as friend of the Sangers, 74; and Margaret Sanger, 73, 84, 87–88; and Upton Sinclair, 118, 119, 120; and William Sanger case, 78–80, 81–83, 84, 85, 86, 87
ACLU, 4, 124, 166
Adams, Annette, 165
Addams, Jane, 128
Agitator (anarchist publication), 54
Alexander, Amerigo V., 162
Alliance for Labor and Democracy, 168
American Civil Liberties Union, 4, 124, 166
American Defense Society, 141, 244n77
American Federation of Labor, 156, 168, 191
American Newspaper Publishers Association, 129–30
American Patriots, 164
American Red Cross, 163, 183
American Socialist, 130–31
American Socialist Party. *See* Socialist Party of America
anarchists: anti-anarchist sentiment, rise of, 48; arrests of, 48, 186; Boyd case, 63–66; Fox case, 52–63; and Free Speech League, 48–50, 52, 66; Home Colony, 52–53, 54–55, 58; and IWW, 63–64; publications of, 48, 53–54, 55; Roe, relationships with, 46, 66–69; and Schroeder, Theodore, 46–47; Turner case, 49–50; violent acts of, 48, 53, 68, 232n104. *See also* Berkman, Alexander; Goldman, Emma; *Mother Earth Bulletin*
Anderson, James J., 56, 57–60, 63, 218n53
Anderson, Margaret, 220n106
anti-Semitism: and Brandeis, 26; and DeWitt Clinton High School teachers, 178; in Glassberg case, 181, 182, 183; and Red Scare, 178
antiwar movement. *See* pacifists; World War I
AP. *See* Associated Press
Appeal to Reason, 120, 131
Arden, Delaware, 161
Armour Company of Chicago, 32
Associated Press: Eastman on, 106–7, 118; and La Follette, 104–5, 151, 154, 155; Mary Craig Sinclair, 121; Senate investigation of, 107–8; and Upton Sinclair on, 105–6, 117, 120; West Virginia coal miners' strike, coverage of, 105, 106, 109–10
Axtell, Silas Blake, 195

Babushka, Grandmother of the Russian Revolution, 50
"bad tendency" test, 159, 160

Baker, Ray Stannard: and *McClure's*, 31, 36; railroad series, 32–33; "The Right to Work," 31; "Some of the Difficulties Encountered in Investigating the Railroad Problem," 36. See also *McClure's* libel case
Baldwin, Roger N., 130, 132–33, 166, 171, 175
Bamberger, Charles J. ("Heller"), 3–4, 76, 78, 87, 205n5
Barnes, Earl B., 132, 133, 134
Beard, Charles A., 179–80
Beck, Carl, 125–26
Bell, Josephine: case against, 146–47, 148; "A Tribute," 133, 134
Bellows, George, 82
Berger, Victor, 191, 195, 199
Berkman, Alexander: and anarchists, 48; in *The Masses*, 134; and *Mother Earth Bulletin*, 131–32; *Prison Memoirs*, 67; and Roe, 68–69, 80, 198–99
Bernstein, Jacob, 92
Bettman, Alfred, 159
Birch, Henry C., 17
Bird, Hobart, 199
birth control: Agnes Smedley, advocate for, 172, 177; Comstock's views on, 74; in *Family Limitation*, 75, 77; feminist and suffragist view on, 73; Goldman's views on, 74–75; Henrietta Rodman, advocate for, 93; Roe's views on, 69, 73, 88, 93. See also Sanger, Margaret; Sanger, William
Birth Control League, 84
Birth Control Review, 172, 175
Bishop, Emily Mulkin, 14, 15, 71
Blaine, James, 25
Blaine, John J., 45
Blast (anarchist magazine), 69
Blatch, Harriet Stanton, 72
Block, S. John, 187
Bolshevik revolution, 167–68, 178
Bolshevism, 169, 181, 182–83
Bond, John C., 106, 110, 114
Boyd, Frederick Sumner, 63–66
Boyden, Albert, 36
Brandeis, Louis, 10, 24, 26, 160, 202
Brass Check, The, 105–6, 117, 121, 231n89

Breen, Matthew P., 78, 107
Breshkovskaya, Catherine, 50
Brisbane, Arthur, 108
Brundin, Thorberg, 171
Bryan, Williams Jennings, 19, 150–51, 153
Bull Moose Party. See Progressive Party
Bull Moose Special incident, 105. See also Sinclair, Upton
Burleson, Albert Sidney, 130, 133, 140, 141, 142–43. See also U.S. Post Office
Burmeister, A. O., 58, 63
Burr, Charles L., 37, 38, 39
Butler, Nicholas Murray, 151

Cabin Creek strike. See West Virginia coal miners' strike
Caffey, Francis G., 137, 143–44, 146, 173, 174–75
Call (New York), 65, 74, 79–80, 81, 183, 231n89
Campbell, Rachel, 48; "Prodigal Daughter," 48
Capital Times (Madison, WI), 197–98
Caplan, David, 68
Cardozo, Benjamin N., 24
Carnes, Thomas, 109–10
Caron, Arthur, 232n104
Cass, Lawrence, 53
Catt, Carrie Chapman, 28
censorship. See freedom of the press; freedom of the press cases; U.S. Post Office
Chafee, Zecharia, 10, 202
Chamberlain, Edward, 48
Chapman, W. O., 56–57, 63
Chattopadhyaya, Virendranath ("Chatto"), 175
Chicago, Milwaukee & St. Paul Railroad, 32, 33
Circuit Court of the Southern District of New York, 33, 37
Clayton Antitrust Act, 26
"clear and present danger" test, 10, 160
Collier's National Weekly, 20, 106
Colorado coal miners' strike, 118–19
Colorado Fuel and Iron Company, 118, 171
Comintern, 147, 170, 175, 177
Commission on Industrial Relations, 8–9, 202
Committee for the Suppression of Vice, 47
Committee on the Civic Service of Women, 91

Index

communists, 167–70, 178, 186. *See also* Bolshevik revolution; Red Scare; Smedley, Agnes; Teachers Union of New York City cases
Comstock, Anthony: background of, 47–48; death of, 88; and William Sanger case, 4, 74–78, 82, 83–84, 86, 87
Comstock Act, 47, 48, 49, 69, 74
Conboy, Martin, 187–88
Conference for Progressive Political Action, 191
"Conscription," 101
Conscription Act, 138, 141, 143, 164, 165
contraception. *See* birth control
Cooley, Thomas, 61
Coolidge, Calvin, 191, 192
Cosgrave, John O'Hara, 111, 112, 114, 117
Cothren, Marion, 92
Court of General Sessions (New York City), 78, 79, 81, 83
Court of Special Sessions (New York City), 78, 81
Coxe, Alfred Conkling, 44–45
Craddock, Ida, 49
Crain, Thomas C. T., 122–23
Crowder, Enoch, 134
Crownhart & Wylie, 153, 163, 164
Culberson, Charles, 127
Cunnea, William, 157

Darrow, Clarence, 49, 53, 132–33, 144, 234n35
Das, Tarak Nath, 172, 173
Davis, John W., 191, 192
Dayal, Har, 171
Dean, Harriett, 220n106
Debs, Eugene V., 156–60, 81, 191
Defrem, Herman (Herman de Fremery), 89, 90, 173, 175
Dell, Floyd, 103, 146–47, 148; "Conscientious Objectors," 133–34
Demonstrator (anarchist journal), 53, 55
Department of Justice, 132–33
De Valera, Eamon, 177
Dewey, John, 179–80, 191, 197
DeWitt Clinton High School cases, 178–81
Dillingham, William P., 151

Discontent (anarchist newspaper), 48, 53
Dodge, Mabel, 79, 113, 169, 170, 241n14
Dow, Lorenzo, 61
Drake, Carolyn M. (Carrie Roe), 13, 14
Drake, Henry C. (father of Carrie Roe), 19
Dr. Foote's Health Monthly, 47, 48
due process. *See* Fourteenth Amendment
Dunn, Nellie, 115
Dunne, Finley Peter, 36, 65

Eagle (Brooklyn), 119
Eastman, Max: on the Associated Press, 106–7, 111, 117; on Debs, 156; on the end of *The Masses*, 147; and the founding of *The Masses*, 104; "Is the Truth Obscene?," 79; and John Reed, 170; and Learned Hand, 147–48; and Margaret Sanger, 88; *The Masses* criminal case, 146–47; photograph of, 100; "A Question," 134; "The Worst Monopoly," 79, 106. See also *The Masses*, AP libel case; *The Masses*, Espionage Act case
Eddy, Mary Baker, 37
Elkins Act, 33, 41, 42, 43
Emporia Gazette, 21
Espionage Act: enactment of, 127–30; and evolution of First Amendment doctrine, 156; in La Follette expulsion case, 154, 155; progressives on, 9; Roe's arguments on, 134, 135, 144–45, 158–59, 176; Roe's views on, 10, 128–29, 130, 160–61; rulings on, 133–35, 135–37, 139, 142–43, 145–46, 202–3. *See also* Espionage Act, cases; Espionage Act, charges brought under; *The Masses*, Espionage Act case
Espionage Act, cases: Amerigo Alexander case, 162; *Debs*, 155–60; *Frohwerk*, 160; *The Masses* criminal case, 147–48; *The Masses* Espionage Act case, 131–47; *Nagler*, 162–64; *Schenck*, 159–60; *Smedley*, 170–76; *Stephens*, 160–62; *Sugarman*, 160
Espionage Act, charges brought under, 146, 147, 156, 157, 161, 163, 164, 172, 172
Ettinger, William L., 185
Evans, Evan A., 163
Everybody's, 106

Fall, Albert B., 151
Family Limitation, 3, 75, 76–77
feminists, 70–71, 73. *See also* Rodman, Henrietta; Sanger, Margaret; Sanger, William
Ferguson, Isaac E., 157
FFI. *See* Friends of Freedom for India
Fifth Amendment, 57, 145, 146, 161, 174
Finegan, Thomas E., 181
Finley, John H., 92, 180, 184
First Amendment: in *Debs*, 157–59; Espionage Act as violation of, 145; and Fourteenth Amendment, 58–59; in *Fox*, 57–58, 61; in freedom of speech doctrine, 4–5, 9, 28–29, 61, 156, 202–3; in *The Masses* Espionage Act case, 135, 144–46; in *Near v. Minnesota*, 202; in *Patterson*, 58–59; in *Schenck* (Holmes), 159–60; in *Stephens*, 161; in *Turner*, 49–50. *See also* Roe, Gilbert E.
Fisher, Walter, 112
Flagg, Jared, Jr., 26, 196
Flynn, Elizabeth Gurley, 63–64
Foote, Edwin Bliss ("Foote Sr."), 47, 48, 50, 75
Foote, Edwin Bond ("Foote Jr."), 47, 48, 50, 51, 216n30
Forum, 194, 195
Fourteenth Amendment: and First Amendment, 58–59; in *Fox*, 57–58, 61–62; in freedom of speech doctrine, 7–8, 9, 61, 201–2; language of, 205n10; in *Patterson v. Colorado*, 58–59; in *Smedley*, 174
Fourth Amendment, 174
Fox, Jay, 52–63; appeal, U.S. Supreme Court, 60–63; appeal, Washington Supreme Court, 57–60, 217n33; arrest and charges against, 55–56; background of, 52–55; "The Nude and the Prudes," 54–56; trial, Superior Court for Pierce County, 56–57
freedom of speech: Brandeis, approach to, 10; Debs on, 156–57; doctrines and evolution of, 7–11, 61, 201–3; as First Amendment issue, 4, 202, 203; as Fourteenth Amendment issue, 7, 8, 61, 201–2; in jury instructions, 56–57, 165; Red Scare, effects on, 9; state laws on, 56, 58, 64, 217n44; tests of, 10, 136, 160; World War I, effects on, 9, 28–29. *See also* Espionage Act; First Amendment; Fourteenth Amendment; freedom of speech opinions; Free Speech League; Roe, Gilbert E.
freedom of speech opinions: in *Debs* (Holmes), 159–60; in *Fox* (Holmes), 59–60, 62–63; in *The Masses* Espionage Act case (Hand), 135–37; in *New York Times v. Sullivan*, 202–3; in *Sinclair*, 122–23; in *Terminiello v. Chicago*, 202; in *Turner*, 49–50
freedom of the press: American Newspaper Publishers Association on, 129–30; James C. Garrison on, 25; state laws on, 56, 58, 59, 64, 217n44
freedom of the press cases: *Fox*, 52–93; *The Masses*, AP libel case; *The Masses*, Espionage Act case; *McClure Co.*, 30–45; *New York Times v. Sullivan*, 202–3; *O'Connell*, 164–66; *Sanger*, 73–74, 75–87. *See also* Sanger, Margaret
Freeman, Elizabeth, 119, 120
Free Religious Association, 47
Free Silence League, 120
Free Society (anarchist newspaper), 53
Free Speech League: background of, 47, 48–49; and Edwin Bond Foote, 51, 216n30; and *Fox*, 52, 57; and Goldman, 50, 66; mission of, 49, 51–52, 217n33; and Roe, 50–51; and *Turner*, 49–50
French, W. H., 112, 113–14
Frick, Henry Clay, 48
Friends of Freedom for India, 175, 176, 177
Frierson, William L., 164
Frohwerk, Jacob, 160
Fuller, Melville, 49
Fusion ticket, 23–24

Garrett, Phillip L., 161
Garrison, James C., 24–25
George, Henry, 161
Germany: claims of American citizens against, 193; and the Indian nationalist movement, 171, 172, 176; La Follette on, 150; and the *Lusitania*, 126; and Smedley, 177; Upton Sinclair on, 167
Ghose, Sailendra Nath, 172, 173, 174, 176, 242n27
Gilman, Charlotte Perkins, 92, 110

Index

Glassberg, Benjamin, 181–85
Glasscock, William E., 105
Glintenkamp, H. J., 146–47; "Conscription," 101, 133, 137; "Liberty Bell," 133
Goggins, B. R., 163
Goldman, Emma: arrest of, 88; and Berkman, 67, 68; on birth control, 74–75; on Craddock, 49; on death of Roe, 198; finances of, 66–67; and Fox, 53; and Free Speech League, 50, 66; as lecturer, 50; in *The Masses*, 134; *Mother Earth Bulletin*, 66, 67; *Mother Earth Bulletin* case, 131–32; photograph of, 99; Roe, relationship with, 66–67; and the Sangers, 74–75; and Turner defense, 49; and William Sanger case, 77, 79
Gompers, Samuel, 168

Hall, A. R., 212n10
Hall, Bolton, 51, 88, 161
Hallinan, Charles T., 128
Hand, Augustus, 140–41, 148, 174
Hand, Learned: candidate for New York Court of Appeals, 25; candidate for U.S. Court of Appeals for the Second Circuit, 147; on common-law rule on obscenity, 132; on freedom of the press, 147–48; and *The Masses* criminal cases, 148; opinion in *The Masses* Espionage Act case, 135–37; photograph of, 101; and *Smedley*, 174–75
Hannan, John, 27, 142, 153
Harding, Warren G., 160, 190
Hardwick, Thomas, 141
Hardy, Ruth Gillette, 185
Harlan, John Marshall, 58–59
Harmon, Moses, 48, 49
Harper's, 241n17
Hatfield, Henry D., 105
Haymarket Affair, 48, 53
Haywood, Bill ("Big Bill"), 74, 156, 169
Hazel, John R., 75
Heller (associate of Comstock). *See* Bamberger, Charles J.
Herbert, Henry W., 87
Heubsch, Ben, 199
Hickey, Thomas, 133

Hillquit, Morris: cases of, 147, 157, 187, 188; and La Follette, 191; and *The Masses*, 132–33; and Roe, 188, 199
Hindu Defense Fund, 175
Hindustan Ghadr Party, 171
Hitchcock, Samuel M., 173, 174
Holmes, John Haynes, 172
Holmes, Oliver Wendell, Jr.: "clear and present danger" test, 10, 160; opinion in *Debs*, 159; opinion in *Fox*, 62–63; opinion in *Schenck*, 159–60
Home Colony, 48, 52–55, 58
Hoover, J. Edgar, 186
Hough, Charles M.: *The Masses* Espionage Act case, 137–38, 139, 140, 146; *McClure Co.*, 37–39, 42, 43
House, Edward M., 25–26
Howe, Frederick C., 72
Howe, William F., 194
Hughes, Charles Evans, 202
Huntington, Francis C., 37
Huntington, Rhinelander & Seymour, 37
Hunziker, Gustav, 64
Hurd, Richard M., 141–42
Hyams, Sarah, 185

Independent, 106
Indian nationalist movement, 171–72, 175, 177
Indian Nationalist Party, 172
Industrial Relations Commission, 8–9, 202
Industrial Workers of the World. *See* IWW
Insurgents Club, 20, 21
Intercollegiate Socialist Society, 113, 118, 171
International Socialist Review, 131
IWW, 55, 63–64, 156
IWW silk workers' strike, 63–64

James, Ollie M., 151
Jews. *See* anti-Semitism
Johnson, Hiram, 22
Jones, Burr, 163
Jones, Mary Harris ("Mother Jones"), 105, 113, 171
Judiciary Committee of the New York State Constitutional Convention, 26
Jungle, The, 118

Karlin, William, 187
Kellogg, Frank B., 151
Kennaday, Paul, 82, 84
Kennerley, Mitchell, 82
King, Alexander C., 175–76
King, Gwyneth D. *See* Roe, Gwyneth King
Klenert, Abram, 64
Knights of Labor, 53

Labor Forum, 125
Lacombe, Emile Henry, 44
La Follette, Belle Case: on birth of Roe children, 18–19, 20; and Emily Bishop League, 14; on La Follette, 18, 21, 71; on La Follette law firm, 14; letter from Roe on Janet Roe, 27; letter from Roe on La Follette article, 32; on Roe, 26, 192; work of, 27–28, 70, 192–93
La Follette, Fola (daughter of Belle and Robert M. Sr.), 15, 21, 27, 89, 92, 111
La Follette, Philip (son of Belle and Robert M. Sr.), 115, 195, 199
La Follette, Robert M., Jr., 153, 195, 198
La Follette, Robert M., Sr.: and Brandeis, 26; death of, 192–93; expulsion case of, 149–55; law firm of, 14; legislative work as senator, 130, 138, 168, 190; and *McClure's* case, 30–32; photograph of, 102; presidential campaigns of, 19, 20–23, 191–92; and railroads, 18, 30–31, 104–5; Roe, personal relationship with, 5, 6, 13, 14, 104–5; Senate, election to, 26–27; and Spooner, 17–18; St. Paul speech, 150–51; and the suffrage movement, 70–71; U.S. Supreme Court, views on, 191–92; and Wisconsin politics, 15, 32, 25, 41, 45
La Follette's Magazine, 25, 187, 192, 198
La Guardia, Fiorello, 191, 196
Laidler, Harry W., 194
Lamar, William H., 131, 133, 134, 139, 140, 143
Lefkowitz, Abraham, 185
Leitner, Donia, 119, 120
Levy, Isaac, 16
Lewis, Marx, 199

Liberator (anarchist newspaper), 53
Linville, Henry R., 93, 198
Lister, Ernest C., 63
Lovett, Robert Morss, 175
Lucifer: The Light-Bearer, 48
Ludlow Massacre, 118–19
Lusitania, 27, 126, 150–51, 154
Lusk, Clayton R., 186
Lusk Laws case, 185–86

MacDowell, Mary E., 181
Magistrate's Court (New York City), 4, 76, 78, 120
Manhattan Liberal Club, 47, 48, 50, 81, 110, 119
Manton, Martin, 148
Marelli, Henry, 64
Martin, Frederick Roy, 113, 155
Masses, The: background of, 103–4; criminal cases, 146–47, 148; the end of, 147; finances of, 114–15, 116–17; and New York public libraries, 141–42; Roe, financial support for, 36, 80, 116–17; Ward & Gow, refusal to distribute, 147–48. *See also* Eastman, Max; *The Masses*, AP libel case; *The Masses*, Espionage Act case
Masses, The, AP libel case, 105–17; background of, 105–7; dismissal of charges, 117; finances of, 114–15, 116–17; indictments in, 107, 108; pretrial proceedings, 107, 108–10, 111–14, 115–16; publicity campaign, 108–9, 110–11
Masses, The, Espionage Act case, 131–48; arguments and opinions, 133–37, 138–39, 140–41, 143–46; bill of complaint, 132, 135; post office orders and rulings, 131–32, 139–40, 142–43; repercussions, 146–48; supporters, 132–33, 142. *See also* Hand, Learned
Masters, Edgar Lee, 49
Maurer, James Hudson, 124–26; *The American Cossack*, 125
Maxwell, William, 91
Mayer, Edward, 182–83
Mayer, Julius M., 145, 146–47, 173

Index

Mayer, William E. C., 179
McClure, Samuel S.: and *McClure's*, 31, 36, 43; photograph of, 98; testimony in *McClure's* libel case, 39, 40
McClure's, 30, 31, 32–33, 36, 118. See also *McClure's* libel case
McClure's libel case, 30–45; appeal in, 44–45; background of, 30–33; complaint in, 33–34; pretrial proceedings, 34–36; trial, 37–43
McCombs, William F., 18, 20, 37
McInerney, James W., 87
McIntyre, Charles, 179
McKinley, William, assassination of, 48
McReynolds, James C., 165–66
Men's League for Woman Suffrage, 72, 104
Milholland Boissevain, Inez, 92, 110
Miller, Nathan L., 186
Milwaukee Free Press, 34–35, 43
Milwaukee Leader, 131
Milwaukee Sentinel, 34
Mixed Claims Commission, 193
Morgan, E. M., 75
Morgan, J. Pierpont, 47, 105, 117
Morton, James F., 53
Mother Earth Bulletin, 66, 67, 131, 133
Mother Jones. *See* Jones, Mary Harris
Mount, Wallace, 59
muckrakers, 4, 30–35. *See also* Baker, Ray Stannard; McClure, Samuel S.; *McClure's*; *McClure's* libel case; Sinclair, Upton; Steffens, Lincoln
Mufson, Thomas, 178–81
Mukerjee, Jadu Gopal, 172
Mulker, Frederick G., 131, 140
Municipal Court of New York, 107
Murphy, Charles, 24
Mutual Reserve Life Insurance Co., 16
Myrick, H. P., 43–44

Nagler, Louis B., 162–64
National American Woman Suffrage Association, 28, 70
National Civil Liberties Bureau, 175
National Defense Association, 47, 48
National Liberal League, 47
Nearing, Scott, 161
Nelles, Walter, 148, 173, 187
New Era, 53
New Jersey Court of Errors and Appeals, 65
New Jersey Court of Pardons, 65
New Jersey Supreme Court, 65
New York Bar Association, 26
New York City Board of Education, 90, 91, 178–80, 182–84
New York Court of Appeals, 25, 89–90, 92
New York Evening Journal, 90
New York Evening Mail, 129
New York Evening Post, 155
New York Secular Society, 81
New York Society for the Suppression of Vice, 4, 47, 74
New York State Assembly: expulsion of socialists, 186–88; impeachment of William Sulzer, 24–25
New York State legislature, 185–86
New York Supreme Court, 23–24, 25
New York Supreme Court Appellate Division, 83, 84, 85–86, 89
New York Telegram, 150
New York Times: on Comstock speech, 86; on Glassberg, 184; on La Follette, 150; on *The Masses* and Pinchot, 110–11; on Maurer, 125; on *McClure's* staff resignations, 36; *New York Times v. Sullivan*, 203; on protest of *The Masses* libel indictment, 110; on Roe candidacy for a Supreme Court nomination, 24; on William Sanger case, 87; and William Sulzer impeachment, 24
New York Tribune, 91, 119, 125, 140, 184
New York World, 49, 196, 231n89
Nolte, Grover C., 55, 56, 58
Norris, Jean H., 91, 92
Northern Refrigerator Transit Company, 35, 40, 42, 45
Noyes, Frank B., 107, 108, 109

O'Brian, John Lord, 159, 175
Obscene Literature and Constitutional Law (Schroeder), 58

O'Connell, Daniel, 164–66
Ohio Socialist Convention, 156
Orr, Samuel, 187
Our Judicial Oligarchy (Roe), 7, 23

pacifists: antiwar advocacy in *The Masses*, 133–34; *Debs*, 155–60; La Follette; expulsion case, 149–55; *The Masses* Espionage Act case, 131–47; *Nagler*, 162–64; *O'Connnell*, 164–66; Preparedness Day bombing, 69; *Stephens*, 160–62; *Sugarman*, 160. *See also* Espionage Act; World War I
Paint Creek strike. *See* West Virginia coal miners' strike
Palmer, Mitchell, 176, 186
Palmer raids, 177, 186–87
Parker, Charles Wolcott, 65
Parsons, Albert, 53
Parsons, Lucy, 53
Paterson, New Jersey, 63
Paterson silk workers' strike, 63–64
Patten, Thomas G., 131, 132, 139, 140
Peixotto, Bridget, 91, 92
Pelham Manor, 23, 27, 69
People's Council of America for Democracy and Peace, 162, 168
Perkins, Charles A., 68, 115–16
Pew, Marlen E., 116
Philipp, Emanuel: and *McClure's* libel case, 32–45; in Wisconsin politics, 25, 45
Phillips, John S., 31, 36, 39–40
Pinchot, Amos: on the Associated Press, 110–11; and La Follette presidential campaign of 1912, 20, 21; and *The Masses*, 104, 115, 116–17; and *The Masses* AP libel case, 108, 112, 116; and *The Masses* Espionage Act case, 132–33; *New York Times* on, 110–11
Pinchot, Gifford, 20, 21
Pinol, Gertrude, 181
Pollack, Simon H., 75
Pomerene, Atlee, 150, 151–52, 153, 155
Post Office. *See* U.S. Post Office
Price, Will, 161
Progressive, 198
Progressive Era. *See* progressives

Progressive La Guardia Non-Partisan Committee, 196
Progressive Party ("Bull Moose Party"): candidates for the Court of Appeals, New York, 25; formation of, 22; Fusion ticket, 23–24; in presidential campaigns, 22, 191; Roe on, 194–95, 196
Progressive Republicans, 20, 23–24, 26, 30
progressives: on Espionage Act, 9; Federal Trade Commission, appointment to, 25–26; freedom of speech, views on, 9–10; and La Follette, 6, 30–31; laissez-faire capitalism, views on, 7–8; Progressive Era defined, 6; in U.S. Congress, 155; in Wisconsin, 6; and World War I, 27–28. *See also* Progressive Party; Progressive Republicans
Pullman Palace Car Company, 156

Quarles, William C., 38, 39, 40, 41
Quinlan, Patrick L., 63

radicals. *See* anarchists; Berkman, Alexander; Goldman, Emma
Rai, Lajpat, 171, 172, 175
Rand, William, 107, 109, 113
Rand School of Social Science, 175, 183
Recht, Charles, 148, 173, 174
Red Cross, 163, 182
Red Scare: and freedom of speech, 9, 29; rise of, 168, 178; and Roe, 4, 5, 168, 178, 190. *See also* Lusk Laws case; Maurer, James Hudson; New York State Assembly: expulsion of socialists; Palmer raids; Teachers Union of New York City cases
Reed, John ("Jack"): on Bolshevik cause, 168, 169; and Boyd, 65, 66; career of, 169–70; and *The Masses*, 104; and *The Masses* criminal case, 146–47, 148; and Netha, 170, 241n17; and Steffens, 169; *Ten Days That Shook the World*, 169
Reid, W. Bruce, 110
Robinson, Boardman, 133–34
Robinson, Joseph T., 151
Rockefeller, John D., Jr., 31, 119, 120, 232n104

Index

Rodman, Henrietta, 89, 90–93, 104, 173, 174
Roe, Carrie. *See* Drake, Carolyn M.
Roe, Gilbert E.: anarchists, relationships with, 46; background and early career of, 12–13, 15, 16–17, 18, 20; Berkman, relationship with, 68–69; on birth control, 73, 93; and Brandeis, 24, 26; on capital punishment, 194; career of, later years, 193–95, 196; career of, overview, 4–5; death of, 197; death of, responses to, 197–99; Emma Goldman, relationship with, 66–67; Espionage Act arguments, 134, 135, 144–45, 158–59, 176; Espionage Act, views on, 10, 128–29, 130, 160–61; family life, 19, 21, 23, 27, 189–90, 192, 193; Federal Trade Commission, potential appointment to, 25–26; finances of, 16, 80, 116–17; First Amendment arguments of, 135, 145, 157, 158–59; First Amendment, role in evolution of, 4–5, 28–29, 203; Fourteenth Amendment arguments of, 61–62; freedom of speech, approaches to, 10–11, 201–2; freedom of speech arguments, 61–62, 153–54, 158–59; freedom of speech, views on, 8–9, 127–28; and the Free Speech League, 50–51; and impeachment of Sulzer, 24–25; and Indian nationalist movement, 175, 177; and La Follette expulsion case, 149–55; La Follette, legislative work with, 18, 130, 138, 168, 190; La Follette, personal relationship with, 5, 6, 13, 14, 104–5; La Follette, political work with, 19, 20–23, 25, 45, 191–92; legacy of, 201–4; and Lusk laws, repeal of, 185–86; marriage to Carrie Drake Roe, 13; *The Masses*, financial support for, 36, 80, 116–17; and muckrakers, 5, 30; Netha, relationship with, 14–15, 195–96; in New York politics, 26, 194–95, 196; New York Supreme Court, candidate for, 23–24; obscurity of, 5–6; on patriotism, 180–81, 184; personal activism, basis for, 18; photograph of, 95, 96, 102; on prohibition, 194; on religion, 195; socialists, relationship with, 5, 93, 113, 124, 178, 194–95, 196; and suffrage movement, 70, 71–73; Teachers Union of New York City, relationship with, 5, 93, 124, 168, 193, 198; on Theodore Roosevelt, 20, 22–23; on Trading with the Enemy Act, 142; at U.S. Supreme Court, 61–62, 158–59, 165–66; U.S. Supreme Court, views on, 195; Walsh Commission, testimony to, 8–9; on women's rights, 72; on Woodrow Wilson, 22–23; World War I, views on, 9, 27–28, 129. *See also* Roe, Gilbert E., cases of; Roe, Gilbert E., works and speeches of; Roe, Gwyneth King

Roe, Gilbert E., cases of: Alexander, representation of, 162; Axtell, representation of, 195; Berkman, representation of, 68; *Birch*, 16–17; *Boyd*, 63–66; *Debs*, 155–50; DeWitt Clinton High School cases, 178–81; *Flagg* cases, 26, 196; *Fox*, 52–63; Garrison, representation of, 24–25; Glassberg case, 181–84; Hyams case, 185; La Follette Expulsion case, 149–55; Mary Craig Sinclair, advisor to, 121–22, 124; *The Masses* AP libel case, 105–18; *The Masses* Espionage Act case, 131–47; Maurer, representation of, 124–26; *McClure Co.*, 30–45; Mixed Claims Commission cases, 193; *Nagler*, 162–64; New York State Assembly case, 186–88; *O'Connell*, 164–66; Rodman case, 89–93; *Sanger*, 73–74, 75–87; *Sinclair*, 118–20, 122–24; Singh, representation of, 176–77; *Smedley*, 170–76; *Stephens*, 160–62; *Union Central Life Insurance*, 16

Roe, Gilbert E., works and speeches of: "Discriminations against Women in the Laws of New York," 72; "The Espionage Law," 160–61; "Freedom of Speech in Times of War and Industrial Disputes," 113; "Memorandum Dealing with Cases Wherein Women Are Not on an Equality with Men Under the Law," 72; "The Menace of English Imperialism," 177; *Our Judicial Oligarchy*, 7, 23; "Reasonable Restrictions on Freedom of Assemblage," 67; "Reminiscences of Ten Years Association with Mr. La Follette in the Practice of Law,"

Roe, Gilbert E. (*continued*) 192; *Selected Opinions of Luther Dixon and Edgar Ryan, Late Chief Justices of the Supreme Court of Wisconsin*, 19; "Senator La Follette and the World War," 193

Roe, Gwyneth (daughter of Gilbert and Netha), 20, 27, 190, 192, 195, 199–200

Roe, Gwyneth King ("Netha"): background of, 14; and Bishop, 14, 15, 71; career of, 14, 15, 20; on Carrie Drake, 13; family life, 21, 23, 189–90, 192, 193; "Go Tell the Emperor," 241n17; later years and death of, 199; photograph of, 97; pregnancy and birth of children, 18–19, 19–20; and Reed, 170; on Roe's illness and death, 197; Roe, relationship with, 14–15, 195–96; and suffragists, 71; on Upton Sinclair, 124; on World War I, 28

Roe, Janet (daughter of Gilbert and Netha), 19, 23, 27, 190, 192, 199

Roe, John E. ("Jack"; son of Gilbert and Netha), 19, 189–96, 199

Rogers, Alfred, 16, 19, 21, 34, 35

Rogers, Henry W., 145

Rogers, Marie. *See* Smedley, Agnes

Rogers, Merrill, 131, 138, 139, 140, 146–47, 148

Roosevelt, Franklin D., 194, 196

Roosevelt, Theodore, 20, 21, 22–23, 31, 65, 151

Roy, M. N., 172

Rublee, George, 26

Russian revolution, 167–68, 178

Salmon, Arthur C., 87

Sanger, John. *See* Sanger, William

Sanger, Margaret: *Birth Control Review*, 172, 175; children of, 84; and Comstock law, 74; *Family Limitation*, 3, 75, 76–77; feminists, schism with on birth control, 73; and Goldman, 74–75; and Margaret Anderson, 220n106; photograph of, 99; on Rodman, 89; and Smedley, 171, 172, 173; social circle of, 74; "What Every Girl Should Know," 74; and William Sanger, 3, 75, 76, 80; *Woman Rebel* case, 75, 84, 87–88

Sanger, William, 3–4, 73–75; background of case, 75–76, 205n5; Comstock complaint, 76–77; financing of case, 78–80, 81, 84, 86; hearing in Magistrate Court, 78; pretrial proceedings, 81, 82–86; trial, 86–87

Schmalhausen, Samuel D., 178–81

Schmidt, Matthew A., 68

Schneer, A. Henry, 178–81

Schroeder, Theodore: background of, 17–18; and Craddock, 49; and Fox case, 59–61; freedom of speech, views on, 8, 61, 201–2; *The Free Speech Case of Jay Fox*, 217n33; and Free Speech league, 50, 51–52, 166; and Margaret Sanger, 75; on *The Masses* AP libel case, 107; *Obscene Literature and Constitutional Law*, 58; philosophies of, 46–47, 216n30; on women's suffrage, 71

Scoble, John M.: and death of Roe, 198; and Dutchess Land Company, 196; and Mary Craig Sinclair case, 122, 123; and William Sanger case, 76, 78, 79

Scott, Alexander, 63

Seabury, Samuel, 25

Sedition Act of 1798, 128

Sedition Act of 1918, 9

Sharts, Joseph, 157

Sherman Antitrust Act, 26

Simms, Charles E., 120

Sinclair, Mary Craig Kimbrough ("Craig"), 119–20, 121–22, 123, 124

Sinclair, Upton: and American Socialist Party, 118, 167–68; on the Associated Press, 106, 117, 120; background of, 118; *The Brass Check*, 105, 106; on Colorado coal strike, 119, 120; John D. Rockefeller Jr. protest of, 119–20, 120–222–24, 202, 232n117; *The Jungle*, 118; later career of, 124; Netha on, 124; photograph of, 100; and Smedley, 171; on violence, 119, 232n104; on West Virginia coal miners' strike, 105–6, 231n89; on World War I, 167–68

Singh, Bhagwan, 171, 172

Singh, Gopal, 176–77

Sixth Amendment, 161, 174

Sloan, John, 103–4

Smedley, Agnes: background of, 171–72; case against, 172–75, 176; and Comintern, 170–71, 242n23; on death of Roe, 199; and

Indian nationalist movement, 171–72, 175; later career of, 177
Smith, Alfred E., 186, 188, 195
Smith, E. G. *See* Goldman, Emma
Smyth, Herbert C., 178, 179
Socialist Labor Party, 125
Socialist Party of America: candidate for president, 194; Debs, member of, 160; disloyalty, accusations of, 187–88; La Follette, support for, 191; Margaret Sanger, member of, 74; and *The Masses*, 104; New York City teachers, affiliation with, 181, 183, 185; New York State Assembly, members expelled from, 186–88; and Smedley, 175; Stedman, member of, 157; Upton Sinclair, member of, 118, 167–68. *See also* socialists
Socialist Revolutionary Party (Russia), 50
socialists: in Arden, Delaware, 161; birth control, views on, 73; and the Bolshevik Revolution, 167–68; on death of Roe, 199; and Indian nationalist movement, 175; and IWW silk workers' strike, 63; Mary Craig Sinclair libel suits, 121–22, 123, 124; *The Masses*, AP libel case, 104–18; *The Masses* Espionage Act case, 132–33; and *The Masses*, founding of, 103–4; Maurer case, 124–26; in New York City mayoral race, 196; New York City teachers, affiliation with, 181, 183, 185; New York State Assembly, expelled from, 186–88; publications of, banned from the mails, 130–31, 132–33; and Red Scare, 178, 186; Roe, relationship with, 5, 93, 113, 124, 178, 194–95, 196; Upton Sinclair case, 118–24; on World War I, 167–68. *See also* Debs, Eugene V.; Hillquit, Morris; *The Masses*, Espionage Act case; Red Scare; Sinclair, Upton; Socialist Party of America; Sugarman, Abraham L.
Solomon, Charles, 187
Soviet Union. *See* Comintern; Smedley, Agnes
Speer, Emory, 143
Spielberg, Harold, 68
Spooner, John C., 17–18
S. S. McClure Publishing Co., 32

Stalwart (faction of Republican Party), 17, 32, 41
Stedman, Seymour: and Debs, 157–58; and *The Masses* criminal case, 148; and *The Masses* Espionage Act case, 132–33, 234n35; and New York State Assembly case, 187, 188
Steffens, Lincoln: and Boyd, 65, 66; on death of Roe, 198; "Enemies of the Republic" series, 31–32; and Free Speech League, 50, 51; and La Follette, 30, 31; and *The Masses* AP libel case, 110, 112; and *McClure's*, 31, 36; photograph of, 98; and Reed, 169; Russian Revolution, views on, 168–69; "The Shame of Minneapolis," 31; *The Shame of the Cities*, 30, 31; and Upton Sinclair, 118
Stephens, Frank, 160–62
Stephenson, Robert P., 173, 174
Stewart, Robert P., 176
Stokes, Rose Pastor, 157
Stone, Melville E., 108, 109, 111–12
Strauss, Jacob, 16
strikes. *See* Colorado coal miners' strike; IWW silk workers' strike; West Virginia coal miners' strike
suffragists, 28, 69, 70–73
Sugarman, Abraham L., 160
Sullivan, L. B., 203
Sulzer, William, 24–25, 199
Sun, 110, 111, 125
Superior Court for Pierce County, Washington, 55–57
Susan B. Anthony Amendment, 70–71
Swann, Edward, 83
Sweet, Thaddeus, 187

Taft, William Howard, 19, 20, 22
Tammany Hall, 23, 24
Tanner, W. V., 62
Tarbell, Ida M., 31, 36; "The Oil War of 1872," 31
teachers, right to marry in New York, 89–90
Teachers Council (New York City), 178, 186
Teachers Union of New York City: Lusk Laws, campaign to repeal, 185–86; Roe, relationship with, 5, 93, 124, 168, 193, 198

Teachers Union of New York City cases: DeWitt Clinton High School cases, 178–81, 244n77; Glassberg case, 181–85; Hyams case, 185; MacDowell and Pinol cases, 181
Teapot Dome scandal, 190
Thomas, John W., 38, 40; railroad report of 1904, 32, 33, 35, 39, 43; railroad report of 1906, 34–35, 41
Thomas, Norman, 175, 194, 196
Tildsley, John L., 178, 179
Trachtenberg, Alexander L., 184–85
Trading with the Enemy Act, 142, 146, 147
Train, Arthur C., 108, 109, 112, 115–16
Tresca, Carlo, 63
Truth Seeker, 198
Turner, John, 49–50

Union Central Life Insurance Company, 16
Union Refrigerator Transit Company of Kentucky, 34
Union Refrigerator Transit Company of Wisconsin, 32–33, 34–35, 36, 40–41
United Mine Workers of America, 105, 168, 171
United States Court of Appeals for the Second Circuit: and appointments to, 37, 147; and *The Masses* Espionage Act case, 137–38, 143–46; *McClure's* case, 44–45
United States Criminal Code, 75
University of Wisconsin, 13, 17, 70
Untermeyer, Louis, 103–4
Untermyer, Samuel, 88, 111, 117
U.S. Congress: Armed Ship bill, 150; Associated Press, investigation of, 108; Clayton Antitrust Act, 26; Committee on Privileges and Elections, 151; Comstock Act, 47; "Espionage and Interference with Neutrality," H.R. 291, 128–30; House Committee on Post Office and Post Roads, 140; House Committee on Ways and Means, 193; La Follette expulsion case, 151–55; Mixed Claims Commission, 193; Passenger Act, 154; progressives in, 191; Senate Committee on Manufactures, 190; Senate Committee on Post Offices and Post Roads, 141; Senate Committee on Public Lands, 190; Trading with the Enemy Act, 142; Walsh Commission, 8–9, 202; war resolution, 28; War Revenue bill, 138, 150. *See also* La Follette, Robert M., Sr.
U.S. District Court for the Southern District of New York, 132, 173
U.S. District Court for the Western District of Washington, 60
U.S. Post Office: and banning of publications, 74, 75, 130–31, 139–40; and Comstock Act, 47–48; mailability, rulings on, 131–32, 133–34; Trading with the Enemy Act, response to, 142. See also *The Masses*, Espionage Act case
U.S. Senate. *See* U.S. Congress
U.S. State Department, 151, 152
U.S. Supreme Court: Brandeis, appointment to, 26; and common-law rule on obscenity, 132; on Espionage Act and seditious libel, 202–3; on First Amendment, 49–50, 159–60, 203; La Follette's views on, 191–92; post–Civil War jurisprudence of, 7; on Sherman Antitrust Act, 26; and U.S. Congress, 191–92
U.S. Supreme Court, cases of: *Birch*, 16–17; *Brandenburg v. Ohio*, 203–4; *Debs*, 155–60; *Flagg*, 26; *Fox*, 52–63, 81; *Frohwerk*, 160; *New York Times v. Sullivan*, 202–3; *O'Connell*, 164–66; *Schenck*, 159–60; *Sugarman*, 160; *Terminiello v. Chicago*, 202; *Turner*, 49–50

Van Fleet, William C., 165
Villard, Oswald Garrison, 194
Vlag, Piet, 103

Wadhams, William H., 115
Wagenknecht, Alfred, 156–67
Walker, E. C., 48, 49
Walsh, Frank P., 8, 133, 175, 234n35
Walsh, Thomas J., 151, 155
Walsh Commission, 8–9, 202
Wappinger's Falls, 189–996
Ward, Henry Galbraith, 44, 145, 146
Ward, H. S., 44
Washington Supreme Court, 57, 59, 60–61, 62

Index

Washington Times, 21
Webb, Edwin, 126
Weeks, Rufus, 103
Weinberger, Harry, 128
Weinstock, Harris, 9
West Virginia coal miners' strike, 105, 228n15. *See also* Sinclair, Upton
Whalen, John, 178, 179
Whalen Resolution, 178
Wheeler, Burton K., 191, 192
White, William Allen, 21, 31, 36
Whitehouse, Mrs. Norman de R., 28
Whitlock, Brand, 51
Whitman, Charles S., 68, 107, 116
Wilcox, William G., 178
Wile, Ira S., 92–93
Wilmot, Floyd, 85, 86
Wilson, Woodrow: and Armed Ship bill, 150; and Espionage Act, 130; and Federal Trade Commission appointment, 26; and Hough appointment, 37; and the *Lusitania*, 150–51; and *The Masses* Espionage Act case, 133, 142; politics of, 32; and presidential campaigns, 18, 22, 27; Roe on, 22–23; and World War I, 27, 28, 115
Winterbottham, John M., 39
Wolf, Morris H., 157
Wolfe, Albert C., 163

Woman Rebel, 73, 75, 88
Woman's Peace Party, 28
Women's Political Union, 72
women's suffrage. *See* suffragists
Woolley, Victor B., 161, 162
World War I: approval of war resolution, 28; and freedom of speech, 9, 28–29, 127–28; and labor movement, 168; and La Follette, 27–28, 130, 138, 150–51; Netha on, 28, 241n17; progressives on, 27–28; Roe's views on, 9, 27–28, 129; and socialists, 167, 168; Upton Sinclair on, 167–68; and Wilson, 27, 28, 115. *See also* Espionage Act; *The Masses*, Espionage Act case; pacifists; Trading with the Enemy Act

YMCA, 47, 162–63
Yorkville Magistrate's Court (New York City), 4
Young, Art: "Congress and Big Business" ("War Plans"), 134; and *The Masses*, 103–4, 147; *The Masses*, AP libel case, 106–9, 113, 117, 118; and *The Masses* criminal case, 146–47, 148; "Poisoned at the Source," 106–7, 118
Young, Cal, 106, 110, 114
Young Men's Christian Association. *See* YMCA

Zimmerman, Albert, 14, 15

www.ingramcontent.com/pod-product-compliance
Lightning Source LLC
Chambersburg PA
CBHW070838160426
43192CB00012B/2229